LOVE YOUR LIFE!

O's Handbook for Your Best Today—and Tomorrow
From the editors of **O, THE OPRAH MAGAZINE**

LOVE YOUR LIFE!

O's Handbook for Your Best Today—and Tomorrow

From the editors of **O, THE OPRAH MAGAZINE**

Oxmoor House®

contents

HERE WE GO

7 INTRODUCTION BY OPRAH

YOUR MIND/YOUR BODY

9 DIET AND EXERCISE

30 HEALTH

54 BEAUTY/STYLE

66 BALANCE

92 HAPPINESS

108 CONFIDENCE

140 SPIRITUALITY

DATING/MATING/RELATING

153 COUPLES

173 TALKING AND LISTENING

184 FAMILY

YOUR LIFE/YOUR WORLD

205 MAKE A CONNECTION

233 GETTING THROUGH IT

267 GIVING BACK

314 ABOUT THE CONTRIBUTORS 316 PHOTOGRAPHY AND ART CREDITS 317 INDEX

here we go

HOW CAN I STRETCH MYSELF to my greatest potential? That's a question I ask myself every day. With each step on my career path, with every city I've lived in, I've known it's time to move on when I've grown as much as I can grow. Taking leaps, forging ahead, pushing yourself toward your very best: It's the only sure way to stay vibrant. It's how you become the person you were meant to be.

When the O team pulled together this year's brightest of the bunch—the stories that most thrilled and inspired us—we had just one thought in mind: You. I want exactly the same thing for your life that I've always wanted for my own: a journey filled with purpose.

In these pages, you'll find plenty of practical advice—from Dr. Oz's insights on getting in shape for all this dream chasing ("9 Numbers That Count," page 36) to Amy Bloom's big lesson in chutzpah ("But What If I'm Scared to Change?" page 113). And because living your best life includes nurturing your closest connections, we've assembled lots of good stuff on dating, mating, and relating—as in Dr. Helen Fisher's "How to Make the Romance Last" (page 162), Gretchen Reynold's "Honey, I Shrunk the Argument" (page 182), and Darby Saxbe's "Between a Talk and a Hard Place" (page 174). We've even included my favorite conversations with some of the most fascinating women I know, from master of comedy Tina Fey to the dazzling Michelle Obama.

This book is meant to help you let your own life shine. And when your dreams grow dim (at some point, they always do) and you're low on gusto (I've been there, too), I hope you'll use this compendium as a guidebook to get back on track. Loving your life begins with how you perceive your possibilities—and as long as you never put a lid on your options, I can tell you that they are vast. You, me, and every other person on the planet are taking this trip together—one step, misstep, and comeback at a time.

Oprah

YOUR MIND/
YOUR BODY

diet and exercise

10 WEIGHT LOSS, FAMILY STYLE | BY TIMOTHY GOWER

13 THE FAT FIGHT | BY ROBIN MARANTZ HENIG AND JESS ZIMMERMAN

18 THE PICTURE OF HEALTH | BY SARI HARRAR

20 THE WAY TO EAT | BY DAVID L. KATZ, MD

22 BATTLE OF THE DIET PLANS | BY NAOMI BARR

24 THE GREAT WEIGHT DEBATE | BY SARAH REISTAD-LONG

26 POSTURE POWER | BY JOHN HASTINGS

28 AND NOW A WORD ABOUT EXERCISE | BY POLLY BREWSTER

29 DECODE (AND DEFUSE) YOUR EXERCISE EXCUSES | BY SELENE YEAGER

Weight Loss, Family Style

Can the family that gains together lose together? Timothy Gower finds out.

Priscilla Marquard was resolute: Her family was going to eat healthier than she did as a kid. "Being American, I ate McDonald's. Being Southern, I ate fried food," she recalls in the soft drawl that betrays her Georgia upbringing. So Priscilla shopped at the organic grocery. She served balanced meals. She even planned menus 30 days in advance to make sure her husband and four children (three of them triplet girls) were consuming a variety of nutritious foods. And Priscilla did it all while trying to accommodate the tastes of each child, including the one who turned up her nose at leafy greens and refused to eat any dish that even resembled a stew.

But by the time the triplets turned 10, it was obvious that the Marquards, who live in Orlando, had weight issues. One of the girls, Alexandra—the picky eater—was slender. Audrey and Caroline, however, were "verging on chubby," says Priscilla. Her son, Philipp, was already there; at 14 the boy weighed 260 pounds. Meanwhile, Priscilla, 42, had her own troubles: After having kids, the former Ford model found that she was carrying an extra ten to 20 pounds that seemed impervious to diets.

While each of us has a special relationship with the scale, in many cases the family factor weighs in (literally). Inheritance plays a part in determining your size, but unlike red hair or blue eyes, DNA doesn't tell the whole story: Psychologists and doctors have found that family dynamics—the way you and your brood interact and relate to one another—can have a major influence on weight.

"We need to change how we look at food, and it all starts with families," says former FDA commissioner David A. Kessler, MD, author of *The End of Overeating: Taking Control of the Insatiable American Appetite*. Too often, parents offer treats in an attempt to placate children, and the food—chips, sweets—tends to be high in fat, sugar, and salt. These substances set off reward centers in the brain, says Kessler, creating a sense of pleasure and a desire to overeat.

Using food to brighten a child's mood can jump-start emotional eating, adds Duke University psychologist Nancy L. Zucker, PhD. "Whenever the child feels sad, she'll

think, for example, sweets," Zucker says. "Sadness is a signal that they need a hug, not a cookie."

Another trap parents fall into is using treats to bribe a child into eating healthier fare—as in, "Eat your broccoli, and you can have a bowl of Ben & Jerry's." "That sends the signal that ice cream is great and broccoli is bad," says Karen Miller-Kovach, MS, RD, chief scientific officer for Weight Watchers International, which is developing workshops for parents of obese and overweight kids.

And children can undermine parents' efforts to eat well. Anyone who has ever been on a weight loss plan knows that controlling your desire to eat foods that are off-limits can drain your resolve. "The kids are complaining about getting grilled chicken for dinner instead of bacon cheeseburgers," says Zucker. "It can really wear you down."

On occasion, spouses can also interfere with their partners' efforts to shed pounds. "You might have a wife who wants to lose weight, but her husband doesn't, so he won't change the food he buys," says Zucker. Or, say psychologists, a husband may feel threatened by his wife's slimming success, possibly out of fear that he could be abandoned for another, fitter man. In response, he might start coming home with boxes of chocolates, complaining that he feels lonely when his wife is at the gym, or making fattening dinners he knows she can't resist.

Fortunately, family can be part of the solution. Scientists who study families and obesity say that when someone in the household has a weight problem—even just one member—he or she is far more likely to shed pounds if everyone adopts a healthy diet and exercises. "If you have an alcoholic in the family, you're not going to serve wine for dinner. You have to change the entire home environment," says psychologist Daniel S. Kirschenbaum, PhD, clinical director of Wellspring, an organization that runs weight loss camps, retreats, and schools for overweight kids and adults in the United States, Canada, Australia, and the United Kingdom, including an annual family camp in Pinehurst, North Carolina. In a recent study, Kirschenbaum followed successful young graduates of Wellspring camps and their overweight parents for about a year and found that 80 percent of the kids who continued to lose weight had parents who also changed their diet and activity levels and lost weight with them. But if the parents stuck to their old habits, everyone was

The first meal was a shock. "We were like, 'Mom, what are you doing to us?'"

more likely to start adding pounds. This kind of research helps explain why Wellspring and other weight loss companies, including Weight Watchers, are developing and launching family-targeted programs.

Priscilla Marquard had read about a "family immersion" camp at Pritikin Longevity Center & Spa in Aventura, Florida, where she'd visited for weight tune-ups during her modeling days and had also brought her mother—who has type 2 diabetes. Priscilla decided that she and the triplets would give the two-week family program a try. (Her ex-husband and Philipp were traveling in Europe at the time.)

Run like a summer camp for kids and their parents, the Pritikin Family Program includes tennis, swimming, and other activities, along with nutrition and culinary classes that emphasize the health benefits of a nutrient-rich, high-fiber, low-sodium, very-low-fat approach. (The diet consists of fewer than 20 percent calories from fat; the typical American diet is about 35 percent.) The first meal the Marquards ate in the Pritikin dining room was a shock to their palates—vegetarian meatloaf, "French fries" that were actually baked sliced sweet potatoes, and no salt shakers on the tables. "We were like, 'Mom, what are you doing to us?'" recalls Alexandra. The girls were initially resistant to the new foods, but they adjusted quickly. This was a revelation to Priscilla: Despite her attempts to feed the family healthy fare, she slipped at times—meeting the triplets after school bearing bags of potato chips or Happy Meals, for example. "They'd get into the car and have huge smiles on their faces," she says. With the help of the camp counselors, Priscilla realized there were better ways to keep her girls happy. And the triplets had frank discussions about what they needed to lose and the habits they would have to change. "The staff helped us get on the same page nutritionally and mentally," says Priscilla.

Improving communication should be a top priority for spouses as well, says Zucker. Dieters assume that others know what sort of support to give—and often end up disappointed and frustrated when they don't get it. "Be specific in terms of what you really need," says Zucker. For some women, that may mean asking a spouse to do the grocery shopping—and making sure he buys plenty of fruit and vegetables, not corn dogs and cupcakes. Other women may be more in need of emotional support. Simply hearing the words "Honey, I know how hard this is—and I'm proud of you" can make all the difference.

The Marquards' time at Pritikin was a success. Priscilla managed to lose 16 pounds; three years later, she had kept the weight off. Audrey arrived at camp weighing 106 pounds; despite a six-inch growth spurt, she held to a trim 102 pounds. As a result of the program, Caroline lost 15 pounds. Philipp also benefited from the lessons Priscilla and the girls learned: He shed 60 pounds through diet and exercise.

The Marquards' experience demonstrates the best way to lose weight is together. Today the Happy Meals and potato chips after school are a distant memory. "Now it's fruit and more fruit," says Priscilla. "And nobody turns their nose up and says, 'Oh, gosh, what's that?'" ◻

A Few More Ways to Help Your Family Fight Fat

■ **SET AN EXAMPLE.** "Kids model their parents—they learn healthy, as well as unhealthy, behaviors from them," says State University of New York at Buffalo psychologist Leonard Epstein, PhD, a pioneer in family-based obesity prevention. Telling a child to go out and get some exercise is far less effective than asking him or her to join you for a bike ride.

■ **SET GOALS.** Consider having everyone in the family sign a healthy-living contract. In the short term, don't focus on weight loss. Instead, have everyone agree to specific daily goals, such as recording a certain number of steps on a pedometer.

■ **USE NONEDIBLE WEEKLY REWARDS,** says Daniel S. Kirschenbaum, PhD, clinical director of Wellspring weight loss programs. A small gift or a few dollars—or even allowing a child to have a friend sleep over—will help reinforce the importance of working toward specific goals.

■ **SIT DOWN FOR A FAMILY DINNER.** Kids who do this at least five or six nights a week are a third less likely to be overweight than children who never eat dinner with their families, according to a 2006 University of Alabama study. Other research shows that kids who eat more family meals consume less fried food and artery-clogging trans fat and saturated fat.

The Fat Fight

What's the most treacherous ground for a mother and daughter to navigate? Robin Marantz Henig and daughter Jess Zimmerman weigh in.

"I wanted to spare her pain."

THE MOTHER'S STORY

Watching my daughter belly dance a couple of years ago brought tears to my eyes. Jess was 28 at the time, and she was splendid. She wore a costume of bright blue and a gold hip scarf with jiggling coins. Her midriff—also jiggling—was bare. She was graceful in her shimmies, graceful with her arms, graceful when she flicked her naked feet. I loved watching her.

All the years of sitting through the plays of Jess's childhood came back to me, plays in which she spoke her lines in a sweet, clear voice but could never get over the awkwardness of being herself. I had thought that at the heart of Jess's discomfort, on stage and off, was the fact that she felt bad about being fat. Yet everything I did to spare her insecurity about her weight turned out to be a source of pain for her—and a thorn at the heart of our relationship that we're still trying delicately to extract.

As a baby, Jessie was spectacular. Huge blue-gray eyes, a corona of golden curls—my husband, Jeff, and I were delighted with the way she looked, the way she laughed, the way she smelled. To us, she was perfect.

Which is why I was so surprised by an offhand comment made one evening at a local restaurant. The owner's wife was fussing over Jessie, who was about 9 months old. "Ooooh," the woman said happily, "I love fat babies."

Fat babies? What baby was she talking about? My baby? I had a fat baby?

The authors, New York City, September 2009.

I was 26 at the time, and I had body issues of my own. Growing up, I was always aware of being chunkier than other girls, and the misery that came with that awareness had never quite left me. I didn't want my little girl to grow up with that kind of unhappiness. Maybe—smarter in 1980 than my mother had been in 1953—there was something I could do to spare her that psychic pain.

By the age of 4, Jessie weighed ten pounds more than the charts said she should. Not fat, just chubby—and I knew I shouldn't overreact. "I'm trying very hard to ignore it," I wrote in my journal, "so I don't make her self-conscious and create a problem where there is none."

Of course, that's exactly what I did: create a problem where there was none. I was on the heavy end of my own lifelong weight-seesaw then; our second daughter, Samantha, had just been born, and my postpregnancy weight was stubbornly hanging on. When I dreamed one night that I was shopping at a plus-size store, I woke up in a panic. In the grip of this self-disgust, I turned to my beautiful Jessie and decided I had to fix her.

Meals soon became a battleground. I packed abstemious school lunches—half a sandwich, a fruit, no junk—and used smaller plates at dinner to limit her portion size. I hid the cookies I bought for Sam, and wouldn't tell Jessie where they were. And when Jessie asked for seconds, I'd say, "Are you really hungry?" I thought that sounded supportive. I see now how harsh it was. If she asked for the food, she was hungry. I should at least have trusted her to know her own body's cues.

I should pause here to point out that despite my body-loathing, I'm not fat. My BMI is at the low end of the "healthy" range, I wear a size 8, and because I'm flat-chested I give off a pretty slim vibe.

But when I look in the mirror, what I see is not a small waist but massive thighs. When I was 21, I wrote a list on yellow legal paper: "What I need to be happy." Years later I found it again, crinkled with age. At the top of the list,

Robin at age 13, 1967, and daughter Jess (*near right*) at age 9, 1989.

number one—ahead of a rewarding career, a loving family, a house with lots of windows—is the single thing I thought would make the rest of my life fall into place: thin thighs. I wrote that list a long time ago. I am 56 years old, I still don't have thin thighs, and, dammit, I still want them.

Things were tough for us when Jessie was in her early teens—tougher than they were for the typical mother and teenage daughter. When I took her to a dermatologist to be treated for acne, she had a tantrum in the waiting room. I was mystified. I didn't see that this doctor visit was, to Jessie, yet another indication that my love was conditional. She thought I loved her only when she was clear-skinned and slim.

When she was 16, Jess—she had by then put a stop to "Jessie"—sat me down one night and told me she'd been bulimic for years. My first thought was she couldn't be, or she wouldn't be so fat. But I held my tongue and listened as she told me that it was my fault. She was bulimic, she said, because of my emphasis on being thin, my embarrassing comments about food in front of her friends, my obvious disappointment in her body.

"I'm not disappointed in your body," I said. "I think you're beautiful." Jess looked at me skeptically. "I do," I insisted. "Your eyes, your hair, your manner, everything about who you are—it's all beautiful." But my perceptive daughter heard the roar of words unsaid. I never said "your body," because to say I found it beautiful would have been a lie.

The summer after her freshman year in college, when she was 18, Jess suggested we try Weight Watchers together. I leaped at the chance, and we bonded over food restriction, each losing about 20 pounds. But by Thanksgiving Jess had regained every pound. I saw this as a setback. I failed to see what was really happening: that by eating normally instead of dieting, she was finally learning to love her

She thought I loved her only when she was slim.

body, however fat or lumpy. This emerging attitude was about to transform not only her relationship with herself but our fractious mother-daughter relationship, too.

Shortly after her 27th birthday, Jess and Dan, her fiancé, came for a visit. A few days earlier, she had sent me a link to a video called *A Fat Rant,* by Joy Nash, a proponent of the fat acceptance movement. As we sat around the coffee table with wine and hummus, I mentioned having watched the video, and before I knew it, we were discussing the prejudice fat people deal with every day and how a person's weight is nobody's business but her own. It felt surreal to be able to talk to Jess about weight this way, and to hear her and Dan call themselves fat without flinching.

"Would you rather weigh less than you do?" I finally dared to ask. My husband stared at me wide-eyed, sure that this time I had really gone too far.

Jess thought about it. Dan thought about it. And their answer was, essentially, no.

A few months later, Jess and I went shopping at a plus-size store in Brooklyn—so much hipper than the store of my nightmare—to look for a wedding dress. After trying on a few, Jess decided she also needed a new bra and jeans. How many mothers and their daughters can go jeans shopping together without a dressing room meltdown? Amazingly, we could.

After seeing the *Fat Rant* video, I'd steeped myself in fat acceptance blogs and had finally become able to accept that Jess was not only fat but beautiful. Her weight was no longer the first thing I saw, or fretted about, or even thought about, when I was with my brilliant, funny, sexy, sensitive daughter. We seemed to have crossed some significant barrier.

But there's a catch: As much as I can embrace fat acceptance for Jess and Dan and their friends, I still can't embrace it for myself. The thought of letting go and just weighing whatever I'm destined to, no matter how much—well, it's scary. I think this bothers Jess. I think it interferes with our ability to be completely candid when talking about weight—but I can't help it. I'm just not there yet.

Oh, but Jess—she's there, emphatically so. That skilled, self-confident shimmy I watched at her belly dance recital did not come easily, but come it did, and it was a lovely thing to behold. That's the image that comes to me when I think about Jess's weight: her body in motion that evening, with a grace and a beauty I had never seen before. It didn't bother me that the midriff she exposed was fat. It didn't bother me because it so clearly didn't bother her.

Big and beautiful: Jess Zimmerman, 2009.

"I was gross, lazy, and unfixable."

THE DAUGHTER'S STORY

When I was 6, my mother, a journalist, wrote an article for *Woman's Day* called "Kids Get Fat Because They Eat Too Much…and Other Myths About Overweight Children." Under the main article was a sidebar about how she'd turned me from a slightly chubby 4-year-old into a slightly less chubby

6-year-old...by feeding me less.

This was typical. When Mom wrote about children and health, I appeared in the role of Fat Kid Saved by Diet or Exercise. The reality might have been that I ate no more than other kids, that I read a lot but also played a lot outside, that I wasn't even particularly fat. But such complexities weren't part of my role in my mother's narrative. I was an object lesson—proof that even fat kids could be salvaged.

The diets never worked for long, so my permanent role in real life became Fat Kid Who's Also a Failure. The 6-year-old in that first article is shown dancing ballet, eating yogurt for lunch, gazing joyfully out onto a slimmer future. In fact she couldn't bear to look at herself in a leotard, and was terrified that her mother would catch her using her milk money for chocolate milk instead of skim.

It's not that I had the world's biggest complex, or the worst food issues, or the most poisonous self-image. And I'm not the most textbook illustration of how fixation on a daughter's body can destroy her self-esteem. But this isn't only about the harm my mother unwittingly did me; it's about the harm the weight loss fantasy does to everyone.

Mom didn't allow me to eat fast food (which I've never missed) or dessert (which, lord, I did). When I was 9, I bargained with myself that if I went a month without sugar, I could have an ice cream sundae, something I'd never eaten before. But when I still stayed fat, all food became suspect.

At a sleepover in fifth grade, I was served sweetened cereal and was simultaneously repulsed and fascinated—it tasted awful, but it looked like dessert for breakfast, and I didn't even get dessert for dessert. Food took on a mystical but terrifying appeal, desirable and dangerous, and safe only when nobody was looking—and I resorted to sneaking and hoarding it. On average, I didn't eat more or worse than other kids, but I didn't have to. If you think you don't deserve food, everything starts to look like a binge.

And there was no question in my mind that I didn't deserve food. I was oversize, clumsy, monstrous—like a different species—though pictures from my preteen years show that the biggest thing about me was actually my prescription glasses. My body was an albatross that marked me as slovenly, ugly, unworthy of love. I fantasized about sloughing it off, like the boy in the Narnia book who turns into a dragon and doesn't become human again until he painfully sheds his skin.

My mother never intended this—she only wanted a happy ending for me. But the ending she envisioned was the same one that played out in every kid's book with a fat character I had ever read: the one where the troubled chubster solves her inner turmoil and ends up svelte. Mom never envisioned an ending where the fat kid discovers that there was nothing wrong with her in the first place. Why would she? Nobody ever wrote that story.

It's difficult for a child to differentiate between someone who wants to armor her against an unjust world and someone who thinks that she's damaged. *What,* I wondered, *is so deeply wrong with me that my mom, who only wants to love me, can't bring herself to love me how I am? And why can't I fix it?*

I kept waiting for the day when I'd reach the happy, skinny ending and get to start on the sequel. I'd diet myself thin at last, and then I'd be vivacious and graceful and sought after, and I would be allowed to wear tank tops and eat, and my life could begin. As I ate less and got fatter, these scenarios became more drastic: They now involved wasting away from a serious illness, which I suspected was the only way I'd become as gaunt as I wanted to be. When I started getting brutal stomach pains in high school, my heart leapt—maybe this was it!

It wasn't. The stomach pains happened because when the life-threatening disease failed to materialize, I had turned to another twisted weight loss strategy: disordered eating. Sometime around the age of 13 I started to read first-person stories about anorexia for ideas on how to control my food intake. I hid behind fussiness—suddenly I didn't like anything with more than three ingredients, or red meat, or fish, or cheese, or anything strongly spiced. (As late as college, a friend bet me that he could recite my entire grocery list. He named six items and got it basically right.) My teen magazines were full of tips on how to throw up without attracting notice. I didn't binge, but I would throw up because I'd had a full meal, or because I'd scarfed a contraband late-night bowl of ice cream, or just because it was the end of the day.

The eating disorder stories tended to harp on the fact that girls who couldn't control their eating couldn't control anything in their lives, and as I got older I started to believe that everything about me was wrong. Though I often exuded a toughness that was mistaken for confidence, I doubted not only my attractiveness and right to exist in the

> I discovered that fat people could be happy, healthy, even loved.

world as a fat person but also my intelligence and talent and general worth. Once I started dating, I sought out boys and men who shared my low opinion of myself. One praised me for recognizing that my weight was "a problem"—he didn't care so much whether I was fat, as long as I knew I wasn't okay.

When I went away to college, I was still on a semipermanent diet punctuated by furtive eating, still pretending to be picky to hide my food restriction, and still looking for people to tell me how lousy I was. I caromed from asceticism to sugar overdose, and gained weight despite spending eight hours a week at fencing practice. (Around this time, I also had my metabolic rate tested. Based on my height and weight, it was significantly slower than average. It's possible that this was always the case. On the other hand, I know from Mom's own articles that restrictive eating can do a number on a person's metabolism.)

In my mind I was still the gross, lazy, unfixable kid. But in the tiny empowerment bubble of a women's college, there were a host of new narratives I hadn't considered. I discovered books, articles, and indie zines offering strange new ideas: that fat people could be happy and healthy and even loved, that we weren't necessarily damaged, that beauty ideals controlled women by making them waste their energy on hating themselves. That the desire to eat food was sometimes just the body's way of taking care of itself. The old narrative—in which I would remain trapped in a loathsome body until I earned love and happiness through slimness—started to fade.

Sophomore year, Mom wrote an article tut-tutting about how the people on campus who told me to "honor my hunger" were only ruining my diet. I ran a campus-wide campaign for Love Your Body Day and asked Mom to quit writing about me.

> And the word *health,* so often used as a club to beat fat people with, needed redefining, too. There's nothing healthy about fearing food and using exercise as a whip.

And eventually *I* started to write. Books, magazines, and literature on campus had planted the suspicion that there was a less painful way to live, and when I rediscovered these ideas in the blogosphere, I found myself repeating and reformulating them. In communicating with others, I started convincing myself.

Along the way, I retooled my vocabulary. *Fat,* the word I'd scrawled accusingly in marker on my offending thighs in high school, was just a neutral way of describing a body. If there's nothing inherently shameful in fatness, there's no reason to hide behind euphemisms. And the word *health,* so often used as a club to beat fat people with, needed redefining, too. There's nothing healthy about fearing food and using exercise as a whip.

A better goal is to exercise for fun and truly eat well—not less, not using different rules, but in a way that's more nourishing and more conscious. By my mid-20s, I was not only eating more normally—I had even added new kinds of exercise to my routine for the sheer fun of it: belly dance, yoga, hula hooping. My weight stayed the same, but I started to really live in the body I was now feeding and taking out to play. I realized that I wasn't trapped in the old cycle of failure, denial, and shame.

These days I can write about my body—and even, cautiously, let my mother write about it—because I've jettisoned the old narratives and started to scratch out a new one. It's a complicated story, with an unpredictable plot—good days, bad days, a pervasive sense of shame that's hard to shake. But I'm finding that the main character is much more healthy, stable, and worthwhile than I'd ever known. **O**

The Picture of Health

Can your cell phone help you shed pounds? New research says yes. Sari Harrar reports on three subtle—and surprising—strategies for achieving your ideal weight.

Ever heard of the twilight zone diet? It's the one where you swear you're doing everything right but still can't drop a pound. Part of the problem may be that your intentions don't match your actions: Recent Cornell University research found that people tend to underestimate the calories they're eating by as much as 38 percent. And they exaggerate how much exercise they get, overestimating calorie burn by as much as 62 percent, according to a University of Texas study. Add these findings together, and you could be 100 percent stuck.

But researchers are finding new ways to help you get back to reality. With the following strategies, you can start winning at the losing game.

Turn Every Meal (and Snack) into a Photo Shoot

When 43 women and men agreed to photograph every morsel before they ate it for one week (and keep a written food diary as well), researchers at the University of Wisconsin–Madison found the results eye-opening—and diet-changing. The mealtime shutterbugs, all of whom considered themselves healthy eaters, discovered that their portions were too big, their meals bereft of fruit and vegetables, and their snack choices calorie-laden. Rather than continue to photograph their bad choices, many chose to eat something else instead.

"The act of taking a photo made them so much more aware of what they were eating," says lead researcher Lydia Zepeda, PhD, a professor of consumer science at the university. "They weren't trying to lose weight, but many said they didn't want an unhealthy snack or a second helping at a meal if they had to take a picture of it."

Though the success of keeping written food diaries is well documented (they doubled weight loss in a recent study from the Kaiser Permanente Center for Health Research), Zepeda theorized that a photo diary might be even more motivational. "With a written diary, there is nothing you do in the moment. You eat the food and write it down later," she says. "With a photo diary, you can still change your mind and choose fruit over cake."

Or as one study volunteer said, "Who wants to take a photo of a jumbo bag of M&M's?"

Zepeda's group used film cameras, but she recommends going digital—the camera in your cell phone may be the simplest option, and you'll have images to look at immediately. To get a handle on what you're eating, take a picture of everything you consume over the course of an entire day, she suggests. "Don't change anything. Choose the foods you would normally eat so you can see your eating habits," Zepeda says. Then continue to snap for at least a week as you improve your diet. (If you're concerned about your food choices, Zepeda recommends reviewing your photos with a registered dietitian.) And anytime your weight loss plateaus, bring out the camera again.

Beat the "Weekend Effect"

Everyone needs a break. But relax your diet and exercise efforts too much on the weekend and you could offset the hard work you put in Monday through Friday, report researchers from the Washington University School of Medicine in St. Louis.

Susan B. Racette, PhD, assistant professor of physical therapy and medicine at the university and the lead study author, documented this phenomenon by carefully tracking the weight, eating habits, and physical activity levels of 48 women and men before and during her 12-month diet and exercise study. Participants kept food diaries (they weighed and measured everything they ate), weighed themselves on laboratory-grade scales every morning, and wore monitors equipped with sensors to measure physical activity.

The results surprised Racette: Before the study began, volunteers were eating enough additional calories each weekend—compared with their weekday regimen—to result in a gain of 9 pounds in a year.

Once the study started, participants who were supposed to be following a reduced-calorie diet had a steady weight dip from Monday through Thursday. But beginning on Friday, they simply stopped losing weight. The study also had an exercise-only group, and these people actually gained weight.

The reason for the gain was that on Saturday and Sunday, nearly everyone cheated a little—eating an extra 100 to 300 calories a day, mostly from higher-fat foods. And while physical activity increased on Saturdays, it was lower than average on Sundays.

"We thought weekends would present a problem for some people, but it was actually a problem for almost everyone—and these were motivated people who knew they were being watched closely," Racette says.

The good news is that the gain each weekend was, on average, less than half a pound, the kind of small increase that only becomes a problem over months. Preventing the gain should be easy, Racette says, provided you plan for it. "Set aside some time for a walk on Sunday," she says. "Eat before you leave the house to run errands so you don't end up at the drive-through or the mall food court. Bring snacks if you're going to sit at a child's soccer game all day so you don't buy nachos from the snack stand."

Track Every Step, Measure Every Calorie

Keeping tabs on all the calories your body burns—at rest, working out, and living life—used to mean joining a research study, becoming a *Biggest Loser* contestant (they wear calorie monitors on their arms), or shelling out big bucks for a high-tech, bulky armband.

No longer. GoWear Fit, a sleek monitor, tracks motion, steps, sweat, skin temperature, and heat flux from your muscles, then calculates the input with an equation that takes into account your age, gender, height, weight, and other personal details to reveal your daily calorie expenditure. Worn on your upper arm, the nifty device collects data that you download to your computer via a USB cable, and the data is whisked to a password-protected Web page that displays your calorie information, total daily activity, total daily steps (from running or walking), and sleep time. Manufactured by BodyMedia—the same company that makes the Bodybugg, used by *Biggest Loser* contestants—the armband costs $199 plus monthly online costs ranging from $7 to $13. For on-the-spot feedback, a $99 display you wear on your wrist will track your data in real time.

Exercise researcher Stephen Yang, PhD, an assistant professor of physical education at State University of New York College at Cortland, says this innovative armband takes the guesswork out of one side of the weight loss equation. "Until recently, mainly research labs used devices that measured calorie burn this way," he says. "Seeing the numbers can be a real motivator and will help keep you from missing workouts." Use the GoWear Fit to figure out how much additional activity you need to burn an extra 500 calories a day. If you keep up that effort, you should drop about a pound a week. ◑

This quick, easy meal is an antidote to fast food—and it's cheaper, too.

The Way to Eat

David L. Katz, MD, shares his top 10 rules for eating right.

One question I'm frequently asked is "What's the secret to a healthy diet?" The answer isn't all that mysterious. You just have to keep some basic guidelines in mind, beginning with:

1 Use smaller plates. Whether you're already trim or trying to lose weight, one of the best things you can do for your waistline and your health is to downsize your dishware. Cornell University nutrition researcher Brian Wansink, PhD, has found that switching from a 12-inch to a ten-inch plate leads people to eat 22 percent fewer calories. If you downsized only your dinner plate,

you'd be eliminating more than 5,000 calories a month from your diet. It really is that simple.

2 Make half of every meal fruits or vegetables. The U.S. Department of Agriculture recommends five to nine servings of produce a day, but if you follow my rule, you won't have to count. At breakfast, fill your bowl halfway with cereal, then top it off with berries or sliced banana. At lunch, eat a smaller—or half—sandwich, and add two pieces of fruit. At dinner, make sure your plate is at least 50 percent salad, broccoli, asparagus, cauliflower, or whatever veggie you choose. This ensures that you get enough nutrients and automatically reduces the amount of fat and calories you consume (provided you don't go crazy with fatty dressings and toppings).

3 Don't eat on the run. The first problem with grabbing and gulping is that it usually means fast food. And even a smallish fast food lunch (small burger, medium fries, diet soda) delivers around 800 calories—more than the average woman would want to get at dinner. When we eat on the go, our brains tend to register the food as a snack—regardless of how many calories we consume—leading us to overeat at our next meal.

4 The shorter the ingredient list, the better. Most of the healthiest foods have only one ingredient: Think broccoli, spinach, blueberries, etc. Longer lists generally mean more sugar, more salt, more artificial flavors. More unhealthy stuff.

5 Nutritious food doesn't have to be expensive. Some colleagues and I recently completed a study in Independence, Missouri, comparing prices between a diverse list of healthy grocery items and a list of less nutritious ones. (This was part of a program we've developed—see nutritiondetectives.com—to help kids make healthier choices about what to eat.) With rare exception, we found that the smart choices cost no more. In fact, there was a potential small savings associated with the healthy selections. And that's without considering such economical options as occasionally substituting beans or lentils for meat, or making a sandwich at home rather than spending money at a restaurant.

6 Take an extra ten minutes a day to prepare healthy meals. By devoting a few minutes to planning for more nutritious eating, you invest in your own health and that of your family. And when I say *few,* I mean it: Studies from UCLA suggest that a wholesome, home-cooked dinner takes only about ten minutes longer to prepare, on average, than serving processed or ready-made food. If you make enough for leftovers, you'll save time in the long run. And don't forget: Obesity, diabetes, and heart disease all lead to doctor and hospital visits—which take a lot of time.

7 Retrain your palate. As any 5-year-old or picky eater can attest, familiarity is a powerful driver of dietary preference. But taste buds *are* malleable and can be taught to appreciate new

and subtler flavors. When you swap processed, high-fat, sodium-packed, and oversweetened food for healthier fare, it can take one to two weeks before your taste buds acclimate. Don't expect to love new flavors right away (and certainly don't expect your kids to). Just keep serving the new dishes, and soon neither you nor your palate will recall what all the fuss was about.

8 Stop eating before you feel full. Slow the pace of your meals. Pay attention to what you're eating. And call it quits when you're about 80 percent full. After a pause, you'll likely find that "mostly full" is full enough. Studies indicate that simply by eating at a leisurely pace, you could drop up to 20 pounds a year.

9 Sit down to dinner with the entire family. Whether it's just you and your spouse or a family of 12, demand that everyone treat the dinner hour as holy. Kids who eat with their parents are less likely to consume junk, less likely to overeat, and less likely to be overweight. Parents who eat with their children report greater satisfaction with family life.

And families who eat together are far less likely to be plagued by eating disorders, drug use, smoking, and alcohol abuse, according to several studies conducted by the University of Minnesota and the National Center on Addiction and Substance Abuse at Columbia University. That's a remarkable benefit to something as simple as sitting down together for a family meal.

10 You really are what you eat. You want radiant skin? Consider that your skin depends on the flow of blood for nutrients and oxygen—which, in turn, requires healthy blood vessels and a steady supply of red blood cells generated by your bone marrow.

The best way to keep your body humming is to eat a well-rounded, nutritious diet. Want to-die-for, salon-style hair? Then you need healthy hair follicles to build hair in the first place—and that, in turn, depends on having a healthy heart to pump nutrients to those follicles, and healthy lungs to give them oxygen.

As for better mental acuity—well, you get the idea: Your brain depends on the vitality of your heart, lungs, liver, kidneys (you name the organ) to be in tip-top shape. The best way to bring out your best attributes is to foster your overall health through smart eating—a diet that favors produce, grains, legumes, and lean sources of protein, such as fish and soy. ◖

> Simply by eating at a leisurely pace, you could drop up to 20 pounds a year.

Battle of the Diet Plans

Three studies try to establish, once and for all, the best way to drop pounds.
Naomi Barr has the results.

Americans spend $60 billion a year on diets, pills, and programs in the hope that the weight loss approach they choose will ultimately triumph over others. Although there are many diets in contention, a clear winner has yet to emerge. As obesity rates continue to rise dramatically worldwide, scientists have recognized the need to test the effectiveness of the most widely used plans. Over the past few years, three notable university-based studies (one from Stanford, a second from Harvard and the Ben-Gurion University of the Negev, and a third from the University of Missouri) have pitted some of the leading diets against one another—and, in the last case, against exercise—to determine which approach offers the best results. Their conclusions may surprise you, so before you spend any more money or time fretting over the most recent diet aid, check out the results of the matchups.

THE CONTENDERS:

LOW CARB

(e.g., Atkins) advises lots of protein, mostly in the form of meat at every meal, and restricts carbohydrates. Thirty percent of your calories will come from protein, 50 percent from fat, and about 20 percent from carbs, especially good ones like veggies and fruit.

LOW FAT

(e.g., Weight Watchers) emphasizes grains, fruits, and vegetables, and allows modest servings of meat. Portion control is key. About 50 percent of your calories will come from carbohydrates, 30 percent from fat, and 20 percent from protein.

ZONE

balances carbohydrates, fat, and protein, theoretically to stabilize hormones that trigger hunger and weight gain. Thirty percent of the calories you eat will be fat, 40 percent carbohydrates, and 30 percent protein.

MEDITERRANEAN

prescribes grains, vegetables, and sources of healthy fats such as olive oil and nuts. About 45 percent of your calories on this plan will come from carbohydrates, 35 percent from fat, and 20 percent from protein.

ORNISH

is an extremely low-fat vegetarian diet that recommends forgoing nuts, meat, and fish. Roughly 70 percent of your calories will come from carbohydrates, 20 percent from protein, and 10 percent from fat.

OFFICIAL SCORECARD

MATCH 1
Low carb vs. Low fat vs. Mediterranean

- ☑ **NUMBER OF DIETERS:** Low carb, 109; low fat, 104; Mediterranean, 109.

- ☑ **POUNDS LOST AT SIX MONTHS:** Low carb, 14; low fat, 10; Mediterranean, 10.

- ☑ **FINAL LOSS (TWO YEARS):** Low carb, 12 pounds; low fat, 7; Mediterranean, 10.

- ☑ **THE DETAILS:** Most of the dieters in this 2008 study published in *The New England Journal of Medicine* (and paid for in part by the Atkins Research Foundation) were men. The women actually lost more pounds on the Mediterranean approach, but the finding wasn't conclusive. As is true in most diet studies, weight loss peaked at around six months, after which dieters began to put pounds back on. All groups saw improvements in cholesterol, insulin, glucose, triglyceride, and blood pressure levels.

MATCH 2
Low carb vs. Low fat vs. Zone vs. Ornish

- ☑ **NUMBER OF DIETERS:** Low carb, 77; low fat, 79; Zone, 79; Ornish, 76.

- ☑ **POUNDS LOST AT SIX MONTHS:** Low carb, 14; low fat, 9; Zone, 6; Ornish, 6.

- ☑ **FINAL LOSS (ONE YEAR):** Low carb, 10 pounds; low fat, 6; Zone, 4; Ornish, 5.

- ☑ **THE DETAILS:** Low carb (Atkins) was the victor in this 2007 study published in the *Journal of the American Medical Association.* These dieters also saw their heart disease risk factors—blood pressure, cholesterol, triglyceride levels—plummet at least as much as they did for people on the heart-healthy low-fat and Ornish diets. Again, most of the pounds were shed in the first six months, with many people gaining back some weight. By the end, in fact, many had stopped following their prescribed diets closely.

MATCH 3
Low fat vs. Exercise

- ☑ **NUMBER OF DIETERS:** Low fat, 24; exercise, 19.

- ☑ **POUNDS LOST AT SIX WEEKS:** Low fat, 6; exercise, 2.

- ☑ **FINAL LOSS (THREE MONTHS):** Low fat, 9 pounds; exercise, 3.

- ☑ **THE DETAILS:** In a 2008 study published in the *Journal of Exercise Physiology,* a group of dieters followed a low-fat plan, while exercisers stuck to their usual eating patterns and worked out at least three days a week for 50 to 60 minutes at a gym. Though the dieters shed more pounds, some of the loss was in the form of calorie-burning muscle (the exercisers kept their muscle mass). As the researchers point out, muscle is key to helping dieters maintain weight loss. The results demonstrate the need to combine exercise and dieting.

AND THE WINNERS ARE... *Low carb and Exercise*

☑ A low-carb diet consistently produced the greatest weight loss, so this plan—combined with exercise—seems to be a good place to start. "I'm a proponent of that approach if it means you'll eat fewer junky carbs," says

Christopher Gardner, PhD, associate professor of medicine at Stanford University and lead author of the study in Match 2 (*above*). But Gardner says dieters may need to try more than one plan before they find success. "We are all so

different—a diet that works for me may not work for you," he says. Although low carb won in terms of average weight loss, each diet had a few adherents who managed to lose 30 to 40 pounds. "What's more important than diet type is how closely you

can adhere to it," says Gardner.
The truth is, says Meir Stampfer, MD, of the Harvard School of Public Health and an author of the Match 1 study, "there is more than one way to go for weight loss, so don't get discouraged." ⬤

The Great Weight Debate

Surprise: The latest research shows you can be overweight and fit, and thin but carrying too much fat. Sarah Reistad-Long sorts it out.

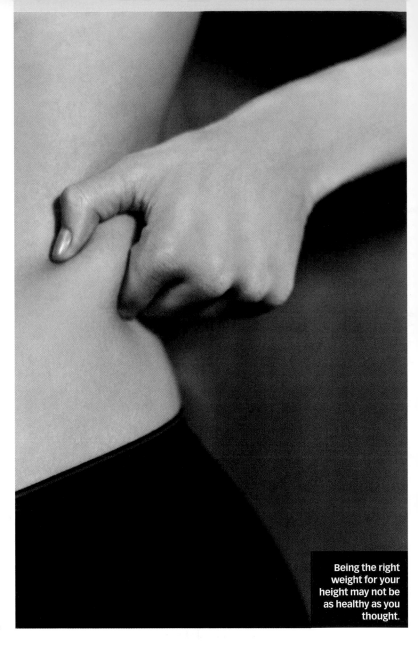

Being the right weight for your height may not be as healthy as you thought.

Leah Dawson is unhealthy—at least that's what public health guidelines would have you believe. The 41-year-old mother of three, who manages her husband's athletic career (he's Olympic skier Toby Dawson), works out four days a week and carefully monitors her diet. Her cholesterol and blood pressure are enviable. But never mind all that: Leah Dawson is considered "unhealthy" because at 5'8", her weight has hovered near 170 pounds. That puts her at 26 BMI (body mass index—the height-to-weight formula doctors use to diagnose weight problems), which is in the overweight category. "My doctor would tell me that I needed to lose weight," she says. "My lab work would come out fine; I've even passed a stress test. But I'm never 'okay.'"

Thirty-nine-year-old Teresa Holler, on the other hand, is considered "healthy." As a physician assistant, Holler knows she needs to monitor her weight. But after a tough pregnancy six years ago, she slowed down her normally rigorous exercise program. Initially, the trim 5'3", 128-pound, size-5 Holler wasn't too concerned: Her BMI remained at 23, putting her in the healthy range of 18.5 to 24.9. Still, she began to worry that something was amiss. "I felt like I was getting this ring of fat around my midsection," she says. "And I was just less energetic." This led her to request a body-fat test from her doctor. She was shocked to find the amount of fat she was carrying on her diminutive frame—30 percent—qualified her as borderline obese, dramatically elevating her risk for diabetes and heart disease. "Here I was, spending my days telling other people how to get healthy, and I'd missed this," she remembers.

Health experts have been too strict with heavy people like Dawson, and too lax with normal-weight people like Holler: Researchers at the Mayo Clinic have found that about half of American adults in the normal-body-weight category still have too much body fat—and given that these people also tend to have many of the risk factors associated with heart disease, that assessment is probably correct. "I'm a cardiologist, and I was seeing too many patients whose BMI checked out as normal but who didn't look right," says Francisco Lopez-Jimenez, MD, the Mayo doctor who headed the study. "Some had a big belly, some had low muscle mass. And they had high blood sugar and cholesterol. It became clear to me that the measurements we were using weren't working for these people."

How risky is it for a normal-weight person to carry too much fat? The answer lies in the way the body stores the stuff. "All fat isn't created equal," says Timothy Church, MD, PhD, a professor at Louisiana State University's Pennington Biomedical Research Center. "The deeply deposited kind—visceral fat—produces three times more bad chemicals than other types, and it drains directly into your liver."

Visceral fat bulks up the trunk of the body, and it has been directly tied to increased risk of diabetes and heart disease. (People who carry fat on the hips and thighs seem to have a lower risk.) Importantly, visceral fat tends to be the type normal-weight people have. It sneaks up on a person because it's not especially visible and it can build up without altering weight—replacing muscle that is naturally lost with aging. And that stealthy buildup of fat may help explain the results of a 2005 study in the *Journal of the American Medical Association (JAMA)*: Researchers analyzed mortality data of people in different weight categories, from underweight to obese, and found that there were fewer deaths among overweight people than those in the normal-weight group.

That finding may come as quite a shock for Americans, who have had it drilled into them that being heavy will take years off their life. But evidence

to the contrary has been mounting, and a 2008 report on the U.S. population published in the journal *Archives of Internal Medicine* made the issue impossible to ignore: Half of Americans who are in the overweight BMI category and a third of those in the obese one (30 or greater BMI) are actually healthy—they have plenty of "good" cholesterol, normal blood pressure and glucose levels, and no other risk markers for heart disease.

"In other research I was doing, I was seeing a lot of people who were heavy but fine," says MaryFran Sowers, PhD, a professor of epidemiology at the University of Michigan who coauthored the study. "What was surprising about the study results was that the number of healthy overweight people was *so prevalent.*"

Lopez-Jimenez agrees. "We've long assumed that all people who are overweight have a lot of fat, and that people with normal weight have less fat and more muscle," he says. "We now know that's not always true. There are fewer unhealthy overweight people out there, and many more at-risk normal-weight ones than we thought." In other words, BMI is an imperfect standard. A simple height-versus-weight number can't account for how a person is built, lean or stocky, big breasted or not.

So if BMI is flawed, what is the best predictor of who is healthy and who isn't? In Sowers's study, there was one reliable answer. People who qualified as heavy but still healthy tended to report being physically active. Indeed, her study isn't the first to note this. Findings published in *JAMA* in 2007 indicate that fitness level—regardless of weight—is the single strongest predictor of mortality risk. People with the lowest level of fitness were four times more likely to die than those with the highest. Longevity didn't require superhuman effort, either; people who could pass a minimal fitness test of walking for longer than five and a half minutes on a treadmill had half the risk of an early death as those who failed the challenge.

Taking all the new findings together, the lesson is that even at 170 pounds, Leah Dawson had it right: Eat a good diet and drop any unhealthy habits you might have. Then focus on exercise and forget about striving toward some standardized ideal of weight. "Fitness is the critical piece we're losing sight of," says Church. "People get so caught up with weight—they start to exercise, the scale doesn't move, and they get discouraged. They're not noticing that their pants fit differently, that they've actually lost dangerous visceral fat. When you become active, you're not just adding muscle, you're getting healthier." And that's what will help you live longer. ◖

Fitness level— regardless of weight—is the single strongest predictor of mortality risk.

Posture Power

Slouching brings you down in more ways than you might think. Here's a plan for upright living.

S tanding up straight is like drinking eight glasses of water a day: Nice if you can do it, but it's not as though slouching will kill you, right? You'd be surprised. In a review of more than 100 studies, scientists from UCLA found that poor posture is associated with breathing problems, falls, depression, and decreased quality of life, all of which shave years off life expectancy.

One of the biggest contributors to slumping is weak muscles in the abdomen and back. "Even people who exercise regularly can have poor posture," says Lesley Powell, director and founder of Movements Afoot, a Pilates wellness center in New York City. "But if you practice good posture, it will carry over to your workout."

Powell's graceful, powerful exercises borrow elements of Pilates, yoga, and dance to target your legs and core. Don't let their elegant appearance fool you, though: They'll quickly strengthen the muscles you need to achieve good alignment.

Powell's program is shown here and on the next page. Hold each position for three to five seconds, resting a few seconds between moves. Then go through the whole series twice more for a total of three sets. As the moves get easier, try holding them longer. —*John Hastings*

1. Standing side kick

(Strengthens abdominals, back, hips, thighs)
Extend your arms to the sides, straight out from your shoulders. Lean forward while lifting your right leg, toe pointed, out to the right. Lift your foot four inches off the ground and balance. Repeat with the left leg.

The Straight and Narrow Plan

More moves that will help you maintain good posture and keep you on the road to health.

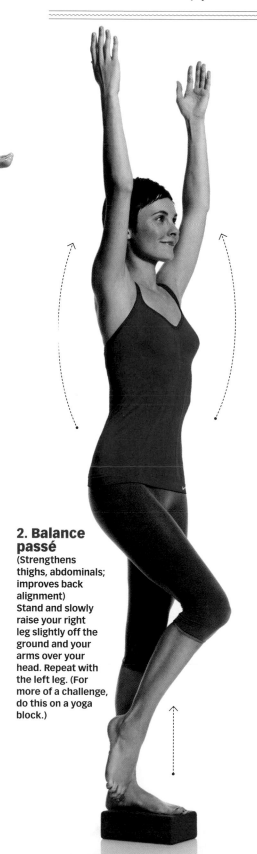

2. Balance passé

(Strengthens thighs, abdominals; improves back alignment)
Stand and slowly raise your right leg slightly off the ground and your arms over your head. Repeat with the left leg. (For more of a challenge, do this on a yoga block.)

3. Bridge

(Strengthens abdominals, thighs)
Lie on your back, arms at your sides, knees bent, feet flat on the floor. Press your feet down as you contract the muscles in your legs. Lift your pelvis up; keep your neck relaxed, and let your legs—not your back—do the work.

4. Side leg lift

(Strengthens hips, thighs)
Lie on your right side with your back touching a wall. Rest your head on your right arm, bend your right leg, with the sole of your right foot facing the wall. Straighten your left leg and lift it about a foot off the ground while pressing the left heel into the wall. Then switch sides.

5. Kneeling side kick

(Strengthens shoulders, abdominals, thighs, back)
Kneel down on the floor, back straight, and then lean to your left until your left hand is on the floor. Lift your right leg straight out to the side until it's parallel to the floor; move that leg slowly backward and forward for three to five seconds while maintaining a straight spine. Repeat on the right side. 🔘

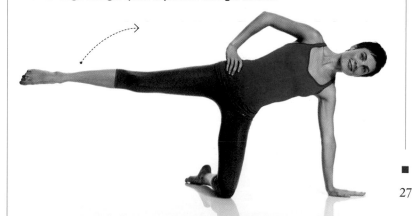

And Now a Word About Exercise

Sure, you can use commercial breaks for quick trips to the fridge. But those 15-plus minutes of ad time per hour are a great opportunity to burn calories. The moves below require no special equipment—just the floor space in front of your TV.

WALL SIT

"Holding this position strengthens your core, quadriceps, and glutes, which in turn helps prevent pain in your low back, knees, and hips," says Vonda Wright, MD, an orthopedic surgeon and author of *Fitness After 40*. Stand with your back against the wall, feet shoulder-width apart, and squat down until your knees are at about 60 degrees; hold for 30 seconds—about the length of one commercial.

PLANK AND SIDE PLANK

"This move is meant to work your core, but it's amazing for your upper body," says Wright. Using your elbows and forearms to support yourself, hold a push-up position for 30 seconds; work up to two minutes. For side plank, face the television, propping yourself up on your bottom forearm. Hold for 30 seconds, working up to two minutes. Repeat on the other side.

STANDING LUNGES

"By doing lunges slowly, you increase intensity," says personal trainer Pete Cerqua, author of *The 90-Second Fitness Solution*. Standing, take a big step forward with your right leg. Sink halfway into a lunge (right knee at a 45-degree angle) and hold for five seconds. Sink further (your knee at a 90-degree angle); hold for five seconds. As you rise up, pause halfway and hold five more seconds, then return to a standing position. Repeat, alternating legs. —*Polly Brewster*

Decode (and Defuse)
Your Exercise Excuses

If finding excuses to skip workouts made us fitter, we'd all be triathletes. Sports psychology consultant Kristen Dieffenbach, PhD, at West Virginia University, says we avoid exercise because "we've robbed it of any joy. We've transformed it from a natural, stress-relieving activity to something we have to schedule, plan, and create goals for. In other words: another form of stress." Here, some common exercise excuses, and advice on ditching them once and for all.

"I'm already too busy—I can't deal with one more thing I'm 'supposed' to do."

TOO MANY WOMEN put their jobs, obligations, and the people they care for before themselves, says Dieffenbach. "Most wouldn't say out loud, 'I am not as important, and I don't deserve the time,' yet that's the only way to translate their actions." Try justifying regular trips to the gym by reminding yourself that unless your needs are met, you'll have trouble meeting the needs of the people counting on you. "Self-care is key to caring effectively for others," says Dieffenbach. "If a friend called and requested some of your time, you'd make it available. Be that kind of friend to yourself."

"How can I exercise when I'm always tired?"

"FIRST YOU HAVE to realize that there are two types of energy—physical and mental—and that they feed off each other," says New York City–based trainer Kacy Duke, author of *The Show It Love Workout*. "Chances are, you're mentally tired from sitting at your job all day, and you need to get your blood circulating to rev your engine again," she says. "Tell yourself, *I will do just ten minutes.* And grant yourself permission to call it quits if you're still slogging after ten full minutes. Eventually, you'll make the connection that feeling tapped out means you need to move more, not less."

PREDICTING FAILURE is a classic way of protecting yourself, says Dieffenbach: "Rule out success, and you don't have to try." Find out what's behind your pessimism by listing the negative thoughts that occur when you picture yourself exercising, she says. One common roadblock is a fear of failure; a new routine can be daunting. If you're put off by the thought of setting up an effective—and safe—workout, consider spending a bit extra on a personal trainer to get you through the challenging first few weeks of an exercise regimen. —*Selene Yeager*

"I'll start out gung ho, but I know I'll get bored and quit."

health

31 A BETTER YOU I BY SARAH BOWEN SHEA

33 YOU DON'T HAVE TO GAIN IT ALL BACK! I BY BOB GREENE

34 "BACK TO BUSINESS" PLAN I BY BOB GREENE

35 THE TRUTH ABOUT THE THYROID I BY JOHN HASTINGS

36 9 NUMBERS THAT COUNT I BY MEHMET OZ, MD

39 ON CALL I BY MEHMET OZ, MD

40 TWO FAMILIES, TWO CHALLENGES I BY GRETCHEN REYNOLDS

46 YOURS FOR THE PICKING I BY MICHELE OWENS

48 EVERYTHING YOU NEED TO KNOW ABOUT MENOPAUSE I BY MARY DUENWALD

    53 SHOULD I TAKE HORMONES OR NOT? I BY JOANN MANSON, MD

A Better You

Discover the Web's smartest health advice for women. By Sarah Bowen Shea

We all know to go to Zappos for shoes or Amazon for, well, anything nowadays, but where do you turn when you get diagnosed with a heart condition, or you're wondering whether your symptoms add up to irritable bowel syndrome, or you want to do a little digging on the drug your doctor prescribed? Sure, you can google yourself silly, but with so much contradictory—and in some cases flat-out wrong—information on the Web, how do you make sure the advice you collect is reliable?

"When patients ask me about Web resources, I'm always nervous because there's a lot of incorrect informa-tion out there, or it's industry sponsored," cautions Alice Domar, PhD, founder of the Domar Center for Mind/ Body Health, which specializes in integrative medicine. And indeed, studies funded by the Robert Wood Johnson Foundation and others have found that information on health Web sites is often inaccurate or incomplete.

The good news is that there is valuable information if you know where to look; even the professionals troll the Internet to learn about cutting-edge studies or unortho-dox treatments. "The Web is wonderful for finding news that's not so mainstream," says Christiane Northrup, MD, the ob-gyn who wrote *Women's Bodies, Women's Wisdom.* "Alternative viewpoints can be just as useful in treating ill-ness, only we don't hear about them as often."

Northrup told us she recently used the Web to research the latest science on vitamin D and fish oil, which inspired us to reach out to other prominent health professionals for their picks for the best women's health Web sites.

Untangling the Web
America's top wellness experts name their favorite health sites.

THE ISSUE	THE EXPERT	THE PICK
GENERAL HEALTH	**Mehmet Oz, MD,** host of the *Dr. Oz Show* and coauthor of the best-selling *You: The Owner's Manual* series	"For one-stop women's health advice, I recommend **healthywomen .org**. Experts are available to answer questions, and you can read about women with similar concerns. It's a great place to start researching health issues; they offer a bunch of useful fact sheets on topics like diabetes and aging that you can download."
PRESCRIPTION MEDS AND SUPPLEMENTS	**Kristen Binaso,** a pharmacist and spokesperson for the American Pharmacists Association	"The most reliable information on prescription drugs is at the U.S. National Library of Medicine and National Institutes of Health's MedlinePlus site [**nlm.nih.gov/ medlineplus**]. You'll find drug interactions, the latest black box warnings about serious adverse effects, and extensive information on supplements, including efficacy."
HEART HEALTH	**Lynne Shuster, MD,** founding director of the Women's Health Clinic at the Mayo Clinic	"**Womenheart.org** is the Web site of the National Coalition for Women with Heart Disease, founded by three women who had heart attacks in their 40s. The site provides a wide range of information that is unique to women with heart conditions, and it's carefully reviewed by a committed team of heart disease experts."
MENTAL HEALTH	**Robert Klitzman, MD,** professor of clinical psychiatry at Columbia University College of Physicians and Surgeons and the author of *When Doctors Become Patients*	"A lot of mental health sites focus solely on depression, but **webmd.com** gives good background on everything from stress management to ADHD. The site, however, could do a slightly better job of making it clear that in many instances the best treatment for mental health disorders may be talk therapy, by itself or combined with medication."
INFERTILITY	**Alice Domar, PhD,** founder of the Domar Center for Mind/Body Health and author of *Conquering Infertility*	"For unbiased, comprehensive, and up-to-date information on infertility, the best site is **resolve.org.** It combines medical information, tips, and strategies for coping with the emotional impact of infertility, plus information on all family-building options. It has links to local resources and state-by-state insurance coverage."
DISEASE RISK	**Tara Parker-Pope,** author of the *New York Times* Well blog	"**Yourdiseaserisk.com** is a guide for assessing your chances of developing cancer, diabetes, heart disease, osteoporosis, and stroke. You answer questions and it gives you an indication of where you fall on the spectrum. It was created by a Harvard doctor, and it's based on all the scientific evidence out there."
CANCER	**Paula A. Johnson, MD,** chief of the division of Women's Health at Brigham and Women's Hospital	"I really like **womenshealth.gov,** a Web site of the U.S. Department of Health and Human Services. It's broad, with a lot of factual information, but it also has a lot of vetted links. Unlike many other sites, it will steer you to trustworthy places. Think of it as a gateway to the best cancer resources on the Web."
MENOPAUSE	**Susan Love, MD,** president of the Dr. Susan Love Research Foundation and author of *Dr. Susan Love's Menopause & Hormone Book*	"For support and community, I have always liked **power-surge.com.** The message boards tend to be good, and the site does a better job of describing women's experiences than anything else out there. I caution people, though, that the site uncritically recommends bioidentical hormones even though the safety data doesn't exist yet."
PEDIATRIC HEALTH	**Harvey Karp, MD,** author of *The Happiest Toddler on the Block* and a professor of pediatrics at the University of Southern California School of Medicine	"**Healthychildren.org** was just launched by the American Academy of Pediatrics. This is a well-developed health-oriented site that's there to give you advice on raising your child and also to calm your mind about medical concerns. It talks directly to parents, not below them or over their heads."
FITNESS	**Bob Greene,** exercise physiologist, trainer to Oprah, and founder of thebestlife.com	"The American Council on Exercise has added an extensive library of exercises to their site, **acefitness.org.** Click on the Get Fit tab and you'll find many moves for every muscle group. The instructions are easy to follow and the information is free." **O**

You Don't Have to Gain It All Back!

From avoiding food triggers to managing stress, **Bob Greene** weighs in with what he knows about relapse—and how to prevent it.

"You don't have to be perfect. If you do something most of the time, you'll be successful."
—Bob Greene

The majority of the American population either wants to be thinner or is actively trying to become so. Yet why do we have such a hard time controlling our eating and sticking to an exercise program? In the 25-plus years that I've been helping people slim down, I've noticed a few common traps that cause people to fall off the wagon. (Incidentally, they're similar to the reasons we fail to lose weight in the first place—and I'll tell you about them on the next page.) Science, too, is starting to help us understand why certain people may be wired to relapse.

That research has to do with the way we respond to pleasure. Food, sex, a glass of wine, certain drugs—they all raise levels of the reward chemical dopamine in our brain. Nora Volkow, MD, director of the National Institute on Drug Abuse, believes that for some people, eating cookies or french fries raises dopamine levels in a way that keeps them going back for more. In other words, these people can become as hooked on food as alcoholics are on booze and smokers are on nicotine, although even in the worst cases, a french fry never delivers the same kind of high.

One reason the craving to overeat may occur is that the brain is deficient in dopamine receptors. In someone like this, it would take more food than normal to get the same hit of satisfaction. According to Volkow, dopamine is also a major player in the frontal cortex, the area of the brain that puts the brakes on destructive behavior. So being low in dopamine hits your weight control efforts with a double whammy—you're driven to eat more and it's harder to stop once you start. That's why when you relapse, it's not with just a slice of pizza; it's with the entire pie.

At this point, there's no way to test your brain to determine whether it's dopamine deficient. But if you suspect that's the case, you should try adopting new sources of pleasure. Hanging out with people you enjoy, for example, is a great start. Also, exercise (I'm not making this up) appears to raise dopamine levels. And avoid foods you can't stop eating (ice cream, cookies, french fries) the way you would stay away from bars and happy hours if you were trying to quit drinking.

Recently, in fact, experts have started comparing the struggle to slim down with the difficulty of breaking an addictive habit. Research suggests that it often takes a number of attempts before people are able to kick cigarettes or give up alcohol for good; this might also be true for weight loss. The National Weight Control Registry is conducting an ongoing study of more than 5,000 men and women who have succeeded in maintaining an average loss of 66 pounds for more than five years—and among them, 91 percent had tried and failed before. The average total number of pounds lost (and relost) by a participant through various diets is a whopping 565!

So here's the good news: Instead of thinking, *I've failed over and over again, why bother trying again?*, take your relapse in stride and stay positive no matter how many attempts it takes you. Each new effort brings you closer to the one that might really work. The key is to stick with it until you achieve your weight and health goals—that's my definition of a true success story. ◐

Bob Greene's "Back to Business" Plan

Whether you're starting from square one or have landed back there, don't kick yourself: I've put together a 12-week program to encourage you on your way to successful weight loss. You'll make six simple diet changes and ease into exercise slowly because I want you to stick with it and avoid injury. (Log on to oprah.com for intermediate and advanced programs.) I've also included the traps you may fall into as you begin to take off weight. But first, let me say congratulations—you've decided to improve your life!

WEEKS	FOOD SWITCH	CARDIO	STRENGTH	TRAPS TO AVOID
1 & 2	Replace soda with water, unsweetened iced tea, or fat-free milk. Diet soda is okay, but limit the amount, as it may encourage cravings for sweet foods.	15 minutes of activity such as walking or riding a stationary bike five times a week. You should be working hard enough so that you can talk, but not for very long.	None. Starting a strength-training program can stimulate hunger. That's why I recommend waiting until you get a few healthy diet changes under your belt.	Don't be tempted by a shortcut (a fat-burning pill, a fad diet). It may work for a while, but to lose weight permanently you need to move more, eat less, and figure out the emotional reasons you turn to food.
3 & 4	Trade in your white bread for 100 percent whole grain. In addition, try incorporating whole grain pasta and brown rice into your diet.	Add five more minutes of cardio to each workout session, for a total of 20 minutes, five days a week.	None at this time.	Exercise is tough. You can shed pounds by just cutting calories, but among successful long-term weight losers, 90 percent exercise regularly. Physical activity also improves mood, sleep, even sex.
5 & 6	Cut out trans fat (look for it on labels—or for "partially hydrogenated oil"). Find baked goods and spreads without it, or make your own, using healthy fats such as olive and corn oil.	Add five more minutes of cardio to each workout, for a total of 25 minutes, five days a week.	Start with eight moves that work the major muscle groups: triceps extension, biceps curl, squat (see oprah.com). Do one to two sets of eight to ten reps for each, three times a week.	Have you thought about the emotional reasons behind why you overeat? You'll keep relapsing if you don't. Try keeping a journal to help get at the deeper issues you need to address.
7 & 8	Switch from fried foods to roasted, sautéed, or baked. Try roasted potatoes, baked (and lightly breaded) chicken, vegetables sautéed in olive oil.	Add five more minutes of cardio to each workout session, for a total of 30 minutes, five days a week.	Continue with your strength-training routine.	Your initial enthusiasm may be wearing thin—so sudden work demands or an injury can throw you off your program. Figure out now how you'll respond to such setbacks.
9 & 10	Skim the fat from dairy: Go from whole or 2 percent milk and yogurt to 1 percent or fat-free versions. Also try calcium- and vitamin D–enriched soy milk with no more than 100 calories per cup.	Add five more minutes of cardio to each workout, for a total of 35 minutes, five days a week.	Add another set of eight to ten reps to each of the moves in your routine.	You're beginning to appreciate the work involved in weight control. Many people set out to lose 20 to 30 percent of their total weight, but 10 percent is more realistic. You may want to revisit your initial goal.
11 & 12	Consider cutting out alcohol as a way to eliminate calories. Instead of beer, wine, or a cocktail, order sparkling water with a splash of fruit juice (or another low-calorie drink) and see if it doesn't make a big difference.	Add five more minutes of cardio to each workout session, for a total of 40 minutes, five days a week.	Continue with your strength-training program.	The pounds have come off—great! But now you find yourself skipping a workout and allowing a second helping here and there. Remember, weight loss is not a finish line but the beginning of a process in which you learn about yourself and improve your life. The longer you persist, the easier it gets.

The Truth About the Thyroid

Sometimes you can blame your weight on your glands. John Hastings investigates.

The thyroid has a big job: The hormones it secretes help regulate heart rate, maintain healthy skin, and play a crucial part in metabolism. When the gland is sluggish (hypothyroidism), it can rob you of energy, dry out your skin, make your joints ache, cause weight gain, and kick-start depression. When it becomes overworked—hyperthyroidism—and produces too much hormone, it can cause racing heart, sleep disturbances, and weight loss. That's a lot of grief for a gland the size and shape of a buckeye butterfly.

Given what can go wrong, you may be surprised to hear that about half of the estimated 27 million Americans with thyroid disease remain undiagnosed, according to the American Association of Clinical Endocrinologists. The seemingly unrelated symptoms are partly to blame. People can spend years going from internist to specialist trying to get a diagnosis. They're often prescribed skin creams and antidepressants when what they really require is thyroid medication.

Most people with thyroid disease, about 80 percent, have the hypo version. Should symptoms drive you to make a doctor's appointment, one of the first things your physician will ask is if you have a relative with the disease, since thyroid disease tends to run in families. Your risk also increases as you get older; in addition, being female

> You may be surprised to hear that about half of the estimated 27 million Americans with thyroid disease remain undiagnosed.

(the disorder is as much as eight times more common in women), or having another autoimmune disorder such as type 1 diabetes or rheumatoid arthritis can worsen your odds.

Depending on your risk profile, your doctor may recommend a thyroid-stimulating hormone (TSH) blood test. TSH is released by the pituitary gland; when the thyroid bogs down, the pituitary releases more TSH. If you have normal levels of TSH, your test score will be from .4 to 2.5. A score between 0 and .4 is hyperthyroidism. Between 2.5 and 4 means you are at risk for hypothyroidism, and should be retested within a year. Above 4 means you have a mild case. Doctors used to resist treating patients in this category (clinical hypothyroidism starts at 10). But a 2007 British study in *The Journal of Clinical Endocrinology & Metabolism* suggests that treating such patients can help prevent cardiovascular disease by reducing bad LDL cholesterol and the risk of hardened arteries while improving waist-to-hip ratio and increasing energy. So if your symptoms led to a TSH test and you scored higher than 4, you and your doctor should discuss treatment.

Most people with hypothyroidism face a lifetime of managing the gland. You'll get a prescription for synthetic thyroxine, which does an excellent job of replacing the missing hormone. Once you and your doctor work out the proper dosage—and that can take some time—you *will* feel better. ▣

9 Numbers That Count

Every woman should strive to meet these optimal goals to make this your healthiest year ever: Mehmet Oz, MD, does the math.

R esolutions are like teenage hearts: They get broken an awful lot. So for the next year, let's make a pact. No more false promises, no more extreme measures, and no more white flags being raised. Here are nine key numbers you can easily tweak to make a huge difference in your overall health. You'll see that resolutions work much better when you take off the "re."

115/75 BLOOD PRESSURE

Hypertension is a cunning thief; left unchallenged, it can steal a decade of quality life. The average American's blood pressure in middle age is about 130/80, but since the average American dies of heart disease, that number isn't good enough. Instead, aim for 115/75. Measure your blood pressure monthly at the same time of day with a home monitor or one at a local drugstore.

TO LOWER BLOOD PRESSURE: Exercise hard enough to sweat for at least an hour each week. If you're used to 30-minute workouts, this means you'll need to do three, since it takes at least ten minutes to start sweating.

83 RESTING HEART RATE

Before you get out of bed to commune with the coffeemaker, take your pulse: Put two fingertips on your wrist or carotid artery (in your neck under your jaw) and count the beats per minute. This is your resting heart rate. Anything higher than 83 means you're at increased risk for a heart attack.

TO SLOW YOUR RESTING HEART RATE: The key, ironically, is to make your heart beat faster for an hour per week (to calculate your ideal number of beats per minute while exercising, subtract your age from 220, then multiply the result by .8). So, just as you'll be doing for healthy blood pressure, simply work up a good sweat.

2 to 1 CHOLESTEROL

When it comes to cholesterol, the total level isn't as predictive of heart disease as what's known as the ratio. To explain, cholesterol is carried in the blood by two different lipoproteins: The bad one, LDL (think *L* for lousy), spews the waxy, fat-like substance in your arteries, gunking them up; the good one, HDL (*H* for healthy), gathers up cholesterol so it can't clog. If you have some risk for heart disease (family his-

tory, high blood pressure, diabetes, smoking), keep your LDL under 100. Otherwise you're okay aiming for under 160; better yet, below 130. Ideally, your HDL should be more than 50. Doctors love it when the ratio of LDL to HDL is less than 2 to 1; they're tolerant if it's 3 to 1.

TO IMPROVE YOUR RATIO: Include soluble fiber in your diet from sources such as oatmeal, kidney beans, and apples, aiming for 25 grams a day. To spice things up, try a whole grain called quinoa. It contains a nearly perfect balance of proteins, as well as the mineral manganese—low levels of which are associated with hypertension.

4 to 1 OMEGA-6S TO OMEGA-3S

Omega-6s and omega-3s are called essential fatty acids for a reason: Their work includes building cell membranes and nerve insulation. But since the body doesn't produce these fats, you must get them from your diet—and the balance makes all the difference. American drive-through cuisine includes huge amounts of omega-6s (irritating in high levels), yet hardly any omega-3s (particularly beneficial for the heart). Although the optimum ratio is 4 to 1, ours is often 20 to 1, which puts us at increased risk for cardiovascular disease, arthritis, asthma, and some cancers.

TO RIGHT THE OMEGA BALANCE: Eat more fish, seafood, whole grains, beans, nuts, and ground flaxseeds to increase omega-3s. And cut back on processed foods—along with oils made from corn, safflower, cottonseed, and peanuts—to ease off the omega-6s.

1 INFLAMMATION

If you've ever seen an apple slice turn brown 20 minutes after being cut, you can picture what inflammation does to your body: It causes the rusting of tissue. You can gauge your level of inflammation with a blood test that measures C-reactive protein (CRP), which is produced by the liver and is part of the body's battle response. A healthy level is under 1—mean-

Hypertension is a cunning thief;
left unchallenged, it can steal a decade of quality life.
Measure your blood pressure monthly.

If you've ever seen an apple slice turn brown 20 minutes after being cut, you can picture what inflammation does to your body.

ing you've got less than half the chance of heart disease than if your level is greater than 3. A number above 10 suggests you may have another ailment (such as an autoimmune disease) that should be diagnosed.

TO REDUCE CRP: Try to eliminate low-grade irritants like gingivitis (floss daily) and vaginitis (see a doctor, especially if it recurs). Also move toward a Mediterranean-style diet (lots of fruits, vegetables, and whole grains; fat from olive oil; moderate amounts of wine).

32.5 WAIST SIZE

Ideally, your waist should measure less than half your height (do it at the belly button—go ahead and suck in). That means if you're 5'5", yours would be less than 32.5 inches. The reason: The omental fat beneath your stomach muscles causes inflammation, which drives many of your body's other critical numbers in the wrong direction.

TO LOSE INCHES AT YOUR WAIST: Focus on slicing off 100 calories a day. Since salad dressings sabotage many a good intention, one idea is to make this nutty recipe part of your routine:

1. Mix 1 tablespoon each of walnut (or hazelnut) oil, olive oil, and balsamic vinegar; add salt and pepper to taste.
2. Chop 1 small tomato, ¼ cup diced onions, and 6 sliced mushrooms.
3. Pour the combo over 1 head of Boston lettuce.
Makes 2 servings, about 150 calories each.

125 BLOOD SUGAR

The other danger of omental fat is that it can block insulin's ability to work, which increases blood sugar and puts you at risk for diabetes. Your blood sugar should be less than 100 after an overnight or eight-hour fast and less than 125 if you aren't fasting.

TO LOWER BLOOD SUGAR: Try chia seeds, which contain

omega-3s and fiber (sprinkle them on yogurt or salads). It's believed that they form a gelatinous substance in the stomach that helps slow the speed at which sugar is absorbed.

-1 BONE DENSITY

It's a good idea for all postmenopausal women to get a bone density scan, especially those who are not on hormone replacement therapy, stand taller than 5'7", or weigh less than 125 pounds. You should also be tested at around age 50 if your mother has had osteoporosis or either of you has had a hip fracture, if you take steroids, or if you drink excessively or smoke. The standard DEXA (dual energy X-ray absorptiometry) scan provides a T score—your bone density compared with that of a healthy young woman: Above -1 is normal; between -1 and -2.5 indicates osteopenia, which may lead to osteoporosis; below -2.5 means you have osteoporosis.

TO STRENGTHEN YOUR BONES: Along with 1,000 IU of vitamin D, take 1,200 milligrams of calcium and 400 milligrams of magnesium (to prevent the constipation that calcium can cause)—half in the morning, half in the evening. Also, start a program of resistance training (using gym equipment, dumbbells, or exercises like pushups and squats) for at least 30 minutes a week.

30 VITAMIN D

When you're deficient in vitamin D, you may be at increased risk for heart disease, cancer, multiple sclerosis, and immune disorders, not to mention osteoporosis. To make sure you're getting enough, take a blood test for vitamin D: Your level should be greater than 30.

TO BOOST VITAMIN D: If you can't get 15 minutes of sun exposure daily, take a supplement containing at least 1,000 IU of D3, the most potent form of the vitamin, or chug a tablespoon of cod liver oil every morning. ◖

On Call

Mehmet Oz, MD, explains how to avoid cell phone dangers.

Dr. Oz will see you now.

I got my first wireless handheld in 1990. It was as big and clunky as a brick, but the mobility it offered made it indispensable. There are now more than 270 million cell phone subscribers in America, and on average we spend about 11 hours a month with the gadgets glued to our heads. But as we've become more reliant on cell phones, experts have grown concerned about the health implications of heavy exposure—specifically, the radiation that the devices emit.

Cell phones expose us to a form of electromagnetic radiation called radiofrequency (RF) energy. Scientists have suspected that this radiation might increase the risk of brain cell damage leading to tumors, and in 1995 they found this to be the case in rats. Most studies since then have failed to show a similar correlation in humans, and last December the Danish Cancer Society released results from a 29-year study that found no solid association between increasing cell phone use and brain tumors. Yet just months earlier, an analysis of the most rigorous studies found convincing evidence linking the use of handheld phones to brain tumors, especially in users of a decade or longer.

The medical community is paying attention, and so is the U.S. government. Last fall a Senate hearing on cell phones and health coincided with an international conference on the same subject. While more conclusive evidence is needed before we start clamoring for the return of pay phones, there are some simple ways you and your family can limit exposure to the radiation:

USE A HEADSET OR SPEAKERPHONE.
No reliable data exist on the upper limit of safe talk time, but corded headsets can reduce any potential risk. These emit much less RF energy, and allow you to move the phone away from your body. One study shows that using a headset lowers radiation exposure eightfold.

KEEP YOUR PHONE OUT OF YOUR POCKET.
A study published last year in the *Journal of Craniofacial Surgery* linked cell phone radiation to decreased bone density in the pelvis, and a 2008 study conducted by the Cleveland Clinic found that it lowers fertility in men.

STOP TALKING WHILE DRIVING.
In addition to creating a potentially deadly distraction, using your phone in the car forces your cell signal to jump between wireless towers. Since RF is highest when a connection with a tower is first established, talking while traveling can increase exposure.

DON'T CHAT WITH A POOR SIGNAL.
The harder your phone has to work to get reception, the more radiation it emits. This is the reason you should avoid using so-called radiation shields (the shiny stickers that claim to block radiation); they actually force the phone to transmit at a higher power.

DON'T WEAR WIRELESS HEADSETS AS IF THEY WERE JEWELRY.
Earpieces don't emit as much radiation as a phone, but they release some—even after your call ends. Remove the device between conversations.

LIMIT CHILDREN'S USE.
Kids have a thinner skull, and their brains are still developing—which may make them more vulnerable to any potential harmful effects of RF radiation. **O**

THE LEWIS-BATTEYS
Busy lives mean Rosalind and Earl Lewis-Battey of Los Angeles (in their kitchen with kids Taylor, *right*, and Evan) often grab packaged or fast food on the run. "We eat wherever we can, whenever there's time," Rosalind says. "But there's never enough time."

Two Families, Two Challenges

One is short on time, the other is short on money. Can they still eat well? We asked a team of experts for their best tips on making healthy meals that are fast and cheap—and still taste great. By Gretchen Reynolds

Breakfast at the Lewis-Battey household in suburban Los Angeles requires all of Rosalind Lewis-Battey's extensive training as a systems engineer. There's scant room for variance or miscalculation. At 6:20 A.M., Rosalind, 46, wakes up her 13-year-old daughter, Taylor, who, after dressing, washing, and primping, has barely ten minutes to gobble cereal, yogurt, or maybe a granola bar before she and her mother rush off to her bus stop.

Rosalind, whose husband, Earl, is just finishing an overnight shift as a detention officer, then returns and wakes 10-year-old Evan. His later school start affords him a comparatively leisurely 15 minutes to wolf down cereal before another mad dash to his school. After dropping him off, she then stops at a 7-Eleven to grab coffee before heading to

work at an aerospace company. There, she's a principal director, with weighty responsibilities. Almost every day, she eats a bowl of instant oatmeal for breakfast and a hastily swallowed take-out lunch.

"There was a time when I cooked," Rosalind says with a sigh. "I liked cooking. I don't cook anymore. I assemble."

Several states away, geographically and metaphorically, the Rogerson family of Santa Fe faces a very different mealtime dilemma. Until recently, Hank Rogerson, 42, earned a respectable salary as an assistant professor of moving image arts at the College of Santa Fe, a private liberal arts school. But the college, rocked in part by the recession, slashed employee salaries in February, which for Hank meant a 78 percent drop in monthly wages. Food shopping for the family became a minefield. "On days when we've just paid bills and there's not much left in the checking account," Hank says, "I'll find myself standing in the store thinking, *Okay, if I buy eggs now, can I get milk, too? If I can't buy both, which do we need more?* We have two small children. How am I supposed to make those choices?"

Food is where many of the most reverberant, of-the-moment issues of family life and recessionary economics meet. How can you feed your family well when you're busy and exhausted? How can you buy healthy foods when your budget has drastically shriveled? "Those are almost universal problems right now," says organizational expert Julie Morgenstern, author of *Shed Your Stuff, Change Your Life.* "I doubt if there's a single family out there that isn't wrestling with either not having enough money or not having enough time to eat well, and probably both."

Enter the pros. *O* went to a lineup of top chefs, organizational experts, nutritionists, and even the secretary of the department of agriculture, asking them: How can these two families—and all the rest of us who are strapped for time and money—prepare meals that are healthful, speedy, inexpensive, and, not least, good? The advice that came back was, in part, philosophical, touching on the emotional import of food. But most of it was flat-out, you-can-do-this practical, with a surprising emphasis on pork shoulder. "Anyone can cook pork shoulder," one chef said. "It's easy to prepare. It's very, very cheap, and one shoulder can feed an army."

"These are tough times, financially and emotionally," Morgenstern says. "But they're also a chance to redefine our relationship to food and family and community."

The Too-Busy-to-Eat-Well Family: THE LEWIS-BATTEYS, Los Angeles

A 10-Step Time-Saving Plan

"When we remodeled our kitchen I didn't bother with a high-end stove, because I would never use it, anyway," Rosalind Lewis-Battey admits. The always-on-the-move family also rarely sits together for meals at either of the two large dining tables in their home.

"Way too many families are in that situation," says Cat Cora, the nation's first and only female Iron Chef, as well as a busy mother. "But it doesn't have to be that way. My mom was a nurse with three kids. She was busy, but we had family meals. Now, even though I'm always swamped

with work, my family cooks and eats together."

Eve Felder, an associate dean at the Culinary Institute of America in upstate New York, agrees.

"I have three girls under the age of 9," she says, "and I work full-time, but we manage to have home-cooked meals together virtually every night. I don't want to sound smug. But it can be done."

The experts' suggestions:

1 LEARN TO COOK. It may sound counterintuitive, but learning to cook, or refreshing rusty skills, is the quickest way to fit healthy foods into a jam-packed life. "If you know how to sauté, braise, and stir-fry, you can make a variety of meals very quickly," Felder says. "Stir-fry beef and asparagus with oyster sauce one night, then chicken and peppers with hoisin sauce the next. It will seem like a completely different meal, but the methods are exactly the same." Don't have time for cooking classes? "YouTube has videos covering every technique you can possibly imagine," says Mark Rubin, the director of the Culinary Arts Center for the Second Harvest Food Bank of Middle Tennessee in Nashville. "Type in 'Dice an onion.' There are dozens of video demonstrations. I watched one the other day on how to clean a squid. Fascinating."

2 SET ASIDE BLOCKS OF TIME. "Think of your weekend as seven distinct three-hour blocks of time," says Julie Morgenstern. "There's Friday evening, Saturday morning, Saturday afternoon, and Saturday evening, and the same for Sunday. If eating healthy is important, you need to devote one of those blocks to cooking and family time."

3 LET YOUR FINGERS DO THE SHOPPING. Grocery stores are a time drain. Avoid them. Instead, "plan the meals you want to have in the coming week or two, including snacks, make a comprehensive list of what you need, and get on the Internet," Morgenstern says. Almost every city has at least one grocery store that allows online ordering. "Most deliver for free, too." In later weeks, you can conveniently reorder with a single click, adding or subtracting ingredients as you go.

4 ORGANIZE YOUR KITCHEN. "Take one weekend afternoon to tear through your kitchen drawers. Throw out everything you don't need. Be ruthless," says Lori Greiner, an organizational expert. Ditto for cupboards and fridge.

Then reorder drawers and your refrigerator with hard-nosed precision: "Line up cans of tomatoes, front to back." Do the same with all your staples. "If you're going to assemble meals quickly," Greiner says, "you have to be able to see exactly what you have and what you need."

5 **PREP, PREP, PREP.** "Run your home kitchen like a restaurant kitchen," Rubin says. "Cut things up in advance." During your weekend block of time, clean and chop carrots, celery, onions, spinach, and broccoli (all of which keep well after being prepped), stuff them in ziplock bags, and put them in the refrigerator. Your meals are now half-complete.

6 **INVOLVE THE KIDS.** Turn over some tasks to your children; drastically cut your workload. Even the youngest can contribute. "My 5-year-old tears up the lettuce for salads," Felder says. Older kids, like 13-year-old Taylor Lewis-Batty, can and should cook entire meals, Cora believes: "I was cooking meals when I was 10," she says. Buy each child a cookbook of her or his own (such as Cora's *Cooking from the Hip: Fast, Easy, Phenomenal Meals*). Or let them google recipes. Buy the ingredients, then supervise, but don't hover. "You're only there to put out fires," literal and figurative, Cora says. "They probably won't need you. And kids enjoy eating what they cook, including vegetables, which is a big plus."

7 **SIMMER—AND THEN FORGET ABOUT IT.** Every expert stressed that cooking can be faster, easier, healthier—and more convenient—than eating carry-out foods. "Throw a pork shoulder or a chicken in the Crock-Pot," Felder says. Then ignore the kitchen for hours. "At the end of the day, you'll have enough meat for three or four different meals. All you have to do is make some rice and steam your cut-up broccoli. Fifteen minutes and you're done." Or have your children help you make lasagna, freeze it in meal-sized portions, and, during the week, have a microwaved Italian feast.

8 **DON'T BE AFRAID TO USE FROZEN VEGGIES.** "The frozen vegetables you can buy today are so much better than even five years ago," Cora says. "They're not those blocks of spinach that you had to break against a table." Look for flash-frozen, unprocessed corn, peas, spinach, beans, or broccoli in microwave-ready steamer bags, she says. Avoid presauced varieties, which tend to be over-processed and salty.

9 **ESTABLISH MEALTIMES.** "Being busy can be paralyzing," Morgenstern says. Structured mealtimes ameliorate some of that anxiety. "Set a family dinner hour, at 6 or 7 or whenever," she says. "Then stick to it. If one parent can't be there, leave it to the other." Kids' activities impinge? Talk to coaches about rescheduling. "Kids need order and consistency in eating habits," Morgenstern says. "We all do." Plus, it can be liberating to have boundaries, "to know that at this hour, dinner takes place. You can't control everything in your family's life. But you can control that."

Feeding Active Kids: Don't Sweat the Sugar

Between them, Taylor and Evan Lewis-Battey play softball, soccer, and basketball (and Taylor dances). Each has one practice a day. Their interstitial snacking consists of candy bars, cookies, or fruit roll-ups. "That's fairly typical" of the diets of active kids today, says Nancy Clark, a sports nutritionist and author of *Nancy Clark's Sports Nutrition Guidebook*. But, she says, even though the snacks are suboptimal, "you have to look at the overall diet," not just the sugary portions. The best current nutritional science suggests that "about 10 percent of calories can be sugar," she says. Since active children should be consuming around 2,000 calories a day, she says, that leaves them about a 200-calorie daily sugar allowance. The remaining calories should be more nutritional. For snacking, stock peanut butter, English muffins, yogurt, raisins, and cut-up fruit and vegetables. And avoid blanket prohibitions. "There's no science showing that forbidding sugar or anything else is healthy or desirable," Clark says. "Everyone will be better off if you allow treats but encourage healthful meals that reduce the desire for sweets."

No-guilt snacks: Keep cut-up fruit and veggies on hand, plus other healthy items like yogurt and raisins.

10 RETHINK WHAT "EATING WELL" MEANS. "I grew up having a sit-down family dinner every night," says Tom Vilsack, the U.S. Secretary of Agriculture. "But I know it's not realistic for most people to spend 90 minutes every day preparing dinner and sitting down together." Maybe instead, he says, "try family breakfast." The type of meal counts less than the context. "A shared meal is one of the last bastions of ritual," says Ted Allen, host of Food Network's *Chopped.* "It gently reaffirms your affection for the people you feed." So go ahead and "buy a prepared rotisserie chicken if you're too busy to cook that day," Morgenstern concludes. "It's healthier than fast food. Just be sure to sit and talk with your family while you eat it. That's what we should mean by 'eating well.'" ◐

THE ROGERSONS Hank Rogerson and his wife, Jilann Spitzmiller, of Santa Fe (with Isabel and Dane) have suffered a huge cut in wages. "Gone are the days of buying whatever we want," says Jilann. "Now we agonize over every choice."

The Family on a Tight Budget: THE ROGERSONS, Santa Fe

A 10-Step Money-Saving Plan

Jilann Spitzmiller was talking recently with friends who had vacationed in Los Angeles. "I kept asking, 'Where did you eat? What did you have? How did it taste? Tell me more.'" She's wistful. "We used to go out to restaurants all the time. It was our primary form of entertainment." Since her husband, Hank Rogerson, suffered a big salary cut, eating out has become a luxury. The family has also canceled vacations and phone services, reined in extravagances (like a birthday party for their 6-year-old daughter, Isabel), and made, for the first time, a weekly spending budget.

That process was revelatory. "I was shocked by how much we'd been spending on food," Hank says. Between grocery stores and restaurants, their family of four had easily been dropping $1,500 a month. "That's not supportable now." Cutting back, though, is wrenching. "It's not that I mind giving up things," Jilann says. Imported chocolate bars? Gone. Wine? Rarely. "But as a parent," she says, "I cannot cut down on the quality of what we feed our kids. Or ourselves." You shouldn't, agree our advisers, many of them professional chefs. Interestingly, their tips for how to maintain high food standards on a frugal budget focus on thinking like a professional chef, for whom every meal is an attempt to do exactly that:

Organics: When are they worth it?

Since her husband's salary was gutted, Jilann Spitzmiller has begun openly voicing the questions that bedevil many of us when we shop in the pricey organics aisle: "Does our milk really need to be organic?" she wonders. "If we can afford only some organic produce, which?"

In answer, the Environmental Working Group (EWG), a Washington, D.C.–based advocacy group, annually publishes a list of the most and least pesticide-contaminated produce, using data from the USDA.

Last year peaches headed the "dirty dozen," followed by, in order: apples, sweet bell peppers, celery, nectarines, strawberries, cherries, kale, lettuce, imported grapes, carrots, and pears. The least

contaminated vegetables were onions, frozen sweet corn and peas, and asparagus. Avocados, pineapples, and mangoes were the cleanest fruit. (For the complete list, visit foodnews.org.)

As for milk, the direct health benefit of buying organic remains unclear. However, Consumer Reports recommends that families with babies or small children stick with organic when they can to avoid any unnecessary exposure to antibiotics, synthetic growth hormones, and most synthetic pesticides.

But if, even with careful shopping, organics are still too costly, "have a traditionally grown apple," says Richard Wiles, executive director of EWG. "Better to have some fruit than none."

1 **EAT LESS MEAT.** "No one needs a 20-ounce rib eye," says Ted Allen, host of Food Network's *Chopped.* Current nutritional guidelines suggest, in fact, that about five to six ounces of meat or any other kind of protein per day is sufficient for most adults. Since meat is one of the costliest food items, "making meat part of the meal, not the centerpiece of the meal, can save you lots of money," says Cora. "It's also more interesting, tastewise." Make at least one meal a week vegetarian, she adds, to save even more.

2 **EAT DIFFERENT CUTS.** "Ask chefs what their favorite cut of meat is and they never say 'beef tenderloin,'" Allen says. "They say pork shoulder or flank steak or brisket"—cheaper, more flavorful cuts. "Flank steak needs only a quick sear, whereas meats like pork shoulder require longer cooking time," Allen says. When they are braised, the result is tender and ample. "You can get a lot of meals out of one pork shoulder," says Culinary Institute of America's Felder.

3 **EAT DIFFERENT PROTEINS.** "Beans are sorely underrated," at least by home cooks, Allen says. "Chefs love them. Black beans are a restaurant staple. And you see adzuki beans even in desserts now." Whatever your bean preference, try to buy the dried variety, not pricier cans. "A bag of dried beans and some rice will feed a family of four for at least two meals," says Rubin of the bustling Second Harvest Food Bank. Soak the beans for several hours or in a pressure cooker for a few minutes. Cook them with spices and "maybe a few slices of bacon or a ham hock," Allen says, add some rice, and you have dinner, for a few cents per person.

4 **GAME THE FARMERS' MARKETS.** Farmers' markets are an unparalleled source of fresh, local, organic produce and meats. They can be pricey, though. So time your shopping. "Go near the end of the day," Cora says, in the last hour or so of the market's schedule, when some farmers drop their prices. The selection of goods may be scantier, "but you can get some bargains," Cora points out. "The farmers will be glad to sell their goods before they close up."

5 **WASTE NOTHING.** This is the essence of chef-think. "In a professional kitchen, you use everything," Rubin says. "There's no waste. For a long time, most Americans haven't had to consider how to use all of the pig or cow or chicken. Now we do. That's one silver lining of the recession." As Felder says: "There's no reason you can't get at least three meals out of one chicken. You have chicken and rice one night, Vietnamese chicken salad another, and chicken soup, using stock you made from the carcass, another." Even if you buy $7 natural, free-range chickens, she says, "each dinner costs well under $10."

6 **HAUNT ETHNIC MARKETS.** "At Asian or Hispanic groceries, you'll find aisle after aisle of unusual spices and produce," Allen says. "You may not be able to pronounce the names, but they're usually markedly less than the cost of similar goods at conventional stores."

7 **SHARE.** "I recently bought a quarter of a cow," Felder says—100 pounds of natural, grass-fed beef at $5 a pound, which she keeps in a five-foot upright freezer in her basement. "It will feed us for two years." To buy grass-fed meat from farms or ranchers directly (at a price that may be much lower than what you pay for natural meats in grocery stores), try eatwild.com.

8 **GROW YOUR OWN.** "Gardening is so easy," Vilsack promises. Thanks to the example set by First Lady Michelle Obama and her compact, organic garden on the White House lawn, it's also hip. And it is mind-bogglingly frugal. For tips on how to fertilize, compost, and naturally repel insects, visit www.nrcs.usda.gov/partners/for_homeowners.html; to learn how to plant a vegetable garden, go to weekendgardener.net. And you don't have to stop with growing greens, either. "I have a childhood friend, once a very urban guy, who's now keeping chickens," Allen says.

9 **SAVOR THE SMALL, GOOD THINGS.** Don't forsake every beloved food. Just rethink portions. "Buy a good chocolate bar once a week, if that's what makes you happy," says Morgenstern. "Then eat only one square a night. Good things should be appreciated. We had so much for so long. Now it's time to savor and enjoy the little things."

10 **RETHINK WHAT "EATING WELL" MEANS.** "One of the big lessons of this economic downturn is that we need to revalue things," Morgenstern says. "All those jars of fancy sauces and gourmet salad dressings that we were buying before? We never needed them, and if we did, we could have made them ourselves. Self-sufficiency is being thrust on us. But that's not bad. Frugality is in our bones as Americans. We can make our own salad dressings and they will be better than anything we could buy." Or, as Cora says of feeding her young sons, "Eating a peanut butter sandwich with them—now *that's* eating well." ◑

From seeds to edible greens: A gardener reaps the bounty.

Yours for the Picking

Forget the myth of the $20 tomato—raising your own fresh, luscious, sun-ripened fruits and vegetables isn't the backbreaking, budget-busting hassle you'd think. Michele Owens digs in.

I hate to break it to you, but the best-tasting food in the world cannot be bought at any price. Not even the nicest farmers' market produce can compete with salad greens that land in the bowl a few minutes after being picked, or tomatoes sliced still warm from the sun, or lemon basil leaves thrown onto roasted vegetables within a moment of being pinched off their stems. If you want food this fresh and flavorful, you have to grow it.

And if you are after culinary adventure and consider the kitchen an endless frontier, that, too, argues for growing your own food. Farmers must be conservative and plant those vegetable varieties they can transport and sell. If there's no demand for hairy melon from cus-

tomers, they're not going to grow hairy melon, no matter how wonderful it may be in a curry.

Home gardeners, on the other hand, are free to experiment with strange Indian gourds, odd Italian leaf broccolis, and strawberries so delicate they seem to consist entirely of perfume. Brilliant seed purveyors like Fedco Seeds and Baker Creek Heirloom Seeds are constantly seeking out the new, the forgotten, the extra-flavorful, and the just plain weird. With even organic seed available for two or three dollars a packet, this is one of the few areas of life where crazy extravagance is the only sensible way to proceed.

Plus, if you hope to eat sustainably as well as beautifully, few things are kinder to the planet than to grocery shop the backyard. Unlike industrial farms, which collectively use tremendous amounts of fossil fuels and cause an array of ecological problems with their overreliance on artificial fertilizers and soil-crushing machines, the home garden requires nothing that upsets the balance of nature. It requires almost no energy input, either, other than the energy of the gardener.

Ah, but that's the problem, you might say! Gardening is hard work, right? Actually, the most successful gardening methods require the least labor. If you manage your garden intelligently, it can take less time than pushing a cart down your supermarket's miles of aisles twice a week. In other words, it's *easy* to grow a flood of beautiful food. Of course, there are many 400-page guides on the bookstore shelves that make it sound as if a vegetable garden has to be managed with the same precision as a graded college chemistry lab. Ignore them. Here's the cheerful truth: Push a seed into the earth and it *wants* to grow. Here is something else the how-tos may not make clear: There is no one right way to make a vegetable garden. The finer points will vary tremendously depending on where you are doing it.

But the basic principles are simple:

1. Pick a spot, any sunny spot, for your garden. It
doesn't have to be large. My first garden was just six by ten feet. It's safe to say that as a first-time gardener, you will be astonished at the amount of food that can be grown in a small space.

The spot also does not have to be perfect in other ways. If your yard is contaminated by lead, or the drainage is terrible, or the ground is undiggable, raised beds are probably the answer. If you are gardening in an arid place, you can always plant your seeds in trenches. Even if your soil has the texture of beach sand or modeling clay, you can eventually turn it into gorgeous loam by adding lots of organic matter to it, something we'll discuss in a minute.

A fence, however, may be a prerequisite for happiness, depending on the ambitions of your local deer and rabbits. And the sun is not negotiable. In my experience, even vegetables that don't like heat need a full day of sun to thrive.

2. Dig once. Then let the worms do the digging for you
forever after. When you first make a garden, you are generally trying to accomplish two things—remove a piece of lawn and dramatically increase the fertility of your ground. Both argue for an initial plowing. Ripping up sod by hand is a brutal job, so I'd recommend borrowing a gasoline-powered tool like a tractor or Rototiller this one single time.

Then pull any visible clumps of grass out of your garden and dig lots of organic matter into it, such as composted kitchen scraps, composted farmyard manure or bagged manure from the hardware store, lawn mower clippings, spoiled hay, straw, or ground-up fall leaves. Scientists parse the subtle advantages of one over the other. In my experience, they all work and are magical in combination.

Here is the important concept: Garden soil is ideally intensely alive, full of more species than you can bend your mind around, including various worms, bacteria, fungi, protozoa, and insects. They will eat the organic matter you have deposited (or each other), and in the process make nutrients available to your vegetables in a form the plants can use. They will also aerate your soil, keep it free of disease, and improve both its drainage and ability to retain water. In other words, they are subtler gardeners than you will ever be, so once the garden is made, let them manage everything below the surface.

In the future, apply your organic matter as a sheet of mulch on top of your soil several inches deep, with the coarser stuff on top. Do it every year, and this blanket will not only feed your underground allies, it will make your life easy by keeping down the weeds and keeping the soil moist. Push this mulch aside to plant a row in spring, pull it back when your seedlings are sturdy plants.

3. Be bold and panoramic in your planting. My first
small vegetable garden contained only the holy triumvirate of tomatoes, basil, and arugula. I had nice salads and pesto from that garden for months. But now I plant a slew of crops, and in any given year, you can always find me taking a flier on things I've never tried before, like black garbanzo beans or tatsoi, an Asian salad green. Not only am I constantly discovering new tastes, I'm spreading the risk with this diversified portfolio, because even experienced gardeners suffer through years when their potatoes rot in the wet ground or the groundhogs eat every broccoli relative for lunch. Plant different things—and plant them in different spots every year to befuddle pests and diseases—and something is sure to thrive, no matter what nature throws at you.

4. Water, weed, and pluck the fruits of your labor. In a
well-mulched garden, neither watering nor weeding will be an arduous proposition. Both will give you a chance to bask in your handiwork, to admire the powdery blue blush of the red cabbages, the graceful arching posture of the chard leaves, the intensely colored little sprays of flowers on the scarlet runner beans. Is there any kind of garden more beautiful than a vegetable garden? Not if your idea of happiness is similar to mine: a good meal on a lovely evening in late summer with family and friends. ◑

Everything

(but were

you need to know
about menopause
too hot, tired, confused,
and cranky to ask)

Is estrogen safe this week? Does it matter when you start hormone therapy? What does "bioidentical" mean, anyway? **Mary Duenwald** scours the latest science for the answers even your doctor may not have.

In a windowless high school auditorium a few blocks from where Highways 6 and 50 intersect in Delta, Utah, you could hear the rain and thunder picking up steam. But for 100 or so women attending a menopause workshop one Sunday, the storm was inside, where the topic of a lecture was about how changing hormones affect sex drive—not the sort of thing people usually talk about in this rural community of alfalfa hay farmers. The speaker was just opening the discussion for questions when the power went out. "It was just so perfect. Suddenly, hands went up

everywhere and the women were asking all kinds of questions they wouldn't have been willing to ask when the lights were on. One wanted to know about orgasm—really personal questions," recalls Linda Ekins, 60, the registered nurse who organized the event.

That was six years ago; today the workshop has expanded into an annual conference called Women in Motion that draws 250 to 300 attendees. The idea came to Ekins when she realized she wasn't alone in having to bushwhack her way through menopause. All across the country, millions of women are dealing with the end of fertility, many of them muddling along in discomfort and frustration. It isn't just a jarring reminder that one is aging; it can also wreak havoc on the body—and the mind. Sudden outbursts of temper, creeping anxiety, depression, loss of passion, or foggy thinking sends many sufferers in search of psychological help; others rush to trainers when their waistlines start expanding; still others go crazy buying supplements to combat thinning hair and painful joints. And often these women don't realize that the real cause of these symptoms—not to mention hot flashes, night sweats, vaginal dryness, and insomnia—is the onset of menopause, which officially starts after 12 consecutive months of having no menstrual periods.

Scientists have yet to figure out why declining levels of estrogen (which occurs when the ovaries stop producing eggs) should have such wide-ranging effects. But they do know that cells throughout the body have receptors for the hormone and that its withdrawal impacts everything from the blood vessels to the brain. "The layperson has very little information about this," Ekins says. "My women are confused. They're having hot flashes. They're bitchy with their husbands, grouchy with their kids, angry at the world, absolutely miserable." And ebbing libido—particularly how it's affecting their marriages—is a huge concern (a course called "Hormones in the Bedroom" drew a standing-room-only crowd a couple of years ago). "My aim is to give women information, so they can visit with their physicians and intelligently come up with a plan," she says. "We do not need to be afraid. We need to be educated."

And yet even smart, well-informed women often hit a wall when it comes to deciding which symptoms *are* menopausal and how to deal with them. Hormone therapy (HT)—specifically supplemental estrogen, alone or combined with progesterone (usually progestin)—is the most studied and effective form of treatment to date for symptoms such as hot flashes and night sweats. But the treatment developed a bad reputation in 2002 after the Women's Health Initiative (WHI)—which conducted the largest, most rigorous study ever on HT—issued alarming findings that taking estrogen and progestin could increase the risk of both breast cancer and heart disease. In addition, it later came out that the hormones didn't seem to help much with sleep, depression, energy, or sexual satisfaction compared with a placebo. "There is still a lot of confusion even among physicians about hormone therapy, and many avoid prescribing it," says JoAnn Manson, MD, chief of preventive medicine at Harvard's Brigham and Women's Hospital and a principal investigator of the WHI study. "It can be a real problem for women to find a doctor who is willing

to discuss all the benefits and risks of hormone therapy."

To more safely and comfortably navigate this major phase of life, it helps to understand a bit about past hormone research and what science is discovering even as we speak.

Hormone History

It was back in 1966 that Robert Wilson, MD, a Brooklyn gynecologist, published his best-selling book, *Feminine Forever*, and declared that taking estrogen was a postmenopausal woman's best chance to lead a healthy, happy, and sexually active life. In the ensuing decade, prescriptions for the hormone almost doubled. But then came evidence that taking estrogen could lead to uterine cancer, and prescriptions dropped off dramatically.

Hormone therapy regained its popularity, however, after the discovery that adding progestin headed off the risk of uterine cancer. In the early 1980s, scientists began to focus on how estrogen could protect women's bones against osteoporosis. By the '90s, research seemed to confirm its long-suspected link to preventing heart disease, at which point the American Heart Association and the American College of Physicians came onboard. Once again, hormone therapy looked like a smart idea.

But in 2002, the Women's Health Initiative caused scientific whiplash. According to its findings, the hormone pills in question—Prempro, the most popular brand of estrogen and progestin—not only failed to protect against heart disease but actually raised the risk. Crunching the data, the researchers projected that among 10,000 women taking these hormones for a year, compared with a placebo, there would be seven more cases of coronary heart disease, eight more cases of stroke, and 18 more cases of blood clots. "There was much rending of clothes and gnashing of teeth when this study came out, because the results were very unexpected," says Nanette Santoro, MD, director of reproductive endocrinology and infertility at Albert Einstein College of Medicine, in the Bronx.

Less shocking but more unnerving for many: Among 10,000 women on Prempro, there would also be eight additional cases of invasive breast cancer. (The fact that there was a lower risk of colorectal cancer and hip fractures got lost in the shuffle.)

The WHI findings made major headlines and were particularly scary to the public, given that researchers stopped the study three years early to protect participants' health. Women by the millions threw out their hormone pills. To this day, many are still wary. "I can understand the mistrust," says Carla Lupi, MD, an assistant professor of clinical obstetrics and gynecology at the University of Miami Miller School of Medicine. "These women grew up being told that hormone therapy was the greatest thing since sliced bread, only to wake up and be told that there actually are some risks."

Unfortunately, scientists have yet to unearth a more effective remedy than estrogen, and that may reflect what's been a relatively narrow approach to the profound mind-body shifts that occur during menopause. "All of this focus on estrogen may be a bit misplaced," says Lisa Sanders, MD, clinical instructor at Yale University School of Medicine. "Women exist in an incredibly complicated hormonal milieu during menopause. Estrogen declines, but so does testosterone, which is why libido goes down. We're also losing hormones that we really don't know much about, and we haven't asked the questions."

The fact is, however, researchers do know a lot more about hormone therapy today. Since the WHI shake-up, they have begun to explore—and shed light on—how the formulation and timing of HT may lower its risks and improve its benefits. And the result is a more nuanced knowledge of how the treatment might be most safely applied.

The Bioidentical Option

Vivian Torres-Suarez, 54, a healthcare executive from Queens, New York, was one of millions of women suspicious of hormone therapy in the wake of the WHI findings. But her symptoms were getting to her—not only hot flashes but also a hot temper that had prompted her to lash out at a colleague during a staff meeting. "I don't remember exactly what he said, but I must have turned into a wicked witch," Torres-Suarez recalls. "Then he said, 'Are we having a bad menopausal day?' And I just blasted him."

Torres-Suarez's gynecologist recommended the estrogen pill Premarin, which contains the same type of estrogen used in the WHI study. "I don't feel comfortable with that, I really don't," Torres-Suarez told her doctor. And there are experts who would agree with that choice, arguing that Premarin and Prempro are not ideal products because they're derived from the urine of pregnant horses. Instead, these doctors prefer a synthetic estrogen, estradiol (found in Estrace, Climara, Estring); it's chemically identical to the kind made by women's ovaries, which is why it is described as "bioidentical." Between 2003 and

A 2002 report suggesting hormones were risky scared the bejesus out of women. Millions tossed their pills.

2008, prescriptions for bioidentical estradiol-based products rose from 22 to 35 percent of the supplemental estrogen market while those for Premarin tablets fell from 53 to 35 percent, according to IMS Health, a healthcare information and consulting company.

Manhattan internist Erika Schwartz, MD, prescribes estradiol made by pharmaceutical companies or orders a transdermal cream from a compounding lab, which customizes it for individual patients. When Torres-Suarez visited Schwartz for a second opinion, the bioidentical hormones made sense to her, and she liked the idea of a cream (hers includes bioidentical progesterone), which she applies to her chest twice a day. "My hot flashes haven't disappeared, but they're much better," she says. "And I'm no longer like the girl in *The Exorcist*. I felt like I was losing my mind, and I'm not like that—I'm really a nice person. This has absolutely made me better."

Yet, whether bioidentical estrogen and progesterone are safer or superior is unproved. It's entirely possible that they have the same risks that Prempro does. "There was a flight from reason when the WHI results were published," says Santoro, referring to the illogical assumption that if a hormone product wasn't used in the study it must therefore be safe. She adds: "To prescribe something more physiologic may make sense, but what's really physiologic for a 55-year-old woman is to have less hormone, period."

Kirtly Parker Jones, MD, a professor of reproductive endocrinology at the University of Utah, in Salt Lake City, points out another important fact of biology. The body often takes the estrogen it's given and changes its form, so that a woman may use estradiol only to have her body turn it into estrone sulfate, the main ingredient in Premarin and Prempro. "Some well-meaning practitioners probably don't know the endocrinology," Jones says. One trial in the works called the Kronos Early Estrogen Prevention Study (KEEPS) is giving some subjects estradiol patches and others Premarin pills, with the goal of determining whether the patch is as effective as, and potentially safer than, the pill. But the results aren't expected until 2012.

In the meantime, a number of practitioners who are deeper into the bioidentical movement are stirring up controversy by measuring the hormone levels in women's saliva, a method unproven by mainstream science, in order to concoct products that may contain mixtures of various kinds of bioidentical hormones, as well as ingredients that have not been approved by the Food and Drug Administration. In January of 2008, the FDA took action, sending warning letters to seven compounding pharmacies stating that their claims of producing drugs that are safer, more natural, and superior to FDA-approved HT drugs are "false and misleading" and unsupported by medical evidence. In particular, estriol, one form of estrogen used by these pharmacies, has never been approved by the FDA, and its safety and effectiveness are unknown.

The Risks of Hormone Therapy

For many women, the specter of breast cancer is what drives them away from HT—and for those who have a higher-than-average risk of the disease, such fears make sense. The link between HT and breast cancer has been supported by studies conducted in the United States, Sweden, and the United Kingdom.

While finessing the chemistry of estrogen won't likely mitigate the breast cancer risk, tinkering with the progestin component of HT might. "Study after study seems to indicate that the increased risk of breast cancer is not related to estrogen but to progestin," says Steven R. Goldstein, MD, a professor of obstetrics and gynecology at New York University School of Medicine. A separate component of the WHI study in which subjects were not given progestin (because they'd had hysterectomies and stood no risk of uterine cancer) did not show an increase in breast cancer risk.

Goldstein has begun to experiment with prescribing his patients much less progestin, while regularly monitoring their uterine lining with ultrasound—the idea being that a smaller amount of the hormone may be enough to prevent cancer there. Still, he makes clear, "there has been no long-term study of this methodology."

When it comes to heart disease risk, the research is most promising. Because the WHI was designed in part to investigate HT's effect on heart disease, the researchers chose mostly women who were older (and more likely to have cardiac events); the average age of the 27,347 subjects was 63, and a majority of them were at least ten years past having their last menstrual period. But now a new theory has taken shape and steadily gained credibility: that hormones

might be less dangerous, and perhaps even beneficial, if started closer to the time women reach menopause (the average age is 51). According to this new theory, estrogen introduced before too much plaque begins to build in a woman's arteries might actually help keep blood vessels healthy. Only after the plaques have gained a foothold might HT make things worse. Further analyses of the WHI data support this idea. As it turns out, a subgroup of younger women in the estrogen-alone study had a significantly reduced risk of heart attacks and cardiac death; those with the increased risk were the ones who'd started hormones more than ten years beyond menopause.

A New Approach: Start Early

Starting HT earlier might also positively affect memory, concentration, and cognition. Alas, here again there is no good clinical trial data. But a half-dozen small studies have had promising results, says Sarah Berga, MD, chairwoman of the department of gynecology and obstetrics at Emory University School of Medicine in Atlanta. "Estrogen seems to lubricate the brain, in some ways, for thinking," she explains.

Better evidence for—or against—early timing may arrive when the KEEPS study, whose subjects range in age from 42 to 58, is completed. "What I hope the study will show," says Santoro, one of its principal investigators, "is that for women close to menopause, the risks of hormone therapy are low and they may get some cardio protection."

There is already a growing consensus around this idea. Many of the leading experts now recommend HT at the lowest dose and for the shortest time possible—the first few years of menopause—along with regular checkups and mammograms for women with debilitating symptoms (assuming they don't have high risk of heart disease or breast cancer). Manson recommends staying on hormones two to three years, five at the most (see "Should I Take Hormones or Not?" on the following page), after which hot flashes usually subside. "Five to 10 percent of women have persistent significant symptoms more than ten years after menopause," she says; in those cases, doctors and patients must weigh the individual health risks against quality

> Now a new theory has taken shape and steadily gained credibility: that hormones might be less dangerous, and perhaps even beneficial, if started closer to the time women reach menopause.

of life benefits. "But the vast majority of women can come off HT after a few years and do fine." This, by the way, is now the position of the North American Menopause Society and the American Association of Clinical Endocrinologists.

But we still have a long way to go in terms of getting the answers we need—which means that women really must take the steering wheel in directing their care. For Linda Ekins, the nurse in Utah, menopause has been a challenging journey. "It's not just about medication," she says, explaining that her menopausal troubles started 20 years ago with depression. "I couldn't figure out what was going on. I went into therapy and realized that part of it was menopausal." When hot flashes came soon after, she was able to keep them at bay by taking the herbal supplement dong quai (although research has failed to prove it a reliable treatment). "But at 55," she says, "the hot flashes were breaking through, and I wanted information." She'd read about bioidentical hormones and found her way to the University of Utah's Kirtly Parker Jones, who prescribed them to her in a progesterone pill and estrogen patch. "I asked for the lowest dose possible, and Dr. Jones said I could try cutting the patch in half. I did, but then I started having hot flashes again, so I've gone back to the full dose. The hormones have done really well for me, including helping vaginal dryness, which I don't choose to experience because I'm still sexually active; as long as my husband is happy and I'm happy, things are good." But, she adds, there's so much more to managing menopause on an emotional and spiritual level. To that end, Ekins has expanded her conference by bringing in experts in yoga and energy work. "Find friends and support systems," she urges. "A pill or patch can certainly help, but it won't be the answer to everything." ◐

Should I Take Hormones or Not?

JoAnn Manson, MD, author of *Hot Flashes, Hormones, and Your Health,* suggests asking yourself three questions *before* going to the doctor.

Amid all the recent confusion about hormone therapy (HT), it is still an appropriate option for some women. Although it's been proven as a treatment only for hot flashes, night sweats, and vaginal dryness, it may also improve sleep, mood, and concentration.

But like most medications, HT carries risks, including higher rates of stroke, blood clots in the legs and lungs (perhaps less of a problem with patches or gels than pills), breast cancer (especially with combination estrogen and progestin), and, for older women, heart disease. So it's worth trying other options first—layered clothing, portable fans, exercise, relaxation techniques, and avoiding dietary triggers such as alcohol, caffeine, and spicy foods. And although research findings are decidedly mixed, some women report hot flash relief from soy, black cohosh, and certain antidepressants.

If, however, none of these strategies work, and you want to consider HT in consultation with your doctor, ask yourself:

1. Do I have hot flashes or night sweats that disrupt my sleep or quality of life? If the answer is yes, HT may be a good option for you, especially if you have recently entered menopause. If, however, vaginal dryness is your sole complaint, try low-dose topical or vaginal estrogen products, which do not have the same systemic absorption as pills or patches and can be used safely for longer. If you're concerned about bone health, be sure to get adequate calcium, vitamin D, and weight-bearing exercise, and ask your doctor about the nonestrogen medications available for preventing osteoporosis.

2. Does my health profile make hormone therapy too risky? Any woman who has a history—or high risk—of breast, uterine, or ovarian cancer should avoid hormone therapy. The same is true for those with liver or gallbladder disease or unexplained vaginal bleeding. And if you're more than ten years past menopause or have an elevated risk of heart disease or stroke, HT is not a good choice for you either. If none of these

health issues applies to you, then you may be a good candidate for HT.

3. Am I comfortable with the idea of using hormone therapy? If—and only if—your symptoms and health profile suggest that hormone therapy is appropriate, you'll need to rely on your own information gathering and instincts to make the decision. Despite society's tendency to "medicalize" menopause, keep in mind that it is not an "estrogen-deficiency disease" but rather a natural stage of life. Interestingly, we no longer refer to hormone therapy as HRT, because the R stood for "replacement"—when, in fact, there is nothing missing. (Premature menopause due to surgery or ovarian failure is different: In these cases, HT is treating a medical condition.) If you are hesitant to take hormones for any reason, you should firmly resist pressure from your doctor, partner, or peers to do so.

On the other hand, if you decide to try HT (and have no risk factors), keep in mind that it is best taken for only two to three years and, as a general rule, no more than five. ◐

beauty/style

55 OTHER PEOPLE'S GLANCES

    56 SPLIT IMAGE | BY NOELLE OXENHANDLER

    58 THE LADY VANISHES | BY VALERIE MONROE

    60 SWEATING IT OUT | BY JESSICA WINTER

62 LISA KOGAN TELLS ALL

64 SOMEONE LIKE YOU | BY BETSY BERNE

"I've always preferred a rather wistful, pensive image of myself… maybe my friends appreciated something about me that didn't penetrate my self-critical radar."

Other People's Glances

They can make you feel loved and understood. Or utterly invisible. Or chronically mortified. Three women take a good look at themselves from another perspective and come out happier, wiser, calmer, and, yes, drier.

Split Image

Why was her least favorite picture of herself the one her friend cherished most? Noelle Oxenhandler discovers that there are some things your mirror won't tell you.

There's a moment when a friendship is deepening that a face changes before your eyes. It feels like a kind of shimmer, as if a veil has dropped away, and you can suddenly see the face behind the face of the person you're getting to know. If you spoke a language like French, it would be the moment you moved from formal to familiar, from *vous* to *tu*. Whatever language you speak, it's the moment when the person before you, and the connection between you, becomes more real.

It's a moment I've always loved. But the sad thing is, I can't seem to get to it with myself. No matter how often I've seen my own face in the mirror or in photographs, I always approach it with the gaze of a stranger—a suspicious stranger. Or, worse, I approach it from the absolute opposite end of the spectrum, as if in the very moment when a close connection shatters. It's the sort of moment one writer so chillingly captured in a passage I read years ago and have never forgotten: A man is having tea with the woman he has passionately loved for quite some time. She lifts a teacup to her lips, makes a slight smacking sound— and suddenly he finds her unbearably coarse and common, drained of any redeemable features. There's something particularly bitter about such moments, a quality of be-

trayal: Someone for whom we had such hopes has turned into an object of disgust. Isn't it true that, on really bad days—and perhaps especially as we get older—many of us look at ourselves this way?

Just the other day, I was having a cup of tea with a friend when I looked up and noticed a photograph of me on her kitchen bulletin board. The moment I saw it, I could feel myself recoil. It's a photograph in which I am outside in the full sun, my eyes crinkled tight and my cheeks about to burst in a fit of laughter.

"Why on earth do you have to display that hideous picture of me?" I asked. "It makes me look like a squirrel with mumps."

Irrational as it was, I actually did feel as though she must have put the photograph there with the intention of humiliating me.

"It isn't hideous," she said—and now it was her turn to sound hurt. "When you laugh, you have a way of losing yourself in the laughter. And that's something I've always loved about you."

Her words made me see something I'd never seen before. I saw that, in blurting out my dislike for the photograph, I had rejected a gesture of affection: as though I'd tossed away a gift, or turned up my nose at a gracious invitation. Even more than that, I had invalidated the moment we'd long ago passed through together, the moment our friendship deepened, when the social veil dropped and our connection became more real.

Suddenly it struck me that several of my close friends kept, somewhere in their houses, an image of me dissolving in laughter. I've always preferred a rather wistful, pensive image of myself. Now, for the first time, I let it sink in that maybe my friends appreciated something about me that didn't penetrate my self-critical radar.

"What do you think?" I asked another friend, Christine. "Do we see ourselves as accurately as those who care for us do?"

She didn't even need a moment to reflect. "When my father died ten years ago, it was such a surprise to see the photograph that he'd kept of me in his wallet."

"Why was it a surprise?"

"Because it was a photograph of me at age 11, just before I became anorexic, and I was so round and smiling."

I heard the sadness in her voice, and I knew that it was many layered. It included the loss of her father, her long struggle with anorexia, and something else as well—a retroactive appreciation of her lost self. And though she didn't say the words aloud, I could hear them in the air between us: "If only I had known how endearing I was then, when I was round and smiling." If only...

As I've begun to ask other women about their ability to see themselves, I've heard the sound of this "if only" again and again. Just the other day, I heard it in my aunt's voice when I showed her the photograph of herself that I had come across in a box of old treasures. "Gosh, I was pretty then," she said. She and I looked a few moments at the long wavy hair and dark doe eyes of the young woman she had been—and then she thrust the photograph back in the box. "I really had no idea. My three best friends were classic beauties, and I always compared myself with them."

Sometimes it's not a retroactive appreciation that's needed but the reverse. If we're nostalgic for a certain lost image of ourselves, it's important to remember the full context. One friend told me that, on her refrigerator, she kept a photograph of herself at her absolute thinnest. "When was it taken?" I asked. There was a long pause, and then she confessed: "It was taken after my trip to India, after I had dysentery that lasted for three months."

Saddest of all was the friend who showed me her favorite photograph of herself, thin as a rake and leaning against a tall oak tree. Remembering the context, I gasped. "But that's when you nearly died of heartbreak! Look how pale and fragile you were. Don't you remember how we had to feed you like a baby bird?" For weeks several friends and I had taken turns stopping by her house with soups and puddings and canned pears because nothing else could make it past the giant lump in her throat. Now I actually felt betrayed that she could possibly admire the photograph that was evidence of this desperate time.

Of course, we can't always rely on our family and friends to protect us from our distortions and reflect our true selves. Sometimes they, too, get attached to a certain image. My neighbor Susan, who's 65, complains that the only photograph her father keeps in his room is one of her as a teenager, in a bikini. Every time she encounters this photograph, she experiences it as a kind of reproach to the adult woman she's become. "It's like, for him, the teenager I haven't been for more than four decades now is the real me. He can't make a space for the person I am."

There's the sadness of trying to keep up with an idealized version of ourselves, every time we look into the mirror or the lens of a camera.

There's the sadness of trying to keep up with an idealized version of ourselves, every time we look into the mirror or the lens of a camera. There's the sadness of realizing—like my aunt, or my friend Christine—that we failed to appreciate the face that was there, behind the veil of the ideal, for those who could truly see it. Several times, when I've found myself watching one of those "extreme makeover" shows on television, I've been fascinated to observe the reactions of the family members in the audience—especially if there are young children whose parent has been transformed. In these cases, I have noticed that when the parent steps out on the stage, there's a moment when the children look absolutely horrified. After weeks of separation while the parent was going through one medical, dental, and cosmetological procedure after another, the children are looking for the familiar face of the person they love—and they're not finding it in the face of this glamorous stranger.

When my own daughter was small, she simply adored her grandmother Rose. Though Rose was wrinkled, white haired, and stoop shouldered, my daughter saw her as physically beautiful. Rose's white hair was luminous to her, like the fine-spun angel's hair that goes on your Christmas tree, and her wrinkles were what made her cheeks as soft as the velvety petals of a flower. Once, while sitting in my lap, my daughter gently stroked my cheek and said, "You're pretty, but you don't have enough wrinkles."

We say that "beauty is in the eye of the beholder," but what would it mean to look at ourselves as though we really believed this were true? The Tibetans have a saying: Who looks not with compassion sees not what the eyes of compassion see. Today, when the suspicious stranger looks into the mirror at her own reflection, I'm going to remind her of that. And who knows? If she can summon enough compassion to let go of her critical gaze, maybe she'll catch a glimpse of a woman dissolving in laughter—and see her with the eyes of a friend. O

"She wasn't flashy or glamorous; but she had a smooth, milky, 20-something complexion and the sweet, expectant, wide-eyed look of youth. Thirty years ago, I might have been her."

The Lady Vanishes

Valerie Monroe was used to being seen—and appreciated. Until she reached an age when the glances stopped. Then what? An invisible woman begins her search for a new identity.

A few months ago, I spent an afternoon helping out an art-dealer friend at a print fair. At a table in front of his display, I sat on one side of him while his assistant sat on the other; we greeted prospective buyers as they walked by. "Hi there!" I would say with warmth and (what I thought was) a touch of modest charm when I saw one coming. Time and again, from the men, I got a limp, dismissive "hi" in response, occasionally a nod. It wasn't the Whistlers or the Chagalls that were diverting the art-lovers' attention; it was my friend's lovely assistant. She wasn't flashy or glamorous; but she had a smooth, milky, 20-something complexion and the sweet, expectant, wide-eyed look of youth. Thirty years ago, I might have been her.

Today, however, I'm 58 and I look it, by which I mean that I haven't had any work done to make me appear younger. I'm trying to get down with the aging thing, to accept it—at least till I've decided that I can't. Almost every morning I discover some other small reminder that I am growing older: an age spot, another wrinkle or wisp of gray in my (thinning) brows.

If you're going through this, you already know that watching your face mature is not the most gratifying spectator sport—because no matter how constantly or enthusiastically you root for the home team, eventually age will win the game. Which is a good way to think about it, because the bottom line is that the process of aging involves a certain amount of loss. And what I discovered at that art fair is that if you have benefited from the currency of your looks, when that currency loses its value, you can end up feeling pretty bankrupt. Entering a room of mixed company—a meeting, a party—or walking down a crowded street, I've learned to expect that I'll attract a little attention. I don't mean that people stop in their tracks, open-mouthed, and stare (as they have when I've walked down the street with my 6'2", striking young niece), but I've been banking on appreciative glances for a long time. They make me feel pretty, which makes me feel happy. Not in the way, certainly, that motherhood has made me happy, or my work, but there is a small feeling of satisfaction attached to receiving these looks; it's as if, at least on the face of it, I know how to do this female thing well.

So I guess it shouldn't have been shocking to me how difficult it was to be distinctly ignored. I hadn't been aware that the glances I'd been accustomed to had been falling off. That afternoon, I felt as if I had been stripped of all color, and was the only gray-and-white figure in a richly tinted painting. I was Marion Kerby, one of the ghosts in *Topper,* all dressed up and nowhere to…be seen.

Becoming invisible is disconcerting enough. But I am beginning to feel obsolete differently, too, maybe more profoundly. I'm almost embarrassed to admit how much I still miss the fundamental, quotidian tug of a child's needs, the grounding responsibilities of parenthood. When I was actively child-rearing, my life had a purposefulness I grieve to this day. My son, at 25, now lives away from my home and is stunningly, happily independent. Which is exactly what I'd always aimed for in raising him, so I am deeply grateful. I just didn't know that along with a joyful sense of accomplishment, I would feel, in some persistent, incontrovertible way, useless. Not pandemically useless; I work, I'm productive in the ways one has to be in order to fall into the category of functioning adult, but the comforting sense of knowing my purpose from the moment I open my eyes in the morning has been replaced with a kind of disquiet. I have, if I'm lucky, a third of my life left. How am I going to spend it so that I feel the fulfillment I felt in the previous third? What can I do that matters?

And here is where the issues of being ignored and feeling obsolete converge. The art fair men—unconsciously, surely—disregarded me in part because I'm no longer fertile, unable to provide them with proof that they are still capable of reproducing. The emotional impact of having it so ungraciously pointed out that I have outlived my reproductive value was like having a bucket of cold water thrown at my face—or, rather, a cold grave opened before me. Because that means, in a Darwinian sense at least, I'm over.

Gentlemen, I feel your pain. The thing is, though my production line has shut down, the factory is still very much open. And I believe there is more work to be done before it closes for good. The psychologist Erik Erikson suggests that there are many ways to express what he calls "generativity"—the need to produce something that contributes to the betterment of society, which not only helps others but makes us feel more content as we get older. That will be my focus, as I march, largely invisible, into my future.

I can tell you this: Even if you don't see me, you will know that I am here. ◖

"I'm left drenched, sheepish, and cursing my neurotransmitters for being such drama queens."

Sweating it Out

She loves a good party. Her (very) nervous system begs to differ. After years of perspiring through cocktail hour, Jessica Winter finally finds drier ground.

It begins, always, in the groove of flesh just above my upper lip—what the Greeks named the philtrum. Tiny beads of moisture collect there, like morning dew on a leaf. More stipples appear under the awning of my lower lip, then above my brow. At this point, I start mopping my forehead preemptively with whatever's at hand—a tissue, a cocktail napkin, a sleeve—but a few rivulets usually manage to trace a brief course along my hairline before I can catch them. There isn't much I can do about the thin, cold streams trickling down my spine, pooling in the sway of my lower back.

I take precautions. I wear lots of black. No silk. Never mascara.

I have a repertoire of camouflaging gestures—secret wiping maneuvers. I'll raise a hand to my mouth, as if for a dainty clearing of the throat. I'll duck my head and do a meditative forehead rub. I'll cup my lips with thumb and forefinger while nodding sagely at the floor—my version (or so I imagine) of Rodin's *Thinker.*

I find that people are exquisitely nice. The couple I met at a birthday celebration last summer were adorable, their faces softening with bemused concern as the temperature settings rose on my internal sauna. Later, peering into the ladies' room mirror, I understood their bewilderment: I looked literally wrung out. Last autumn, at a bustling event for a friend's new book, I chatted with a college classmate who, after perhaps ten minutes of catching up, reached back to take a paper towel off the drinks table. She gave it to me without comment—I'm not sure she even broke eye contact—and with matter-of-fact graciousness, as if she were handing her business card to a prospective client.

Which is all to say: I sweat a lot at parties.

Thankfully, it's not a smelly sweat; it's diluted and benign. And, unlikely as this sounds, the sweating is not a manifestation of churning dread and anxiety—not directly, anyway. I like parties! I like people, and music, and free drinks! But somewhere, somehow, my nervous system seems to have put itself on red alert for any large social gathering, because my fight-or-flight mechanism kicks into overdrive at the first hint of crowds nibbling canapés. I'm left drenched, sheepish, and cursing my neurotransmitters for being such drama queens (but also relieved that they're so well-behaved when I'm consciously nervous—oddly enough, I don't perspire if I'm, say, interviewing for a job or speaking in front of a group).

After the Paper Towel Incident, I resolve to do all I can to dehydrate the party experience. I see an herbalist in New York City's Chinatown who gives me a small paper bag of *huang qi* (each piece resembles an oversize, misshapen emery board) and another of *bai zhu* (which looks like jigsaw pieces carved out of ginger). I cook the herbs into a tasteless soup, guzzling cup after cup of the stuff before I head over to a magazine launch party on a freezing winter night. The venue turns out to be a converted public bathhouse under renovation; the roof isn't completely installed yet, and the space is dotted with heating lamps. The guests keep their coats on. And yet, despite the herbs and the chill, in midconversation I find myself striking that modified *Thinker* pose so I can dab furtively at my mustache of sweat.

I wonder: Could I manage to sweat in a blizzard, provided the blizzard involved 50 people standing around with plastic cups of beer?

A few days later, at the suggestion of my editor, I visit the ebullient New York City dermatologist Cheryl Karcher, who injects Botox into my philtrum and the groove under my lower lip, blocking the nerve signals that stimulate the sweat glands. Three mornings later, I dribble Listerine down my chin and know that the Botox has taken hold. At cocktail hours to follow, my stiff upper lip stays as dry as the martinis. My habits, however, aren't effaced so easily: My hand keeps fluttering needlessly to my mouth in that professorial cupping gesture. And because I was too wimpy to let Karcher zap my hairline, my forehead remains in dire need of another Paper Towel Incident.

Among all my quick-fix experiments, the most effective involves the sedative Xanax, which is typically prescribed for anxiety disorders and panic attacks. I swallow half a milligram about an hour before arriving at a packed benefit where there's plenty of cheerful complaining about the heat and close quarters. Yet I stay supernaturally crisp and dry all evening, and as a surprise bonus, I temporarily gain the ability to achieve intense, almost sensuous eye contact with anyone I meet.

Now, I have no plans to begin popping tranquilizers every time I report for party duty. But the crystalline success of the Xanax trial confirms the obvious: that my sweating problem is definitely a case of displaced anxiety—anxiety I'm not even aware of until it liquefies!—rather than a purely physi-

cal malfunction. (Xanax does not target norepinephrine, one of the stress hormones that undergirds the fight-or-flight response; rather, it enhances the action of the same soothing neurotransmitter that gets along so well with alcohol.)

For a therapist's perspective, I call Roger Granet, a psychiatrist based in New York and New Jersey. "Somewhere along the line, you learned some distorted thinking related to specific social situations," he says. "What's at play is a conditioned behavioral response." In other words: Pavlov's dogs had their dinner bell; for me, it's a swarming loft and a DJ. But how—and when—did I learn to respond this way? How did my nervous system train itself to associate parties with panic? Granet asks me to think back "to high school or even grammar school—maybe something happened on the playground, or at a Bar Mitzvah?"

Eureka! At last, a creation myth for my sweating syndrome. It is June 1990, the day of my friend Rachel's Bat Mitzvah. But for me, a gangly 13-year-old upholstered in Laura Ashley chintz, it is an outtake from *Mean Girls*—you know the deal, where you show up and none of the other girls will talk to you, and you have no idea why, but apparently a bunch of them are "mad" at you, and you're assigned to the end of one table with no one sitting across from you, and you flee the scene and spend the evening loitering around the guy they've hired to sketch caricatures of the guests. You tell this kind man that you like to swim, so he draws you diving into a goldfish bowl—which is apt, because this is the night when you are ordained to spend every social occasion of your adult life soaking wet.

Well, okay, I can't place *all* of the blame for my Nixonian flop-sweat disorder on one Bat Mitzvah. But it's a start. Granet reckons that a judicious course of beta-blockers (which can modulate the fight-or-flight response in stressful situations) paired with cognitive-behavioral therapy would help me reorganize my scrambled thought patterns, freeze my supply of trigger memories, and, as a result, dry me out.

Part of me (the lazy part, I suppose) is disappointed: I wanted an insta-solution inside a pill or a syringe. On the other hand, I'm impressed that the human brain has such a long, stubborn memory—that it's so committed to learning from past mistakes and keeping me safe from emotional harm, however ineptly. And I must admit, there are moments when I'm delighted by the spectacular Keystone Kops incompetence of my neurotransmitters, forever shouting "Fire!" in a crowded party space and setting off my sprinkler system. Just because it's happening to me doesn't mean it's not hilarious.

But maybe the joke's over. Maybe I should give the wilted wallflower that is my nervous system a makeover. It's been ordered around by a mortified 13-year-old long enough. And my party face could use some mascara. ◻

Lisa Kogan Tells All

Our 40-something columnist isn't getting older, she's getting…oh, the hell with it—all right, she's getting older! But she's also getting a few other things: resilient, resourceful, and, if she's really lucky, maybe James Franco.

H ere's a little fact of life that took me by surprise: Roughly 23 million women in this country are 40 to 49 years of age and about 6,000 of us turn 50 every single day.

We are a thoroughly undefined constituency. Some of us are what the wonderful Wendy Wasserstein used to call "bachelor girls," some of us are married, and a lot of us have had trial separations that seemed to go just fine…at least for the husband (with the struggling rock band), who went on to become the ex-husband (with the thriving law practice). Many of us have demanding kids or aging parents or a little of each. We juggle jobs, mortgages, student loans, and cancer treatments with low-fat diets, low-impact aerobics, low-grade depressions, a strong sense of irony, a dark sense of humor, and a full-bodied cabernet.

We are tired. We are *very* tired—we've thought seriously about penciling in a nervous breakdown for ourselves, but we've been through everything the world has to throw at us so many times that it's damn near impossible to get nervous about much of anything.

Despite (or perhaps because of) all the coulda, woulda, shoulda moments that have come and gone, we've learned how to have a good laugh, an impromptu party, and an impure thought (or two) on a semiregular basis. We consider our options, our alternatives, our exit strategies. We take notes, we plan ahead, but we always leave room for serendipity. We are an entire generation of women who are making up our lives as we go along.

I know that it's human nature to want to glorify the past and preserve it in a delicious, if often inaccurate, cotton-candied haze. But the truth is that part of me (that would be the part of me that now needs an underwire bra and a pair of Spanx) really does miss my 20s. I still had that new car smell. I still thought terrorism would stay confined to the other side of the world. On the home front, I still kept standing up for brides (as if they needed my assistance to stand) while waiting politely for it to be my turn. And because it never occurred to me that my turn wouldn't come, I devoted an inordinate amount of time to trying to decide whether my wedding gown should be white or ecru—by the time I hit 35, I'd have been okay with paisley.

The Web had not gone mainstream when I was in my 20s, so any surfing I did (and coming from Detroit, that wasn't much) was in the ocean. And I grant you, my rearview mirror might be a little bit rose-tinted, but if memory serves, those oceans were fairly clean. Come to think of it, the glaciers were glacial, the bees were alive and well, a can of tuna didn't require a warning from the surgeon general, and the climate wasn't making any sudden moves. Color me crazy, but I've always been a sucker for a nice solid layer of ozone parking itself between me and a death ray.

I'm also a great believer in time off for good behavior. I crave solitude. I like being unreachable once in a while, and in those days it was no big deal if somebody couldn't track you down for half an hour. You see, in the 1980s, we didn't know from e-mail or cell phones or Facebook or GPS, and a BlackBerry was nothing more complicated than a healthy treat that was high in antioxidants—only guess what? Nobody had ever heard of antioxidants.

I didn't need a baby aspirin every night or a Lipitor every morning. And I swear to God (that's another thing, God was still around when I was in my 20s), the closest anybody seemed to come to a genuine eating disorder was picking at a mixed green salad on a blind date until it was okay to go home and scarf down the contents of your refrigerator.

But before I start turning into my great-uncle Saul, who never fails to tell me how he could've bought the entire Upper East Side of Manhattan for $225 back in 1936 ("when an ear of corn still tasted like an ear of corn"), let me say this: As much as I miss those days, I'm delighted and relieved to be done with being young.

One quick glance in the mirror is all I need to know that time is most definitely a thief. Wait, strike that: One glance and I usually think I'm holding up pretty well—it's upon closer inspection, that moment when I take a deep breath, put on my glasses, and turn up the dimmer switch, that I'm reminded gravity is not my friend. But if time has robbed me

We are an entire generation of women who are making up our lives as we go along.

of a little elasticity and a lot of naïveté, it's left a few things in their place.

Thanks to nearly 48 years at the big dance, a million mistakes, and one extraordinary psychiatrist, I've finally achieved the occasional touch of clarity. I'm getting to be resourceful. I'm getting to be resilient, and I hope that on my better days, I'm getting to be a little more calm, a little more contemplative, a little more compassionate.

Sometimes I think being middle-aged isn't about learning a lot of new lessons so much as learning the same old ones again and again. Here are a few of the lessons I keep learning:

• It is never a good thing when a shrinking portion of the population controls a growing portion of the money. It tends to make incredibly decent, hardworking, middle-class people sort of jumpy, and the next thing you know Kirsten Dunst is playing Marie Antoinette in a Sofia Coppola extravaganza.

• Anyone who looks okay in ochre will look even better *not* in ochre.

• War and famine bad, James Franco and spaghetti carbonara good.

• What doesn't kill me does not make me stronger. It makes me anxious, bitchy, and vulnerable...but nobody wants to see that embroidered on a pillow.

• This isn't exactly an old lesson I keep learning, but given that I'm lucky enough to have my own column, I'd like to use it to set right an unfortunate mistake. Remember a few years ago when we all got together and decided that sleep was the new sex? I've come to believe that we were dead wrong. What do you say we make actual ouch-you're-on-my-hair, did-you-hear-the-baby, jeez-that-was-my-eye, messy, intimate, life-affirming, really, really fun sex the new sex?! Because here's the thing: Between the economy, the environment, and the powder keg that is Pakistan, nobody's getting any sleep anyway—so as long as we're all lying there wide awake...

• Dorothy Parker was a genius. She wrote a gem of a poem called "Indian Summer." It's very short, but I'm low on space, so I'll just cut to the end:

But now I know the things I know,
And do the things I do;
And if you do not like me so,
To hell, my love, with you!

Bravo, Ms. Parker. And, finally, deep into my 40s, I couldn't agree with you more. ◘

Here's looking at you, kid: Betsy Berne and her daughter, Brookti.

Someone Like You

Classmates were teasing Betsy Berne's adopted African daughter for being "different"—but now her mother has suggested the perfect comeback.

Brookti, my 6-year-old daughter, gets teased a lot. She gets teased because her skin is brown and we live in a predominantly white neighborhood. She gets teased because she's adopted. She gets teased because she has a white mother. She gets teased because she doesn't have a daddy. She gets teased because she's from Africa.

I can usually handle the teasing. I'm willing to reach across the aisle, as they say, and so is Brookti. All kids tease, Brookti included; it's part of growing up. And really, the teasing has only become problematic in the past few months or so, since kids younger than 6 don't usually engage in this kind of "nuanced teasing," shall we call it—that is, teasing with a very deliberate, not-so-hidden agenda.

I've never been part of the species of overprotective, helicopter, whatever you want to call them, modern mothers who pounce over the slightest provocation. I let Brookti fight her own battles. And fortunately she is no slouch, which I suspected the moment I received my first picture of her five years ago from the AFAA (Americans for African Adoptions) foster home in Ethiopia. Dressed in, or rather swallowed up by, a gigantic mismatched T-shirt and shorts ensemble, her tiny, elegant head held high, Brookti stared at me with insouciance, her perfect mouth set in a pout, as if to say, *What's it to you?*

Indeed, she's been a diva since she touched down on American soil, barely able to walk and completely unable to speak English, or any language, for that matter, although "talk" plenty she did, with dramatic gestures to drive her many points home. Suffice it to say, she is even more of a diva now: She walks with a strut and teases with Hannah Montana–inspired impunity. Brookti is a member of the proud Tigray tribe, and it shows. She carries herself ramrod straight, like the queen she is possibly descended from (unlike her Jewish "older parent" mother, who hails from a different tribe, Eastern European peasants, not so royal but just as proud, in their own hunched-over way).

But the teasing is starting to get to both of us. The other day a classmate of Brookti's who's seen us together for over a year asked me if I was Brookti's babysitter. I held my temper, looked her straight in the eye, and said, "I think you know better than that." But when the little girl persisted and asked me again, not once but twice, I had to walk away rapidly so she wouldn't hear me cursing under my breath.

A few months ago, Brookti was fiercely proud to be from Africa (she can't really pronounce Ethiopia, so we generally stick with Africa), fiercely proud to have "two countries" just like the man in the newspaper I was always talking about—Obama. But then, after one particular teasing bout, she made me promise not to tell anyone she's from Africa or that she has two countries.

A few months ago, Brookti didn't mind talking about being adopted, but then she made me pinky-promise not to tell anyone, and when I told her more stories about Obama, she interrupted anxiously to say, "Are you sure he's not adopted, too?"

A few months ago, she didn't give her brown skin or my white skin a whole lot of thought. We talked about our different colors all the time, but she was perfectly fine with being brown. The other night, though, she started sobbing, just as I was applying lipstick in the mirror before going out, and through her tears, she blurted, "I want white skin, too!" I said, "Brookti, are you crazy? You have the best skin color! White people would much rather have brown skin; look at them—and me—in the summer trying so hard to get brown skin like yours!"

As the tears kept coming, I told her yet again that, yes, she was different from a lot of other kids but it was a great thing to be different. I said, "You have to be proud to be different." Try telling that to any kid who is 6, when your greatest goal in life is to fit in. So I tried a new tack. I told her that I, too, was different because I didn't have a husband, but I didn't care; I was proud to be different. (To which she replied—bless her loyal heart: "Mommy, I'm glad I don't have a daddy!")

Now, in light of our current president, I tried yet another tack. "Brookti," I said, "when white kids tell you your brown color is yuck, you answer, 'Well, our president is brown'—and see what they say. When brown kids tell you that I can't be your mother because I'm white, you answer, 'Well, our president is brown and his mother was white'—and see what they say. When kids tease you about being African because Africa only has wars and poor people, you answer, 'Well, our president is part African and he's proud of it'—and see what they say. When kids tease you because you don't have a daddy, you answer, 'Well, our president had a single mother'—and see what they say."

And here's something I haven't told her yet, but I will. I'll say, "Hey, Brookti, tell the kids it's a whole new world out there now, things are going to change; we should be proud of our differences and what we have in common, and we should celebrate them, just like our president—and see what they say." ◖

> I told her yet again, it was a great thing to be different.

balance

67 MASTERY PLAN I BY KELLY CORRIGAN

70 JUST WHAT YOU NEED! I BY MARTHA BECK

73 ANIKA NONI ROSE'S AHA! MOMENT

74 BACK TO BASICS I BY ALLISON GLOCK

82 OPRAH TALKS TO ELLEN DEGENERES

89 NINE SMALL STEPS THAT WILL PAY OFF BIG IN THE FUTURE I BY SUZE ORMAN

Mastery Plan

A photography business, a newspaper column, a published memoir: Kelly Corrigan thought life was about dabbling in many things—until her daughter showed her the satisfaction of perfecting just one.

This is it!" I'd call to my husband, Edward. "Get the video camera!" Georgia was a year old. "Come on, baby! Take a step." She'd been torturing me for weeks, slowly lifting herself up and then freezing—studying the terrain, considering the consequences. I was the queen of diving in, of *hey, why not?*, and I guess I'd assumed that my daughter would be the same. "You can do it!" I'd cry. "One little baby step!" But it would be another six weeks before Georgia summoned the nerve to lift one foot off the ground and set it down in front of the other. Naturally it happened when I wasn't looking, perhaps even *because* I wasn't looking.

Right around this time, I found an old Pentax in our storage space and started taking pictures. A few weeks later, I told Edward I was thinking of quitting my job designing educational software. "I want to be a photographer," I announced, handing him a set of black-and-whites. "Candid portraits." He responded with his signature squint, a look of derision, skepticism, and superiority all rolled into one. (Edward is a person who dares not begin anything that might not end with excellence, whereas I've been known to swing by the art supply store on the way home from the museum because "how hard can it be?")

I landed one photography client, then another. A nice man at the camera shop walked me through my contact sheets, showing me which frames to print. After my first big assignment, I ran back to the lab waving my check. "She couldn't believe this was my first job!" I reported. "I can't, either," said the nice man, beaming. That was all the confirmation I needed to say goodbye to educational software.

A year or two later, though, expectations had reset. Clients started asking if I did my own printing, if I would bring lights, if I could shoot in medium format. Nope, not me. If there are ten steps to mastering photography, medium format is probably around step eight. It's advanced. You are no longer taking big, easy strides, but rather inching ahead so slowly you wonder if you've moved forward at all. Too much work for too little gain, I thought.

By this time, Georgia was in preschool, distinguishing herself as the girl who drew flowers. Not hearts, or stick people, or big firecracker suns—just flowers. And really just one flower: a daisy-ish blossom that she honed and refined over the course of a year, like Monet and his water lilies. "Want me to show you how to draw a house?" I would ask. "I'm not finished with my flower," she'd answer. Really? It looked good enough to me. If I were Georgia, I'd have moved on months ago. I like the huge payoff of the steep learning curve. One day you're stumbling around and the next, you're doing it (skiing down the bunny slope, playing chopsticks on the piano, drawing a tree). I like impressing people ("Wow, you've never done this before?"). And I love always having a fresh answer to my favorite question, "What's new?"

Clearly, Georgia felt differently. And since I had some strong opinions on the matter—and was unwilling to devote myself to the finer points of photography—I put down my camera and picked up a pen. I had read enough poorly written newspaper columns to believe that I could beat the average. I whipped up a sample essay (about teaching kids to approach new things with optimism); one month later, my name and photo were on the front page of *The Piedmonter*, my California town's weekly paper. Just like that, I was a "columnist": $50 per column, two columns a month. People at cocktail parties seemed

> I like the huge payoff of the steep learning curve. One day you're stumbling around and the next, you're doing it.

impressed. Edward stopped squinting. When I walked Georgia to school, she ran from driveway to driveway looking for my face on the morning's paper.

In second grade, having finally taken her flower as far as she could, Georgia dedicated herself to the cartwheel. Weeks became months. "You've got it!" I'd tell her. "Not yet," she'd reply. She wanted to start and end on an imaginary balance beam, like her friend Amelia did. I'd say, "Try a headstand." But she wasn't looking for a quick win. She was working on something small and specific, something well beyond basic proficiency. "No," she'd say, tossing her legs over her body again.

Meanwhile, after a year of writing my newspaper column, it was getting harder and harder to produce 800 original and meaningful words about family life. That's when I came up with my coolest party trick yet. I decided to write a book—a memoir about growing up; I called it *The Middle Place*. Each week I'd bang out a new chapter, which I'd oblige Edward to read the minute he walked in the door on Friday nights. Eventually, my story had a beginning, middle, and end. My sister-in-law found me an agent, the agent found me an editor, the book was published. True, in every chapter, there's a phrase or a paragraph or a whole page that I wish I'd worked harder on. But to everyone's astonishment, for one splendid week, the book was tied for 15th place on the *New York Times* best-seller list. (Special thanks to Aunt Peggy, who bought 15 copies that week instead of ten.) It did okay with reviewers, too. All in all, pretty good *for my first time.*

A year after *The Middle Place* came out, my agent wants to know how the second book is coming. "I'm thinking about it," I say, as I flip through my rough outline for *Hello, World* (so much easier to name a book than write one). I look at the document almost every day—sometimes touching up sentences, more often just tweaking the formatting. I want to write it, I do. The subject matter—deciding what faith to teach our children—feels important and provocative and worthwhile. But when I get inside a chapter, I can't get any momentum going.

So rather than suffer through the hopeless periods that every decent writer has, rather than delete and rewrite, outline and restructure, rather than advance by those tiny increments my daughter seems to relish, I've started something new: *Saving Fairyland,* an original screenplay! Step one: Buy special software. *Check.* Step two: Bang out a draft. *Voilà!* Step three: Drag my friend Betsy into the project. *Done.* Right this minute, we have 89 index cards on my dining room table, one for each scene; by the time you read this, the fifth draft will be complete. That's right, *finished!* If this were *Hello, World,* I'd still be suffering through the first chapter. "You're too much!" my friends say. "What next—an opera?"

Of course, as I'm busy reinventing myself, Georgia is still working on her cartwheel. The same damn thing, over and over again. Except, as Edward points out, her cartwheel has actually changed—a lot. She can do it anywhere now: on a grassy hill, in a crowded living room, on a painted line on concrete. Where it was once mostly momentum, it's now controlled and exact. What appeared to be fruitless repetition has turned out to be...mastery.

"That's some cartwheel, honey," I say. And I mean it.

For 15 years Edward and I have been going to a San Francisco lecture series that features writers talking about their life's work. One night we listened as the novelist Charles Frazier described how writing *Cold Mountain* took him six or seven years, two or three of which he spent in the Blue Ridge Mountains, cataloging Appalachian plants, tracking down headstones on forgotten hillsides, reading the letters and journals of 19th-century farmers. On the way home from the lecture that night, Edward and I agreed that Frazier's gift was not only genius but will. And persistence. And discipline. And hard, hard work. The work, by the way, seems not to have gotten any easier the next time around: Nearly ten years passed before Frazier's second novel, *Thirteen Moons,* came out. I liked it even more than *Cold Mountain.*

Writers like Charles Frazier are moving slowly, even imperceptibly, toward some hard-to-come-by, maybe even impossible, goal that they refuse to forsake. They haven't been on the steep part of the learning curve in years. They're not susceptible to the *look at me!* lure of having something new to announce. And they wouldn't abandon their craft any

sooner than they would their children. How rich their satisfaction must be.

After about a thousand cartwheels, Georgia knows something of that satisfaction. And watching her, I finally see that although I've always prided myself on fearlessly jumping into one new project after another, I'm the one who's been doing the same thing over and over: finding a way to be a beginner. I keep starting at zero and making it to six or seven but never going any further, never knowing the gratification of levels eight, nine, and ten, never reaching the place where the cartwheel becomes elegant.

When I think about writing another book *(It couldn't possibly go as well; I've told all the best stories already),* what worries me is that I may have already done my personal best—and that whatever worked about *The Middle Place* was nothing more than beginner's luck. For the first time, I'm wondering if all of the commotion that goes with continually—and "fearlessly"—reinventing myself might just be an elaborate smoke screen, a way to distract myself from my greatest fear: failure. The truth is, I'd like to sit down for however many years it takes and write one clear and beautiful thing, one book worthy of a world that already has too many books in it. The other truth is, I'm just not sure I can.

Georgia is too young to have found her life's work, but when I watch her study the terrain and consider the consequences, it's clear that if she felt as though she had something big to say, she'd write a second book. She'd slip off quietly, and while no one was looking, she'd summon the nerve to lift one foot off the ground and set it down in front of the other.

So here I go, opening the *Hello, World* file again. One sentence at a time. If I can get myself through this, it will be the most truly daring thing I've ever done. And while I think and stare and occasionally type, Georgia sits at the kitchen table, directing her considerable focus to writing in cursive. The stylish capital *G.* The Laverne and Shirley *L.* Over and over again, she writes her name, Georgia Corrigan Lichty, until it perfectly reflects the indomitable, inspiring girl she is. ◖

All the commotion that goes with reinventing myself might just be a distraction from my greatest fear: failure.

Just What You Need!

There are two ways of going through life: Gather everything in sight, just in case you need it. Or trust that you'll find exactly what you need, just in time. Guess which one lets you really stop and smell the roses? **Martha Beck** on when—and how—to say "enough!"

Shortly after World War II, executives at Japan's Toyota Motor Company made a decision from which, I believe, we all can benefit. They decided to make cars the way they'd make, say, sushi. Unlike most manufacturers, which bought and stored massive stockpiles of supplies, Toyota began ordering just enough parts to keep their lines moving, just when those parts were needed. This made them spectacularly productive, and turned the phrase "just in time" into business legend.

I know of the Toyota case because in my former life as an academic, I taught international business management. My students and I had some rousing discussions about just-in-time (JIT) manufacturing, as well as its alternative, which is known as just-in-case (JIC) inventory. These students were the first people who hired me as a life coach (perhaps because I could never resist applying business theory to everyday life). When we discussed JIT versus JIC management as a lifestyle strategy, we concluded that Toyota's business innovation could positively impact all of our lives. If you feel overburdened, overstressed, and anxious, I'm betting the same is true for you.

Why Just-in-Case Is Just Crazy

Most people live with a just-in-case mind-set because for most of human history, it made sense. The primary fact of life for just-in-case processes is: "Everything good is scarce!" By contrast, just-in-time systems rely on the assumption "Everything good is readily available." Well, until quite recently, the former claim was true for most humans—it's still true for many. But most of us live in settings where basic necessities, like food, clothing, and other humans, are plentiful.

Living in an abundant environment but operating on the assumption that good things are scarce leads to a host of dysfunctions that can be summed up in one word: excess. Most of us are living in some kind of excess; we work too much, eat too much, rack up debt buying too much stuff. Yet, driven by the unconscious, just-in-case assumption that "everything good is scarce," we just keep doing and accumulating more. We've all seen some of the unfortunate results, and I've found that most fall into the following four categories:

STARVING OFF THE FAT OF THE LAND

For years I noticed that my clients who lived in a mind-set of scarcity had trouble controlling their weight, even though they dieted assiduously. I also read studies showing that poor women—particularly those who periodically starved themselves to feed their children—were particularly plagued by obesity. Researchers hypothesize that when the body knows it may be starved, whether by poverty or by dieting, it activates automatic just-in-case mechanisms that store fat on the body to get through the next "famine." Ironically, this biological just-in-case mechanism puts fat on precisely the people with the discipline to starve themselves.

STUFF TSUNAMIS

Just-in-case thinking triggers primal, unconscious impulses to hoard good stuff, fat supplies being just one example. Combine JIC attitudes with a superabundant culture, and things can go wildly off kilter. There have been several cases like the one in Shelton, Washington, where a woman recently suffocated under a pile of her own possessions. To recover her body, police reported having to "climb over [clutter] on their hands and knees. In some areas, their heads were touching the ceiling while they were standing on top of piles of debris."

MONEY MADNESS

My wealthiest clients have taught me that having lots of money doesn't quiet scarcity-based, JIC anxiety. This point was reinforced for me when I heard about the suicide of the German billionaire who lost hundreds of millions of dollars in the recent financial crisis. Now, this poor guy wasn't literally a poor guy. He still had a personal fortune. But to a just-in-case thinker who's used to billions, it wasn't enough to keep him from throwing himself in front of a train.

LOVE'S LABOR'S LOST

Just-in-case thinking destroys relationships faster than—and sometimes with the assistance of—a speeding bullet. Along with the impulse to hoard objects, it also triggers excessive attempts to control our supply of love—that is, other people. So anxious lovers have their partners followed. Parents micromanage children. People-pleasers try to manipulate everyone into liking them. This behavior isn't love; it's a fear-based outcome of believing love is scarce. If you've ever been on the receiving end of such anxious machinations, you know they make you want to run, not bond.

Why Just-in-Time Just Makes Sense

As Toyota execs and my graduate students concluded so many years ago, hanging on to a just-in-case worldview in abundant environments is plain bad business. And as I've seen in countless coaching scenarios since, switching to a just-in-time mind-set ("Everything good is readily available") restores health and balance to our lives.

The great news is that just one mental shift—focusing on the abundance of your environment—switches your psychological settings so that your life automatically improves in many areas you may think are unrelated. This is essentially a leap from fear to faith; it's not religious faith but the simple belief that we'll probably be able to get what we need when we need it. When the issues above are considered through abundance-based, just-in-time thinking, it's a whole different ball game:

FOOD FULFILLMENT

I've never been a weight loss coach; my focus is on helping people go from fear and suffering to relaxation and happiness. So I was baffled when many of my clients told me, "I'm finally losing weight—and I'm not even trying." This intrigued me so much that I spent years researching and writing a book about it [*The Four-Day Win*]. After reading thousands of studies and interviewing dozens of experts, I'm convinced that the thought "Everything good is readily available" kicks the body out of its panicky, fat-storing mode and into a state that helps it shed excess fat.

STUFF SUFFICIENCY

Dianne is 50-ish and newly divorced. Part of our coaching work helped her develop just-in-time confidence about money (which allowed her to leave the financial security of her emotionally dead marriage). During our final session, she said, "Something weird is happening. All of a sudden, I'm tidy. I've always been a stuff person, but now I don't add clutter. It's a wonderful, spacious feeling." Dianne didn't achieve this by forcing herself to clean up. She simply developed the confidence of a just-in-time manager, and her behavior changed almost on its own.

MELLOW MONEY MANAGEMENT
"I got really panicky when the economy went south," says Jackie, one of my fellow coaches. "All my business dried up, and I was really scared. But I hate feeling scared, and I'm a coach, so one day I coached myself back to trusting life. I felt better immediately, but what's strange is that clients started coming out of the woodwork. I had to start a waiting list."

This, as any Toyota alum will tell you, is what happens to people who have enough confidence to run a just-in-time operation. I can't quite explain this; it often seems nothing short of miraculous. Perhaps this is why the authors of the Bible included the story of the wandering Israelites who were given manna from heaven, but only permitted to gather enough to supply their needs until the next "mannafestation." Whether you take it literally or metaphorically, this tale was considered important enough to become holy writ. Why? I believe it's to counteract the just-in-case anxiety that makes billionaires keep hoarding more money. The Israelite story-keepers wanted to remind readers that, miraculous as it seems, just-in-time confidence keeps supply lines clear and prosperity flowing.

LASTING LOVE
I've done my share of just-in-case controlling when it comes to love (I'd like to apologize to anyone who once wandered into my danger zone). Happily, I've learned that setting people free, not trying to control them, ensures a lifetime supply of love.

Here's the closest thing I know to a genuine love spell: "I'll always love you, and I really don't care what you do." This is not a promise to stay in a relationship with someone whose behavior is destructive. It's a simple statement that you aren't dependent on the other person's choices. That means you can respond to someone as he or she really is, instead of trying to force a fallible person to be infallible.

> The great news is that just one mental shift switches your psychological settings so that your life automatically improves in many areas you may think are unrelated.

Knowing that love (like all good things) is readily available, we don't need to control any individual. And oh, how people love being loved without a care.

Making the Switch
When I meet someone who's a mess of excess, I just itch to coach them. I know that if they'd reroute a few simple brain habits, their lives would improve almost effortlessly. The transformation wouldn't take much work—no need to exhume childhood traumas or hook up an antidepressant IV. We'd just throw the neurological toggle switch that exchanges fight-or-flight mode (the sympathetic nervous system) for rest-and-relaxation mode (the parasympathetic nervous system). Most animals experience this switch in response to environmental conditions. We humans possess an unparalleled ability to create it with our thoughts.

It's almost too easy: Simply by taking your attention off thoughts of scarcity and persistently focusing on observations of abundance, you can replace the nervous, just-in-case mind-set that kept our ancient forebears alive but is killing many of us. The best way to effect this shift is to use these simple exercises:

1. List ten times you thought that there wouldn't be enough of something and you survived.
2. List ten areas where you have too much, not too little.
3. List 20—or 50, or 1,000—wonderful things that entered your life just at the right time, with no effort on your part. Start with the little things (oxygen, sunlight, a song on the radio). You'll soon think of bigger ones. Most of my clients realize that the most important things in their lives showed up this way.

I started doing exercise 3 several years ago, and I still haven't finished my list. Once you deliberately focus on abundance, you'll be overwhelmed by all the good things that show up like manna in the desert, without much effort on your part. If this seems too easy, you can go back to fearful, just-in-case thinking (you'll need a diet counselor, a housekeeper, and a financial planner, but that's okay—they can substitute for friends). But if, like me, my business school students, and my clients, you decide to try just-in-time thinking, you'll find yourself struggling less and accomplishing more in ways you'd never expect. You may kick yourself for not discovering this sooner. Relax. I promise, you're just in time. ◍

Anika Noni Rose's Aha! Moment

Everyone wanted a piece of her, and how could she refuse? Then one day—sick, in tears, and totally overwhelmed—the actress realized the value of one simple word: no.

I respect people who work hard and juggle well. But at some point, you've got to figure out that six balls in the air might be too many, so try two.

I learned that lesson in December 2008. I had just returned to New York after filming *The No. 1 Ladies' Detective Agency* in Botswana for four months, and I got sick. An awful stomach virus took me down so hard that I couldn't leave my couch for days. The illness really should have been a period of forced relaxation. But even though I wasn't physically leaving the house, I was mentally leaving it, because I was still fretting about my work. Since I had just returned to the States, I was getting phone calls left and right. That may not sound particularly *taxing*, but when you're on the verge of exhaustion, taxing is subjective—even talking to the FedEx man to give him directions to your apartment can be taxing!

I was feeling overwhelmed, and when I was invited to sing at a fund-raiser in New York, I forgot to respond. I heard that they were going to replace me, and my survival instinct kicked in. Even though I needed to slow down, I just couldn't because my mind-set was: *You have responsi-bilities. This is your job. Do it. Do it. Do it.* So I started rearranging my schedule. I had a trip to Vietnam planned, and I began making calls to reschedule it.

But every time I picked up the phone to change that vacation, I started crying. And I thought, *It's very special to be able to do what I do, and it's a blessing. Performing is the only thing I've ever done, and I'm crying over this gift—the thing I love.* I realized in that moment that I was operating out of fear—the fear that if I didn't continue putting myself out there, all of a sudden I wouldn't exist in entertainment anymore. But what would happen if I missed one event? Nothing. Somehow in the whirlwind that had been my life for the past five years, my moorings had loosened.

So I just stopped. I didn't postpone my trip to Vietnam, because I realized: How often would I have an opportunity like that? Maybe not for years, but I will be able to sing a song onstage again. Instead of rearranging my life for work, I said no. I turned down projects. I took naps. I healed. I said no to save my health, my peace of mind, and life. It's so natural to say no that it's one of the first words babies learn. It may be one of the most important tools in our linguistic arsenal. —*As told to Crystal G. Martin*

BACK to BASICS

Overwhelmed by consumerism and sobered by the economy, more Americans are embracing the less-is-more philosophy of "voluntary simplicity," trading possession obsession for personal fulfillment. **Allison Glock** drops in on a few devoted followers and discovers that for them, enough really *is* enough.

A ll Kristen Martini wanted was a simpler life. Not a simpler way to make a goat cheese omelet. Not a simpler way to drop five pounds. Not a simpler mop and broom system that traps lint in those hard-to-reach places. No, the goal was nothing less (or more) than a simpler way to be.

"Essentially, I wanted to stop consuming so much. I wanted to let what I have be enough."

Kristen, 37, a good friend, tells me this as we drive to Orlando, Florida. We are headed to meet two members of the Simple Living Institute, an organization devoted to helping people attain happiness through a lifestyle called voluntary simplicity, or simple living, whose most devout followers whittle down their possessions to only what they need to get by. The movement has been gaining momentum recently, advanced not only by the faltering economy but by a persistent ennui many Americans are feeling. Hounded by the nagging suspicion that no matter how many cars, coffee presses, or perfect-fit T-shirts they own, their personal fulfillment remains elusive. Many of us are coming to recognize that time spent watching *Real Housewives of Atlanta* is not time that buffers the soul. We are experiencing the dawning, sometimes painful realization that stuff, even really cute stuff, in the end is kind of a drag.

"A few years back," Kristen continues, "I was married

GARDEN PARTY Terry and Tia Meer on their farm in Florida, where they help spread the gospel of voluntary simplicity.

and doing the country club thing, and I met some friends who were living very simply. I saw how much happier they were than me. They were authentic. I realized then that the endless shopping was not making me happy."

Not even a tiny bit?

"Maybe for a few minutes. But then what? I saw there was more to being alive than collecting possessions."

Kristen gives me a wan smile. She knows I am a collector, that I am drawn to stuff like dogs to ripe garbage. Old things, mostly. Crappy, kitschy, vintage bric-a-brac. Linens. Mason jars. Handknit doilies. Kristen is aware that I have never, not once, passed a yard sale without stopping.

She was once like me, but for the past 14 months she has been teaching herself how to be free of the burden of *too much*. "How many Florida-themed salt-and-pepper-shaker sets can you own?" she asks wryly. (I stop my mental count at seven.)

We met last year at our children's school. I noticed her immediately. She was wearing jeans and a cotton tank top, her hair loosely pulled back with a gauzy scarf. She looked pretty, bohemian. More, she looked peaceful. We quickly discovered we had more in common than third-grade children: We are both liberal do-gooders. We both enjoy a stiff cocktail. And we are both single moms, a boot-camp bond if ever there was one.

Kristen lives with her 8-year-old twins, Aidan and Ellie, in a stucco cottage in the woods. The house is miniature and remote, at the end of a long unpaved drive. It is 800 square feet, with low wood ceilings and stone floors. The family of three shares one bedroom and two beds. The single bath is the size of a telephone booth. The first time I visited, I was both impressed and appalled. "Maybe you shouldn't have put the house in the dryer?" I teased.

Before renting the cottage, they had lived in a 3,600-square-foot, five-bedroom house with two kitchens. There was a playroom. There was a laundry room. There was enough space not to see each other for hours at a stretch. "I didn't even use some of the rooms," Kristen says. In the cottage, privacy is nonexistent, yet she loves her home with unbridled fervor.

Her new lifestyle has a precedent. "I lived in the woods when I was 21, 22," she says. "I had my own garden. I was really into my nice, quiet, cheap life."

Then she got engaged to a businessman and told herself grown-ups didn't live in the woods, without a television or a set of china. So after she got married, she found herself in a huge home, full of things, which she took great care in placing here and there, while ignoring the signs that all was not well beneath the surface.

The babies were a distraction for a time. Then they weren't. Depression followed. And insomnia. Then medications, therapy. None of it worked. Kristen found herself unable to get out of bed. She lost 20 pounds. Her husband, earnest and traditional, was confused by her unhappiness. After all, they were supposed to be living the American dream.

"I knew it was time to get out when my life started to make me physically sick," she says now.

Kristen realized that to become the person she longed to be, she had to leave her marriage. So, after much soul-searching, she abandoned her old life in its entirety—her spouse, her furniture, excess clothes, collectible salt and pepper shakers—and returned, with her children, to the woods of her youth.

"The day I moved, I brought only my car, a few clothes, and food," she says. "I got to the cottage around 4 in the afternoon and went out looking for firewood. As I made a big pile by my door, I kept thinking, *I'm getting my do-over!*"

Kristen started keeping a journal.

"I want to explore, to climb trees, to kayak different rivers," she wrote. "I want to continue building strong, healthy friendships. I want to make a difference. I want to sleep on my own. I want to grow spiritually and emotionally. To have more patience and stillness. To be quiet inside. I want to be at ease with myself, to create, to give, to love, and to laugh my ass off."

"So, how's it going?" I ask as we zip down I-95.

She smiles. "So far, really, really good. My electric bill went from $150 to $35."

"You can't warm that place with body heat alone?" I joke.

"You're just bitter because your bill is $500 a month," she shoots back good-naturedly.

True, I am one of those Americans whose house is too big for their income. One of those poor schmucks who have to work long hours at jobs they wish they didn't have just to pay to heat rooms they don't need. Meanwhile, Kristen, who earns a small salary as an elder caretaker, has cash to spare. This keeps her high on the juice of freedom. So intoxicated, in fact, that she craves more. Hence our trip to learn more about the Simple Living Institute, a group she hopes will offer additional ideas for paring down her already austere life.

"I can do more," she says excitedly. By which she means, have less. Such is the heart of the simple living phi-

losophy: Become conscious of what you genuinely need, and the rest, punt like a rotten apple.

"I do have friends who just don't get what I'm doing," she says with a shrug. "Many of my friends from my old life think I'm a little nuts. But my true friendships are getting much deeper. The other people who do this, we make time for each other. We care about community. We volunteer. We create time to do the things we believe in, in lieu of just mindlessly accumulating."

Instead of shopping, Kristen now gardens. Instead of buying new clothes, she trades with friends. Instead of racing to get her kids new bicycles from a big-box store, they prowl the thrift shops until the right one turns up.

"I also stopped dyeing my gray hair, which has mortified some of my girlfriends," she says, laughing. "I don't care. I don't want to spend time altering myself anymore. I want to be happy as I am, with who I am and what I have."

Me too, I think. I'd like to feel cage-free, unburdened. Minus the gray hair—I draw the line at voluntary aging.

The notion of voluntary simplicity has been around for centuries; see: Buddha, Jesus, Thoreau, the Shakers, the Amish. In 1936 a Quaker named Richard Gregg published an essay titled "The Value of Voluntary Simplicity," thus coining the term. Over time the concept evolved into a movement, though it remained a fringe lifestyle. But 2008 was something of a perfect storm for the voluntary simplicity movement. The mortgage crisis, the banking meltdown, the spike in gas prices, and the unfettered baking of our atmosphere has led an unprecedented number of folks to put down the credit cards and start thinking about plan B. According to Wanda Urbanska, 52, the amiable host of PBS's *Simple Living with Wanda Urbanska* and the de facto Martha Stewart of the voluntary simplicity movement, the lifestyle is gaining mainstream appeal. At least 10 percent of the population, by some estimates, have embraced the tenets of living simply.

"This isn't a fringe thing anymore," Urbanska says from her home in Mount Airy, North Carolina, considered a simple-living hot spot. "There is a shift going on. When I first started talking about this in 1992, I was seen as a wacko zealot. Now simple living is fashionable."

Urbanska's ratings have gone up each of the show's four seasons, and PBS just upped her viewership range to 75 percent of the country. "People keep telling me this is just what we need at this time," she says. "They want to get back to basics, assume financial independence and environmental stewardship. For the first time, the culture is saying bigger isn't better. When you are in debt, it's hard to live with any pleasure. People are starting to feel there is so much more to life. Everything you bring into your house becomes a responsibility. You have to care for it, clean it, and ultimately, dispose of it." She sighs. "I don't want to say it's empty to shop, but to me, a great conversation is worth way more than anything I could pull off a shelf."

One of the movement's pioneers is Vicki Robin. In 1980 she and her business partner, the late Joe Dominguez, began running frugality seminars around the country, traveling in a motor home and staying with friends. They donated all their profits to other causes. They later wrote *Your Money or Your Life*, a seminal book that espoused the benefits of spending less. The Pacific Northwest is one of the movement's original strongholds, and in the 1980s Robin, now 63, moved to Seattle. Today she lives in a small apartment above a garage on Washington's Whidbey Island and drives a two-seater Honda Insight hybrid. "For me, frugality equals freedom," she explains. "I don't have any debt, I know how to live within my means. I am not scared by the economic boogeyman."

"Money doesn't buy you happiness" may be a cliché, but science supports the idea. In 2005 Tim Kasser, PhD, associate professor of psychology at Knox College in Galesburg, Illinois, and the author of *The High Price of Materialism,* with his colleague Kirk Warren Brown of Virginia Commonwealth University, published a study that compared 200 voluntary simplifiers with 200 typical Americans. Though the simplifiers earned an average of $26,000 per year, about $15,000 less than the typical group, they were found to be "significantly happier."

"You hear that in order to be happy you need lots of money or stuff," says Kasser. "That just didn't turn out to be true."

In fact, Kasser says those results suggested that the very things society teaches us to crave—wealth, status, prestige—can actually lead to persistent feelings of depression and dissatisfaction.

"People who pursue intrinsic values—self-acceptance, making the world a better place, helping polar bears—are much happier than people who chase popularity, money, and image," says Kasser. "If you orient your life around personal growth and family and community, you'll feel better."

Consider that even though the average family income has more than doubled since the 1950s, our level of happiness has essentially remained stagnant. "Take a deeper look at what you are really after with all this stuff," suggests Kasser. "Love? Acceptance? Feeling competent? Find more direct ways to achieve those goals. Live your values. In our sample of typical Americans, 27 percent said they'd made a voluntary income reduction already. To me, the good news is that fixing this is something that is accessible to everybody. We can shift our goals."

Other voluntary simplicity advocates are seeing similar results. "This past year, more than 100,000 people have expressed interest in the tenets of simple living," says Carol Holst, cofounder of Simple Living America, a Los Angeles–based nonprofit that offers advice for people looking to "find the satisfaction of enough."

"We take the stand that you can be fulfilled without things," says Holst. "Once you reach that conclusion for yourself, life really changes. What used to seem empty and futile becomes joyful and exciting."

She reiterates that this is *voluntary* simplicity. "Listen, if there was something I really wanted, I'd do it," says Holst. "No guilt. Ed Begley Jr. jokes about how this movement isn't about living under a rock in Topanga. It's about feeling satisfied, not deprived. It's about filling up, not emptying out. Our approach is to empower the individual. There isn't any finger-wagging. This isn't a high bar. It can vary greatly, depending on your needs. Maybe you stop watching television. Maybe you join a gardening club."

Or maybe, like Kristen, you flush your whole past down the composting toilet.

The Simple Living Institute's Econ Farm is a five-acre parcel in the central Florida woods, about 40 minutes from Walt Disney World. A marshy woodland thick with mangroves, moss, and wild ferns, it's named after the Econlockhatchee River, which flows through the land. This is where Tia and Terry Meer help spread the simple living gospel. The couple has just finished building a 1,024-square-foot log cabin, where they intend to become as close to self-sufficient as possible. Harvesting rainwater and solar power. Eating food they farm on the property and bass they catch in the river. The Meers already grow a lot of what they consume. "The first thing we did was put in 50 blueberry bushes," says Terry, a lithe, apple-cheeked blond who smiles as he talks. "Then orange, lemon, and lime trees."

Terry, 34, and Tia, 29, met in college in Florida and formed an instant bond. After graduation they moved to Hawaii, where Tia, who was raised on a family farm in Pennsylvania, became a gardening consultant while Terry designed solar-energy systems. They ate papaya picked from trees, biked to Waikiki Beach, and "had a very simple island life," Terry says.

In a way, the Meers have re-created a version of that life in central Florida. They built the cabin from a kit. Costing only $50,000, it is a no-frills square structure held aloft by stilts and built of sustainable materials, with shelves and counters found on Craigslist or at the local "freecycle" site. They don't use air-conditioning, yet the space remains cool and breezy.

"Our next-door neighbor pays $400 a month for electricity," says Tia. "Our bill is about $30." Their grocery bill is equally lean, about $100 a month (which may explain why they look as fit as greyhounds).

The Meers do not own a television. They have reduced their possessions to what can fit comfortably in a few duffel bags. They ask for nothing at Christmas. "I grew up on a houseboat," says Terry. "On a boat you really see how little you need very quickly. Everything has a purpose. There isn't space for anything else."

Yet in the quest for less, compromises have to be made. The couple wanted to run their appliances on solar power. But since the county required them to install electricity in order to get a certificate of occupancy, they spent their budget to meet the mandate and plan to convert to solar later. "We weren't allowed to be off the grid," Tia says. "We couldn't use our own water exclusively. We had to clear more trees than we wanted. It was disheartening. It conflicted with the whole concept of the house."

Tia and 11 other community members started the nonprofit Simple Living Institute in 2002. Its mission: "to provide cooperative education empowering individuals and organizations to be responsible stewards of their well-being and the environment." They hold workshops and educate people about organic gardening, worm composting, and alternative energy. The group has about 1,000 people on its e-mail list, and a recent Simple Living Kids' Festival saw 32 families racing around the Econ Farm, gleefully looking for raccoon tracks and snake skins.

"Economically, people are starting to understand the benefits," says Terry of the voluntary simplicity movement. "I had lost hope for a while there, to be honest. But now I see people coming around. They understand that if you don't have clean air or water or soil, money isn't worth a whole lot."

Over lunch at Tia's sister's vegan restaurant near downtown Orlando, I notice Tia's flawless skin and enviably radiant hair. I want to ask if showering with rainwater or eating homegrown grapefruit keeps her looking so fresh, but I don't want to appear superficial. So instead I ask her what voluntary simplicity means to her.

"I want to live in a way that preserves the Earth for future generations," she says, picking up a spinach leaf from her salad.

"We are making these choices consciously," Terry adds. "But I think in the future, people will have to make some of these choices whether they want to or not. I feel very good being able to go out into my garden and pick dinner or catch a fish. I don't have to spend money or time driving to a grocery store. Once you simplify and localize, you save so much. And in these troubled times, people see the logic of that approach."

Today Terry owns his own company, Alternative Concepts and Technology. He installs solar panels and

> "I stopped dyeing my gray hair. I don't want to alter myself anymore. I want to be happy as I am, with who I am and what I have."

JUST ENOUGH
Kristen Martini downsized from a large home with two kitchens to a cottage with one bedroom, which she shares with her twins, Ellie and Aidan.

makes $40,000 a year. Tia works in habitat restoration and makes $24,000. Their bills, including student loan payments, health insurance, and food, run about $1,500 per month.

"I've never liked money," says Terry. "I'm happier when I'm not spending it. I've never been motivated to make it. That's why we built our house ourselves. No mortgage. Our retirement is what we are doing: the location, the cabin, the fruit trees. They'll grow as we grow."

To Tia and Terry, the cabin represents the ultimate sovereignty, a true test of self-reliance, and a chance to spread the word. Kristen finds the whole visit inspirational, especially the talk of "humanure"—human waste recycled as compost. (That this portion of the conversation happened over lunch distressed no one but me.)

"It comes down to a personal philosophy," Terry tells Kristen as he crunches on an organic blue corn chip. "You don't need to have as much as you can get. People work 50 hours a week to afford all this stuff. But you end up with only an hour to spend with your kids or your wife. That's not living; it's living to work. I'd rather harvest sweet potatoes than work all day at a job I hate."

I ask the Meers if either one of them was ever tempted to buy an item they didn't need. They look at me with something akin to pity.

"I worked at a convenience store once," Terry offers helpfully. "That hurt."

"We drive a pickup truck," Tia says, head lowered. "Cars are our biggest vice."

"In the future, we're going to build a garage with solar panels on top so we can plug in an electric car," Terry adds quickly. "I mean, that's the long-term goal."

It's dinnertime when we leave the Meers' cabin. Kristen and I decide to find a hotel. We have not made a reservation, preferring the enlivening randomness of spontaneity. After all, this is Orlando, a tourist Mecca. Finding a modest hotel should be as easy as crossing the street. Ninety minutes of interstate driving later, we grasp our misjudgment.

I do want more meaning in my life, I think. I do crave the freedom of less. But right now, I am exhausted. I stink of marsh and hummus. And I have to pee. I am a single mom, riding with another single mom, on possibly the only free night we will have for months. "Call information," I tell Kristen. "And ask for the address of the nearest Ritz-Carlton."

Kristen shoots me a look.

"You'll get a bath!" I add. "With bubbles. And wine."

She dials. With gusto, I might add. It occurs to me that sometimes the simplest thing to do is to treat yourself.

The next day, back in her tiny cottage in northern Florida, Kristen has decided to unload even more furniture. The space feels crowded, she says. And how many places do you need to park your butt, anyway?

"Depends on the butt," I say.

Kristen squints and hands me a chair. She says she has been having a struggle with her daughter, Ellie. She has told Ellie all about the importance of soil, of reducing waste, of the impact on the environment, about consumerism. "But you know, those are pretty big concepts for an 8-year-old. Especially one who only really wants new school clothes."

Even so, Kristen is confident she made the right choice for her family. "At first there was a lot of 'I'm bored.' They didn't have their own rooms, or a million toys, or computers. But since then, we've found games to play, we go for walks, we talk more, we lie in bed and draw, we are literally closer together."

Kristen is also healthier. No more sleeping pills. No more antidepressants. Her journal wish list is coming true.

And then there are the nights when she cooks dinner and, through her open windows, hears the sound of her children running in the woods, the piercing, manic joy of kids throwing stones and kicking leaves and squealing at ghosts behind every windblown tree. "When I hear them playing outside, I think, *This is exactly what I wanted. This is the experience I was looking for.*"

She runs her fingers through her short, graying hair. Her face is calm, relaxed.

"Some people say one person can't make a difference, but I like that expression about how throwing one sea horse back in the ocean makes a big difference to that sea horse. I wanted to sleep at night knowing I'd done my part."

She smiles, wistful for a moment. "I do miss sleeping in my own room."

"That would certainly make some things simpler," I say with a wink.

We laugh. And then the two of us walk outside to the garden, talking about whether or not we'd have sex with Bill Maher, and winter flowers, and what sort of old ladies we'll be, all the while consuming nothing but the easy joy of each other's company. **◐**

Oprah Talks to Ellen DeGeneres

She's known for her sharp wit and easygoing attitude (and, of course, the sneakers and funky dance moves). But behind the comedy is a woman who's had to muster her courage to get where she is today. **Ellen DeGeneres** tells Oprah about her balanced life, her loving wife, and how she takes her job as an *American Idol* judge *very* seriously.

In January 2009, when I first heard that Ellen DeGeneres wanted to be an *O* cover girl, I was sure it was a joke. She started with an announcement to the four million viewers of *The Ellen DeGeneres Show:* "Goodbye to the resolution to read," she quipped, "and hello to the resolution to be on the front cover of *O* in '09!" Then the crusade intensified. In March she launched an "O, Yes I Can!" campaign, and, in between unsuccessful attempts to reach me at the Harpo studios, she unveiled a series of mock *O* covers, including one on which she and I are riding a tandem bicycle through the countryside. The campaign was so funny, I actually hesitated to make the call that finally ended it. But last May, during Ellen's 1,000th show, I surprised her by Skyping into the broadcast and inviting her to share December 2009's cover with me.

Of course, as far as covers go, this one is nothing compared with the one she did in April 1997, when she appeared on the front of *Time* magazine next to the headline "Yep, I'm Gay." In those days, Ellen—a Louisiana native who broke into stand-up comedy in the early '80s by performing at small clubs in New Orleans—was the star of her own sitcom, ABC's *Ellen.* As the show gained popularity and critical acclaim, Ellen, now 52, chose to reveal the secret she'd been carrying for years. What followed was a media circus leading up to the most-watched episode of her series: an estimated 42 million people tuned in to see Ellen's character also come out of the closet. But just as quickly, the crowds went away. The show's ratings started to crash, and a year later it was canceled.

In September 2003, Ellen came back to television as host of *The Ellen DeGeneres Show,* now in its seventh season. When she's not delighting viewers with her quick wit and spontaneous dance moves, she's squeezing in one of her side gigs—like, say, hosting the Academy Awards (which she did in 2007) or taking a spot on the judges' panel on *American Idol* (which she has done this year). Away from the limelight, Ellen shares her life with the actress Portia de Rossi. The two began dating in 2004, and four years later, in a private ceremony at their home, they married. Despite the passage of California's Proposition 8 (which made same-sex marriage illegal in the state), the couple's union is still valid because it occurred before the November 4, 2008, vote.

When Ellen arrived at the photo shoot for our cover, I didn't have to ask her how she was doing; it showed on her face. She radiated the kind of peace and satisfaction that come only when you're living at your highest potential. That's why, a few days after our cover shoot, I gave Ellen a call—to talk about the balance she's achieved in her life, and to get the story behind the glimmer in her eye.

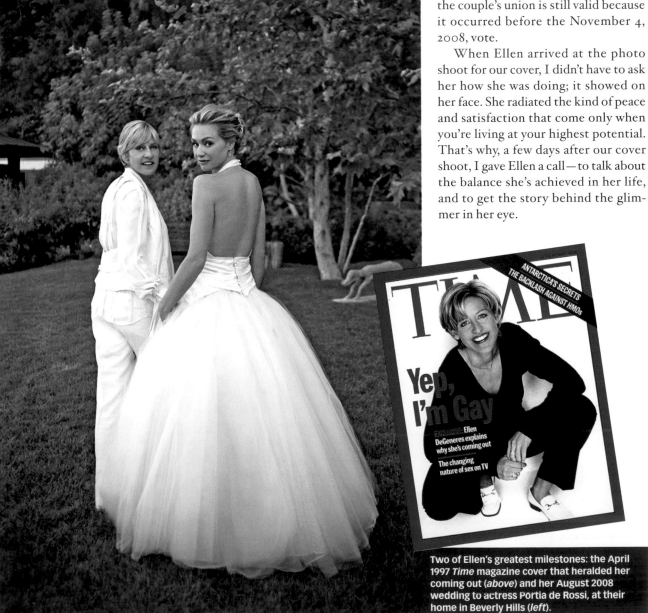

Two of Ellen's greatest milestones: the April 1997 *Time* magazine cover that heralded her coming out (*above*) and her August 2008 wedding to actress Portia de Rossi, at their home in Beverly Hills (*left*).

O! What I Know for Sure...I Think

Performing at The Improv, circa 1991. *Below:* One source of Ellen's wisdom (see number 2 on her list).

BY THE WAY, I SHOULD POINT OUT THAT THERE ARE things I know for sure and things I don't know for sure. Also, there are things I wish I never knew. Like did you ever see that *Primetime* report about hotel rooms and what's on the bedspreads? Exactly.

Actually, there's nothing I know for sure because I know for sure that things change.

For a long time I thought I knew for sure who I was. I grew up in New Orleans and became a comedian. And there was everything that came along with that. The nightclubs. The smoking. The drinking. Then I turned 13.

While I was doing stand-up, I thought I knew for sure that success meant getting everyone to like me. So I became whoever I thought people wanted me to be. I'd say yes when I wanted to say no, and I even wore a few dresses. And it worked. I got my own sitcom.

The show was very successful. I had everything I'd hoped for, but I wasn't being myself. So I decided to be honest about who I was. It was

strange: The people who loved me for being funny suddenly didn't like me for being…me.

I had a really tough time for a few years. My show was gone. My phone wasn't ringing. There wasn't one job offer. And at that point, I thought I knew for sure that I wouldn't work in Hollywood again.

Eventually, I decided to go back to how I started my career, and I wrote an HBO special. Then I got my talk show. And look at me now…I'm on the cover of *O*. And that's the highest honor we give in this country.

I know for sure I would never change any of the hard times I went through in my life. Because it was in those times that I grew the most and gained the most perspective.

It's our challenges and obstacles that give us layers of depth and make us interesting. Are they fun when they happen? No. But they are what make us unique. And that's what I know for sure…I think.

ELLEN DEGENERES: [*After checking her caller ID*] Harpo Inc.

OPRAH: [*Laughs*] I love it. Are you awake?

ELLEN: I am. I just woke up. I had a horrible night. The weirdest thing happened. We had some huge pop in the wall at 2:30 in the morning, and then it sounded like our whole house was going to explode. I don't know if a speaker blew or what—it was just this crazy loud vibration that went on forever, and I lay in bed thinking that the house was going to catch fire because there'd been an electrical short. So I went down to the basement—I haven't been down to the basement since we moved in two years ago—and lying next to all the audiovisual equipment is an audiobook called *Being in Balance.*

OPRAH: Oh my goodness. Isn't that just how the world works?

ELLEN: There's always a reason things happen.

OPRAH: You're exactly like I am. I know that everything happens for a reason, so I look at everything like, *Okay, what does that mean,* and *What am I supposed to be getting from* that?

ELLEN: Right.

OPRAH: You know, you can make yourself nuts doing that, though. But it's also the way to live, I think. How long have you been living this way?

ELLEN: Well, I think I have always been a searcher. But right before I decided to come out, I went on a spiritual retreat called "Changing the Inner Dialogue of Your Subconscious Mind." I had never been to anything like it before, and all my friends were taking bets on how long I'd last with no TV, no radio, and no phone. But for me that was the beginning of paying attention to all of the little things.

OPRAH: Would you say that coming out was the seminal moment in your life?

ELLEN: Oh yeah, because it stripped everything away. The whole world was talking about me. You know, if you're going to be honest with yourself, you have to admit that you go into show business wanting people to talk about you and wanting everyone to know who you are. But that also means there are going to be a whole bunch of people who don't like you. No matter *who* you are. I'm sure there's somebody out there who doesn't like Betty White because she's short and has white hair.

> "I cry often and easily. You're supposed to laugh, you're supposed to cry, you're not supposed to shove your feelings under the rug."

OPRAH: Refresh my memory: At what point did you make the decision to come out? You were three years into your sitcom?

ELLEN: I was four years in, because the fifth year is when they canceled me. I think I've told you about a dream I had. I was struggling with the idea of coming out—what it would do to my career and to me—and in this dream, I was holding a tiny finch in the palm of my hand. I could feel how much I loved this bird and that it was safe in my hand, and I was reaching in to put it back in its cage—one of these thin, bamboo, beautiful, multitiered cages—and as I was putting the bird back in, I realized that the cage was against a window and the bird could fly out. The bird realized it at the same time I did, and I became the bird. And the bird looked at me and wanted to fly out, but I looked at the bird and said, "But you're safe in here in a beautiful cage. Don't leave." And the bird just looked at me and flew out the window.

OPRAH: Wow.

ELLEN: So I was like, *Okay, I know what that means.* Until then I'd had no idea I was in a cage. I was in this beautiful setting, and I was making money and had everyone taking care of me.

OPRAH: So once that veil lifted, did everything change?

ELLEN: Well, there were lots of different veils and lots of different layers—but just to say the words was so huge for me. You know, people say, "Why do you have to tell everybody, who cares, and why do you have to announce it?" It's because it's your truth and the truth shall set you free.

OPRAH: To be able to say it out loud to the world.

ELLEN: But then it turned into everybody telling me to shut up. I was on your show and I was on the cover of *Time,* and there was article after article, and then articles reporting on articles, and it became this storm. I was getting attacked for talking about it so much, and I was like, *"I* am not talking about it, *you* are." And then everybody was hating me and "Oh, shut up already," and that's when the show went down in flames. I actually think the show got better after I came out. The season that no one watched—

OPRAH: ...turned out to be the best season. I remember. But it's so important to say that out loud so people can also see for themselves how the things that broke you open actually allowed you to be set free.

ELLEN: I think Diane Sawyer told me she read something

that said the cracks in your heart let the sun shine through. I just thought that was beautiful. And it's all part of balance. I'm a comedian, and I definitely see the humor in a lot of things. I am also sad a lot. I cry often and easily. I think you're supposed to feel all kinds of things. You're supposed to laugh, you're supposed to cry, you're not supposed to shove your feelings under the rug. I was raised in an atmosphere of "everything's fine." But as I got older, I was like, "Well no, everything's not fine. There is stuff that's sad." I am a really sensitive person. I think I am too sensitive sometimes, especially in this business.

OPRAH: But you do laugh more than you cry, don't you?

ELLEN: Oh, sure. I'm not like a depressed person. But I am saddened by how people treat one another and how we are so shut off from one another and how we judge one another, when the truth is, we are all one connected thing. We are all from the same exact molecules.

OPRAH: Is that why you became vegan?

ELLEN: I became vegan because I saw footage of what really goes on in the slaughterhouses and on the dairy farms. As Linda McCartney used to say, if they had glass walls, no one would eat meat. And let me tell you, I loved eating meat. I loved lamb, I loved chicken, I loved my cheeseburgers....

OPRAH: Did you notice a difference when you became vegan?

ELLEN: Well, I felt better about myself, and I felt healthier living in a cruelty-free way. I haven't been sick since, I am not as tired, and I've lost weight. And I am lucky: I have a chef, so it's easy for me. For a lot of people, it's harder.

OPRAH: Trying to do it so you stay balanced—back to that word, *balance*—is work. You've got to know what you're doing to get all your nutrition.

ELLEN: Right.

OPRAH: Okay. So, when I saw you at the photo shoot for the *O* cover, what I was the most struck by was the light in your eyes.

ELLEN: Well, of course there was a light—I was with you!

OPRAH: [*Laughs*] No, there really was a twinkle in your eye that comes only from a sense of well-being. I'm telling you, I recognize it when I see it. What's that all about for you?

ELLEN: You told me you wanted to talk about this, so I was thinking about it.

And I asked my massage person: What is it about me that you think is balanced?

OPRAH: [*Laughs*] That's like when Gayle was invited to speak about self-esteem and she calls me and says, "How do I feel about self-esteem?" So your massage person said...

ELLEN: She said I constantly challenge myself. She has known me for 11 years, and she said when something goes wrong, instead of running away from it, I look at it and go, "What's my part in it, what's my responsibility?"

OPRAH: And are you able to challenge other people to accept their responsibility?

ELLEN: Oh yeah, and that was such a huge thing for me, because I was raised to be quiet about things like that—you know, just keep your mouth closed. Not in a strict way—my parents were very passive. My father would never confront anybody about anything and is just kind and gentle. And my mother is really funny and sarcastic. But in my family, nothing was ever confronted. Yet now it's easy for me to tell other people what they're doing and how it makes me feel.

OPRAH: You don't have the need to please.

ELLEN: Well, sure, I want people to like me—but not at my expense. I just learned that there are too many people who are going to have an opinion about me whether I am kind to them or not. I can't control what they're feeling. I am not a yeller and I don't have a temper, but I do want people to do their best. And if someone is a friend and I see that they're doing stuff that is not helping them grow, I will make it a point to talk to them about it.

OPRAH: Nongrowth seems to be a real deal breaker for you.

ELLEN: I think you need to be around people who stimulate you.

OPRAH: What was really delightful and heartwarming was to see you in the presence of Portia and vice versa. When she first walked into the shoot, your face lit up. Tell me about this relationship and how it has enlightened your life.

ELLEN: Well, we're perfect for each other. She is so beautiful and so smart and so funny, and with her, I have that sense of "I'm done now." I'm settled. I know that part of my life is taken care of. I've got love. I've got someone who

"Sure, I want people to like me—but not at my expense. I just learned that there are too many people who are going to have an opinion about me whether I am kind to them or not. I can't control what they're feeling."

will be with me till the day I die.

OPRAH: Is that why you wanted to be married?

ELLEN: Getting married was more important to her, really. Portia says all the time how lucky we are that we had each other in that short window of time when it was legal to marry, because a lot of people hadn't found their person, and then suddenly that right was taken away. I'm tearing up thinking about it—we got to get married, and have a wedding. I grew up thinking I'd never get to do that.

OPRAH: What do you refer to each other as—"my partner"?

ELLEN: No, it's "my wife." She says "my wife" and I say "my wife."

OPRAH: So there you are on your farm with your wife and your horses and your dogs. So balanced. But are you going to be able to maintain this balance, this time for yourself, with the *American Idol* schedule?

ELLEN: Well, look at you! *I* don't have a radio show or a magazine. For a couple of months, I'll just fly out and do those audition things.

OPRAH: That's what I loved seeing—you, on the road for those auditions.

ELLEN: I started live on the air in February. But I wanted to look at the tapes to see if they missed people who I would have put through.

OPRAH: Fantastic. You're not afraid of confronting!

ELLEN: That's right. And I'm careful about not hurting people's feelings. I know what it's like to stand up there and perform.

OPRAH: Did the *Idol* people come to you, or did you approach them?

ELLEN: They came to me, and it was a total surprise. I like to try new things because I get bored so easily. And I like the show, so I thought it was a great idea.

OPRAH: Okay. So when you're at home, you're not dancing, are you?

ELLEN: I'll dance if there's music on. I like dancing.

OPRAH: I should have said, when you're at home and not shooting covers with me. Speaking of which, how did you come up with this whole get-on-the-cover-of-*O* idea, anyway?

ELLEN: It all got started because I was in a CoverGirl ad that was on the inside cover of your magazine. I held it up

> "The more relaxed I get and the more confident I feel, the more I get to play and be myself and say whatever I feel like saying."

on my show and said, "I'm on the cover of O! I'm on the *inside* cover, but I'm on the cover!" And that rolled into, "Well, if I'm that close, I might as well be on the *cover* cover!" and then I started the campaign. And I guess you felt so guilty about putting Michelle Obama on the cover that you decided you had to put me on the cover, too.

OPRAH: No, this is what happened. We had already planned the cover with Michelle. And then you started your campaign, and I was like, "Well, is she really serious?" So we waited a couple of weeks, and I decided you were.

ELLEN: I was not serious, though, because I didn't think it was going to happen! No one had ever been on the cover with you, so I really thought it was just a joke. But then once the Michelle Obama cover came along, that's when I really started going after it. And I was shocked and thrilled when you actually went for it.

OPRAH: It was fun. Tell me, are you having as much fun as you appear to be having?

ELLEN: It's a lot of work to put a brand-new monologue and a brand-new show on the air and find comedy every single day. It's challenging and it's the hardest thing I have ever done, but it's the best-suited thing for me. The more relaxed I get and the more confident I feel, the more I get to play and be myself and say whatever I feel like saying and not worry about whether I'm being a good interviewer. Although sometimes, I will admit, you're talking to people and you're like, "Oh please, have something to say!" But in general I'm just more and more confident that if I'm myself, people are going to enjoy it more.

OPRAH: You get paid for being yourself.

ELLEN: It's amazing. It's crazy.

OPRAH: That's what happens when you tell the truth. You open that door for that bird to fly out.

ELLEN: It's so weird because I love you so much, and to come to this place and do a photo shoot with you—I'm not surprised I had a brightness in my eyes.

OPRAH: Well, I'm happy to be able to call you my friend. But I know you have to get back to work, so either I'm going to have you up to my house for dinner, or you guys are going to have me down to yours.

ELLEN: You have an open invitation.

OPRAH: Thanks! O

Suze Orman: Nine Small Steps That Will Pay Off Big in the Future

Huge, scary numbers are lurking everywhere these days: The massive federal bailout (now on the taxpayers' tab)...the unemployment rate, which is now at a 26-year high... that daunting sum you are constantly told you will need if you want to retire comfortably...the six-figure mortgage balance you barely chip away at each month.

Listen to me: Stop focusing on the big picture. Given what is going on in the world right now, you'll only fuel your fear and anxiety.

Macroeconomics matter, but your security depends far more on microfinance—the small choices you make with your money. Every financial worry you want to banish and financial dream you want to achieve comes from taking tiny steps today that will put you on a path toward your goals. My list of small moves that yield big dividends:

① Save a bit at a time.

I get so frustrated when people tell me it's unrealistic to create an eight-month emergency savings fund, or have money saved for a home down payment, or pay off their $5,000 credit card balance. I am not suggesting that you can snap your fingers and have everything taken care of. What I'm telling you is to move toward your goals in steps. Rather than get lost in the big picture—"Eight months? Are you crazy, Suze? I can never do that!"—focus on what is within your power: the sums you can sock away every week or month to get closer to what you're trying to achieve. Put $50 a week into a bank savings account earning 2 percent interest, and in three years you will have saved more than $8,000.

② Have a little self-discipline!

Okay, so where do you find the money to put toward your financial goals? If you're dealing with a layoff or furlough, I know you feel stretched to the limit. But often when families tell me they have no money for their goals, I look at their spending and find lots of "wants" to cut. So pull out your three most recent bank and credit card statements, circle every charge or debit that is not a necessity, and ask yourself: *Can I eliminate this cost entirely?* If not, can you scale it back 30 to 50 percent (downgrade the cable, say, or opt for the less-pricey cell package)? Every time you cut expenses, you can put the money toward bigger goals.

③ Automate.

So many financial dreams are thwarted by the failure to act upon good intentions. Even if you commit to step 2 and free up money, using it wisely can be a challenge. Complete this sentence: I had every intention of _____ , but I got sidetracked or couldn't stick with my plan. That blank could be: (a) building an eight-month emergency fund; (b) investing in a Roth IRA; (c) saving

for a home down payment; (d) paying every bill on time; (e) all of the above.

The solution is easy: Put your financial life on autopilot as a form of "forced" saving. Your 401(k) is a great example of auto-investing; with every paycheck, money goes into your retirement account. You can set up the same system at a discount brokerage or fund company to help you invest in an IRA, authorizing the firm to pull money out of your bank account weekly, monthly, or quarterly.

Autopilot is also a great way to save for a home down payment. Have $100 automatically transferred from your checking account to a bank savings account each month and in five years at 2 percent interest you could have more than $6,300 set aside. An FHA-insured mortgage requires a 3.5 percent down payment, so $6,300 would be enough to buy a $180,000 home.

And if you suffer from late-payment-itis, set up auto bill pay through an online bank account. This will save you those $39 late fees on credit card payments and lift your FICO score (on-time payment history accounts for 35 percent of your score).

④ Max out on the company match.

In a 2008 survey of nearly a million 401(k) participants, the investment advisory firm Financial Engines found that 33 percent don't contribute enough to their company plan to collect the maximum employer matching contribution. That's literally turning down free money. The way a match works is that if you contribute to your retirement account, your employer will throw in some money, too. One common system is for an employer to give 50 cents for every dollar the employee contributes to her 401(k), up to a specified limit, such as 6 percent of a salary or a certain dollar amount per year. Under those terms, if the employee contributed $3,000, the employer would kick in another $1,500. Hello! That's a guaranteed 50 percent return on your investment. And $3,000 spread out over 26 pay periods is only $115 every two weeks. That's a small step toward a big goal.

If your company doesn't provide a match—or has opted to suspend its match during the recession—you may still qualify for a Roth IRA. I recommend funding the IRA completely

> Pull out your three most recent bank and credit card statements, circle every charge or debit that is not a necessity, and ask yourself: *Can I eliminate this cost entirely?*

before you contribute to an un-matched 401(k). Without the match, a 401(k) is still a good deal, but a Roth IRA is even better. Details follow in the next small step.

5 Invest in a Roth IRA.

I love the Roth IRA. Tax-free income in retirement is a truly great deal. That's because income tax rates are likely to rise given all the big federal deficits that will need to be repaid. (And remember: Withdrawals from a traditional IRA or 401(k) will be taxed at your ordinary income tax rate.) If you have modified adjusted gross income (AGI) below $105,000 this year ($166,000 for married couples filing a joint return), you can invest the maximum $5,000 in an IRA (or $6,000 if you are 50 or older). Above those income limits, you can make smaller contributions; you lose eligibility if you have a modified AGI of $120,000 or more, or are part of a married couple with a modified AGI of $176,000 or above.

I know $5,000 or $6,000 is a big deal. And I promised small steps. So break that $5,000 into 12 monthly chunks. Does $416 sound more doable? If it's still too much, save what you can. No rule says it has to be $5,000. You can invest as little as $600 a year at some fund companies through an auto-investing plan, or save until you meet the $1,000 to $1,500 minimum initial investment most mutual funds require.

6 Subtract your age from 100; put that much in stocks.

Now we need to talk about asset allocation. For all your long-term investments, such as retirement accounts that you won't touch for at least ten years, you need a mix of stocks and bonds. Stocks offer the best shot at inflation-beating gains. But stocks don't always go up. That's where bonds come into play: They have less upside potential, but they also do not pack the same risk. So what's your Midas mix of stocks and bonds? Subtract your age from 100 and invest that percentage of your retirement savings in stocks. The rest belongs in bonds. For the stock portion, put 70 percent in U.S. stocks and the rest in international funds. As for the bonds: You should definitely have some lower-risk investments in your 401(k), but rather than invest in a bond fund, look for a GIC or Stable Value fund, which offers a guaranteed return. For your IRA accounts, I am all

A small amount of money buys your family protection if you die prematurely.

for owning individual bonds you can hold to maturity instead of bond funds, which are subject to trading and carry more risk.

7 Spend $50 a month for peace of mind.

That's about what it would cost a healthy 40-year-old woman to buy a million-dollar 20-year level term life insurance policy; figure on less if you're younger and more if you're older. But the idea is this: A small amount of money buys your family protection if you die prematurely. You can shop for term life insurance policies at selectquote.com and accuquote.com.

8 Create the four most loving documents in existence.

One of the most tragic disconnects I see is when someone tells me she loves her family to pieces but hasn't set up these four must-have documents: a revocable living trust, a will, a durable power of attorney for finances, and a durable power of attorney for healthcare. I realize these don't sound like a "small" undertaking, since estate lawyers may charge $2,500 to create them. Visit suzeorman.com and click on the Will & Trust link to learn about how you can draw up these essential documents on your own.

9 Add a 13th mortgage payment; pay off your loan five years faster.

If you're in your 50s and plan to live in your current home forever, try to pay off the mortgage before you stop working so you remove that big cost from your postretirement expenses. One way to do so is to make one extra mortgage payment a year. You can even spread the payment over 12 months. Let's say you have a $1,500 monthly mortgage payment and a 30-year fixed-rate mortgage. If you divide $1,500 by 12, that's $125, so instead of paying $1,500, you send in $1,625 each month. That will cut your repayment time by five years and reduce your interest payments over the life of the loan; for a $250,000 mortgage charging 6 percent, you will save $61,000 ($228,000 in interest payments versus $289,000). That $125 a month may be tough, but it's doable. It's one small step now, and one giant leap toward future financial security. ◖

O
happiness

93   NEED A LIFT? I BY JESSICA WINTER

98   SMALL DELIGHTS

   98   PARADISE. 17 CENTS A SPOONFUL I BY MARK LEYNER

   99   TREASURE HUNTING I BY GILLIAN FASSEL

   99   TWO WHEELS, NO WAITING I BY SAÏD SAYRAFIEZADEH

 100 LIFE ON THE PAGE I BY JESSICA HELFAND

 100 TUNING IN I BY CAITLIN MACY

 100 IN MY ELEMENT I BY FARAI CHIDEYA

101 ESCAPE YOUR RAT RACE I BY MARTHA BECK

104 STUCK IN A RUT? ONE SIMPLE TWEAK CAN GET YOU UNSTUCK I BY DR. PHIL

106 "I KNOW FOR SURE THAT LIFE IS FULL OF DELIGHTFUL TREASURES,
     IF WE TAKE A MOMENT TO LOOK AROUND" I BY OPRAH

Need a Lift?

How are you feeling these days? Like hiding your head under the pillows (and your money under the mattress) and saying "wake me when it's over"? We've got something a lot better for you than escape. It's a buoyant blend of warmth, wonder, compassion, and connectedness that'll help you soar over pretty much anything life throws in your path. **Jessica Winter** gives you the recipe to raise your spirits and lighten your heart.

It was a dreary afternoon not long ago, one of those days when the sunlight is wan and somehow sooty, flattening everything into a half-hearted pencil sketch. Sitting at my desk, I quit staring at my cuticles long enough to open a YouTube link from a friend—a newsclip about Jason McElwain. You might remember Jason, the autistic high school student from Rochester, New York, who scored 20 points in four minutes during his one-and-only stint in a game with his school's basketball team. In the clip, the coach gets choked up retelling Jason's story; tears sprang to my eyes, too. As I watched the elated home crowd rushing the court after Jason's final three-pointer, I felt borne aloft on a wave of happy pandemonium.

I started forwarding the video, hoping my friends would feel what I felt: awe, surprised delight, teary joy.

Within a few minutes, the replies started coming in:

"Crying."

"Oh no, I'm crying at work!"

"I'm Facebooking this now. Amazing."

"Wow—just what I needed. Thanks!"

And then I wondered: Does this feeling come in prescription form?

Especially in our current moment of doom and gloom, stories like Jason McElwain's seem like just what the doctor ordered. When forces beyond our control have upended what we thought we knew for sure (about our savings, our homes, our country, our future) and a drizzle of apprehension settles over us, we hunger for uplift. We want a nudge toward happiness, a little magic to open the pressure valve of everyday life—the sublime thrill of transcendence to be found in a Mendelssohn symphony or a Turner landscape, in a perfect kiss or perfect morning jog, in time spent with our families and friends. And then we want to hit Forward on that feeling: because the more we share it, the stronger it grows.

But a yen for uplift isn't just a sentimental reflex (grumps and pessimists, stick with us!). The physiology that makes McElwain-brand exhilaration possible is also the bedrock of our instincts for compassion, caretaking, and connection. The capacity for uplift is part of what makes us essentially, euphorically human. According to a growing body of scientific research, it's critical to our health and well-being. And luckily, lifting our spirits doesn't depend on finding YouTube miracles in our inbox. (Well, not entirely.) For the most part, it's up to us.

We can start in the general vicinity of our cleavage, with that serene warm-chest feeling that washes over us when we're moved by an extraordinary act or by a person of great virtue (whether it's Nelson Mandela, Chesley "Sully"

Sullenberger, or the amazing woman who runs your local soup kitchen). But to reach the physiological root of those sensations, we need to take a close look at the vagus nerve—actually a bundle of nerves that starts at the base of the brain and branches out through the body, linking up with the facial and vocal muscles and the heart, lungs, and gut. Acting as a messenger between the central nervous system and the major organs, the vagus nerve slows the heart rate (through the release of the neurotransmitter acetylcholine), calms the immune response (by controlling the release of proteins called cytokines), and communicates with the muscles that control respiration and digestion.

When we give a reassuring smile or sigh in sympathy with another person, the vagus nerve is quietly at work behind the scenes, "reducing our heart rate to a more peaceful pace [and] enhancing the likelihood of gentle contact in close proximity with others," social psychologist Dacher Keltner writes in his recent book, *Born to Be Good*. The mellowing vagus is also closely associated with oxytocin, the all-important hormone of human trust and devotion. For a study published in 2008, researchers Jonathan Haidt and Jennifer A. Silvers invited nursing mothers to bring their babies and watch a clip from *The Oprah Winfrey Show* in which a musician paid moving tribute to his former teacher for steering him away from a life of crime and gangs. The moms who watched (and, sometimes, cried through) the elevating *Oprah* clip were more likely to nurse and hug their babies—suggesting heightened levels of oxytocin, which cues lactation—than another group who laughed along with a video of Jerry Seinfeld telling jokes. Oxytocin, often released along the smooth and orderly Route Vagus, is essential to uplift, according to Haidt, an associate professor in social psychology at the University of Virginia. (His name, aptly, is pronounced "height.") In his view, human happiness derives neither from external validation nor solely from within, but from "between": through the relationships created by love, work, and "something larger than yourself"—whether it's a religious group, a volunteer organization, or a political campaign. "If happiness comes from between," Haidt says, "then oxytocin is the hormone of between. It's the catalyst that helps bond people together."

Even if we don't know oxytocin from OxyContin or our vagus from Las Vegas, we seem to know intuitively how to prepare our spirits for takeoff—even when the forecast calls for grounding all flights.

For one thing, we're yearning to discover new, deep connections with others. In fact, many of us are investing in the most private form of "between" there is: the oxytocin factory known as romantic intimacy. Memberships at the

online-dating site match.com were up 16 percent in January 2009 as compared with the same period in 2008; in February 2009, Match's competitor plentyoffish.com saw a whopping 94 percent rise in traffic over the previous year. And despite the sharp contraction in most consumer spending since the economic crisis blew up a couple of years ago, Babeland, a sex toys retailer with four outlets in New York City and Seattle, has seen double-digit increases in sales; during Valentine's Day weekend in 2009, sales were up 26 percent over the previous year. "We haven't seen a spike like this since just after September 11," says cofounder Claire Cavanah. "People are nesting. They're looking for a stress reliever. They want to be comforted." (And, evidently,

they want vibrators. Sleek, fuchsia-colored vibrators.)

We're sweating out stress at the gym, too, which also hits the V-spot: Aerobic exercise and yoga enhance vagus nerve output—as does meditation. The Equinox fitness club chain, with locations nationwide, reports an 18 percent increase in usage of its gyms since autumn of 2008; attendance at Curves, a women's-only national chain, was up 22 percent in January 2009 compared with the previous year. Memberships at Life Time Fitness, which has locations in 18 states, are up 14 percent. And yoga teachers appear to be the new first responders to (economic) emergency. Invoke, a yoga and Pilates studio in Indianapolis, has seen higher revenues and attendance since fall

2008, according to owner Amy Peddycord, whose $5 community yoga classes are always packed. David Sunshine, owner of Dallas Yoga Center, laments that he has to keep turning people away from his new yoga-for-stress classes.

Groups of people sun saluting through hard times together is an indicator of what Haidt calls our "hive psychology." "Evolutionary history over the past 15,000 to 20,000 years involves a lot of synchronous movement, chanting, dancing—the temporary creation of larger groups," he says. "It's a way of ramping up the 'between' to make people feel part of something greater than themselves." Joining a hive could be as simple as laughing or gasping along with an audience at a comedy or thriller (movie attendance was up 17.5 percent in 2009). Or as profound as huddling in freezing temperatures with 1.8 million of your fellow Americans at the National Mall on Inauguration Day.

President Obama's call to service has given a big boost to one of the most reliable vehicles for uplift: volunteer work, which forges yet another kind of nourishing "between." Sonya Lyubomirsky, a professor of psychology at the University of California, Riverside, has consistently found that performing acts of kindness is highly correlated with increased happiness, improving both our self-image and—oxytocin alert!—our sense of community. One beneficiary of the service surge, the volunteer organization New York Cares, reports a 30 percent increase in prospective volunteers attending orientation sessions in January 2009 compared with the same period in 2008, and a monumental 75 percent increase from February 2008 to February 2009.

"People will increasingly turn to volunteer work to lift

their spirits during the economic crisis," predicts trend analyst Kiwa Iyobe, of the New York City–based marketing consultancy Suite 2046. "A lot of people seem to have learned through their experiences during the presidential campaign that being part of a community and making a difference—even a small one—is deeply satisfying. No matter how busy or stressed they are right now, volunteers report that they always feel better after taking a few hours to do something positive for their community along with a bunch of like-minded strangers. It has the effect of putting their own lives and problems into perspective."

So, the basic, scientifically proven recipe for raising our spirits appears to be deliciously straightforward: sex, exercise (other than sex), and service (other than...never mind). But for those times when your sweetheart and your running shoes are out of reach and your next volunteering gig is a few days off, uplift is also available in instant fun-size packets.

"Even if you're just sitting in a chair, there are things you can do to change the pace of the day in a way that's recuperative and uplifting," says Karen Bradley, a visiting associate professor of dance at the University of Maryland. "Take a minute to write your name in cursive with your eyeballs, or count your teeth with your tongue, or just hum along with some music. The muscles around your eyes will relax; your jaw will relax; you will start to breathe more deeply." (Caution: All that droning and eye-rolling may not have the same calming effect on observers.) Bradley also loves "the 20-minute 'Google Earth vacation.' You pick an exotic location, choose your resort hotel, decide which restaurants to visit and what you'll eat. I've gone everywhere: New Zealand, Machu Picchu, the Galápagos Islands. It reminds you that you're not the center of the universe—it opens your mind and gives you perspective."

Evolutionary anthropologist Sarah Blaffer Hrdy likewise looks outward to find "momentary joys." "I'll take a walk and wait for little flashes of discovery in the natural world," she says. "Recently, I watched my dog leap through the air, over a creek, to chase a wild turkey—something I'd never seen her do before. I can't jump creeks anymore, so I enjoyed being part of her abandon!"

Any minor shift in outlook—including a little vicarious creek jumping—can make a dismal picture less dispiriting. Yale psychology professor Susan Nolen-Hoeksema, an expert on depression, has studied our penchant for self-punishing rumination when we face a problem—a tendency that many of us have indulged during the past two years. She found that a simple, ten-minute imagery task (such as picturing clouds in a bright blue sky or a cheery stack of watermelons in a pickup truck) can turn brooding into focused action. "The quality of your problem-solving markedly improves," says Nolen-Hoeksema. "When you're ruminating, the negative thoughts are so strong that it's hard to inhibit them. But even after a moment of distraction, those thoughts aren't activated anymore. It's like pressing the restart button when your computer is acting up."

Remember, too, that crafty reprogramming of the mind doesn't necessarily depend on *what* you're thinking about, but *how* you're thinking about it. Harvard psychology professor Ellen Langer once assembled three groups of football-averse women to watch the Super Bowl; the group assigned to make six "novel distinctions" about the game ("It didn't matter if it was about the players' rear ends—anything," Langer explains) enjoyed themselves significantly more than the group that had to take notice of just three things, or nothing at all.

What we can learn from the mindful Super Bowl party, Langer says, is that "when times are tough, the way out is in actively noticing new things. The essence of happiness is that feeling of engagement with the world and with other people."

In other words, instead of waiting for this daunting moment to pass, we can try to seize and shape it, to lighten it—however we please.

So send the link. Start the conversation. Report for duty. Make the novel distinction. Move. Roll your eyeballs around. Go to the game. Grab somebody's hand. And, yes—if you do just one thing—only connect.

A friend tells a story about going to see an exhibit at the Museum of Modern Art in New York City. She was drawn to a room where a crowd had gathered in a semicircle before a canvas, obviously mesmerized. As she approached the painting—Vincent van Gogh's breathtaking *Starry Night*—and joined the group, she felt gathered up into their shared, awestruck stillness. Tears welled in her eyes: For one transcendent instant, she'd found her hive, had found her between.

"We are incomplete creatures," says Jonathan Haidt. "We cannot live alone; we cannot find our own meaning alone. We realize our potential, we become alive, only when we find the 'between.'"

Chances are, the between is closer than you think. It could be waiting for you in someone's eyes, in a phrase of music, in a starry night. You can find it. Just be sure to keep looking up. ◖

Small Delights

What are the things that make you happiest—that don't involve a major transfer of currency? Six writers give us a new appreciation for ordinary pleasures, from supermarket pudding to zingy pop radio.

Paradise. 17 Cents a Spoonful

It doesn't take a forensic psychiatrist to explain the origins of my obsessive love for pudding. For me, pudding is all about the polymorphic erotics of being fed. More than just a cheap thrill in tough times, pudding turns me into a baby bird waiting there, gape-mouthed, for some sweet, pre-chewed pabulum.

What if you could condense the evolution of gastronomic pleasure from the very first mammalian sip of mother's milk to everything savored and swallowed over the millennia into one single alimentary act? Sound crazy? And, friends, I'm not talking about hot, steamy Christmas puddings, bread puddings, figgy puddings, crème brûlées, or zabagliones. I'm talking about the store-bought, ready-made pudding you find in the refrigerated section of your supermarket. I'm talking six plastic four-ounce cups of cold, thick, dizzyingly sweet pudding for around $2. I'm talking Swiss Miss. I'm talking Kozy Shack.

And actually, I've refined the act of pudding eating even further, down to its Eucharistic essence—a single spoonful. Two ounces. Seventeen cents' worth.

Here's how it's done: Scoop out a tablespoon of pudding from the plastic container (butterscotch is regarded by pudding illuminati as the epitome of flavors); put it in your mouth; *do not* move it around or disperse it in any way with your tongue; swallow the glob intact and let Mother Gravity slowly draw it down. Remember—this is as much about how it feels as it is about how it tastes.

Anticipation of that single sweet glob is the fuse that drives me through the day. A tablespoon of pudding is the perfectly titrated dose. It's a fugitive pleasure, swallowing a syllable. That sweet, thick syllable—*pudd*. The *-ing* is simply the slide down the throat, the *pudd* as it bids adieu.... The parting of the pudding is all sweet sorrow.

A cowboy's shot of whiskey in a saloon sends the cowboy west, far from Mama, toward trouble, exile, and ultimately into the sunset. But the spoonful of pudding has a completely opposite vector. It sends you back, back east, back to Mama, toward the dawn, all the way to Eden...before the fall of mankind. Prelapsarian paradise at only 17 cents per glob! That's what I'm talking about. —*Mark Leyner*

Treasure Hunting

I am an estate-sale shopper—equal parts bargain hunter, recycler, voyeur—and I can conceive of no better way to spend a Saturday morning-into-afternoon than on the estate-sale circuit, armed with classified ads, Google maps, and a big, big latte. I've found, among other artifacts, a cache of 1950s Boy Scout memorabilia, a stalagmite shaped like an elephant's foot, a velvet-covered volume titled "Poetry in Costume." That last was a meticulously drawn history of women's fashion, from Grecian to Gibson girl, and its schoolgirl creator had pasted a letter from her teacher on one of its pages:

"This is a beautiful book," the teacher wrote in May 1945. "I am sure it will be something to cherish and pass on to your children. It betrays your artistic nature and your gentle, beautiful character."

But her children did not cherish this book, and I can't resist imagining a novella to explain their heartlessness. Maybe, tragically, she outlived them. Or perhaps they just weren't the kind of people who get sentimental about objects, and when they came across this relic while cleaning out her attic, they thought, *What am I going to do with this old thing?* and tossed it in the "sell" pile.

And sell it they did, to me, for $8.

Sometimes I feel it's the least I can do to honor this stranger, to buy something her own family didn't deem worthy of saving but that she kept, for a reason strong and personal to her. And every time my 5-year-old daughter asks me to pull "Poetry in Costume" off the shelf so she can pore over the wonderful ladies and their lovingly rendered draperies, I'm reminded that the circle of life is also very much a circle of stuff, passing from one gentle, beautiful character to the next.   —*Gillian Fassel*

Two Wheels, No Waiting

My bicycle prefers the errand. Indeed, it has no interest in tranquil rides through the park, around the pond, on to nowhere.... It would die of boredom. No, on sunny afternoons it desires the post office, the grocery store, the library. This is when it is best able to display, conspicuously, its skill and dexterity and forthrightness. After all, who can surpass my bicycle when it comes to a span of ten blocks? Certainly not the foot, plodding clumsily to and fro. Nor the car, halted in traffic, panting with frustration, staring at us with envy as we pedal past. When we finally arrive back home at the end of the day with the sun setting, our basket will be full of the fruits of our journey. "Good boy," I will whisper to my bicycle, and I will rub its handlebars affectionately.   —*Saïd Sayrafiezadeh*

Life on the Page

During the two years I researched my book about scrapbooks, I came across Zelda Fitzgerald's. It had this cacophony of odd, weird, disconnected moments—a review of one of Scott's plays, a picture of Zelda dressed as a clown—which is exactly what her life was. Anne Sexton kept firecrackers in hers. I found her scrapbook in a dusty box at the University of Texas at Austin. I felt as if nobody had ever looked at it.

I travel everywhere with a little notebook, double-stick tape, and a date stamp. That's all you need. A few months ago a giant dragonfly, which had lived for a long time in my studio, dropped down on the table, dead. I was fascinated by its wings; they're so rarely—if ever—not in motion. I taped it into my sketchbook; it resembled a piece of delicate brown lace. I know some people don't trust their ability to express themselves in words, but if they grab something and paste it down in a scrapbook, they can make sense of their life as it changes. The gesture—not just saving something in a box but cementing it into place, saying, "I was here, this happened, here's the date"—that's really what it's all about.

—*Jessica Helfand*

Tuning In

I got a clock radio when I was 8 and experienced an immediate joy of connectedness that's never gone away. I'll listen to anything: country; Keillor; Communist chat. Indie college stations that play bands I've never heard of. Radio France International—the station of the Francophone diaspora—or the BBC. I get supper on the table to *All Things Considered* and clean up to a cheesy "Hits of Yesterday and Today" playlist.

That you can cook and clean to the radio (and drive and dress and endure dental work) is to me central to the appeal of the dial. It's stimulating...but not coercively so. It's pleasurable, but, like tea to television's coffee, the addiction it incites is a mild one. Radio is not only wildly cheap, it's durably so: The machine I listen to now is not remarkably different from my clock radio of 30 years ago. Let your stereophilic husband have his fancy speakers and his subwoofer. Optimum sound quality is not the point of radio. For me, just listening is—tuning in, wherever I happen to be, to this private conversation that always includes me. ◖

—*Caitlin Macy*

In My Element

Water has always shaped my memories: I can remember the times my sister would bring a plastic bucket down to the stream and catch crawfish. (We even had one as a pet for a while.) Recently we decided to paddle out on an ocean kayak tour, a flotilla of amateurs, struggling to stay on course. The swells grew high, and we both started to feel nervous. Then a humpback whale whooshed out of the water a hundred yards from us, sent spray flying, and dove back into the deep. Another awestruck paddler asked, "Why do they do that?" Our guide smiled and said, "If you weighed 30 tons and you could levitate out of the water, wouldn't you?" Renowned children's advocate Marian Wright Edelman titled her recent book *The Sea Is So Wide and My Boat Is So Small.* For her, it's a metaphor; but Marian—I know how you feel.

—*Farai Chideya*

Escape Your Rat Race

Feeling trapped by a job, relationship, or routine, but terrified of making a change? **Martha Beck** shows you how to feel your way to freedom.

Sheila and I are conversing at a drug treatment center, where she's been remanded. Counselors are listening, so we can't plan a way to break her out. As it happens, escape is the last thing on Sheila's mind. I'm not coaching her through the woes of being institutionalized for drug use but prepping her for her upcoming release.

"In here everything's simple," Sheila says. "Outside I'll have to deal with my crazy mom, get a job, pay the bills. I don't know how to handle that without drugs." When I ask her to picture a peaceful, happy life, Sheila draws a blank. "I can't imagine anything except what I've already seen," she says.

The despair in her voice is so heavy it makes me want to huff a little glue myself, but two things give me hope: a fabled land known in the annals of psychology as Rat Park, and a montage of other clients, once as hopeless as Sheila, who went on to live happy, meaningful lives. The concepts I learned from Rat Park, channeled through the behaviors I've seen in those courageous clients, just may transform Sheila's future.

But first, what is this mythic Rat Park? And how might it relate to you? The term comes from a study conducted in 1981 by psychologist Bruce Alexander and colleagues. He noted that many addiction studies had something in common: The lab rats they used were locked in uncomfortable, isolating cages. Testing a hunch, Alexander gathered two groups of rats. For the first, he built a 200-square-foot rodent paradise called Rat Park. There a colony of white Wister rats found luxurious accommodations for all their favorite pastimes—mingling, mating, raising pups, writing articles for newspaper tabloids. The second group was housed in the traditional cages.

Alexander offered both groups a choice of plain water or sugar water laced with morphine. Like rats in other studies, the traditionally caged animals became instant addicts. However, the residents of Rat Park tended to "just say no," avoiding the drug-treated sugar water. Even rats that were already addicted to morphine tended to lay off the hard stuff when in Rat Park. Put them back in their cages, however, and they'd stay stoned as Deadheads.

Alexander saw many parallels between these junkie rats and human addicts. He has talked of one patient who worked as a shopping mall Santa. "He couldn't do his job unless he was high on heroin," Alexander remembered. "He would shoot up, climb into that red Santa Claus costume, put on those black plastic boots, and smile for six hours straight."

This story jingles bells for many of my clients. Like Smack Santa, they spend many hours playing roles that don't match their innate personalities and preferences, dulling the pain with mood-altering substances. Miserable with their jobs, relationships, or daily routines, they gulp down a fifth of Scotch, buy 46 commemorative Elvis plates on QVC, superglue phony smiles to their faces, and head on out to whatever rat race is gradually destroying them.

Sheila was actually a step ahead of most of my clients, in that she knew she was locked up. Most people are trapped in prisons made of mind stuff—attitudes and beliefs such as "I have to look successful" or "I can't disappoint my dad." Ideas like these—being deeply entrenched and invisible—are often more powerful than physical prisons. When we're trapped in mind cages, gulping happy pills by the handful and fantasizing about lethally stapling coworkers, we rarely even consider that our unhappiness comes from living in captivity. And if we ever come close to recognizing the truth, we're stopped by a barrage of terrifying questions: "What if there's nothing better than this?" "What if I quit my job, lose my seniority, and end up somewhere even worse?" "What if I break off this relationship and end up alone forever?" "What if I get my hopes up and the big break never comes?"

When the alternatives are staying in the familiar cage or facing the unknown, trust me, most people choose the cage—over and over and over again. It's painful to watch, especially knowing that liberation is only a few simple steps away. If you suspect that you might need to engineer your own prison break, the following pieces of common-sense advice can set you free forever.

You Don't Have to Know What Rat Park Looks Like

"I just don't think I'll ever find the right life for me," Sheila frets.

"Of course you won't!" I say. "How strange to think you would!"

It amazes me how often people use that phrase: "Find the right life." Would you walk into your kitchen hoping to find the right fried egg, the right cup of coffee, the right toast?

Such things don't simply appear before you; they arrive because you rummage around, figure out what's available, and make what you want. (If you're rich, you can hire a chef and place your order, but you're still creating the result.)

Bruce Alexander's rats were hand-delivered into paradise. Lucky critters, indeed—but not nearly as lucky as Alexander himself, or the rest of us humans, who have the astonishing ability to envision and build Rat Parks. All animals are shaped by their environment, but we, more than any other species, can shape our environment right back. We can cook the egg, brew the coffee, paint the room, change the space. We can fabricate our Rat Parks, and we must, if we want them built to spec.

"But I don't know what I'm trying to build," Sheila protests when I tell her this. "How can I create something when I don't have a clue what it looks like?"

Time for commonsense suggestion number two.

> When the alternatives are staying in the familiar cage or facing the unknown, trust me, most people choose the cage—over and over and over again.

You Don't Need a Map to Find Your Rat Park

I often invite clients to play the dead-simple game You're Getting Warmer, You're Getting Colder. The client leaves the room, and I hide a simple object—say, a key—in a tricky place, such as the inside of a cake. (Not that I would have done this with someone locked up. Like Sheila. Absolutely not.) When the client returns to the room, he almost invariably stands still, and asks, "What am I looking for?"

Obviously, I don't answer him. The only feedback I'll give is "You're getting warmer" or "You're getting colder." Eventually clients will start moving. Guided by the words *warmer* and *colder,* they quickly identify the general hiding area. Then there's a period of confusion, fueled by assumptions like "Well, she certainly wouldn't hide it in the cake." They go back and forth for a bit, then stop and demand, "Where is it?" Again, this gets them nothing. Peeved, they revert to following the "warmer/colder" feedback until they arrive at the object.

I've never had a client who didn't ultimately succeed. Not one.

My point: Life has installed within you powerful "getting warmer, getting colder" signals. When Sheila thought of leaving the treatment center, her tension, anxiety, and drug cravings soared. The time she had to serve was "warmer"; her outside life, "colder." Certain activities were freezing cold—dealing with her mother, working, paying bills. As we examined each of these, we found that her guidance system was giving her beautifully clear messages. For instance, being around sane noncriminals, even officials at the treatment center, felt "warmer" than Sheila's crazy dope-dealing mother. Working in the cafeteria, with its institutional predictability, was "warmer" than her old cocktail waitress job, where she'd flashed her flesh to elicit unpredictable tips from drunken customers. Living within her economic means felt "warmer" than credit card shopping sprees she couldn't afford.

True, Sheila was a long way from her own Rat Park. But with the knowledge that her navigation system was functioning perfectly, all she had to do was play her life as a game of You're Getting Warmer, You're Getting Colder. The same is true for you. It isn't necessary to know exactly how your ideal life will look; you only have to know what feels better and what feels worse. If something feels both good and bad, break it down into its components to see which are warm, which cold. Begin making choices based on what makes you feel freer and happier, rather than how you think an ideal life should look. It's the process of feeling our way toward happiness, not the realization of some Platonic ideal, that creates our best lives.

"My life is so far from perfect," Sheila says as we end our session. "I don't know if it's fixable."

She's ready to hear my third and last piece of commonsense advice.

You Don't Have to Make Big Changes to Get There

This step is something I stole from philosopher and engineer Buckminster Fuller. Bucky, as his friends knew him, chose for his epitaph just three words: CALL ME TRIMTAB. Trim tabs are tiny rudders attached to the back of larger rudders that steer huge ships. The big rudders would snap off if turned directly, but, as Fuller famously said, "just moving the little trim tab builds a low pressure that pulls the rudder around. Takes almost no effort at all. So...you can just put your foot out like that and the whole big ship of state is going to go."

Every life is a series of trim-tab decisions. Should you read tonight or watch TV? Choose what feels warmer. Self-help or thriller? Choose what feels warmer. Cuddle with the dog or banish him from the bed? Choose what feels (psychologically) warmer.

If you make mistakes, no problem; you'll soon feel colder and correct your course. Making consistent trim-tab choices toward happiness is what steers the mighty ship of your life into exotic ports, safe havens—in short, into every Rat Park you can imagine, and then some.

I say goodbye to Sheila not knowing whether she'll set her trim tabs toward happiness or back to her drug-abusing cage of a life. I've learned not to get my hopes up with humans, who aren't nearly as clear-sighted and authentic as rats. But our session reminds me to keep following my own tiny feelings and impulses to their distant and amazing destinations. So instead of worrying about Sheila—or me, or you—I'll choose to trust our powerful instincts, our desire to be happy, our amazing human capacity for invention. You may choose cynical despair instead—it's all the rage in intellectual circles—but if you care to join me, I think you'll find it's a whole lot warmer over here in Rat Park. ◘

> It isn't necessary to know exactly how your ideal life will look; you only have to know what feels better and what feels worse.

Dr. Phil: Stuck in a Rut? One Simple Tweak Can Get You Unstuck

Whether your problems are large and overwhelming or small and annoying, you often don't need a major overhaul to go from where you are to where you want to be. Simple tweaks can set you on the right path. Many of the issues I hear about over and over again involve inertia, the tendency for a body at rest to remain at rest. If you're stuck in a rut, you need to build some momentum to get out of it, and that means knowing the critical first step to take. Here are nine problems I'm often asked about and my advice on how you can address each of them with just a slight change—a simple shift—that can lead to lasting transformation.

① **Sex with my husband has become ho-hum.**
My experience is that bored people are *boring!* Look in the mirror and ask, *Might I be the one who's blah in the bedroom?* If the answer is yes, then take the initiative to change things. Vary the place, the time, or the positions, or come up with a new kind of foreplay (there are lots of books that offer suggestions). Fantasy is more than okay, so give yourself permission to enjoy it. Just changing what you do in bed will likely change the response you receive and thus your overall experience.

② **I have trouble setting big career goals and sticking with them.**
First, make sure you have a measurable, identifiable goal rather than some hard-to-define "vision" of the future. Don't just say "I want to be happy" or "I want a better job"; instead, set forth exactly what you mean by "happy" or "better." If it's a new job you aspire to, define precisely what you want to do, how much more money you hope to make, and what kind of coworkers you'd like to have. Next, set up a timeline of specific steps you need to take to get from A to Z. Your first step might be putting together your résumé by the end of week one; next could be sending it to five industry contacts each week for six months; then you might set up a deadline for your first interview. Bottom line: The difference between dreams and goals is clarity and a timeline. The next year will go by whether or not you take small steps toward your goal, so hold yourself accountable every inch of the way to create the results you deserve.

③ **I'm so shy it kills me to go to parties.**
That's a trait you and I share. Here's my secret: Before you head to a party, literally script out a conversa-

tional plan. Come up with five topics drawn from pop culture, politics, news, sports—whatever interests you or the people you'll be seeing—so you'll have talking points to help you break the ice. Another trick: When you talk to people, ask them questions about themselves, because I promise you it's their favorite subject! Ask about their job, hometown, or how they spend weekends; you'll find that from there on, they'll do all the heavy lifting.

④ **Other people use me like a doormat, but I hate to be rude in return.**

You teach people how to treat you; nobody else is responsible here. Your problem is that you're confusing aggressiveness and assertiveness. By being aggressive, you protect your rights but at someone else's expense. When you're assertive, you protect your rights without trampling on anybody else's. You may think that passivity is the moral high ground and you may want to avoid being as rude as your abuser, but you can be assertive without being aggressive. Here's a technique to help you take on a bully: Make eye contact. It forces people to recognize you one-on-one as a thinking, feeling human being. Make eye contact with anyone who treats you as a doormat, and I guarantee they will start to see you as someone worthy of dignity.

⑤ **I try to be a good mother, but there's no time for me!**

Remember how I just said we teach people how to treat us? Well, guess what? Your kids are people. And here's a shocker: They are *not* helpless. They have arms! Legs! Brains! They can pick up their own toys; they can do any number of things for themselves. We have a generation of entitled children, but you need to claim some entitlement of your own by learning to say no. If you love your kids—and I know you do—then take care of their mom. They need a mother, not a martyr. So get them in the game by teaching self-sufficiency, and stop feeling guilty if you're not doing everything for them every minute of every day.

⑥ **My husband and I seem to be growing apart.**

Ask yourself if the two of you are too problem oriented. If problems are all you ever deal with, then you're going to have a problem relationship! You can't let arguing or worrying about your issues go on all day or night. So compartmentalize: If you must have a talk that you think could turn contentious,

choose a window of time, address the issue, and move on. And you may actually need to schedule time for the two of you to have fun. (By the way, the more contrived that feels, the more likely it is you need to do it.) And remember the "four-minute rule": What happens in the first four minutes of togetherness sets the tone for the rest of your day or evening. So use that time to connect, acknowledge each other, and have fun.

⑦ **I'm single and burned-out on dating.**

The oldest definition of insanity is doing the same thing over and over again and expecting a different result. If you want a different outcome, you have to choose different behaviors. Are you going only to bars to meet guys? Maybe you need to stop. Think you'd never join a tennis league because that's not your thing? It is now. The point is: Get out of your comfort zone because what you've been doing isn't working. Try new activities that put you in a target-rich environment, and I promise new opportunities will come.

⑧ **If I'm faced with any decision, I freeze.**

You are playing the "what if" game. What if you make the wrong decision? What if there's a better option? But if you're going to play that game, play it all the way to the end. Ask yourself, *If I went down this road, what is the worst thing that could happen?* You'll see that the results are not as bad as you might imagine. There is no insurance policy in life—and no guarantee you'll always make all the best decisions. But that's all right. Bottom line: Give yourself permission to call your own shots, even if you may be wrong.

⑨ **I feel as if everyone is somehow dissing me.**

The truth is, you're not really responding to what anyone is saying or not saying about you. What you are responding to is what *you* are saying to yourself about what you *imagine* people are saying about you. If you want to address this issue, you have to change what you're saying to yourself, and start being your own best friend. You have to say: *I'm going to do the best I can. Sometimes people will like me, and sometimes they won't. But I accept who I am, and not everyone has to like me for me to be okay.* And keep in mind the advice my dad used to give me: "Son, you wouldn't worry so much about what people thought of you if you knew how seldom they did." Good point, Dad! ◖

> There is no insurance policy in life— no guarantee you'll make all the best decisions.

Proof of growing old gracefully: This sweeping beauty of an oak tree in my California backyard… just gets better with time.

WHAT I KNOW FOR SURE: OPRAH

"I know for sure that life is full of delightful treasures, if we take a moment to look around."

I'm sitting in my favorite spot on Earth…under the oaks in my yard on a sunny Sunday, chillin' with my dogs, Luke, Layla, and Sadie, who are chowing down on rawhide chew sticks while I savor every lick of a lemon Popsicle.

I call this layered pleasures. When a good thing—Sunday—just gets better, with sunshine and dogs and a yummy treat.

I know for sure that life is full of delightful treasures, if we take a moment to look around. So I decided to actually do that instead of just telling you about it. I went on a pleasure quest with my camera, and found that the wisdom Dorothy picked up in Oz remains true: I didn't have to look any further than my own backyard.

Oprah

Sadie (*far left*), the newest member of the family, relaxing with Layla.

A lemon-drop martini I made with fresh lemons from the garden.

One of my favorite places to read is beneath this tree.

A field of lavender near the oaks.

Calla lilies on the back fence make me happy.

I start the day with Irish steel-cut oatmeal and affirmations from Daily Word *magazine.*

Luke, lying in wait.

A rose at first bloom in my garden. Smells like love.

confidence

109 HOW TO BECOME THE PERSON YOU WERE MEANT TO BE

   110 ANSWERING THE CALL I BY OPRAH

   112 WHERE DO I START? I BY ANNE LAMOTT

   113 BUT WHAT IF I'M SCARED OF CHANGE? I BY AMY BLOOM

   115 NOW WHAT DO I *DO* WITH ALL THIS YOU-NESS? I BY ALAIN DE BOTTON

   116 WRITE ON! I BY JUNOT DÍAZ

   118 WHO AM I MEANT TO BE? I BY ANNE DRANITSARIS, PhD

121 "WHAT MONEY HAS TAUGHT ME ABOUT PERSONAL POWER" I BY SUZE ORMAN

124 10 WAYS OF LOOKING AT POWER

133 OPRAH TALKS TO TINA FEY

How to Become
the Person You Were
Meant to Be

Answering the Call

Every person has a purpose.
The real work of our lives is finding it.

It's not that I've always known who I would be. It was just very clear to me from an early age who I wouldn't be.

The opportunities for a girl born black in Mississippi in 1954 were limited. You could teach in a segregated school. Or be a maid. A cook. A dishwasher. A servant. I never thought that would be the life for me.

I vividly remember standing on my grandmother's small screened-in back porch, churning butter while she boiled clothes in a big black cast-iron pot in the yard. As she pulled the steaming clothes from the pot to hang on the line to dry, she called to me, "Oprah Gail, you better watch me now, 'cause one day you gon' have to know how to do this for yourself."

I did what she told me. I watched carefully as she pulled the clothespins from her apron, held them two at a time between her lips, and placed one and then the other on opposite ends of the sheets and towels and shirts and dresses she hung on the line.

A still, small voice inside me, really more a feeling than a voice, said, *This will not be your life. Your life will be more than hanging clothes on a line.*

The certainty of that divine assurance got me through many a difficult moment during my growing years.

I wanted to be a teacher. And to be known for inspiring my students to be more than they thought they could be. I never imagined it would be on TV.

I believe there's a calling for all of us. I know that every human being has value and purpose. The real work of our lives is to become aware. And awakened. To answer the call. O

Who are you meant to be?

Carrin Gramke, 5, Nebraska
Princess

Sofia Mena, 5, California
Brain Surgeon

Sydney Tucker, 8, Kentucky
Special Education Teacher

Nathonya Chery, 11, Georgia
Fashion Designer

Gentry Kincade, 10, Oklahoma
Pastry Chef and Baker

Cecilia Rose Trella, 9, Illinois
Talk Show Host

Danielle Riley, 14, New York
Forensic Scientist

Brooke Harrison, 13, Florida
Writer

Ricaylah Citizen, 16, Nevada
Doctor

Where Do I Start?

By Anne Lamott

We begin to find and become ourselves when we notice how we are already found, already truly, entirely, wildly, messily, marvelously who we were born to be. The only problem is that there is also so much other stuff, typically fixations with how people perceive us, how to get more of the things that we think will make us happy, and with keeping our weight down. So the real issue is how do we gently stop being who we aren't? How do we relieve ourselves of the false fronts of people-pleasing and affectation, the obsessive need for power and security, the backpack of old pain, and the psychic Spanx that keeps us smaller and contained?

Here's how I became myself: mess, failure, mistakes, disappointments, and extensive reading; limbo, indecision, setbacks, addiction, public embarrassment, and endless conversations with my best women friends; the loss of people without whom I could not live, the loss of pets that left me reeling, dizzying betrayals but much greater loyalty, and overall, choosing as my motto William Blake's line that we are here to learn to endure the beams of love.

Oh, yeah, and whenever I could, for as long as I could, I threw away the scales and the sugar.

When I was a young writer, I was talking to an old painter one day about how he came to paint his canvases. He said that he never knew what the completed picture would look like, but he could usually see one quadrant. So he'd make a stab at capturing what he saw on the canvas of his mind, and when it turned out not to be even remotely what he'd imagined, he'd paint it over with white. And each time he figured out what the painting wasn't, he was one step closer to finding out what it was.

You have to make mistakes to find out who you aren't. You take the action, and the insight follows: You don't think your way into becoming yourself.

I can't tell you what your next action will be, but mine involved a full stop. I had to stop living unconsciously, as if I had all the time in the world. The love and good and the wild and the peace and creation that are you *will* reveal themselves, but it is harder when they have to catch up to you in roadrunner mode. So one day I did stop. I began consciously to break the rules I learned in childhood: I wasted more time, as a radical act. I stared off into space more, into the middle distance, like a cat. This is when I have my best ideas, my deepest insights. I wasted more paper, printing out instead of reading things on the computer screen. (Then I sent off more small checks to the Sierra Club.)

Every single day I try to figure out something I no longer agree to do. You get to change your mind—your parents may have accidentally forgotten to mention this to you. I cross *one* thing off the list of projects I mean to get done that day. I don't know all that many things that are positively true, but I do know two things for sure: first of all, that no woman over the age of 40 should ever help anyone move, ever again, under any circumstances. You have helped enough. You can say no. No is a complete sentence. Or you might say, "I can't help you move because of certain promises I have made to myself, but I would be glad to bring sandwiches and soda to everyone on your crew at noon." Obviously, it is in many people's best interest for you not to find yourself, but it only matters that it is in yours—and your back's—

and the whole world's, to proceed.

And, secondly, you are probably going to have to deal with whatever fugitive anger still needs to be examined—it may not look like anger; it may look like compulsive dieting or bingeing or exercising or shopping. But you must find a path and a person to help you deal with that anger. It will not be a Hallmark card. It is not the yellow brick road, with lovely trees on both sides, constant sunshine, birdsong, friends. It is going to be unbelievably hard some days—like the rawness of birth, all that blood and those fluids and shouting horrible terrible things—but then there will be that wonderful child right in the middle. And that wonderful child is you, with your exact mind and butt and thighs and goofy greatness.

Dealing with your rage and grief will give you life. That is both the good news and the bad news: The solution is at hand. Wherever the great dilemma exists is where the great growth is, too. It would be very nice for nervous types like me if things were black-and-white, and you could tell where one thing ended and the next thing began, but as Einstein taught us, everything in the future and the past is right here now. There's always something ending and something beginning. Yet in the very center is the truth of your spiritual identity: is *you*. Fabulous, hilarious, darling, screwed-up you. Beloved of God and of your truest deepest self, the self that is revealed when tears wash off the makeup and grime. The self that is revealed when dealing with your anger blows through all the calcification in your soul's pipes. The self that is reflected in the love of your very best friends' eyes. The self that is revealed in divine feminine energy, your own, Bette Midler's, Hillary Clinton's, Tina Fey's, Michelle Obama's, Mary Oliver's. I mean, you can see that they are divine, right? Well, you are, too. I absolutely promise. I hope you have gotten sufficiently tired of hitting the snooze button; I know that what you need or need to activate in yourself will appear; I pray that your awakening comes with ease and grace, and stamina when the going gets hard. To love yourself as you are is a miracle, and to seek yourself is to have found yourself, for now. And now is all we have, and love is who we are. ◐

But What If I'm Scared of Change?
By Amy Bloom

Change can be wonderful. People improve their appearance, improve their marriages, get great new jobs, even great new spouses. Plus, dear little babies become adorable toddlers, and pretty soon the toddlers can read and then they're having a really nice Sweet Sixteen and their skin clears up and they never talk to you, they fall in love with people you wouldn't allow in your house if you had a choice and they move far away and you rarely get to see the grandchildren.

That's what change is for a lot of us—stuff you have to pretend to embrace even as your heart sinks; you know it's going to end badly and you already feel the inevitable loss. The other awful thing about change is that we want it as much as we fear it and we need it as much as we need safety. I hate my marriage but I'm afraid of being alone. I'm sick of being a lawyer but I don't know how to do anything else.

Good news: It doesn't matter whether you like change or not, whether you embrace it or run in the opposite direction. Not only will changes be taking place, they will be taking place all the time, with and without your participation, from the mouse-sized (they no longer make your favorite suntan lotion) to elephant-sized (death, divorce, and disability). It turns out that even if you make no changes in your lousy marriage, your stultifying job, or your painful relationship with your brother, all those things will change anyway. Your only choice is to take steps toward change (you don't have to quit the job or the marriage all of a sudden), or to wait and see what surprises the universe has for you as you cling to what you thought was safety.

Mostly, change is as inevitable as rain in the spring. Some of us just put on our raincoats and splash forward, some of us choose to stay home, a few admirable nuts shed their clothes and cavort in the yard, and some people go out and get deeply, resentfully, and miserably wet. And no matter what, the rain falls. It falls on dry grass, which is the kind of change we love, and it falls, too, on June weddings and the day you began the Appalachian Trail. Sylvia Boorstein is a Jewish grandmother, a psychotherapist, and a Buddhist, which signifies to me that she must know something about complaining (even quietly) and accepting (not just pretending to). She writes: "We can struggle, or we can surrender. *Surrender* is a frightening word for some people, because it might be interpreted as passivity, or timidity. Surrender means wisely accommodating ourselves to what is beyond our control. Getting

> ## Change is as inevitable as rain in the spring. Some of us just put on raincoats and splash forward.

old, getting sick, dying, losing what is dear to us...all of these are beyond our control. I can either be frightened of life and mad at life—or not. I can be *disappointed* and still not be mad." People get old, plans change, and red wine spills on your great-grandmother's tablecloth—there isn't any other way.

It seems to me that the absolute star of accepting change is the Dalai Lama, the easy, gentle master of living in the moment and understanding that life is nothing *but* transition. My sister is not the Dalai Lama; no one has ever gotten them confused. My sister's approach to change, although not approved by the International Council for the Happy-Go-Lucky, is novel and effective.

Me: Hi, it's me. I just wanted to let you know that x (a member of my side of our extended family) wants to bring someone to Thanksgiving/Passover/anything.

She: Oh. Shit. The table will be so crowded.

Me: Umm...

She: It'll be awful. People will be sitting on the patio, practically.

Me: Umm...

She: I'm not making something vegan, dammit.

Me: Umm...

She: Is he/she nice?

Me: Yes.

She: Are they in love?

Me: Looks that way.

She: [*Pause*] Okay.

Me: Okay? It's okay?

She: [*Sweetly*] Well, of course. [*Patiently*] There's plenty of room.

So, maybe, there's an alternative to beatific acceptance of change. Maybe a little grousing helps. Maybe some frank grumbling smooths the way for some genuine acceptance. Maybe the trick is to acknowledge that change is sometimes wonderful, sometimes not, often disturbing, and always happening. Then, make room at the table.

My sister, the Dolly Lama. ◖

Now What Do I *Do* with All This You-ness?

By Alain de Botton

One of the first questions we face when we meet new acquaintances is "What do you do?" And according to how we answer, they will either be delighted to see us or look with embarrassment at their watches and shuffle away. The fact is, we live in a world where we are defined almost entirely by our work.

This can be hugely liberating for people who are happily employed. But the problem for many of us is that we don't know what job we're supposed to do and, as a result, are still waiting to learn who we should be. The idea that we have missed out on our true calling—that somehow we ought to have intuited what we should be doing with our lives long before we finished our degrees, started families, and advanced through the ranks—torments us. This notion, however, can be an illusion. The term *calling* came into circulation in a Christian context during the medieval period to describe the abrupt imperative people might encounter to devote themselves to Jesus' teachings. Now a secularized version has survived, which is prone to give us an expectation that the meaning of our lives might at some point be revealed in a ready-made and decisive form, rendering us permanently immune to confusion, envy, and regret.

I prefer to borrow from psychologist Abraham Maslow, who said: It isn't normal to know what we want. It is a rare and difficult psychological achievement.

To begin to find a more fulfilling vocation, it is not enough to simply ask yourself what you might like to do. Concerns about money and status long ago extinguished most people's ability to think authentically about their options. Instead, I would suggest free-associating around clusters of concerns that delight and excite you, without attempting to settle upon anything as rigid as the frame of a career.

In searching for their aptitudes, people should act like treasure hunters passing over the ground with metal detectors, listening out for beeps of joy. A woman might get her first intimation that her real interest lies in poetry not by hearing a holy voice as she pages through a book of verse but from the thrill she feels as she stands in a parking lot on the edge of town overlooking a misty valley. Or a politician, long before she belongs to any party or has any profound understanding of statecraft, might register a telling signal when successfully healing a rift between two members of her family.

We should also remember that the first ingredient usually missing when people can't choose a life direction is confidence. Whatever cerebral understanding we apply to our lives, we retain a few humblingly simple needs, among them a steady hunger for support and love. It's therefore helpful to identify—and engage with—the internal voices that emphasize our chances of failure. Many such voices can be traced back to a critical instructor or unhelpful parent: a math teacher who berated us for poor algebra skills or a father who insisted that our sister was good at art and we should stick to the books. The forming of an individual in the early years is as sensitive and important a task as the correct casting of a skyscraper's foundation, and the slightest abuse introduced at this primary stage can unbalance us until our dying days.

A useful thought to bear in mind for anyone still struggling with a less than meaningful job: Work may not be where your calling resides. Indeed, for thousands of years, work was viewed as an unavoidable drudge; anything more aspiring had to happen in one's spare time, once the money had been hauled in. Aristotle was only the first of many philosophers to state that no one could both be obliged to earn a living and remain free. The idea that a job could be pleasurable had to wait until the 18th century, the age of the great bourgeois philosophers, men like Jean-Jacques Rousseau and Benjamin Franklin, who for the first time argued that one's working life could be at the center of happiness. Curiously, at the same time, similar ideas about romance took shape. In the premodern age, it had widely been assumed that marriage was something one did for purely commercial reasons, to hand down the family farm and raise children; love was what you did with your mistress, on the side. The new philosophers now argued that one might actually aim to marry the person one was in love with.

> ## To find their aptitudes, people should act like treasure hunters passing over the ground with metal detectors, listening out for beeps of joy.

We are the heirs of these two very ambitious beliefs: that you can be in love and married—and in a job and having a good time. As a result, we harbor high expectations for two areas of life that may provide support but not the deep purpose we ultimately long for. To remember such history while contemplating "Who am I?" can be enormously freeing.

And although that question is one of life's toughest, we should allow ourselves to relish it as we think about our aptitudes, and to open ourselves to all the many sources we can derive meaning and mission from—whether it's writing poetry, leading a neighborhood cleanup, raising children, or daring gravity while flying down an icy slope on a pair of skis. We should also consider that, in the end, the answer to "Who are you meant to be?" is perhaps this: the person who keeps asking the question. ❶

Write On!

Pigheaded determination is no substitute for sheer, amazing talent. But sometimes it helps. Just ask Junot Díaz.

It wasn't that I couldn't write. I wrote every day. I actually worked really hard at writing. At my desk by 7 A.M., would work a full eight and more. Scribbled at the dinner table, in bed, on the toilet, on the No. 6 train, at Shea Stadium. I did everything I could. But none of it worked. My novel, which I had started with such hope shortly after publishing my first book of stories, wouldn't budge past the 75-page mark. Nothing I wrote past page 75 made any kind of sense. Nothing. Which would have been fine if the first 75 pages hadn't been pretty damn cool. But they were cool, showed a lot of promise. Would also have been fine if I could have just jumped to something else. But I couldn't. All the other novels I tried sucked worse than the stalled one, and even more disturbing, I seemed to have lost the ability to write short stories. It was like I had somehow slipped into a No-Writing Twilight Zone and I couldn't find an exit. Like I'd been chained to the sinking ship of those 75 pages and there was no key and no patching the hole in the hull. I wrote and I wrote and I wrote, but nothing I produced was worth a damn.

Want to talk about stubborn? I kept at it for five straight years. Five damn years. Every day failing for five years? I'm a pretty stubborn, pretty hard-hearted character, but those five years of fail did a number on my psyche. On me. Five years, 60 months? It just about wiped me out. By the end of that fifth year, perhaps in an attempt to save myself, to escape my despair, I started becoming convinced that I had written all I had to write, that I was a minor league Ralph Ellison, a Pop Warner Edward Rivera, that maybe it was time, for the sake of my mental health, for me to move on to another profession, and if the inspiration struck again some time in the future…well, great. But I knew I couldn't go on much more the way I was going. I just couldn't. I was living with my fiancée at the time (over now, another terrible story) and was so depressed and self-loathing I could barely function. I finally broached the topic with her of, maybe, you know, doing something else. My fiancée was so desperate to see me happy (and perhaps more than a little convinced by my fear that maybe the thread had run out on my talent) that she told me to make a list of what else I could do besides writing. I'm not a list person like she was, but I wrote one. It took a month to pencil down three things. (I really don't have many other skills.) I stared at that list for about another month. Waiting, hoping, praying for the book, for my writing, for my talent to catch fire. A last-second reprieve. But nada. So I put the manuscript away. All the hundreds of failed pages, boxed and hidden in a closet. I think I cried as I did it. Five years of my life and the dream that I had of myself, all down the tubes because I couldn't pull off something other people seemed to pull off with relative ease: a novel. By then I wasn't even interested in a Great American Novel. I would have been elated with the eminently forgettable NJ novel.

So I became a normal. A square. I didn't go to bookstores or read the Sunday book section of the *Times*. I stopped hanging out with my writer friends. The bouts of rage and despair, the fights with my fiancée ended. I slipped into my new morose half-life. Started preparing for my next stage, back to school in September. (I won't even tell you what I was thinking of doing, too embarrassing.) While I waited for September to come around, I spent long hours in my writing room, sprawled on the floor, with the list on my chest, waiting for the promise of those words to leak through the paper into me.

Maybe I would have gone through with it. Hard to know. But if the world is what it is so are our hearts. One night in August, unable to sleep, sickened that I was giving up, but even more frightened by the thought of having to return to the writing, I dug out the manuscript. I figured if I could find one good thing in the pages I would go back to it. Just one good thing. Like flipping a coin, I'd let the pages decide. Spent the whole night reading everything I had written, and guess what? It was still terrible. In fact with the new distance the lameness was even worse than I'd thought. That's when I should have put everything

> # It was like I had somehow slipped into a No-Writing Twilight Zone and I couldn't find an exit.

in the box. When I should have turned my back and trudged into my new life. I didn't have the heart to go on. But I guess I did. While my fiancée slept, I separated the 75 pages that were worthy from the mountain of loss, sat at my desk, and despite every part of me shrieking no no no no, I jumped back down the rabbit hole again. There were no sudden miracles. It took two more years of heartbreak, of being utterly, dismayingly lost before the novel I had dreamed about for all those years finally started revealing itself. And another three years after that before I could look up from my desk and say the word I'd wanted to say for more than a decade: done.

That's my tale in a nutshell. Not the tale of how I came to write my novel but rather of how I became a writer. Because, in truth, I didn't become a writer the first time I put pen to paper or when I finished my first book (easy) or my second one (hard). You see, in my view a writer is a writer not because she writes well and easily, because she has amazing talent, because everything she does is golden. In my view a writer is a writer because even when there is no hope, even when nothing you do shows any sign of promise, you keep writing anyway. Wasn't until that night when I was faced with all those lousy pages that I realized, really realized, what it was exactly that I am. ⬛

Quiz

Who Am I Meant to Be?

By Anne Dranitsaris, PhD

Forget your career. Forget your role as a mother or a wife. Forget how much money you make or how successful you are. If you're struggling with the question *Who am I meant to be?*, this quiz can help you figure out what really defines you. Based on personality science, I have identified seven "striving styles," modes of thought and behavior that direct us to seek satisfaction in different ways. Although everybody is wired with all seven styles, most people have one that dominates. When you engage this innate style, you've got the best shot at fulfilling your potential; when you don't, you can feel stuck.

After responding to the statements below, you will discover your striving style, learn what to do if it's backfiring from neglect, and find ideas to guide your life in the direction that it was meant to go.

Instructions:
Read each of the following statements and ask yourself how true it is. Then, using the scale at right (from "never" to "always"), mark the appropriate number. If your first thought when rating a statement is *It depends,* think about how you would react on an average day. The more honest you are, the more accurate your feedback will be.

SCALE:
0 = NEVER
1 = RARELY
2 = SOMETIMES
3 = OFTEN
4 = ALWAYS

Style #1

1. Others describe me as nurturing, supportive, and helpful.
⓪ ① ② ③ ④

2. I have a tendency to lose sight of my own needs and focus on others.
⓪ ① ② ③ ④

3. I am more interested in relationships than goals.
⓪ ① ② ③ ④

4. When others don't appreciate my help and support, I tend to do even more for them.
⓪ ① ② ③ ④

TOTAL _____ 11

Style #2

1. I enjoy being the center of attention. It's also important that my work be recognized.
⓪ ① ② ③ ④

2. I am more interested in goals than relationships.
⓪ ① ② ③ ④

3. I am very conscious of my image and work hard to make sure it reflects my success.
⓪ ① ② ③ ④

4. I have a tendency to try to meet others' expectations.
⓪ ① ② ③ ④

TOTAL _____ 10

Style #3

1. I get pleasure from being creative.
⓪ ① ② ③ ④

2. Others have described me as too emotional.
⓪ ① ② ③ ④

3. I don't have time for shallow relationships; I am interested only in making authentic connections.
⓪ ① ② ③ ④

4. I don't feel it is important to adapt to societal expectations.
⓪ ① ② ③ ④

TOTAL _____ 11

Style #4

1. When presented with a new experience, I embrace it enthusiastically.
⓪ ① ② ③ ④

2. Because my interests are so wide-ranging, I often burn the candle at both ends.
⓪ ① ② ③ ④

3. I have a strong need for adventure, excitement, and novelty.
⓪ ① ② ③ ④

4. People sometimes mistake my exuberance for impulsiveness or lack of discipline.
⓪ ① ② ③ ④

TOTAL _____ 12

Style #5

1. Others depend on me for my insight and wisdom.
⓪ ① ② ③ ④

2. I'm driven to be knowledgeable and competent, and to understand how things work.
⓪ ① ② ③ ④

3. Under stress, I tend to withdraw and isolate myself.
⓪ ① ② ③ ④

4. I enjoy the kind of work where I can be on my own to learn or invent.
⓪ ① ② ③ ④

TOTAL _____ 13

Style #6

1. Others would describe me as loyal, hardworking, and predictable.
⓪ ① ② ③ ④

2. A big priority in my life is safety—for me, for my friends, and for my family.
⓪ ① ② ③ ④

3. I strive to do what is expected of me and am respectful of authority.
⓪ ① ② ③ ④

4. I tend to be wary of new things, preferring to stay with the tried-and-true.
⓪ ① ② ③ ④

TOTAL _____ 11

Style #7

1. I like to have the authority and responsibility to make my own decisions.
⓪ ① ② ③ ④

2. Others depend on me to know what needs to be done (and often, to do it).
⓪ ① ② ③ ④

3. I seek opportunities where I can be in charge of people and outcomes.
⓪ ① ② ③ ④

4. I often find myself advising others.
⓪ ① ② ③ ④

TOTAL _____ 13

Scoring: Total your numbers in each Style section. Now take the highest total and go to the corresponding Striving Style below—if you have a few "highest" scores, read each matching description and see which ring most true. Many people have two or three strong striving styles, and they can all be important in leading you to the person you are meant to be.

STYLE #1:
Striving to Help

You are a nurturer: You are caring and supportive in your personal relationships as well as in your job. Unselfish and altruistic by nature, you often anticipate the needs of those around you before they are aware of them. If there is one thing that brings you satisfaction, it's tending to others.

What to watch out for: When you're doing things for people *only* to feel valued, you can become resentful. And if you sense that your help is not appreciated, you may end up playing the martyr. So before giving your time to everyone else, make sure to take care of yourself (physically, emotionally, and spiritually). And practice waiting until someone asks for help: While you may be able to perceive what a person needs, that doesn't mean she wants you to attend to it.

Looking ahead: It's important for you to be genuinely of service in acknowledged ways. Whether you foster a child, care for an elderly aunt, rescue animals, or support a rock star's career as her personal assistant, look for opportunities where you can help other people or bigger causes. Volunteer work has your name written on it, as do many careers: nursing, teaching, customer service, healing, social work. Don't feel pressured to run the company or lead the project; you may be even more effective as someone's right hand. And you'll likely find working with other people more meaningful than flying solo.

STYLE #2:
Striving to Be Recognized

You are an achiever: Ambitious, competitive, and hardworking: That's you. With a clear image of who you are, you work tirelessly to make sure your accomplishments are recognized. Your drive for success extends to your family, and you invest a lot of energy in helping them live up to your expectations. Thanks to your knack for diplomacy and abundant charisma, you often inspire others.

What to watch out for: You are prone to becoming a workaholic, slaving away toward success while neglecting your personal life. Because you're driven to gain approval, you can find yourself performing for others like an actor; if you become overly concerned with your image, you end up feeling superficial. To keep your ambition under control, get involved in group activities that require cooperation. Also practice listening to those around you and think about sharing the spotlight from time to time.

Looking ahead: Any career that allows you to scale the ranks and gain recognition, status, even material rewards, lights you up. Actress, entrepreneur, salesperson,

politician—you get the picture. And consider balancing your professional challenges with personal ones: Run a 10K, train for a triathlon, compete in a tennis tournament, bike from one end of your state to the other; or join a debate team, play in a poker circle, enter your purebred spaniel in a dog show. Whenever you can win at something, you're happy.

STYLE #3:
Striving to Be Creative

You are an artist: You came out of the womb with a paintbrush in your hand. Or maybe it was a flute or a castanet or a fountain pen to go with your poet's imagination. The point is, you're an original, and you know it. Even if you don't have a singular gift, you're drawn to the arts—anything creative, for that matter—and you have a unique way of looking at the world. Your need for depth and authenticity in relationships can lead to both great joy and profound sorrow, depending on whether others reciprocate. You don't care so much about adapting to group or societal expectations; your independence and sharp intuition propel you on your own path.

What to watch out for: When fear of conformity overrides your creativity, you can assume the role of "outsider" or "orphan" and end up feeling alienated. You may even go so far as refusing to vote or pay taxes. This lone-wolf stance might be a defense against feeling vulnerable. Try to be aware that blaming others for your banishment, or pushing away those who want to get close, only makes things worse. Also, dramatizing your emotions can interfere with your creativity.

Looking ahead: As long as you genuinely express yourself, you feel like the person you were meant to be. How you do it is irrelevant. A chef or architect can be as much of an artist as a painter or sculptor.

Many advertising and public relations executives are also highly imaginative. Beyond work, there are opportunities everywhere you look to coax out your inner artist: Design your own jewelry line, create an innovative blog, dream up a comic strip. Relationships are another avenue for self-expression.

STYLE #4:
Striving to Be Spontaneous

You are an adventurer: Action-oriented, curious, outgoing, and often technically gifted, you live for new experiences. You are drawn to risk-taking and aren't afraid to fail. Generally restless, you tend to job-hop or choose a field that offers constant novelty. If you had to name your favorite place, it might be the center of attention—you're a born entertainer, and can easily adapt to any audience. While you collect many acquaintances, you're less likely to develop deep, committed relationships.

What to watch out for: When you can't satisfy your thirst for variety and excitement, you may see yourself as trapped, which can lead to impulsive and self-destructive behavior—drinking, drugs, breaking off relationships, ditching financial responsibilities. Try to find value in some traditions; if you learn to appreciate repetitive experiences, you won't always feel the urge to bust free. And when a new opportunity thrills you, keep in mind that just because it sounds exciting, that doesn't mean it's good for you.

Looking ahead: Life will have meaning for you as long as you feel stimulated. That might mean chasing twisters, exploring the polar ice caps, getting a degree in dance therapy, or becoming an astronaut. It might also mean reading new books, attending workshops, or letting yourself get swept up in an intoxicating romance. As a risk-lover with a lot of energy, you're a natural entrepreneur. You'll be happiest if you change jobs every so often and travel extensively. Movement is what keeps you going.

STYLE #5:
Striving to Be Knowledgeable

You are an intellectual: As a leader, you're often ahead of your time. As an employee, you try to surpass the competence level of peers, even managers. Incisive and curious, you're driven to deeply understand how things work. But that's *things,* not people. Oh, your family and friends are important; it's just that you don't need to spend hours engaging with them. Social validation isn't your goal—you're secure enough in your cerebral pursuits.

What to watch out for: When you can't find a way to be the expert, you may withdraw or simply withhold information, which can make you seem smug or arrogant. If you feel yourself retreating into your own world, seek a friend's help to pull you back. Also balance your cerebral tendencies through physical activities like jogging, hiking, or dance.

Looking ahead: You discover who you are meant to be through accumulating insight and knowledge. So follow your curiosity. Are you drawn to learning Mandarin? Joining a philosophy society? Studying and practicing Buddhist meditation? Delving into the complexities of computer programming? Writing a historical book? Pursuits that place you near the leading edge of technology, science, psychology, academia, or business are good bets. But any situation that allows you to work independently with freedom to investigate and innovate will fuel your drive.

STYLE #6:
Striving to Be Secure

You are a stabilizer: You are the rock in a storm, the one others lean on. Loyal and committed in your relationships, you maintain a support system of like-minded people whom you look out for. (So what if you do it behind the scenes and don't get credit?) You're careful with money, cherish the familiar, and defend the traditions you care about.

What to watch out for: Rapidly changing environments (like a shaky economy) are very hard for you. As a result of such instability, you can spiral into a state where everything seems catastrophic and you're sure life will only get worse. You can also become overcontrolling, rejecting any suggestion that doesn't conform to your idea of the way things should be. To avoid being too rigid, each month try changing one habit. Experiment with clothes, drive a different way to work, initiate conversations about subjects you wouldn't normally discuss. And when the opportunity arises to do something new, avoid the impulse to immediately say no—this may be nerve-racking, but the more you practice, the less anxious you'll feel.

Looking ahead: You find meaning in pursuing safety and certainty. Focusing on family can give you great satisfaction. Also consider planting a vegetable garden, hosting class reunions, volunteering as a lifeguard, teaching at your church or temple. In the work arena, look for positions where you're responsible for others, and for making sure everyone is following the rules. You work well in any environment that is stable and consistent. Careers in government, finance, the military, law enforcement, and product manufacturing are strong options for you.

STYLE #7:
Striving to Be in Control

You are a leader: You approach everything as though you were born to be in charge. Confident, assertive, and decisive, you know what you want and you go after it. You also look out for family, friends, and community—you feel you know what's best for them—and have no fear of confronting anyone who challenges your ideas. Taking the driver's seat, you also generously donate time and energy to people and neighborhood projects.

What to watch out for: When you feel threatened, or others refuse to go along with your agenda, you can become confrontational and domineering, sometimes to the point of being dictatorial. Practice letting someone else take charge on occasion. Also try meditation; it can help you become more aware of your controlling impulses and ease the anxiety that may be provoking them.

Looking ahead: You discover your purpose when you take control of your environment. For you, finding a decision-making role is key. That could mean anything from producing a play to spearheading a global campaign for something you care about. In work, you're suited for leadership positions in education, government, industry, finance, religious institutions, or politics. But you can find satisfaction anytime you're given the autonomy to do things your own way. ◖◗

Suze Orman:
"What Money Has Taught Me About Personal Power"

My street name is "the Money Lady." That's what strangers say when they stop me: "Look, it's the Money Lady!" Emphasis on *money*. Early in my career, they seemed to be commenting primarily on the fact that I was always popping up somewhere giving financial advice. But as the years have gone by, I've sensed that the people I meet are referring to my success—and that I am powerful in their eyes because I've made money.

They've got it all wrong. Money didn't make me powerful. And if it weren't for the fact that I'm usually standing in a crosswalk when people stop me, I'd tell them that when I first had a lot of money, it served the purpose of showing me exactly how power*less* I was. In fact, money has taught me a great many lessons. Let me share them with you.

① POWER COMES FROM WHO YOU ARE, NOT WHAT YOU HAVE. Society has programmed all of us to think that external achievement is what gives us power. But that's only perceived power, and it can be fleeting. I can't tell you how many times my grandfather would say, "Suze, they can take your house, they can take your job, they can take your money, they can even take your mind, but they can't take your heart. So you have to grow up valuing your own heart, who you are."

My grandfather understood the difference between external and internal power. It was something that took me years—and a number of painful experiences—to comprehend.

② MONEY HAS NO POWER OF ITS OWN. You alone are the power source. You are the one who makes the choices to spend money, to save money, to borrow money. That's why I say money is such an amazing teacher: What you choose to do with your money shows whether you are truly powerful or powerless.

When I started to make serious money in my 30s, I was exhibit A for external power. I drove a fancy car, had a closetful of expensive clothes, wore a watch that cost the equivalent (at that time) of a 25 percent down payment on a house. Why did I have all those things? Because I was dating someone who was seriously wealthy, and felt I needed to keep up with the rich crowd I found myself in. I, Suze Orman, took money out of my 401(k) to pay for that pricey Cartier watch. And when I ran through all my money, I started using the bank's: I eventually had more than $60,000 in credit card debt. How could that be?

I'd done the work—made the choice—to earn money, but then I made another choice: to use the money not to build personal wealth or move toward financial security but to try to impress people. Money didn't make me powerful. It just showed me how sadly powerless I was.

③ SELF-WORTH BUILDS NET WORTH. I realized that until I started acting honestly, I would be broke and unhappy. It was my own aha moment: I realized we spend *more than* when we feel *less than*. I felt *less than* because I could not afford what all those rich people could. But look where that got me—in debt and miserable. It was right then that I started to use money as my guide. I began attentively watching how I was using money and how I was feeling when I made money choices.

When I learned to give myself—and my money—the love and respect we both deserved, I felt as if a huge weight had been lifted. I was no longer racing to keep up; I was so happy being right where I was. Being me. I stopped spending money I didn't have and started living within my means. I had found my power. I was clear on who I was, what I wanted, and what I thought. No more letting the external world define me—I defined me. And it was only when that happened that I was able to dig out of debt and build the lasting net worth I now have.

If you have credit card debt and no savings, and you feel miserable, don't attribute your woes to not having enough money; instead see the lessons your money is trying to teach you. Is it possible you have yet to find your self-worth?

④ DO WHAT'S RIGHT, NOT WHAT'S EASY. Believe me, I know how easy it is to run up credit card debt. I have 60,000 memories of what happens when you act without conscience, doing whatever you want rather than pulling yourself back and considering whether it is right. If I had stopped to have that talk with myself, I would have seen my powerlessness earlier. That would have saved me money and gotten me to happy a lot faster.

To know whether something is right or just easy, I turn to my three gatekeeper questions: Is it kind? Is it necessary? Is it true? And I make sure I can answer yes to all three. Is it kind—to me? Is it necessary—for me? Is it true—for me?

I see so many women fail the gatekeeper test when it comes to dealing with loved ones. When a sister asks for a loan to pay off her credit card or a child asks you to cosign a loan for a new car, you jump in and say yes without a moment's hesitation. It is imprinted in your DNA to always give, no questions asked. But if you were to ask yourself the gatekeeper questions, you would often see that what is easy to do is not necessarily right.

If you lend money to someone, are you really solving their problem or just getting them off the hook? My experience is that people who are bailed out of trouble often end up back in trouble. How is that help really kind to them? And if you are lending money that depletes your emergency savings, or prevents you from working toward your own financial goals, is that kind or true to yourself? Repeat after me: Say no out of love rather than yes out of fear.

> Never trust anyone else to care about your money more than you do.

5 **IGNORANCE IS NOT BLISS WHERE MONEY IS CONCERNED.** We all take in financial information from outside sources, whether it's friends and family, professionals we hire, the magazines and blogs we read, or the television we watch. Gathering that information is important, but at the end of the day you must depend on yourself to synthesize it and make your own informed decisions. Seeking out opinions is smart; blindly following those opinions without thinking through whether they make sense to you—and *for* you—will leave you drowning in a pool of powerlessness. When I was a struggling waitress and some amazing customers raised $50,000 to help me open my own restaurant, I blindly "gave" the money to a stockbroker without knowing how he was investing it. Within a few months, my account was worth zero. Zero! Was it the broker's fault? Sure. But it was mine, too. That was the moment I learned how my powerlessness had cost me a fortune. That was when I vowed to never trust anyone else to care about my money more than I do.

6 **HOW YOU RESPECT YOUR POSSESSIONS SAYS A LOT ABOUT HOW YOU RESPECT YOURSELF.** My closets are temples of organization. But they have been a work in progress. When I was just starting to make money as a stockbroker, I would come home after a long day and throw my clothes on the floor; by the weekend I had a pile of disheveled items that I schlepped off to the dry cleaner. I spent a lot of money having clothes cleaned and pressed because I was too lazy to hang them up at the end of the day. Sound trivial? I don't think so. It was symptomatic of my lack of respect for the money I had worked so hard to earn.

Cars are another dead giveaway. I once knew a woman who had serious external power and a super-impressive career. But her car was a disgusting mess: fast food wrappers all over the place and a trunk that was a mini-dump. One day she was driving us somewhere and asked me to pull her

> You alone are the power source. You are the one who makes the choices to spend money, to save money, to borrow money. That's why I say money is such an amazing teacher: What you choose to do with your money shows whether you are truly powerful or powerless.

wallet out of her purse; my hand came back smeared in lipstick. Ick. No surprise, her financial life was a mess, too. I was at her house once when someone from the utility company came by to turn off her service because of lack of payment. Do you really think this was a happy woman? When you can't manage to keep the power turned on, exactly how much are you in control of your destiny?

And buying what you can't afford, regardless of how well you take care of it, is flat-out disrespectful of yourself. Purchasing a home with a tremendous mortgage just because you think it is your right to own a home—and then not being able to keep up with the payments—is not being true to your circumstances. Leasing a big fancy car to keep up appearances when you have to borrow from your 401(k) to make the payments, or don't have enough to fund your Roth IRA? Tell me what that is all about!

If you don't respect what money can buy, then you don't respect money. If you don't respect your financial obligations—paying your bills on time, buying only what you actually have the money for, saving for your future—then you don't respect money. And if you don't respect money itself, that is a sign you are not respecting yourself. It takes hours, weeks, and months working at a job to earn the money you then spend. To turn around and use that money in a wasteful or powerless way is just heartbreaking to me. You deserve better.

I want you to measure your power right now by walking through your home. First, open every closet and every drawer, and take a serious look in the garage, including the interior of the car. Are things organized or a mess? Next, pull out everything that still has a sales tag attached or is in unopened packaging. Why did you buy it? More important, when did you buy it? Perhaps when you were feeling less than? Every possession you bought is waiting to tell you a story. Take the time to learn the lessons that your money can teach you, and you will be on the path to building lasting and gratifying internal power. I'll bet all my money on it. **O**

10 WAYS *of* LOOKING *at* P**O**WER

One definition doesn't do it justice—because real power, like most things multifaceted and complex, is best viewed from many perspectives. Look at it this way, and it's innate. Look at it that way, and it's learned. Over here, it's all about the body. Over there, it's a state of mind. It can be stealthy and quiet. Or vivacious and loud. Transgressive or inclusive. In fact, power can be so *many* things that we're holding it up to the light, the better to see them all. On the following pages, we're exploring the inner workings of power—its voice, its determination, its resolve, and even its fear. We're introducing you to the women who made it on our first *O* Power List—10 remarkable visionaries who wear their power in 10 very individual ways. The women flexing their muscles on our list may not be the names you'd expect. (Do you really need us to bring Meryl Streep or Maya Angelou to your attention? We didn't think so.) So embrace the power of these phenomenal women as we give you a look into their lives and their stories....

THE POWER OF LOUD

ANNA DEAVERE SMITH

Actor and playwright

You've seen her in Nurse Jackie *and* Rachel Getting Married, *but Anna Deavere Smith isn't just an actor. Her one-woman plays (including* Let Me Down Easy, *which premiered in New York in October 2009) are a form of theater unto themselves, brilliantly conjuring the voices of real people. Speaking of voices, we asked Smith what happens when you turn up the volume:*

August, circa 2000, not far from Monte Carlo, at a rehearsal for a concert. The stage—outside in the bright sun and naked except for masses of tangled wires—was on the French-Italian border. Literally straddling the border. Workmen were setting up for a

soloist who would sing that night. I was sitting in the bleachers, enthralled. Suddenly a fast-moving train *loudly* zoomed through on its way from France to Italy. I put down my espresso. Would that train be going through during the concert? Whose idea was it to put a singer in the middle of a train route, anyway?

That night, when the great soprano Jessye Norman stepped onstage, exhilaration was followed by one engulfing human hush. Just at a peak moment, I heard that train approaching. Jessye Norman's voice shut it down.

We don't all have the ability to sing out over a racing train, but we do have the power to speak up—and out. A voice can get a party started, shout down opponents, or lead a country. Vocal cords are like any other part of your body. They are there to be worked.

THE POWER OF FEMALE STRENGTH

VENUS WILLIAMS

Champion

She has earned 17 Grand Slam titles and three Olympic gold medals, and was a critical voice in the successful lobbying effort to win equal prize money for female players at Wimbledon and the French Open (a cause she took up from one of her mentors, Billie Jean King). Both on and off the court, Venus Williams embodies a perfect marriage of power and grace. In the singular artistry of her play, we see that beauty and brawn aren't mutually exclusive. King leads the ovation:

Venus is wonderful to watch. I've known her since she was a little kid, and she still amazes me. I sit in the box at Wimbledon and still don't believe my eyes—how much ground she can cover, how every step is huge and light and elegant at the same time. She runs like a beautiful gazelle.

Her body is so long, but her wrists and ankles are tiny— she's delicate in some ways, and yet so strong.

Her wingspan is enormous. So much leverage—when she swings, the arc is gigantic, and that creates more power. She's held the record for the fastest women's serve ever. I'll say, "Venus, come up to the net and put your arms out." Then I put a racket in her right hand and say, "Okay, how can anyone get by you?" She just starts giggling. "Let's also talk about how tall you are, and how fast, and what kind of vertical jump you have. Do you realize what God gave you?"

Whenever I go to the ballet, I think of how we don't connect dance and sports in our minds as much as we should. Venus reminds me of that, too.

Venus Williams at Wimbledon, 2007.

Donna Brazile, Washington, D.C., 2005.

THE POWER OF AMBITION
DONNA BRAZILE
Political analyst, force of nature

Donna Brazile grew up in New Orleans and discovered campaigning at the age of 9, when she went door-to-door for a candidate who'd promised to build a playground in her neighborhood. Thirty-two years later, she became the first African-American woman to manage a major presidential campaign (Al Gore's, in 2000). Now 50, she teaches in the women's and gender studies program at Georgetown University and is a contributor to CNN, NPR, and ABC News. We asked her to tell us about the many things she has aspired to over the years:

I came into this world anxious to be a part of it. I wanted to find my place at the table. I wanted to be successful. In high school, I wanted to be involved in everything that was happening: I wanted to join the Soul Sisters Club and write poetry and do athletics and student council. I wanted to use my big mouth, and my energy, and my intellect. And today I still want those things—and then some. I want to make a difference in presidential politics. I want to educate and inform. I want to connect to the next generation. One day I want us to put a woman in the White House. I want to write poetry—not like when I was young, about the gory details of growing up poor and black, but poetry that comes from the calming stream flowing in my soul. I want to practice nonviolence. I want to practice joy. I want to learn from my enemies, even if all I learn is not to be like them. I want to get the last word. I want to do a little bit of everything, and when I'm not stirring some pot somewhere or creating some drama, then I want to be alone in my garden.

WHO PUT *YOU* IN CHARGE?
LATEEFAH SIMON
Community leader, change agent

At 15 she was a client at the Center for Young Women's Development, which helps troubled and poor young women transform their lives. By 19 she was the center's executive director. Seven years later she received a MacArthur "genius" grant. Today Simon, 33, is executive director of the Lawyers' Committee for Civil Rights in San Francisco, a senior at Mills College, and the mother of a 14-year-old daughter. We asked her how she claimed her power:

I grew up in the Fillmore, a community in San Francisco that was hit hard by the crack-cocaine epidemic. My neighborhood was at the edge of the Castro, where men were dying of AIDS, and I knew the black community was suffering, too. With all that tragedy around, I began to politicize what I saw—I felt *entitled* to be political. Once you feel that, everything is in your grasp: You think, *I can learn to speak in front of people, write grants, develop policy. It may take me longer, but I can do it.* When I was 18 and eight months pregnant, I would go and speak about HIV, and I knew people were thinking, *Who are you to talk about safe sex?* But I didn't apologize. I want to change the lives of women in this country—and that *should* be done by someone who had a baby at 19, who white-knuckled her way through college, who taught herself to run an organization. When people say, "How do you do it?" I say I'm not doing half the work my grandmother did. If you want to inflict your change, you have to recognize who you're accountable to. The women before me accepted nothing but the best, and I owe it to them to lead.

Lateefah Simon, San Francisco, 2008.

THE POWER OF FEAR
LAUREN AMBROSE
Actor

At first glance, Lauren Ambrose's dewy face and doe eyes suggest an innocent naïveté. But anyone familiar with her devastating performances knows that her exterior belies an extraordinary intensity and a preternatural ability to convey the humanity of her characters. Best known for her Emmy-nominated role in the HBO *drama* Six Feet Under, *Ambrose, 32, recently wowed audiences in a Broadway production of the Eugène Ionesco play* Exit the King, *and can be heard in the film adaptation of* Where the Wild Things Are. *She pulls back the curtain on her favorite emotion:*

I enjoy playing roles that push me to my absolute capacity, emotionally and physically—that feel like a leap of faith. I often take a role without knowing what I'm supposed to do, what's required of me. Figuring that out is a process, and for me that process starts with fear.

Every single time I begin a job I think, *I'm a fraud. I'm going to get fired. What am I doing here? They're going to find me out.* But you can't tell yourself you shouldn't feel that way, because that doesn't help. What helps is really living with what it feels like to be that afraid, and beginning from there. The fear is the way through.

You can't deny, either in life or as an actor, what's really going on. So even though I might be playing the most confident person in the world, if I'm ready to throw up with nerves, that fear has to be present somehow. I think I need it—that daunting feeling like I'm looking up at Mount Everest. It's what lets me go into rehearsal without expecting anything. But I also know that through diligence, and not letting the fear take over, something will come. I love that feeling, like jumping off a cliff—it's a big, powerful, enlivening, animal feeling. I think, *What will come up, what will come out, if I really relinquish? What real, live thing can happen in the room, and go into the art we're making?* That's what's truly scary, but also such a thrill.

THE AWESOME POWER OF EVERYWOMAN
LILLY LEDBETTER
Retiree, hero

For 19 years, while Lilly Ledbetter was a manager at a Goodyear tire plant in Alabama, her male peers' salaries far outpaced her own; by the late 1990s, the highest-paid male manager was making some $18,000 more for comparable work. Though Ledbetter didn't prevail when her discrimination suit reached the Supreme Court, her case led to the Lilly Ledbetter Fair Pay Act, which President Obama signed into law in January 2009. On behalf of women everywhere, we salute her....

Work hard and play by the rules: That cornerstone of the American dream crumbled a bit in 2007 when the Supreme Court ruled against Lilly Ledbetter. The five-four decision boiled down to timing: Five male justices invoked the statute of limitations for pay-discrimination claims, and decided the inequity Ledbetter suffered had expired.

But Ledbetter kept right on fighting. And the new law that bears her name effectively nullified the Supreme Court decision. Today the 72-year-old retiree is championing what she calls "the next logical step": the Paycheck Fairness Act, which would strengthen penalties for equal-pay violations.

Lilly Ledbetter never received the hundreds of thousands of dollars due her in back pay and benefits. But her name is now shorthand for a new, improved American motto: Work hard, play by the rules—and, if necessary, change them.

Lilly Ledbetter, Birmingham, Alabama, 2009.

General Dunwoody, Washington, D.C., 2009.

CRACKING THE BRASS CEILING
GENERAL ANN E. DUNWOODY
Four-star general, U.S. Army

In 2008 Ann E. Dunwoody became the first female four-star general in American military history. (In the U.S. Army, one higher rank exists—General of the Army—but only two officers have ever held it: George Washington and John Pershing.) Dunwoody is in charge of army logistics; around the world, it is her 61,000-plus employees who make sure American troops have everything from beans to bullets, helmets to helicopters, spare parts to spare ribs. We asked her about her code of conduct:

I never intended to make the military a career. I was going to be a phys ed teacher. But I tried a college program—they paid me $500 a month in exchange for two years in the army—and I fell in love. The work offered something new every day. There were physical challenges, logistical challenges. It was hard. It was fun.

When I was commissioned, in 1975, the army was rebuilding after Vietnam, and just starting to integrate women. Early on, at airborne school, where we learned to jump out of planes, they encouraged us to cut our hair. If we kept it long, it had to be pulled back and off our necks. But then they said we couldn't wear barrettes—we had to tape our hair to our head, with what we call 100-mile-an-hour tape. It's like duct tape, but green. Most people cut their hair. I didn't.

A little later, when I was a platoon leader at Fort Sill in Oklahoma, there was a tendency to put me in charge of women only. There were other frustrations, too. Like the time I finished some advanced training, then got a lower job than I should have. All I said was, "I'm going to go in and do my best." I believe when you do that, people recognize your talent. And it worked.

Mayda del Valle,
Los Angeles,
2009.

THE POWER OF
TELLING YOUR STORY
MAYDA
DEL VALLE
Spoken-word artist

*Mayda del Valle doesn't waste words.
Or time. In 2001, at the age of 22,
the Chicago native became the
youngest poet and first Latino to win
the Individual National Poetry
Slam. Since then, her bracing style—
informed by Latin jazz and hip-
hop—has set off sparks on Russell
Simmons's* Def Poetry *HBO series
and Broadway show; in May of
2009 she performed at the White
House at the invitation of the president and First Lady. When* O *asked
del Valle to talk about what she does,
she composed this poem:*

when I would wander into the kitchen
for the third time
in 37 minutes
shoulders curved into a question mark
waiting for the perfect opportunity to ask her
for something
my mother
in all her motherly wisdom
would say

As if I didn't carry you for 9 months
and push you from this body. what is it you
want girl?
el que no habla Dios no lo escucha

if you don't speak God can't hear you

It might have been the fear
of being
so quiet
that my creator would become deaf to my
very existence

the hurry up and spit it out already
that mothers have of forcing their offspring
to speak

Might have been the height the color
of language the how did you learn English
the name that stumped teachers who smelled
like stale coffee and cigarettes
the shhhhhhh not
right now

The 7 A.M. reception desk temp job
at the fancy designer label
I wore the same shoes to every day
where no one noticed my pen and paper
hiding the diary in religion class
mom finding it
under the bed

might have been the you're that *girl*
who beat me at the slam last week
the but
what will people think
if you talk
about that
in public?

might have been stories of grandmas
with a child on one hip
and a silent song swinging from the other

could have been anything
that encouraged the hand the mouth
the loud the shout
the story the telling

must have been something
made me think I was special enough
to speak to scream
to stand up straight
special enough to ask
God to listen
to me

POWER: THE EQUATION

SHIRLEY ANN JACKSON, PhD

Theoretical physicist, university president

Quick—think of a woman whose name is synonymous with science. For a century, the only option was Marie Curie, but the name on the lips of future generations may well be Shirley Ann Jackson. Her résumé is a catalog of firsts: first African-American woman to earn a doctorate from MIT. First woman and first African-American to chair the U.S. Nuclear Regulatory Commission. First African-American woman to lead a national research university (Rensselaer Polytechnic Institute, where applications have doubled in the past four years). We asked Jackson to devise—and explain—a formula for power:

{Preparation^{10}(Passion + Persistence)}
+
{Connection^{10}(Compassion + Courage)}
+
{Excellence^{10}(Achievement + Wisdom)}

= Power

$$\{P_1{}^{10}(P_2 + P_3)\} + \{C_1{}^{10}(C_2 + C_3)\} + \{E^{10}(A + W)\} = Power$$

Follow your passion with persistence, magnified by intense preparation. Use compassion and courage to weave a strong web of connections. Use focused excellence to drive achievements and gain wisdom. It is through the combination of all these things that your power will reveal itself.

The magnitude and reach of your power is up to you.

You must be prepared; you must commit the time, energy, and effort required to achieve. Be persistent. The passion you exhibit for your ideas and ideals and the compassion you show for others will further enhance your power.

Connectivity is key; it is what creates and strengthens your web of opportunity. The more connected you are, and the stronger your connections, the more effective you will be in obtaining and using power to achieve your goals.

All of this requires courage: the courage of your convictions, and the courage to get started, and the courage to keep going.

Shirley Ann Jackson, Rensselaer Polytechnic Institute, Troy, New York, 2005.

THE POWER OF CRYING FOUL
MELANIE SLOAN
Government watchdog

In 2003 Melanie Sloan, then 38, left a plum position as assistant U.S. attorney to start running a new government watchdog group, Citizens for Responsibility and Ethics in Washington (CREW). Working alone for the first 18 months, she gathered evidence that then House Majority Leader Tom DeLay (R-TX) had violated House ethics rules; her efforts helped lead to DeLay's disgraced exit from government in 2006. Since then CREW—now with a staff of 17—has revealed dirty tricks by lobbyist Jack Abramoff, Rep. John Murtha (D-PA), and many others. Politicos, beware: No matter where you fall on the partisan divide, Sloan is looking over your shoulder. We asked her to describe the view....

Mine is a very wearing job—you get rid of bad guys and then more appear. It's never done. But here is what's great: When I pick up the paper and read something terrible, I don't just think, *Wow, that is awful and I hope somebody does something about it.* I read it and go, *Wow, what can I do about that today?* Yes, it's hard to fight for what you believe in, but hard is never a reason not to fight. My mom would say I've always had an innate sense of fairness and justice. But I also went to a Quaker high school and took their values of social justice to heart. So even if I alienate all of Washington, I'm not afraid. In fact, when people start attacking me, I'm happy. It means I'm getting to them, and that means I'm doing my job. ◖

GOOD TIMES: Chatting it up in Tina Fey's Manhattan apartment, November 2008.

Oprah Talks to Tina Fey

We've known her as a favored face on *Saturday Night Live*, as the lovely
Liz Lemon of *30 Rock*, and, for a time, as an unlikely factor in a historic election.
But Tina Fey swears she's just an ordinary working mom who scarfs down
Kit Kats in her sweatpants. Oprah shares a few laughs with this Emmy-winning,
politician-lampooning, child-rearing multitasker extraordinaire.

Exactly one day after the close of the Democratic National Convention in August of 2008, Senator John McCain made a big announcement: Alaska governor Sarah Palin would be his running mate. I was still in Denver at the time, riding the wave of Barack Obama's stirring speech at Invesco Field the night before. The second I saw Governor Palin on my TV screen, I—along with almost everyone else in the world—had just one thought: *That is Tina Fey! Next stop*: Saturday Night Live!

Tina first joined *SNL* in 1997, as a writer (like many of the show's great talents, she came out of Chicago's Second City school of improvisational comedy); within two years, she was promoted to head writer, the first woman to hold that position in the show's then 25-year history. Three years later Tina took on the role that originally made her famous—cohost of *SNL*'s news show parody, "Weekend Update."

In 2006, Tina left *Saturday Night Live* to create the Emmy-winning comedy series she both oversees and stars in, NBC's *30 Rock*. And this is why, when everyone from strangers to her own husband started suggesting that she impersonate Palin on *SNL,* she felt compelled to remind them, "I already have a day job." Luckily that didn't stop *SNL* creator and executive producer Lorne Michaels from wooing her. As Michaels told an interviewer, "The whole world cast her in that role." The result was a *Saturday Night Live* jackpot: The brilliant comedian who has satirized everything from elastic-waisted "Mom jeans" to "the girl with no gaydar" made the presidential campaign as hilarious as it was historic. Her six appearances as Palin, beginning with *SNL*'s season premiere on September 13, were watched by millions of people live and millions more online, and were a genuine international sensation.

On the rainy Saturday afternoon when I arrive for my talk with Tina, she and her husband, Jeff Richmond, and their daughter, Alice, greet me at the front door of their two-bedroom Manhattan apartment (the door, by the way, is plastered with Alice's Crayola artwork). If the Palin impersonations catapulted Tina, 40, into a new stratosphere of stardom, you wouldn't know it from her living room;

only the cluster of golden Emmys standing atop a bookcase hint that she is anything other than an ordinary working mom. Tina and Jeff—a music producer who left *SNL* to become the composer for *30 Rock*—admit that their life is definitely more harried than glamorous: They spend their days racing between the set of the show and their toy-strewn home.

In October of 2008, the couple began jokingly asking their daughter who would be the next president. "Ba-rack O-bama! Ba-rack O-bama!" Alice said. How could a 3-year-old call an election? "I think she just liked saying the name," says Tina. "It's fun." And so is my time with Tina—a funny girl from Upper Darby, Pennsylvania, who has gone from being an early-morning receptionist at a Chicago-area YMCA (a side gig during her Second City days) to one of the most masterly comedians of our time.

OPRAH: Sarah Palin was introduced to the world on August 29, 2008. How soon afterward did you get the call from Lorne Michaels?

TINA: Lorne played it cool, as he always does, and waited until the week of the first show. He called and said, "Think about if you want to impersonate her." I was like, "I'll do a joke about her. I'll do a sketch where I'm myself. I'll do anything except impersonate her!"

OPRAH: Why didn't you want to impersonate her?

TINA: Because even when I was at *SNL,* I didn't do impersonations. I always wanted to be the kind of person who could do them—I always thought they were the coolest thing on the show—but I didn't have any experience.

OPRAH: How did Lorne coax you?

TINA: Lorne is very—what's a word besides *sneaky?* He's very laid-back, but then he slowly corners you. He said that even his doorman had mentioned how much I look like Sarah Palin.

OPRAH: Sometimes, looking at pictures from the campaign, I had to look twice—was that really her, or was it you? So, when you were finally there onstage impersonating her, were you scared?

TINA: No. I just kept thinking, *I don't work here anymore, so if this ends up being lousy, I told you guys I don't do this.* I also felt safe doing it with Amy [Amy Poehler played both Hillary Clinton and Katie Couric in the *SNL* sketches]. I wouldn't have enjoyed doing it alone, because I never did anything alone on *SNL.*

OPRAH: When I'm on TV, I can sometimes feel when a moment transcends the

"When humor works, it works because it's clarifying what people already feel. It has to come from someplace real."

studio and is transported into people's living rooms. Did you feel that energy? All those people watching and thinking, *Yeah, she's doing it!*

TINA: I joked that I should have opened the show with, "Live from New York…are you happy now?" But yes, I did feel that energy in the first show. I always try to focus on the live audience, though, because if I think about the fact that the show really is going out into the world, then I do start to get nervous.

OPRAH: Many people have said that you had a huge impact on the campaign.

TINA: When humor works, it works because it's clarifying what people already feel. It has to come from someplace real. You don't just decide to destroy a person by making up stuff, and no one at *SNL* is writing to go after someone. Governor Palin is a dynamic speaker in a prepared setting, and she was carefully packaged at the Republican National Convention. Because she didn't do many interviews during the campaign, *SNL* was the first to poke a hole in that package.

OPRAH: Were you nervous about meeting her when she came on the show in October?

TINA: A little. But I knew I hadn't done anything I had to be embarrassed about.

OPRAH: How did the sudden celebrity make you feel?

TINA: Weird and vulnerable, especially since it's linked to politics. I don't want some crazy person trying to get to me.

OPRAH: Have people been angry when they've approached you?

TINA: Nobody was angry the first week—not even my Republican parents.

OPRAH: I love that your parents are Republicans.

TINA: Everyone's parents are Republicans! Week one, they loved it; week two, they loved it; week three, they loved it—but by week four? My dad was like, "Enough already!" I told him it was just that Governor Palin was the most fun to play. For a long time, Bill Clinton was the most fun, but in this election Sarah Palin was.

OPRAH: But now you've laid the character to rest.

TINA: I saw her on TV the other day, and I found myself thinking, *How's she saying that—oh, I don't have to worry about it anymore!* You know, in the beginning, it was this special performance I did. But then it turned into a *Flowers for Algernon* thing: Every time I performed, I felt like it wasn't as good as the time before. It was as if I was progressively forgetting how to do it. So even if McCain and Palin had won, I would have had to stop. I'm done.

OPRAH: They say you should never say never.

TINA: Well, if I need a gig in three or four years…

OPRAH: Now let's talk about how you got started in comedy. When did you realize you could make people laugh?

TINA: Around sixth grade. The only way I could get comfortable around people was to make them laugh. I was an obedient girl, and humor was my one form of rebellion. I used comedy to deflect. Like, "Hey, check out my zit!"—you know, making fun of yourself before someone else has a chance to.

OPRAH: I'm surprised at something you've admitted about

FUNNY GIRL: Fey (*left*) with fellow Second City actors Scott Allman and Rachel Dratch, Chicago, 1996, and (*above*) decked out for her second Halloween, 1972.

your high school days: You were mean to the point of being caustic. I know you were in the movie *Mean Girls*—you actually adapted the book it's based on—but I wouldn't have guessed that you were mean yourself.

TINA: It was about lashing out at others to make myself feel better.

OPRAH: Why were you lashing out?

TINA: It was the kind of thing where if I liked a boy and he liked some other girl, then that girl was in trouble.

OPRAH: You were one of those girls!

TINA: Yes—in my circle of loser friends. I don't think I ever truly bullied anyone; it was about jockeying for position and trying to take the attention off myself. But that's a dangerous habit for girls to get into.

OPRAH: If this were *The Oprah Winfrey Show,* I'd be asking if there was anyone you wanted to apologize to…

TINA: Well you know, when I wrote *Mean Girls,* I had some archetypes in my head—like the prettiest girl and the most popular girl. And as I was working on the script, I threw in some names of real people from high school and mixed them up with other random names. I later heard from a friend who went to my high school reunion that some of my former classmates weren't pleased. When they saw the movie, they were like, "What did I do to *her?*" I was inadvertently hurtful. So I apologize to the women whose names I used.

OPRAH: Okay. Changing the subject now: At the University of Virginia you started as an English major and then switched to drama.

TINA: Yes, I studied playwriting and acting, but somehow I knew that serious acting was not really quite what I was intended for.

OPRAH: And when you moved to Chicago in 1992 to do improv at Second City, did you know you'd found your calling?

TINA: Yes. In Chicago improv is a cult. Everyone who's in it is *so* into it—all you do is go out four or five nights a week and watch other people improvise. I can't think of anything else like it.

OPRAH: It's its own art form.

TINA: It is. And when people try to televise it, it shrinks. The thing that comes closest is free-form jazz. Sometimes when you listen to a recording, you're like, "This is quite long," but if you're there hearing it in person, it's so exciting.

OPRAH: A couple of years ago, the cast of *Thank God You're*

> "The only way I could get comfortable around people was to make them laugh. I was an obedient girl, and humor was my one form of rebellion."

Here [an improvisational sketch comedy series that ran on NBC in 2007] visited my show. It was the first time I'd tried improv. You have to be 100 percent in the moment.

TINA: That's right. When I studied acting technique, I could never understand what I should be thinking about when I was onstage. I'd be standing there thinking *Hmm, how does my hair look?* But with improv, the focus is clear: You're supposed to be listening to the other person so you know how to respond. Improv involves a lot of agreement. It's all about saying yes to the person you're across from, because if you don't say yes, the sketch is over. That can even shape your worldview. It breeds positivity.

OPRAH: For many years, I was a news anchorwoman. I hated it, but it was a good job, so I kept it. The day they fired me and put me on as a talk show host, I felt like I'd come home to myself. Is that what happened to you with improv?

TINA: Yes. It's better than acting because you can play people you don't remotely look like. It feels like a sport—and it was the fit I was looking for.

OPRAH: At Second City, does everybody know when the *SNL* scout is coming?

TINA: Oh, yes—like puppies in a pound: "Take me, take me, take me!"

OPRAH: *SNL* is still a sketch comedian's big dream?

TINA: Yes—though these days, the dream could also be to get into a Judd Apatow movie. And yet *SNL* remains the only place where you can make up stuff on a Wednesday that's on the air by Saturday. Comedians who only do movies miss that. *SNL* keeps you tuned up for everything. Nothing freaks you out. But back to the scouts: When they came, they didn't take me. My friend Adam McKay was already working at *SNL,* so I called him. That's how I eventually got a writing job there.

OPRAH: When that happened, did you think you were in heaven?

TINA: Yes! Of course, I also felt pressure. But once I found the rhythm of the place, I liked the competitiveness. It was like, "Let's see what everybody's got this week!"

OPRAH: What's that experience like?

TINA: You're at this crowded table with Lorne Michaels, all the cast and designers and network people, and the week's host. During my first week, Sylvester Stallone was hosting. In this packed room, they finally get to your sketch. It's hard to get laughs when you're new—you get some goodwill after you've been there for a while, but in the beginning, you're just sweating. You may not get a single laugh during your whole piece. A year after I came to the show, I finally had a piece that really killed in that room—and that was almost more satisfying than having it succeed on the air. That's how tough that room is.

OPRAH: But after just two years on staff at *SNL*, you became the first female head writer in the show's then 25-year history. That was a big deal.

TINA: In fairness to the show, there had only been about three head writers over those 25 years. Yet I think there's a perception that the show is misogynistic. I don't doubt that it once was, but it isn't now.

OPRAH: As a writer, did you miss performing?

TINA: A little. At *SNL,* there are lots of frustrated performers working as writers. Lorne often turns actors into writers, and he's smart to do it, because writers who've performed are more sensitive to performers. A writerly writer is like, "What do you mean you can't say that long speech perfectly?" A writer who has performed wouldn't do that—which is good. But it's a little heartbreaking to be at *SNL* and not be on the air.

OPRAH: Speaking of being on the air, you weren't offered the "Weekend Update" spot until after you lost 30 pounds. Tell me about that.

TINA: Well, I'd been writing, which is a sedentary life. And in Chicago, there's a different aesthetic than there is here in New York.

OPRAH: There truly is.

TINA: When I first came here, I was like, *Ohhhh, okay.*

OPRAH: Yes, it's different in New York.

TINA: The only place worse is Los Angeles, where it's just disgusting.

OPRAH: Where if you're over a size 4 or 6, forget it!

TINA: "L.A. obese," they call it. So anyway, when I came to *SNL,* I was increasingly just sitting around eating bad food, but I wanted to get control of my weight. So I did Weight Watchers. And after I lost weight, I did a two-woman show with my friend Rachel Dratch, and Lorne came and saw it and asked if I would test for "Weekend Update." But I don't want to make it sound as if he wouldn't have asked me to test if I hadn't slimmed down. No one ever said, "Lose the weight."

> "Improv involves a lot of agreement. It's all about saying yes to the person you're across from, because if you don't say yes, the sketch is over. That can even shape your worldview. It breeds positivity."

OPRAH: How did it feel to perform again?

TINA: It was great. People were nice to Jimmy Fallon ["Weekend Update" cohost] and me right away. We had the only segment that doesn't get cut. Ever. I had a privileged experience at *SNL.*

OPRAH: Then what made you decide to do *30 Rock*?

TINA: Lorne encouraged me to develop a show for NBC.

OPRAH: And you modeled it after one of your all-time favorite series, *The Larry Sanders Show* [Garry Shandling's satirical comedy series, which ran from 1992 to 1998 on HBO]?

TINA: *The Larry Sanders Show* was a show within a show, and the network wanted me to do that, too. But as much as I loved the series, I was worried it would seem like we were trying to rip it off.

OPRAH: What was your original pitch?

TINA: I wanted to create a show about a cable news producer who has to deal with a conservative, overbearing pundit who is gold in the ratings. I kept thinking, *Wouldn't it be great to get Alec Baldwin?*—but I never felt I could. The network passed on my original idea. They wanted me to make the show feel more like my life as a sketch-comedy writer. I was resistant at first, but then I thought it could be funny to have a crazy triangle of people—especially if it included actors like Alec Baldwin and Tracy Morgan. Tracy is the complete opposite of me. We breathe oxygen, and that's about all we have in common. Well, I suppose there's more than that.

OPRAH: Why did Tracy come to mind? Just because he's a little crazy?

TINA: He's not so crazy. He's funny in a very raw way.

OPRAH: I mean crazy in a nice way.

TINA: Yes. He's crazy in the best possible way.

OPRAH: And why did you want Alec Baldwin so badly?

TINA: I thought it would be fun and funny for Alec to play the complete opposite of his own politics [Baldwin, who is known for his liberal politics, plays Jack Donaghy, a politically conservative network executive]. Also, I knew him as an *SNL* host, and he is great at comedy. Sometimes on *SNL,* you get brilliant actors who just don't take to comedy.

OPRAH: Other than a sense of humor, what do you need to take to comedy?

TINA: A willingness to drop your ego

Fey as Governor Sarah Palin on *Saturday Night Live*, flanked by *SNL*'s Darrell Hammond as Senator John McCain and Will Ferrell as President George W. Bush, October 23, 2008.

and let yourself look foolish. You almost have to enjoy looking vulnerable. You'd be surprised how many people don't want to do that.

OPRAH: They don't even know how! For so many great actors, it's about being in control.

TINA: Exactly.

OPRAH: *30 Rock* wasn't a big hit at first—even though it's so well done. I know what it's like to work on a project and love it—then when you put it out, the world doesn't receive it the way you intended. That's what happened to me with the movie *Beloved*.

TINA: In the beginning, I would just cling to any good review we received. And the fact that when it was over, I'd at least have the DVDs.

OPRAH: When you got an Emmy in 2007, I laughed when you said, "I'd like to thank our dozens and dozens of viewers."

TINA: Our ratings were scary!

OPRAH: Did your show survive only because it received such critical acclaim?

TINA: Yes—any other show would have been gone. Of course,

we debuted at a time when NBC didn't have much else happening. If *Friends* or *Frasier* were still on the air, forget it.

OPRAH: Last year *30 Rock* received 17 Emmy nominations. Did y'all go nuts when the nominations were announced?

TINA: We were working that day, but we did have a little Champagne. Then somebody pointed out that *The Larry Sanders Show* had once gotten 16 nominations but won nothing. I was like, *Okay, I'll get ready to win nothing.*

OPRAH: How many did you win?

TINA: Seven.

OPRAH: And what does it mean to win?

TINA: The first year, it made us feel like a real TV show. Before the Emmys, I had done a lot of downplaying: "It's just a bunch of people who paid 200 bucks to start a club and give themselves prizes." But after we won, I was like, "It's the greatest thing ever—extremely prestigious."

OPRAH: Just like that, it became an honor!

TINA: Exactly! Actually, it's rewarding for everybody who works so hard on the show.

OPRAH: What's your process for creating a script?

TINA: Once we have a preliminary draft, we do a reading. Then I'll have a couple of writers over to my home. We plug the computer into the TV, put the script onscreen, and work on it together. We try to include three story lines in every episode. When I go back and watch the first season of *The Mary Tyler Moore Show,* I'm like, *My God, there's just one story!*

OPRAH: That American Express ad where you're hiding under the table with total chaos around you—is that real?

TINA: My life is not quite that crazy, but it's close. It's a weird mix: I have this job that I love, but I'm also like, *When can I go home?* In a way, that's a good thing, because otherwise, I'd never go home. I would just kill myself doing this show. And even so, the moment we put Alice to bed, Jeff and I go back to work. Sometimes I call a moratorium on talking about work at home, but mostly, we talk about it nonstop.

OPRAH: What's it like to work with your husband?

TINA: We're not literally together all day. That would make anybody crazy. But it's a good situation because we work toward the same goal. Although maybe I'm the one saying it works because I'm the boss! You should ask him. Last year he did have an issue with a particular story for the show. He was like, "Listen, I'm going to tell you something because nobody tells you no—I don't like this."

OPRAH: You've reached that point where nobody tells you no?

TINA: At some point, you realize that people might be laughing at your jokes because they're afraid not to laugh. That's why I still have Lorne as a partner on *30 Rock.* He'll tell me if he doesn't like something.

OPRAH: Do you feel like the big star that everybody says you are?

TINA: Not exactly. One day last week when I was writing, I was in my sweatpants, exhausted, and I realized I'd just eaten six Kit Kats in ten minutes.

OPRAH: Kit Kats are your drug of choice?

TINA: Actually, it's usually doughnuts. When I have a day when my hair is dirty and I'm tired, my friend Kay sings this little song she made up [*Tina sings*]: *TV star, livin' the life, just like Jennifer Aniston!* My life is not at all like Jennifer's. I never walk the dogs on the beach. I'm never in St. Bart's. I'm never on a yacht.

OPRAH: No photos of you smooching with Jeff?

TINA: Noooo! [*Laughing.*] We have a good life—we just don't have a famous person's life.

OPRAH: Do you want that life?

TINA: It's great to have people be nicer to me than they would be if I weren't famous. But the new level of fame that came from the Palin thing makes me anxious. I don't love it that people recognize me all the time.

OPRAH: You've been given the talent of great humor. How do you want to continue using it as the best expression of who you are?

TINA: I want to keep creating comedy that is, as my old improv teacher would say, at the top of our intelligence or higher. It's easy to fall into the trap of just cranking out things that are good enough to sell.

OPRAH: How do you choose the work that's most important to you? By now, I could have had a food line, a furniture line, and a perfume line.

TINA: I choose one project at a time. I'm like, *If I saw this on my shelf a year from now, would I think it was good—or would I think it's b.s.?* People have asked me to put my name on other shows, but I won't do it. The only hallmark I have for what I do is that I've worked hard on it. I can't lend my name to something I didn't work on.

OPRAH: Has somebody asked you to do the Tina Fey doll yet?

TINA: No!

OPRAH: It's coming. But I've always believed that if you say yes to everything that comes along, people won't believe you when you really do have something meaningful to say. Final question: What do you know for sure?

TINA: I know for sure that you can tell how smart people are by what they laugh at. I know for sure that a hard-boiled egg is two points on Weight Watchers. I know for sure that my kid needs my husband and me to be with her more. And I know for sure that I can't get comfortable with all the attention I've been getting because it won't last forever. It's just a moment—and there will be other moments when people don't care what I'm doing.

OPRAH: This was fun—thank you for spending a rainy Saturday afternoon with me.

TINA: Thanks for stopping by! ◖

"Before the Emmys, I had done a lot of downplaying: 'It's just a bunch of people who paid 200 bucks to start a club and give themselves prizes.' But after we won, I was like, 'It's the greatest thing ever—extremely prestigious.'"

spirituality

141 THE CUPPED HANDS I BY PAM HOUSTON

144 HIGHER CALLING I BY PETERO SABUNE

145 SNOW ANGELS I BY ELIZABETH STROUT

146 GANDHI'S GHOST I BY RAJMOHAN GANDHI

148 LET EVERYTHING HAPPEN TO YOU I BY UWEM AKPAN

149 "WHEN YOUR LIFE IS ON COURSE WITH ITS PURPOSE, YOU ARE YOUR MOST POWERFUL" I BY OPRAH

The Cupped Hands

The universe sent her a mystic, a movie star, and a miracle acupuncturist. Then Pam Houston asked for love, and the universe said Yes.

Two years ago, I was lying on my acupuncturist's table with needles sticking into my ears, neck, belly, ankles, and between my toes, when she said to me, out of nowhere, "Well, you know, Pam, you are protected."

Denise was treating me for debilitating lower-back pain, after the MRI had said, "severely degenerated L4/5 disk," and the family doctor had said, "eventual wheelchair," and the specialist had said, "Call me when you become incontinent," and the surgeon had said, "Sure, we can operate, but it probably won't work."

Acupuncture had worked, steadily, deeply, undeniably, and eliminating pain was only the beginning; with each treatment I was becoming calmer, more solidly grounded in the center of my life. Denise is a wonder; smart, hilarious, ultraintuitive, massively tuned in. When she said I was protected, I knew she was talking about something bigger than job security or health insurance.

"I do know," I said, because somehow, unaccountably, I did. Denise patted my arm and I closed my eyes and that is the first time I saw the cupped hands.

Before I go on, let me say that I was born and raised in Trenton, New Jersey. I am an obsessive-compulsive checkbook balancer, I love football and ice hockey, and I got a perfect score on the analytical portion of the Graduate Record Exam. So when serendipitous—even uncanny—encounters occur in my life, I have to squint at them from all angles before I am willing to believe.

There was the time, years ago, when I had missed my plane at LAX Airport and Carlos Castaneda walked up (as if he knew me, though of course he did not), introduced himself, and gave me four essential pieces of advice about my life. There was the time I was sitting in Granzella's, a roadside attraction off the I-5 south of Redding, in California's grim Central Valley, drinking bad coffee, telling a 20-year-old story about William Hurt (whom I didn't know either, but who had once changed my life by the way he read a story onstage), only to look up from my coffee to see that Hurt—all dressed in white like some angel of the interstate—had just walked through the front door.

The cupped hands, though, were on a different plane of uncanny than the sudden appearance of a Yaqui mystic or the ability to conjure an Academy Award–winning actor by saying his name. These hands were not actual, not in the flesh, as William's and Carlos's had been when I shook them. I saw these hands only in my mind's eye, and yet they were as insistent, as undeniable as anything I have seen or felt in my life. The cupped hands were grown-up hands—lined, fleshy, and weathered, poised to receive, possibly water, possibly something water only stands for. They were there, I was given to understand, to catch me if I fell.

A few days later I was walking with my dog in the alfalfa fields outside Davis, California, noticing that in spite of some disappointments I was coping with (a painful but inevitable breakup, severe budget cuts at work), I was feeling happy, almost exhilarated. I recalled the inverse of that moment, times where everything in my life had been going great and I felt unaccountably sad. The possibility of untethering happiness and sadness from circumstance felt frightening and wonderful, like a new brand of freedom.

The sun was setting in the Central Valley haze, leaving a kind of pink mouth against a white sky, and somehow in and through that rose-colored opening, I saw/felt those cupped hands again. What had begun as exhilaration became a quiet, permeating ecstasy that hung around long enough for me to find myself humming, then laughing. I fought the urge (thank God) to turn cartwheels all the way back to my truck.

A few months later I was sitting

> What had begun as exhilaration became a quiet, permeating ecstasy that hung around long enough for me to find myself humming, then laughing. I fought the urge (thank God) to turn cartwheels all the way back to my truck.

on the opposite side of the continent, far out on the long rocky breakwater in Provincetown Harbor, Massachusetts, under a similarly pink-slashed sunset, talking to the sea and the sky. Some people would call this praying, and I might one day, too, so I began, as I believe all prayers should, with gratitude. Thank you for the sunset, thank you for my friends, thank you for the pain that is gone from my back. Thank you, that is, both for the wake-up call of pain, and for its subsequent relief.

I watched the tide rush out under the giant slabs of granite beneath me.

"Okay," I said, out loud this time, which felt both ridiculous and better. "I think I am finally ready for you to send me a big, deep, generous love." I'll admit I didn't know who I was praying to. Something that might be called Ocean and might be called God, and that manifested itself to me occasionally as cupped hands.

"But if you don't think I am ready for big love," I continued, "then maybe just a little romance to keep the conversation going." A great blue heron landed in the reeds nearby. "And if I'm not even ready for that, maybe just a sign that I'm on the right path."

Satisfied with my prayer, I trained my eyes on the heron. A dapper little man was approaching on the jetty, wearing short shorts in psychedelic colors and a yellow shirt, walking a Westie, who was wearing a sweater, even though the day was quite warm. He said, "Lovely place to sit and think, isn't it?"

"Yes," I said, "it surely is."

He never broke stride, but grinned as he passed. "You are a good person," he said. "It's all going to be okay."

I watched him recede along the horizon, the tops of the big rocks turning green and gold and purple in the encroaching twilight. "Thanks," I told the thing that is part God and part Ocean. "That was just what I had in mind."

> "Okay," I said, out loud this time, which felt both ridiculous and better. "I think I am finally ready for you to send me a big, deep, generous love." I'll admit I didn't know who I was praying to.

It was exactly two weeks later when I found myself in Taos, New Mexico, talking with a poet named Greg Glazner, someone I had not known until chance put us on a shared bill at a night full of literary readings. We were in his hotel room—not as salacious as it sounds—but the conversation was having that delicious accelerated quality that can happen sometimes with strangers, and before long I was telling him about Denise, and the alfalfa fields, and the cupped hands.

"These hands?" he said, holding his hands just like the ones in my mind's eye, with a look of such intensity on his face it scared me.

"Well, you know," I said, backpedaling, "cupped hands as metaphor." What had made me want to share my fledgling spiritual realizations with a complete stranger anyway? "Some kind of safety or support."

"Oh," he said, "I know those hands," and he reached into his briefcase and pulled out a greeting card with a photo of hands on the front, fleshy, weathered, cupped, and catching a stream of cold, clear water. "Look," he said, and held the card out to me. "And look," he said, pointing to the yard-sale-quality print over the standard-issue hotel bed. There were the soft lines of a woman's face, below it only the suggestion of a body, and below it, in sharper detail than anything else, her open, waiting hands.

The rest, as they say, is history. Greg and I have been together going on two years now, and though no relationship is made without effort, this one is proving to be that big love I prayed for on the Provincetown rocks. I don't know why and I don't know why now, but I do know I would have to be some kind of arrogant to squint too hard at my good fortune this time. Denise says it is simple: I had to learn how to ask for help before I could receive it. Now when life gets hard and I start to lose faith, I put myself back in that alfalfa field, where a smudged sky opened up and invited me inside it, momentarily illuminating my connection to everything larger than me. ◖

Petero Sabune (*far right*), a prison chaplain, with Reverend James Forbes at Union Theological Seminary in New York City. The two men's chance meeting 34 years ago influenced Sabune's career path.

Higher Calling

Petero Sabune had no desire to become a man of the cloth like his father. A chance meeting with a famous minister and an unexpected family tragedy convinced him to change course.

I remember the encounter as if it were yesterday. On a fall day in 1976, when I was a student at Vassar College in Poughkeepsie, New York, one of my professors asked me to escort a visiting speaker across campus. The visitor was Reverend James A. Forbes, a renowned minister and professor at Union Theological Seminary in New York City, who would later become the first African-American senior minister at Manhattan's Riverside Church.

As we walked, Reverend Forbes asked what I was

planning to do with my life. I told him I was from Uganda; I was studying political science and hoped to go into international relations. He looked at me and said, "Have you ever thought of going into the ministry?"

I burst into laughter, then explained why. My father was an Anglican priest in Uganda, and my five brothers and I grew up as the kids of the local pastor. This was very uncool. As a result, we were the bad kids, always trying to distance ourselves from our father.

Forbes and I reached our destination, and he turned to face me. "My father was a minister, too," he said. "It was the one thing I never wanted to be, either. But I want you to think about this: Being a minister is like being the queen on a chessboard. It's the only piece on the board that can move in any direction—in every direction. If you ever change your mind or have any questions, come and say hello."

I didn't give the conversation another thought at the time. Later that year, in August, my brother James died under mysterious circumstances. He was at Rutgers law school and the president of a Ugandan students association. Idi Amin, our country's dictator, had come to the UN to give a speech, and my brother organized student protests against him in New York. Amin wasn't happy. He invited my brother and some other students to come to Uganda for discussions with the government. We never saw James again.

That fall I went back to Vassar for my senior year. I started preparing my applications for international relations graduate schools. But I couldn't get that conversation with Reverend Forbes out of my mind. After the tragedy with James, the idea of the chessboard took on a new meaning. I wanted to fight injustice and hate. I kept thinking about that queen chess piece. It's an amazing image: You can move anywhere; your presence as a pastor, a preacher, or a minister can change lives. Gradually, it made sense. So I called Reverend Forbes and asked, "Do you remember me?"

"Of course," he said. After I explained my change of heart, he added, "Union Seminary has a theological weekend for interested students coming up. Come and visit."

I enrolled at Union (though I didn't tell my father till later) and was ordained in the Episcopal Church on May 18, 1981. Since then I've served in small, struggling parishes and large, prestigious churches. I've been a cathedral dean, and twice stood for election for bishop. I've done work in Haiti and Sudan and Rwanda. In 2004 I became pastor and Protestant chaplain at Sing Sing, the maximum security prison in Ossining, New York. The inmates are a hidden population, but I pray and hope that I touch at least one of them at Bible study every night. It's the same thing we try to accomplish in our daily life: to take something that has been thrown away and transform it, make it new.

That meeting became the catalyst for my life. Whatever spark was in me, whatever ember was burning there, Reverend Forbes lit it that day. And it still burns. ❏

Snow Angels

Elizabeth Strout and the soldier were from different worlds, yet they shared a haunting insight.

It was January, and I was driving from Portland, Maine, up to Bangor, where I was to speak the next day. The Maine light, so magnificent at that time of year, sliced through the thin-trunked pine trees as I drove up the highway. *What a beautiful world,* I thought. *Stark, pristine—God, what a beautiful world.*

At the hotel (I was staying out near the airport), I was surprised to find the place filled—and I mean the lobby, the hallways, the restaurant—with men and women GIs dressed in fatigues. They seemed so young. They reminded me of the students I had taught for years at Manhattan Community College. These "kids" were on their way to Baghdad. Their plane had encountered a mechanical problem, and no one was sure when the flight would take off. So they were waiting.

All around me young people were playing cards, laughing, eating popcorn, and drinking sodas. *They're going to Baghdad*, I thought. *Their lives will be changed forever.*

That evening it began to snow. I watched through the window of the restaurant as the snow swirled to the ground. And then I saw that a number of the GIs had tumbled outdoors and were playing, lying on their backs, moving their arms, making angels in the snow. I went outside to watch them.

One fellow stood apart from the rest. He was talking on a cell phone, then flipped it shut. He shook a cigarette from a pack. "Do you have a light?" he asked. I saw that he was not as young as the rest. "One second," I told him, and got some matches from someone nearby. As the man lit his cigarette, he said, "I've been there before. Baghdad. Most of these guys haven't. That was my wife on the phone."

"I'm sorry," I said.

He nodded, blew smoke into the cold air. We stood together. Not far off, angels were still being made in the snow. "They don't know," he said, nodding in their direction.

"No," I said. "I mean, I don't know, either. I'm sorry," I said again.

He glanced at me, and it was a look that was a fleeting moment of—of what? A common understanding of something that neither of us could have put into words? I'll never know. I only know that I stood with him while he smoked, and it felt as though we had known each other a long time. Then he tossed his cigarette butt into the snow.

"Take care," I said. I put my fist to my mouth and kissed it—then extended it slightly toward him.

He held the door open for me, shook the snow from his boots. "Thank you," he said. "You, too."

In the morning they were gone. The silence was large. Awful. ◖

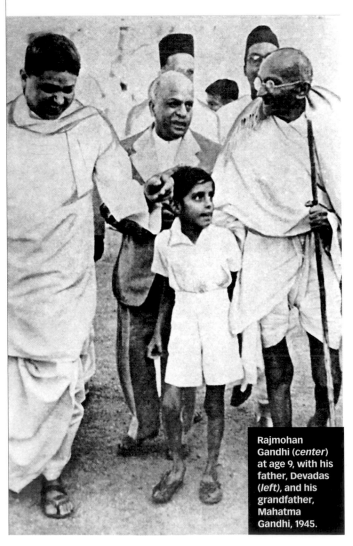

Rajmohan Gandhi (*center*) at age 9, with his father, Devadas (*left*), and his grandfather, Mahatma Gandhi, 1945.

Gandhi's Ghost

A rare recording comes to light, and Rajmohan Gandhi hears a beloved voice from his childhood.

Two years ago the National Press Club in Washington, D.C., invited me to read from my new biography of Mohandas Gandhi, my grandfather, known as Mahatma. Afterward I sat down for a dinner with friends at the club's Reliable Source grill. At one point, Mesfin Mekonen, the impressive Ethiopian who runs the grill, tapped me on the shoulder and asked for a word with me. Leading me away from the table, Mekonen said, "There's a man here at the club, an old-timer, who wants to talk to you. Can I bring him over?" "Sure," I replied.

A few minutes later Mekonen reappeared with an

elderly man. His head carried a precious supply of white hair, and he seemed friendly but also a little cautious.

"I am John Cosgrove," said the man. "I have been a journalist here in Washington for many years. In 1948 a friend of mine, a reporter called Alfred Wagg, gave me a gramophone recording of the speech delivered by Mahatma Gandhi to Asian leaders in April 1947." After hesitating a bit, Cosgrove added, "I still have that recording. Would you be interested in it?"

Would I indeed! I told Cosgrove that newspaper accounts from 1947 had made me well aware of the speech, which took place on the grounds of New Delhi's Old Fort, to a large assembly of Asia's political leaders, all hoping to shed the shackles of colonial power. Gandhi touched on the atom bomb, the clash of civilizations, and the West's need for wisdom. I knew he spoke in English; in fact, I had included a few excerpts in my book. But I had not realized that a soundtrack existed.

As one of Gandhi's 15 grandchildren, I remember, as a schoolboy in New Delhi, sitting close to him as he said his late-afternoon prayers. My grandfather was staying at Birla House as the guest of a wealthy Indian ally, and there, day after day, hundreds of Hindus, Muslims, and Sikhs would gather to hear his short postprayer speech.

It was a dangerous, troubled time. When my grandfather gave this speech, his dream of a free India was four months from being realized. But his triumph was marred by terrible violence, as Muslims and Hindus vented their fears and hatreds. After his prayers, Gandhi would speak lovingly but frankly to his "children," urging them to embrace reconciliation. Angry at his stand for forgiveness, some in the audience would object menacingly. I watched him hold his ground and heard his earnest, friendly voice as he answered the hecklers. *Could I defend him if he were physically attacked?* I would ask myself, even though I was only 11.

Sadly, I was nowhere near him on January 30, 1948, when he was assassinated while walking to the prayer site. I was taking part in a sporting event in my school. When I reached Birla House, his body, surrounded by flowers, was lying on a white sheet on the floor. Three bullets fired by Nathuram Godse, a Hindu extremist, had silenced him.

Yet what was it about my grandfather's voice, the

> The decades compress and I see him, sitting cross-legged against a backdrop of ancient walls, so fragile in appearance yet so strong in spirit.

purring sound that gently but irresistibly entered people's hearts, often persuading them to think afresh?

For most of Gandhi's life his utterances were not preserved, lest the recording company invite the wrath of the British empire. As far as I knew, the only recording of Gandhi speaking in English was made in 1931 in London, where he was in talks with the British. And then, almost exactly 60 years after Gandhi's death, John Cosgrove appeared at my table, with news of another.

"The recording is upstairs in my room," he said. "If you don't mind, I can bring it for you to see." "Please bring it!" I replied. Inwardly I thought, *Oh my God, please!*

A few minutes later, he handed me an album containing two 78 rpm records. In New Delhi, Cosgrove told us, Wagg had recorded the speech. Nine months later, after the assassination, DC Records turned the speech, along with an introduction by Wagg, into these two 78 rpm records and sold them as a "memorial album."

I wanted keenly to hear my beloved grandfather's voice, but the old discs were too fragile to be played. The Press Club offered to have them digitized so that I, and the rest of the world, could hear him.

Returning from D.C. to my university office in Illinois, I find a link in my e-mail. I click on it. First there is a little coughing, and then the voice, clear, gentle, and earnest. And also sibilant, as I remember it always was. A once-familiar cough and voice, as warm now as it had felt 60 years ago. I realize how much I loved that voice, and how much I have missed it. And then I have a stunning recollection: I was actually present, with my siblings and parents, when my grandfather gave that talk before thousands of people. The decades compress and I see him, sitting cross-legged against a backdrop of ancient walls, so fragile in appearance yet so strong in spirit. The realization of what my grandfather means to me, the power of his dream, floods over me once again. I had no idea that Wagg had been there as well, with his recording machine, the needle etching Gandhi's words onto the spinning aluminum disc, just as he couldn't know the emotions and memories his recording would revive in me.

When the recording ends, I click Play again. ◖

Let Everything Happen to You

Inspiration works in mysterious ways. How **Uwem Akpan** found his other calling.

Failure introduced me to fiction writing while I was preparing for the priesthood. I was four years from ordination and teaching 60 preteen-agers per class at St. Francis Secondary School in the slums of Lagos, Nigeria. But my dream lay outside the classroom. I longed to be a columnist for the Nigerian *Guardian,* where I imagined I would write articles criticizing the ills of my country. I'd hoped that if I submitted four articles a month to their Op-Ed page, after six months I could show up and say to the editor, "I am he.... Please, make me a regular columnist!" So I went to work and sent in my first package of four articles. I was well into my second package the following month, when it dawned on me that they weren't publishing any of my pieces. When I phoned them, they said my pieces weren't...well, good enough. I'd failed. I was a miserable 28-year-old. Teaching, which I'd once taken pleasure in, now depressed me. My students complained that I'd become tougher on them. Some days I was even angry attending Mass, and sleep was difficult. I stopped reading the *Guardian* for a while.

Some months later, when I went back to reading the paper, I noticed that the *Guardian* serialized stories on Saturdays. So I decided to attempt fiction. After a few nights of writing, it felt as if a gate had opened into parts of my being I never knew existed. Every night I ran through that gate, like a mischievous child, and played and explored and ran after flying termites all over again.

At night even when there was a power cut (we suffer daily power cuts in Nigeria), sometimes I couldn't sleep. I was thinking characters. It was crazy. I was free to make and to destroy, like Jeremiah. Awesome responsibility. I'd never been so happy, and yet so frightened—except on the day of my First Holy Communion. Which is the easiest way I can begin to describe an earlier turning point in my life, when the faith that called me toward my other vocation—the priesthood—deepened.

I was 11. First Holy Communion, best day of my life. As an Ikot Ekpene morning sun poured its rays into the cavernous Prince of Peace Chapel, I choked with awe, waiting to eat God. Having experienced the indescribable freedom and joy of First Confession the previous day, now I trembled: But how do you eat God? And how do you live after that? Awesome responsibility. The Handmaid Sisters had warned us not to chew but to just let the Communion melt on the tongue. After Mass, the whole day, I walked around feeling this deep peace that finally the Lord was my portion but also anxious I would have to pee or go to toilet, to flush away the Body and Blood of Christ. It was like what Rilke says: "Let everything happen to you: beauty and terror."

So it wasn't too strange for me to begin to believe that I could be a priest, the one who changed mere bread and wine into the Body and Blood of Christ, the one who reconciled people to their God in the confessional. And that Wednesday in January 2000 when, after endless rewrites, I submitted my first short story, "Soaking the Gun," to the *Guardian* (they started serializing it three days later), I could imagine the beauty and terror of being a writer. ◖

"When your life is on course with its purpose, you are your most powerful."

I'm always fascinated by lists of "Most Powerful People," and by the ways they use external things—fame, status, wealth—to define and rank power. It's curious how a person can go from the top of a list one year to unlisted the next—all in the blink of a board meeting. Was that person's power real, or was the power only in the position? We often get the two confused.

For me, there is no real power without spiritual power. A power that comes from the core of who you are and reflects all that you were meant to be. A power that's connected to the source of things. When you see this kind of power shining through someone in all its truth and certainty, it's irresistible, inspiring, elevating. I can feel it in myself sometimes, mostly when I'm sharing an insight that I know will have an impact on someone's life and I can see that they "get it." I get real joy from helping other people experience aha moments. That is where *my* power lies.

Gary Zukav writes in *The Seat of the Soul,* "When we align our thoughts, emotions, and actions with the highest part of ourselves, we are filled with enthusiasm, purpose, and meaning.... When the personality comes fully to serve the energy of its soul, that is authentic empowerment." Fulfilling your purpose, with meaning, is what gives you that electrifying "juice" and makes people stand in wonder at how you do it.

The secret is alignment: when you know for sure that you're on course and doing exactly what you're supposed to be doing, fulfilling your soul's intention, your heart's desire, or whatever you choose to call it (they're all the same thing). When your life is on course with its purpose, you are your most powerful. And you may stumble, but you will not fall.

I know for sure that in every challenging experience there's an opportunity to grow, enhance your life, or learn something invaluable about yourself. Every challenge can make you stronger if you allow it. Strength multiplied = power. For real.

Oprah

■

149

Breathing Space

SUNSET AT ALDABRA ATOLL, SEYCHELLES, INDIAN OCEAN, 2005
Photograph by Stuart Westmorland

DATING/ MATING/ RELATING

couples

154 THE TANGO CHALLENGE | BY MARISA SILVER

157 TERRA INCOGNITA: THE MALE BRAIN | BY CAROL MITHERS

159 WITH THIS RAGE, I THEE WED | BY KIM BARNES

162 HOW TO MAKE THE ROMANCE LAST | BY HELEN FISHER, PhD

163 CUPS OF MEN | BY HEATHER SELLERS

166 SHE'S SO FINE! | BY MARY A. FISCHER

The Tango Challenge

He leads? She follows? Not in **Marisa Silver's** house. But one little dance lesson wouldn't unbalance a blissfully equal relationship…would it?

I was not raised to be a follower.

I was a child in the '70s, in New York City, raised smack in the eye of the feminist storm. My mother was a trailblazer in her work, succeeding in a field in which, at that time, few women had. I went to an all-girls' school that was the antithesis of a finishing school. Far from being tidied and made marriageable, we were wild haired and brazen, clomping around in Frye boots. We studied Mary Wollstonecraft and *The Communist Manifesto,* which, for reasons still obscure, we were made to read nearly every year. We were

taught to have a voice and to use it. There was no implied limit on what we were expected to achieve simply because we were girls. In the ninth grade, I asked a friend of mine what she wanted to "be" when she grew up. "A mother," she replied. I was speechless.

The only capitulation made to any sort of latent social convention was when I was sent to dancing school. The justification was that between my school and my house full of sisters, I was at risk of having no contact with boys whatsoever. Every week I would put on a dress, unscrew a carton of L'eggs, struggle into a dirty pair of white gloves, and take the bus to the Pierre hotel. There, in the ornate ballroom, I would curtsy to the dance instructor and wait to be asked to dance by one or another blazered boys'-school boy. It was horrible, the waiting. Humiliating. I was never first picked. Nor second, nor tenth. More often than not, I would not be asked at all but would be forced, by the pitiless dance teacher, into the arms of some short, sweaty-palmed leftover. We would dutifully execute the boxy waltz or the slightly more jazzy, if anachronistic, fox-trot, always placing the required imaginary body width between us. The teacher encouraged us to make conversation. "So, what grade are you in?" I'd say, launching a brilliant opening gambit. Invariably, my partner was looking over my higher shoulder to see what he was missing.

I hadn't taken a dance class in 30 years when my husband and I entered the tango classroom in Buenos Aires for our inaugural tango lesson. Wearing our sexless American running shoes and loose-fitting jeans, we opened the door to a room filled with three-inch heels and polished brogans. The women wore tight-fitting dresses that flared out at the waist for maximum spin effect. The men wore slim pants and dress shirts, their figures knifelike and precise. The diminutive teacher had a dancer's carriage as she swanned over and looked us up and down. "Your shoes, they will stick," she announced unhappily.

The evening before, we'd been to a *milonga*—one of the many dances around town where regular folk showed up at midnight on any given weekday. I watched, fascinated, as couples moved about the floor, their feet interleaving like a well-shuffled deck of cards, their hips swiveling, their arms raised and frozen as if these limbs were ignorant of the excitement going on below. Couples were stout and slim, clunky and garish—none of them as glamorous or beautiful as the professional dancers we'd seen on another night at a Vegas-style professional tango show. A woman whose legs were poured into gold lamé tights brushed up against another dressed like a conservative grandmother. The men, hair slicked back, redolent with cologne, wore jackets and unmatched slacks. But despite their shabbier appearance, these dancers shared something with their more polished counterparts; they all looked like they were going to murder someone. Couples danced without speaking, their gazes off in the middle distance, their expressions grim and determined. Nothing in their faces communicated the erotic knowingness of

The dance was electric— it was about danger and power and sex.

their ritualized movements. It was no wonder that tango had begun in the bordellos of Buenos Aires. The dance was electric, poised and suggestive all at once. It was about danger and power and sex.

"Hey. We can do that!" I said to my husband excitedly. "I went to dancing school!"

Our instructor demonstrated the basic tango step, put us in a corner, so as not to upset the other more fluent dancers, and told us to practice. Dutifully, we did, counting the eight counts out loud, congratulating each other when we had successfully completed a round. We held ourselves apart from each other, staring down at our feet, as if they were wayward children who might run out of the room if we did not keep a close eye on them. Feeling confident, we called the instructor over and demonstrated our prowess. She nodded with approval and showed us the next step, a slightly more complicated variation that would move us not just in a circle but along the dance floor. I had visions of us at a *milonga,* gracefully sweeping around the room, as adept as New York taxi drivers at weaving in and out among the other couples, our private dance part of a larger tango ballet. Again, we counted, corrected each other gently, and mastered this second step enough to be shown the third, which, thrillingly, included a little hip swivel and a coquettish leg kick on my part. We were on our way.

"Okay," our instructor said once we had polished off the third step. "Now you dance."

Heads down, lips moving, we started with our first step. Satisfied, we made the joint decision to try a few rounds of the second step. When we'd accomplished this, we instructed each other to work on the third. This went on for a while, until it was obvious to us that something was terribly wrong. Why were we not twirling around the floor in fluid synchronicity like the other dancers in the class? Why did we look like a couple of kids from my long-ago days at the Pierre?

"You have to join the steps," our instructor told us, taking my chin in hand and lifting it so that I looked past my husband's shoulders, taking my husband's arm and placing it more firmly around my back.

"But how do we know which steps to do? How do we know when to change?" I said.

"Chest intention."

"Best intentions?"

"Chest intention."

My husband and I were flummoxed. My chest's intentions and my intentions for my chest diverged sharply after nursing two children. My husband—well, he has a lovely chest, but his extra-curriculars run to playing the piano, not to more and more hours at the gym. Our instructor reached up and placed a hand between the shoulder blades of each of our backs and pushed. That imaginary dancer standing between us drew his last breath.

"His chest speaks to you. It is his heart, yes? It tells you what to do. It makes you go where he wants you to go. Your chest listens. Yes?"

In this moment, despite our apt-pupil diligence and our surpassing ability to count to eight over and over again, my husband and I knew we were being challenged at our cores. He would tell me what to do? I would happily surrender to his lead? Every knee-jerk instinct in my body rebelled at the idea of being pushed around against my will. My husband's instincts faltered because it is not in his nature to order anyone around. In his work he is, in fact, a leader. But it would never occur to him to use his authority in a heavy-handed way. He leads by inclusion, by gathering in people and their ideas. It is not a strategy. It is a genuine outgrowth of a kind and generous and emancipated personality. Our relationship is built, in part, on the acceptance of these aspects of our separate characters.

But now, in a basement dance hall in a barrio in Buenos Aires, I found myself calling our dynamic into question. The orthodox feminism I was reared on had become more nuanced over the years. I could have babies and wear feminine clothing, concern myself with issues both frivolous and weighty, and still be taken seriously in conversation and in my work. So, what was so wrong with being led around a dance floor? I watched as my instructor and her male counterpart demonstrated the dance for us. She was nothing if not powerful and in control. You would never know that she was being told what to do by the subtle press of her partner's chest. Would it be better, sexier even, if my husband and I could conform to more traditional roles? Just for one dance? Would it be...dare I say it...a thrill? Were we forever trapped because I read *Mother Jones* when

It takes two: Marisa Silver with her husband, Ken Kwapis.

I was 14 and he read about Gandhi?

"So," I said to my husband when our instructor had moved off to more able couples, "I guess you're supposed to tell me what to do."

"With my chest," he said.

"With your chest."

"Intentionally."

"Right."

It was a comedy. I'd feel him press against me and I'd move in the direction I thought he wanted me to go, try to execute the step I thought he wanted us to do, and he'd move the opposite way. Suddenly, our sneakers were sticking to the floor, our feet were tangled, and where we had been moderately adept in our practice rounds, we were now utterly awkward.

"We can do this," I said, determined. "You just have to push me around more."

"I am," he said.

"I can't tell."

"I'm doing it. But you have to follow."

"I am."

"You're not. You're pulling me the other way."

"Okay. Let's try again."

The music ended. The instructor clapped her hands. Blessedly, the class was over. If it had gone on any longer, it would have become the dance version of couple's therapy. My husband and I looked at each other, accepting the fact that we had failed to achieve any tango mojo whatsoever. We stumbled outside into the vibrant Buenos Aires night. We laughed, we berated ourselves, we took care of each other's bruised egos. We even casually toyed with the idea of taking more classes when we were back home. But we both knew that somehow, in the hurly-burly of kids and work and the stuff of our lives, this wouldn't happen. And there was something else we both knew, something that, for better or worse, our brush with tango confirmed:

As a couple, we don't lead and follow. We stumble forward together. It is not always clear, and only very rarely elegant. After many years of marriage, our journey does not often resemble a well-oiled dance but more the path made by a Seussian machine that rattles side to side and somehow inches forward. It's our particular dance. We're pretty good at it. We do it in sneakers. ◐

> As a couple, we don't lead and follow. We stumble forward together.

Terra Incognita
The Male Brain

Is he truly incapable of putting down the toilet seat? Can he really have passionate sex and not even think about calling you again? **Carol Mithers** goes exploring for answers.

The more science learns about how men are different from us (right down to the structure of their brains), the more we find ourselves hoping it will finally explain some age-old mysteries. For instance:

Why do men tend to keep their cars spotless but live like pigs at home—while for women it's the other way around?

According to Simon Baron-Cohen, PhD, author of *The Essential Difference: Male and Female Brains and the Truth About Autism,* men's neurological wiring tends to make them better at systems, while women are superiorly rigged for empathy. Which could help explain why—although the culture is changing—guys still take such pride in their machines, while women often care more about maintaining a clean home. Another clue comes from a 2007 study (conducted for BMW by a British team that included Oxford psychologists), which found that male drivers actually view their cars as extensions of themselves. Women, whose self-image is tied more directly to their bodies, are likely to think of their vehicles as separate entities, the authors suggest. But because men are less tuned-in to their bodies, they easily project their identity onto an object. If only that object were a sink full of dirty dishes.

Why do men like to watch violent sports, while a good number of women would rather do just about anything else?

The truth is, football has a lot of female fans (44.3 million women watched the 2009 Super Bowl, for example). But guys are drawn to football (and boxing and wrestling) in ways that women aren't. Men tend to be more aggressive, says Lucy L. Brown, PhD, a professor in the departments of neurology and neuroscience at Einstein College of Medicine in New York City. The difference likely involves hormones (like testosterone) and sensitivities to those hormones in parts of the brain such as the hypothalamus—which, in animals, is associated with aggression. Fine, but does he really have to shriek "Kill him!" when the other team's quarterback is about to get sacked? Yes, he does: If you're a guy, watching your team win increases testosterone levels, according to a 1998 study in *Physiology & Behavior.* Viewing combative sports also helps men identify with traditional ideals of masculinity like domination, risk taking, and competition, explains Douglas Hartmann, PhD, associate professor of sociology at the University of Minnesota. "In fact," he says, "the less physically competitive his daily life is, the more sports can become a means toward achieving those ideals, at least in his mind."

Why can a man enthusiastically (very enthusiastically) sleep with a woman he knows he'll never see again?

Well, there's the old Evolution Did It theory: Men are hardwired to spread their seed; women, to find a mate who will protect the children she may bear. Physical differences may play a role, too. According to Lisa Diamond, PhD, an associate professor of psychology and gender studies at the University of Utah, not only do female rats have more extensive brain circuits for oxytocin—which helps mammals to bond—than males but in humans, women show greater release of the neurochemical during sex (especially orgasm) than men. Also, biological anthropologist and Rutgers University professor Helen Fisher, PhD, notes: "The two brain hemispheres are less well connected in men than in women. This gives men the ability to focus on one thing at a time and be very goal oriented, whereas the female brain is built to assimilate many feelings at once, and to connect sex and love much more rapidly." Interesting, plausible theories all, but Lucy Brown cautions that we're still really just guessing. And in the end, the fact that men forever remain a bit of a mystery may be part of what keeps us intrigued. ◐

> Because men are less tuned-in to their bodies, they easily project their identity onto an object. If only that object were a sink full of dirty dishes.

With This Rage, I Thee Wed

When is a marriage troubled, and when is it fatally flawed? Kim Barnes looks back on her husband's temper— and their journey to a more perfect union.

I was sitting at the wine bar with a friend—I'll call her Lacey—who was considering divorcing her second husband, having recently discovered his stash of hard-core porn. "I know that no man's a saint," she said, "but I can't live with lechery."

That takes care of lust, I thought, and made a mental note. Although I hadn't told Lacey, I had a little project going—involving a question I'd been challenging other friends to answer: Given that no person and no marriage is perfect, if you could pick your mate's flaw—the one flaw you could live with—what would it be? Nothing so slight as socks on the floor or a residual jones for Pac-Man. I meant the things we keep hidden from even our closest confidants, the things that can prove fatal to a marriage: lust, gluttony, greed, sloth, envy, wrath, and pride. So far, none of my

friends had been able to pick a "best" flaw; all they'd managed to do was rule out the worst.

"I'd rather die," willowy Meg had said, "than be married to a glutton."

Greed? "Cross it off," Theresa snapped, then hesitated when I suggested pride. "Pride is why my husband left *me,*" she said. "I could never admit I was wrong."

Now, at the wine bar, Lacey sipped and sighed. "I want a husband like yours," she told me. "Someone who reads me love poems over breakfast."

I just smiled. After 26 years, Bob and I do still spend summer days as we did the July we got married: camping along Northwest rivers, fly-fishing, drinking Champagne. The demands of our professional lives (both of us are writers and teachers), the rigors of child rearing, the empty nest we are fluffing, cross-country moves, money woes—the pressures that so often destroy a marriage, ours has survived. To Lacey, it seemed a storybook romance. What she didn't know was how close I had come to leaving the marriage she idealized. I'd never told her the flaw I'd chosen—that Bob was a wrathful man.

When I met Bob, I was 22. He was seven years older, seven inches taller, and I was enthralled by his intellect, his passion, his hair (oh, his hair! dark, thick like an animal's fur, hanging down in his eyes, curling at his collar…). He'd sung in a rock band, been a conscientious objector during Vietnam, and was now a talented poet and teacher. I watched him weep over the death of John Lennon and rail against wrong-minded politicians. And soon after we moved in together, I got my first glimpse of his rage.

The lawn sprinkler that failed to oscillate? Bob beat it into the ground, gaskets flying. The chain saw that wouldn't run, he pitched against a tree until it snapped into pieces. I laughed when I recounted these slapstick incidents to friends. Who was he hurting, after all?

I was 25 when Bob asked me to marry him. Moderate in his consumption, balanced in his ambition, kind to my parents, and lustful only for me: If an occasional temper tantrum was his only flaw, I should count myself lucky.

But one afternoon the summer we married, Bob and I were driving back from the store when we found ourselves behind an elderly woman at a traffic light. She hesitated, not sure if she wanted to turn left or right. Bob grimly rode her bumper. "Get off the road, you old bag!" As we roared by, he flipped her off; on her face was a mix of befuddlement and fear.

I sat stunned. Outraged. Speechless. Silently fuming.

"What's wrong?" Bob asked, truly curious.

It wasn't right, I said, how he had treated that woman.

"But she couldn't hear me."

"But I could." I held my hand to my heart. "And it hurt."

Over the next year, Bob's outbursts became more frequent, until one morning, in the middle of an argument whose subject neither of us remembers, he picked up the wooden table at which we were eating breakfast and brought it down so hard it shattered. I backed to the wall. Mouth twisted, Bob grabbed my arms. "Why are you making me do this?" he said through clenched teeth. I shook my head, unable to make sense of the question, afraid to attempt an answer.

Trying to talk it out only made things worse. Bob insisted that I was

the one being unreasonable. I'd never seen anyone so enraged, but now I wondered: *Were* my expectations unfair? I'd been raised in a family of stoics, after all, and my upbringing was defined by suppressed emotion. But surely I had enough objectivity, enough perspective, to know that busting out a window with your bare knuckles—or kicking a hole in a wall, or denting the car hood with your fist—wasn't standard behavior. And I was beginning to fear that he might turn his rage on me.

I wanted to tell someone about Bob's anger, so someone could tell me what I should do. But who could I tell, and how would I? My friends and family loved Bob for the same reasons I did: his wit, his honesty, his compassion, his loyalty. And those same people had an equally firm sense of me: that I was a strong-minded woman who would never allow herself to be intimidated. Safer to remain silent than to risk their judgment and doubt. *It will get better,* I assured myself. What I really meant, though, was *I will get better.* If Bob's paying the bills incited a loud invective against the obscenity of money, then I would pay the bills. If raising my voice brought out the bully in him, then I would keep my mouth shut.

A few months after our fourth anniversary, our daughter was born; her brother, two years later. Raising children raised the stakes. Waiting in line at a McDonald's drive-through made Bob furious. His rage was like a sudden squall—I spent my energy keeping his anger from swamping us all. Our children sometimes laughed at his tirades, sometimes cowered, and as they grew into adolescents, they often rolled their eyes—even as I worked to hide my increasing fear that I was staying in a marriage I was simply too proud to leave. Torn between self-doubt and shame, I kept on keeping my secret, though I still longed for someone to tell me: How would I know when it had gone too far?

The answer came one day as Bob and I were driving down the highway to the hardware store. I was fretting, imagining the minor mishap that would turn our little jaunt into hell on wheels (a flat tire, someone's badly parked car, an inept clerk), and wondering aloud if I should have just stayed home. I had become that little old woman at the light, unsure of which way to turn.

Suddenly Bob hit the brakes, cranked a U-turn, and brought us to a sliding stop, cursing my indecision so cruelly that I sat paralyzed, afraid he might gun the car back onto the highway.

Back home, I gave him an ultimatum: See a counselor, or our marriage was over.

> I gave him an ultimatum: See a counselor, or our marriage was over.

And maybe this is the difference between a flaw and a fatal flaw. Even though it meant exposing his failures, Bob chose to keep our marriage alive. We made appointments separately and together. Talking to the therapist filled me with dread: dread that the problem was not Bob's temper but my own prideful expectations; dread that I was betraying him; dread that I had allowed myself to be victimized; dread that we were broken and could not be fixed.

"You can save this marriage," the therapist told us, "but you've got to understand what's causing the problem." She explained that when caught in conflict, the brain releases adrenaline and cortisol, inducing the fight-or-flight response. Never one to turn tail and run, Bob chose to bully the world into submission. But when I was the one who defied him, he felt the conflict as rejection. His terror then led him to rage at the very person he feared losing: me.

It wasn't easy for Bob to accept that the anger that puffed him with strength was a shield against vulnerability, or that each act of physical and verbal violence was an indirect threat against me.

Along with assigned readings and exercises, the therapist gave Bob a palm-sized thermometer. "When you rage," she said, "blood is diverted from your extremities to your vital organs, and your fingers turn cold. Count to ten. Focus on calming down, letting your hands warm up by degrees. Make it a habit. Practice."

It's been more than a decade since that initial appointment. At first, when his temper flared, Bob would grasp the thermometer, take a deep breath. "I'm getting better, aren't I?" he'd ask, and he was. He discovered other ways to engage his daily frustrations: taking long walks, imagining that the driver in front of him was someone he loved, remembering that he wanted nothing in the world to frighten me, least of all him.

My change, too, came by degrees, first by revealing

The author and her husband camping in Oregon, 1984, and at home in Idaho, 2005.

Bob's rages to the therapist and then to a few close friends. "There's so much good in Bob," some of them told me. "He wants to do better. That's what makes the difference." Another friend said, "I'd have left him years ago." Later she would confess that she, too, was given to rages, a secret shame that made her sure she could never be wholly loved.

And so, as I sat in the wine bar, listening to Lacey mourn the impending loss of her second marriage, I posed my query, reminding her that she'd already eliminated lust. She twirled the glass in her fingers. "Not pride," she finally said. "My first husband hid his debt and drove us into bankruptcy. I didn't know until I got the call from the attorney. We lost everything. I couldn't live with the betrayal."

"You never told me that," I said.

"I never told anyone."

I've come to realize that you never know the secrets of someone else's marriage—but that when it comes to your own, it's better to break the silence before the silence breaks you. I couldn't hear the truth until I gave it voice, and neither could Bob. By reaching out for help, we chose to leave the isolated island of shame and blame and hitch ourselves to something truer than a perfect marriage: a union defined by our desire to grow beyond our flaws. Today Bob's rages are a thing of the past, the occasional tremors like the fading aftershocks of an earthquake (and my zero-tolerance policy proof of my own shored-up foundation). Still, when Lacey turned the tables on me—"What flaw would *you* choose?"—I didn't give it a second thought.

"Anything but wrath."

And then I told her why. What I saw in her face was disappointment and relief: My marriage wasn't so perfect after all, yet somehow it had survived. Could she, should she allow her soon-to-be ex a chance to redeem himself?

I didn't have an answer, only an ear. ◖

How to Make the Romance Last

The truth about what keeps marriages together. By Helen Fisher, PhD

I have a friend who met her husband at a red light. She was 15, in a car with a pile of girls. He was in another car with a crowd of boys. As the light turned green, they all decided to pull into a nearby park and party. My friend spent the evening sitting on a picnic table talking to one of the guys. Thirty-seven years later, they are still together.

We are born to love. That feeling of elation that we call romantic love is deeply embedded in our brains. But can it last? This was what my colleagues and I set out to discover in 2007. Led by Bianca Acevedo, PhD, our team asked this question of nearly everyone we met, searching for people who said they were still wild

about their longtime spouse. Eventually we scanned the brains of 17 such people as they looked at a photograph of their sweetheart. Most were in their 50s and married an average of 21 years.

The results were astonishing. Psychologists maintain that the dizzying feeling of intense romantic love lasts only about 18 months to—at best—three years. Yet the brains of these middle-aged men and women showed much the same activity as those of young lovers, individuals who had been intensely in love an average of only seven months. Indeed, there was just one important difference between the two groups: Among the older lovers, brain regions associated with anxiety were no longer active; instead, there was activity in the areas associated with calmness.

We are told that happy marriages are based on good communication, shared values, a sturdy support system of friends and relatives, happy, stable childhoods, fair quarrelling, and dogged determination. But in a survey of 470 studies on compatibility, psychologist Marcel Zentner, PhD, of the University of Geneva, found no particular combination of personality traits that leads to sustained romance—with one exception: the ability to sustain your "positive illusions." Men and women who continue to maintain that their partner is attractive, funny, kind, and ideal for them in just about every way remain content with each other. I've seen this phenomenon, known as "love blindness," in a friend of mine. I knew him and his wife-to-be while we were all in college, when they both were slim, fit, energetic, and curious: a vibrant couple. Today both are overweight couch potatoes. Yet he still tells me that she hasn't changed a bit. Perhaps this form of self-deception is a gift from nature, enabling us to triumph over the rough spots and the changes in our relationships. I'm not suggesting you should overlook an abusive husband or put up with a deadbeat bore. But it's worth celebrating one of nature's best-kept secrets: our human capacity to love…and love…and love. ◑

Cups of Men

How many coffee dates with strangers does it take to find one great love? **Heather Sellers** on being alone, being together—and the bravado of the lonesome man.

ne hundred cups of coffee with 100 men.

I got the idea from a lawyer friend, who married a handsome furniture-maker in Maine, a man who owned more books than she did. "Sometimes," she said, "I met three a day. You only need 15 minutes." It took her two months. She quickly lost count.

After six months, I am at four.

We meet in a coffee shop parking lot. He springs out of his enormous red convertible, more like a boat than a car, and thrusts into my hands a fat library book. He looks ten years older than his photo and roughened, like someone has taken the smooth young version he posted and rubbed sandpaper over it. I stare at the book he's handed me, turn it over. It is a book of ideas and complaint. He is ranging

around the parking lot on foot—big loops. Why is he ranging around the parking lot? Why am I holding a fat library book? "Finally," he says, rovering up to me, beaming. "Finally someone in this godforsaken place gets me." I kneel down, set the book on the pavement, pretend to tie my shoe.

The next man wants to go out again. I tell him about the coffees. He wants to know what number he is. "I want the T-shirt," he says. "Number X, with the cup, you know. That's what I want." He pats his front. He says he wants to be 99. He, too, has books, paperbacks in his backpack. Two backpacks. One is his office.

I feel so bad for all of them. The man with a part in a play who could talk of nothing but the play. The play is his life. Both will start soon. The man in white knee-socks and black sneakers who chose a coffee shop across from the mental institution. It was very distracting. The whole time he talked, I kept trying not to think he'd come from across the street on a pass. Then, when I

■

163

talked, at the end, I felt as if I was the one on the pass.

The chef/Hemingway aficionado/sea captain (age 53, two kids at home, blue eyes) who said he would be divorced but the economy was really bad and he couldn't do that to his wife just yet. She had a boyfriend. He was excited about dating.

It's like going to the pound and I am a nice dog from some other pound.

I felt afraid one time. He yelled, stood, holding his coffee aloft in the Buzzatorium, "I'm not a loser! I'm not a loser! I do not think I'm a loser!"

I feel forensic. I feel I should be getting paid, because this feels hard, like a job, all these coffees. And I have to get specifically dressed for it and leave my house.

They behave as though on job interviews or in sales positions, leaning forward, pitching. Maybe it's the caffeine, but the men *do not shut up*. Not nervous-talky, like a girl gets, but sales-talky, rushed, forceful, boasty. They have a few prepared questions, but they aren't wanting the information. They're checking boxes off. *Asks questions*. I'm talkative, and I can't get a word in edgewise. They talk for 30 minutes and I wonder how my friend kept it to 15. She lives in New York. In the Midwest, everything is slower. I listen too much. I need exit strategies. I need less hope. In the Midwest, we're shadowed by hope, enveloped by it.

Part of me wants them to keep talking; it's similar to reading a mediocre novel. I know I'll never finish, but I can't quite put it down. I know it won't get better. Can it get worse?

When I stand up to say goodbye, the men say, as people do when they've felt listened to, "Wow. You are a great conversationalist."

My friends are married people and stunned. "Why are you doing this?" "I could never do it." We say this same thing about tragedy, as though we have a choice. About wheelchairs and Down syndrome babies and cancer and missing limbs. Looking for love isn't a tragedy or a defect. It's a situation.

I'm doing this because I've been divorced three years and I haven't had a single date. No one has asked me out. I called the single father on my street before Christmas and asked him to go out for a drink. He said he didn't have any money right now.

My friends think I am trying too hard. "Stop trying and then it will happen!" "When you give up, that is when it will happen." They think I am so happy alone and I will not admit it. They have also suggested my standards are too low (the mechanic/hunter/libertarian who cursed in every single sentence he uttered) and too high (the baker who

was thrilled to talk about gluten-free, who compared my body to that of a supermodel's. Whom I didn't want to see again—he had so many kids, a long commute, and byzantine ice hockey commitments).

My friends claim they can't imagine dating. If their husbands die, they say, they will make it alone. They pat their mates when they say this. They seem not madly in love but madly in small vague terror. I am helping them remember the good parts of marriage after a long, crabby day.

It's funny to me how many of the divorced men from match.com say to me in conversation, "my wife." How much they talk about the lives from which they have been fired. As though I am a babysitter, guy, shrink, or nice wall.

Fed up with men's ads "seeking women age 18–[one year younger than whatever age they are]," I change my profile. I say I am looking for a man age range 18–41; I'm 42 years old. But my friend who met the furnituremaker says it isn't funny. You can't sound bitter, she says. You can't make a commentary; this isn't the time to make a point.

My friend Ellen met three gorgeous millionaires on match.com. All wanted to study Buddhism with her and ride bikes with her; she picked the cyclist from Italy, who is ten years younger and crazy in love with her. "It's not like dating in your 20s," she told me. She says I need to be in my 50s to really do this right. "You're at just the wrong age," she said.

I do not know if dating in my 20s was like dating in my 20s. I was pretending to be a person similar to myself. The pretend person was much better and much worse than my true self. I had no real beliefs.

Almost a year later, I've made it to a couple of dozen.

Number 31 has, he says, simplified his life. "So tell me your life story in 20 words or less," he says, and I do, and he talks for the next 25 minutes, leaning forward, elbows on the table: his financial statement, his business plan, his recovery program, four children, his "wife." A man pushing an empty wheelchair can't get past our table. My coffee date doesn't see this, because it is taking place behind him and he is talking to me about the $3 million house in Aspen and how it's good he doesn't have it anymore. I stand up, pull the table a bit. The coffee date sees how, moves chairs. The man pushing the wheelchair still struggles. The chair is like a prop—something he has never seen before, much less used. Finally, he gets past us.

"Do you mind getting the door?" he says to my coffee date. My coffee date rushes to the door, gallant. "And the next door?" I hear the wheelchair pusher say. They disappear into the foyer. They're gone a long, long time. I sip my water.

I finish my salad. I enjoy the time alone. I am thinking: *I can't keep doing this. I want to slip out. I do not want to be rude.*

"People are strange," he says when he comes back. The man with the wheelchair kept asking him to open doors. "He didn't really seem to be going anywhere."

One coffee lasted all winter, and how happy I was on the weekends, playing all that backgammon and keeping score and naming things funny names that meant something to us, skiing, then hunting morels and reading *The Reivers* aloud to each other every night.

It's very distracting, a loved person, and it makes the planet manageable. The planet, which is so large and lonely and blue, and also hurtling through dark empty space. All of which you can feel when you are alone.

I'm not un-whole. I'm not half a person. But being with someone is energizing and relaxing, the opposite of coffee. It organizes me. The doubleness amplifies things, but in a way called *softening*.

I love having a boyfriend. Men are not like cars or pets — the opposite. But having a man in one's life is like having a car in America — easier. A home without a man in it? It gets a little museum-ish. Not bad. Beautiful, and very very very still. Stewarded only by a woman, objects, life, can get weird to the touch, overly pristine.

Like most plans, the plan is pretend. I do *not* want a hundred cups of coffee, a hundred men. I do not want coffee. I do not want the wrong man. I do not want to be alone. Yesterday, I doubled down, one at lunch, one at 4 o'clock in the afternoon. Today I am sick in my bed, a summer cold, hell.

Especially good to do with someone one is sleeping with at night: the grocery store, swimming in open water (inside water better alone), dog-walking, talking about the friends, practicing foreign languages, thinking about houses, riding bikes, breakfast. Coffee in bed.

Sometimes I feel like a priest, hearing these men confess their lives and wives. Sometimes I feel like an officer of something, like the town of single people. Sometimes I feel like an ambulance chaser, gaping at their stories.

One day I get a trifecta of bad news — my family, my regular life, so many things can go horribly wrong. I call my ex-husband. Dave and I are divorced, but we are terrible divorced people; we are friendly and helpful and un-mad. We meet at the neighborhood

bar, a place I can cry in if need be. Eight, nine years ago, I met this man, my ex-husband now, on match.com. He wrote, "I do not know if I could keep up with you, but I would enjoy trying." He was the only person I went out with. He was the only person I married.

Then a woman comes in and I recognize her voice; she's a colleague, Joy. I haven't met her boyfriend, and I am happy to now. I introduce my ex, Dave. I happen to know she met her boyfriend on match.com. This was years ago. They settle in next to me, happily, and order four appetizers and begin playing the game at the bar, little cards with embarrassing questions.

Then my friend Ellen comes in. With her online boyfriend in tow. We hug and carry on. Introductions all around. We sit at the bar facing forward and drink our drinks, man woman, woman man, man woman. I whisper to Dave, "Everyone at this bar met online. Match.com." He gives me a shocked look. I finish my martini.

Once, I told someone I was the first match.com divorce. They were stunned and curious. I was just kidding. I'm sure there were others, before me.

Back then, you posted one photo. It scrolled down so slowly, like a creaky roller blind. He was the first person who wrote me. I wrote him back before his photo finished unrolling. I wrote him back while his forehead was still arriving. He was great right away.

I don't think we look or don't look for love; the heart is a receptor, always working. In spite of our best efforts to protect or hide it. Love looks for us, regardless of how we orient ourselves.

All the coffees have pulled me into human presence, out of myself. The coffees are like Empathy Boot Camp. The coffees remind me of short stories I can't stop thinking about. I have heard 41 stories of actual lives: lives bungled, misrepresented, frayed, lit by moments of luck or beauty. Lives a lot like my own life. Raw like this, pitched toward me, hope unclenched. I've mostly wanted to run away. I do not even drink coffee. I drink water.

So I am moving through these coffee shops, Leaf and Bean, Beaners, Cuppe Diem, carefully, a strong, clear woman, cool water. I can't help listening to each man with my heart. Sometimes I think men mistake women for nature. But with each sip, I'm closer, I know I am closer, to finding the place in me where love given comes from. And how it is.

Sweet little mysterious sip by sip.... ◧

Looking for love isn't a tragedy or a defect. It's a situation.

She's So Fine!

Cynthia Nixon did it. Lindsay Lohan did it. TV shows are based on it. Is it our imaginations, or are wives and girlfriends ditching their men and falling in love with other women? New science says that sexuality is more fluid than we thought. Mary A. Fischer gets the details.

At a Halloween party in October of 2008, Macarena Gomez-Barris, dressed as a flamenco dancer, put out a bowl of her homemade guacamole and checked on the boiling pot of fresh corn in the kitchen. She'd recently separated from her husband of 12 years, and the friends streaming in now were eager to meet her new love, who, on this night, was the pirate in the three-cornered hat carving pumpkins outside. After her marriage broke up in 2007, few of those who knew Gomez-Barris had thought she'd be single for long—"a catch," they called her—and they were right.

An animated 38-year-old, Gomez-Barris seemed to have it all—a brilliant career, two children, striking looks. Her family had come to the United States from Chile when she was 2 to escape Augusto Pinochet's military dictatorship and to pursue the traditional American dream. While studying for her master's degree at UC Berkeley, she met a charismatic Chilean exile and fiction writer named Roberto Leni at a salsa club in San Francisco. "We had instant chemistry, and he was my soul mate," Gomez-Barris says. They married and eight years later had their first child, a son.

The trouble began after they moved to Los Angeles, where their daughter was born and Gomez-Barris's academic career took off at the University of Southern California. Leni spent his days caring for the house and children. "I was in the more powerful role," says Gomez-Barris, a PhD and an assistant professor in the sociology and American studies and ethnicity departments. "I made more money and was struggling to balance my work and home life."

"Immersed," is how Leni puts it. "She lived and breathed USC. All her friends were professors, and eventually I was obsolete. I'm nothing the system considers I should be as a traditional man. I'm not ambitious. I don't care that much about money. I was brought up among torture survivors, and the most important values were in the emotional realm of human experience, to soothe and support."

His noble ideals unfortunately clashed with day-to-day realities. "Someone had to care about making money to support our family," says Gomez-Barris. Despite efforts to save their relationship in counseling, they ended up separating.

Single again at 36, Gomez-Barris dated a few men, none seriously. "They were not so sure of themselves in their careers or financially," she says. "It was a time of real exploration and personal independence, and I became very rational about the kind of partner I wanted and

Macarena Gomez-Barris (*left*) was married 12 years before falling for colleague Judith "Jack" Halberstam.

needed"—someone, she hoped, who would match her intellectual ambitions but also take care of her and her children.

At a party one night in March 2008, Gomez-Barris ran into Judith Halberstam, PhD, a professor of English, American studies and ethnicity, and gender studies at USC. They had met in 2004 and admired each other's scholarly accomplishments, occasionally finding themselves at the same campus parties.

But while they shared an affinity for politics and social justice, they were seemingly miles apart in their private lives. Halberstam, nearly ten years her senior, was openly gay.

That night, Halberstam, who had also broken up with a partner of 12 years, spotted Gomez-Barris standing across the room and thought, *Now, there's a really beautiful woman.* "I saw her differently then and developed a big crush on her," says Halberstam. "Yet it made me nervous, given that I have a history of unrequited love with straight women. Then again, you don't choose who you love."

Gomez-Barris noticed that Halberstam was more attentive to her than usual, even flirtatious. "She got up and gave me the better seat, as if she wanted to take care of me. I was struck by that," she says. A few weeks later, Halberstam suggested they go out for dinner, and again, Gomez-Barris was impressed by qualities she liked. "She chose a Japanese restaurant, made reservations, picked me up at my place—on time. I felt attracted to her energy, her charisma. I was enticed. And she paid the bill. Just the gesture was sexy. She took initiative and was the most take-charge person I'd ever met."

Intrigued as Gomez-Barris was, it still never occurred to her that they would be anything more than friends. While she'd been attracted to women at times, she assumed she would eventually fall in love with another man. "I was still inscribed in a heterosexual framework that said only a man could provide for my kids and be part of a family," she says.

On a warm spring night in Malibu, after attending a film screening together, Gomez-Barris and Halberstam walked on the beach, a beautiful pink sunset rounding out a perfect evening. They kicked off their shoes and ran, laughing, through the rising tide. "At that point, things were charged with sex," Gomez-Barris remembers. Her feelings deepened, and not long afterward, they became lovers. "It was great, and it felt comfortable," she says of the night they first became intimate. "What blew me away was that afterward, Judith held me to her chest. So I got passion, intimacy, and sweetness. And I thought, *Maybe I can get all the things I want now.*"

Lately, a new kind of sisterly love seems to be in the air. In the past few years, *Sex and the City*'s Cynthia Nixon left a boyfriend after a decade and a half and started dating a woman (and talked openly about it). Actress Lindsay Lohan and DJ Samantha Ronson flaunted their relationship from New York to Dubai. Katy Perry's song "I Kissed a Girl" topped the charts. *The L Word, Work Out*, and *Top Chef* are featuring gay women on TV, and there's even talk of a lesbian reality show in the works. Certainly nothing is new about women having sex with women, but we've arrived at a moment in the popular culture when it all suddenly seems almost fashionable—or at least, acceptable.

Statistics on how many women have traded boyfriends and husbands for girlfriends are hard to come by. Although the U.S. Census Bureau keeps track of married, divorced, single, and even same-sex partners living together, it doesn't look for the stories behind those numbers. But experts like Binnie Klein, a Connecticut-based psychotherapist and lecturer in Yale's department of psychiatry, agree that alternative relationships are on the rise. "It's clear that a change in sexual orientation is imaginable to more people than ever before, and there's more opportunity—and acceptance—to cross over the line," says Klein, noting that a half-dozen of her married female patients in the past few years have fallen in love with women. "Most are afraid that if they don't go for it, they'll end up with regrets."

Feminist philosopher Susan Bordo, PhD, a professor of English and gender and women's studies at the University of Kentucky and author of *Unbearable Weight: Feminism, Western Culture, and the Body,* also agrees that in the current environment, more women may be stepping out of the conventional gender box. "When a taboo is lifted or diminished, it's going to leave people freer to pursue things," she says. "So it makes sense that we would see women, for all sorts of reasons, walking through that door now that the culture has cracked it open. Of course, we shouldn't imagine that we're living in a world where all sexual choices are possible. Just look at the cast of *The L Word* and it's clear that only a certain kind of lesbian—slim and elegant or butch in just the right androgynous way—is acceptable to mainstream culture."

That said, of the recent high-profile cases, it's Cynthia Nixon's down-to-earth attitude that may have blazed a trail for many women. In 1998, when *Sex and the City* debuted on HBO, she was settled in a long-term relationship with Danny Mozes, an English professor, with whom she had two children. They hadn't gotten married: "I was wary of it and felt like it was potentially a trap, so I steered clear of it," Nixon said in an interview with London's *Daily Mirror*. In 2004, after

> "I got passion, intimacy, and sweetness. And I thought, *Maybe I can get all the things I want now.*"

O ver the past several decades, scientists have struggled in fits and starts to get a handle on sexual orientation. Born or bred? Can it change during one's lifetime? A handful of studies in the 1990s, most of them focused on men, suggested that homosexuality is hardwired. In one study, researchers linked DNA markers in the Xq28 region of the X chromosome to gay males. But a subsequent larger study failed to replicate the results, leaving the American Academy of Pediatrics and the American Psychological Association to speculate that sexual orientation probably has multiple causes, including environmental, cognitive, and biological factors.

Today, however, a new line of research is beginning to approach sexual orientation as much less fixed than previously thought, especially when it comes to women. The idea that human sexuality forms a continuum has been around since 1948, when Alfred Kinsey introduced his famous seven-point scale, with 0 representing complete heterosexuality, 7 signifying complete homosexuality, and bisexuality in the middle, where many of the men and women he interviewed fell. The new buzz phrase coming out of contemporary studies is *sexual fluidity*. "People always ask me if this research means everyone is bisexual. No, it doesn't," says Lisa Diamond, PhD, associate professor of psychology and gender studies at the University of Utah and author of the 2008 book *Sexual Fluidity: Understanding Women's Love and Desire*. "Fluidity represents a capacity to respond erotically in unexpected ways due to particular situations or relationships. It doesn't appear to be something a woman can control." Furthermore, studies indicate that it's more prevalent in women than in men, according to Bonnie Zylbergold, assistant editor of *American Sexuality*, an online magazine.

In a 2004 landmark study at Northwestern University, the results were eye-opening. During the experiment, the female subjects became sexually aroused when they viewed heterosexual as well as lesbian erotic films. This was true for both gay and straight women. Among the male subjects, however, the straight men were turned on only by erotic films with women, the gay ones by those with men. "We found that women's sexual desire is less rigidly directed toward a particular sex, as compared with men's, and it's more changeable over time," says the study's senior researcher, J. Michael Bailey, PhD. "These findings likely represent a fundamental difference between men's and women's brains."

This idea, that the libido can wander back and forth between genders, Diamond admits, may be threatening and confusing to those with conventional beliefs about sexual orientation. But when the women she's inter-

ending her 15-year relationship with Mozes, Nixon began seeing Christine Marinoni, at the time a public school advocate whom she'd met while working on a campaign to reduce class sizes in New York City. Marinoni was a great support when the actress was diagnosed with breast cancer. Far from hiding the relationship, Nixon has spoken freely in TV and newspaper interviews about it not being a big deal. "I have been with men all my life and had never met a woman I had fallen in love with before," she told the *Daily Mirror*. "But when I did, it didn't seem so strange. It didn't change who I am. I'm just a woman who fell in love with a woman."

viewed explain their feelings, it doesn't sound so wild. Many of them say, for example, they are attracted to the person, and not the gender—moved by traits like kindness, intelligence, and humor, which could apply to a man or a woman. Most of all, they long for an emotional connection. And if that comes by way of a female instead of a male, the thrill may override whatever heterosexual orientation they had.

At the Sky Sport & Spa in Beverly Hills, Jackie Warner takes a break in her office between training sessions. Even at rest, the 40-year-old openly lesbian star of Bravo's reality show *Work Out* is charged with energy. Wearing a tight-fitting white T-shirt that shows off her defined arm muscles and sinewy body, she doesn't make small talk. And when she sits briefly for a conversation, she looks straight at me in a way that indicates she wants to get right down to business, while her mind races ahead to the 20 other items she's got at hand.

In early 2007 she got particularly close to one of the trainers she worked with on the show, Rebecca Cardon, 33. Cardon was straight and had a boyfriend, but when he left town for a couple of weeks she started spending a lot of time with Warner, and the two became inseparable. "Even after he came back, I preferred spending my time with her. I was like a starving animal," says Cardon, describing her hunger for connection. "I never had that with men. Jackie's intelligent, articulate, deep, fun, open-minded. We talked for hours. *This woman is my soul mate,* I thought. *She gets me.* I told her my darkest secrets, and she told me hers. We were very there for each other."

When sex came up, Cardon was hesitant at first. "I was scared about being that intimate and felt like a 12-year-old, very nervous," she says. "But afterward I thought, *Oh my God, this feels completely normal and not wrong.* The experience opened up my world and made me see how stuck I'd been." After three months, the two women drifted apart, although they remain good friends, and Cardon returned to dating men.

Meanwhile, with the show having completed its third season, Warner finds herself an unusual pinup girl. She gets hundreds of love letters and e-mails from straight women all over America (some posted on her Web site), and the refrains are similar: "I'm

married. I have never been attracted to another woman, but I have a huge crush on you." One entry in a social network group reads, "If Jackie hit on me, I'd definitely reconsider my sexuality." Other women offer to fly out and spring for her ($200 an hour) personal training sessions, hinting they'd like to have sex with her.

"Many of them are in the second part of their lives, their kids are grown, they're still in their sexual prime, and now they're looking to expand and have excitement," says Warner of her fans. "Also, these women are attracted to the masculinity in me. I'm physically strong. I succeed in business, and they see my confidence."

Ironically—or not, as some might argue—it is certain "masculine" qualities that draw many straight-labeled women to female partners; that, in combination with emotional connection, intimacy, and intensity. This was definitely true for Gomez-Barris, whose partner, Judith Halberstam, 47, says she has never felt "female." Growing up in England as a tomboy who had short hair and refused to wear dresses, Halberstam says people were often unable to figure out whether she was a boy or a girl: "I was a source of embarrassment for my family." As a teenager, she was an avid soccer player—not that she was allowed on any team. And her 13th birthday request for a punching bag and boxing gloves was met with the demand to pick something more feminine. "Throughout my youth," she says, "I felt rage at the shrinking of my world." Halberstam channeled her anger into a distinguished academic career and authored several provocative books, including, in 1998, *Female Masculinity*. It was during the past few years that she started calling herself Jack and answering to both "he" and "she."

"Men can't understand why I want to be with Jack, a lesbian, when I could be with a biological man," says Gomez-Barris. "And at first I thought it would be threatening, but I have a rebellious spirit. He's powerful, accomplished, and appealing. And in some ways, the experience is better than in heterosexual sex. Sex with most men is phallic-centered and revolves around intercourse, and that can be limiting and unsatisfying."

Bridget Falcon, 32, administrator of programs for Family Service of Greater New Orleans, grew up dating boys but felt a pull

> Certainly nothing is new about women having sex with women, but we've arrived at a moment in the popular culture when it seems acceptable.

toward women that ebbed and flowed. She remembers having fleeting crushes on girls in elementary school. And at the end of high school, while openly going out with a boy, she began seeing a girlfriend. "I enjoyed sex with men," she says, "but there was a lack of emotional intimacy with them, and I had cravings for female connection. Still, I was uncertain about my sexuality, trying to figure it out, which is why I was at first drawn to dykes. I liked their masculinity. When I went out, I wanted to be with someone who, unlike me, was secure in her gayness. There was no mistaking who I was. I'm the girly girl, the one who wears skirts, dresses, and makeup." By the time she was 25, she began to date women exclusively.

In 2004, after earning her master's degree in counseling at Loyola University New Orleans, Falcon met April Villa, now 34, who works as a civil engineer for the U.S. Army Corps of Engineers. "April is a beautiful, feminine woman," says Falcon, "yet she's so much like a guy, analytical but not overly introspective, and, just like my dad, she likes to build things and can fix anything." Over the next several years, they supported each other through a series of storms—the literal hurricane, Katrina, and the emotional one that slammed into them as they struggled to come to terms with becoming a couple. "Being different, especially in the South, has never been easy," Falcon says. Villa felt the same way as a civilian working in the military, uncomfortable about freely exposing her gay lifestyle. After they bought a house together, there was friction between them. "Neither of us was really ready to come out as a couple. We hid our relationship from certain friends and from April's colleagues at work. It made both of us feel small, like we weren't proud or committed to each other." At one point last year they put the house up for sale and lived on different floors. But they decided to try to stick it out. In therapy—individually and as a couple—they began to deal with their fears: "Now we can tell each other, 'I'm still really afraid of being public in certain situations, but I can count on you to talk about this without taking it personally,'" says Falcon. "Because in the beginning, we did take it personally, as in you are ashamed of me, you are ashamed of our love. We've really broken the intimacy barrier."

"In this crossroads of ambiguity, we might be able to get something really fascinating happening," playwright Anna Deavere Smith once put it. Jennifer DeClue, a 37-year-old Los Angeles yoga teacher, agrees. "Having more options feels like the most natural thing in the world," says DeClue, who fell for her first girlfriend in her early 20s while living in New York City. After moving to Los Angeles and starting film school, she dated one other

Jennifer DeClue (*left*) lived with the father of her daughter, Miles, 8 (*center*). Now she's in a happy relationship with Jian Chen.

woman, but at 27 became involved with a man. They moved in together, and she got pregnant. "I found pleasure with men," she explains, "but I never liked the hierarchy of heterosexual relationships. And after sex, I usually felt empty and almost incidental, as if the man really didn't see me for me, and I could have been anyone. I discovered that my gender and sexuality can be fluid, and that my role changes depending on who I'm with." She broke up with her boyfriend when their daughter, Miles, was 9 months old, and DeClue focused on being a single mother, paying the rent, and pursuing her studies. In the fall of 2007, at a Buddhist gathering, she met Jian Chen, now a 36-year-old graduate student who identifies as a "boi," a place somewhere between butch and transsexual. "I'm interested in androgyny," DeClue says with a playful smile. "I like a masculine exterior and feminine interior."

Feminist theorists were among the first to begin to uncouple sex from gender. In 1949 French philosopher Simone de Beauvoir published her groundbreaking book *The Second Sex,* with the famous line, "One is not born, but becomes a woman," suggesting that classic female characteristics—passivity, shyness, nurturing—aren't just biological but are embedded by parents and culture. Today, after the women's liberation movement's crusade for equality between the sexes, thinkers like Halberstam are challenging the very definition of gender roles. And as with sexual desire, the idea of fluidity is gaining currency, as evidenced by an ever-expanding vocabulary: transgender, transsexual, transvestite, boi, heteroflexible, intersex. And many who embrace fluidity are adopting the term *gender queer* with pride. But as passionate as they are, those who live by their newly won gender freedom still find themselves at odds with the prevailing culture.

"I may hold Jian's hand in public," says DeClue, who doesn't live with Chen, "but I am very aware of the looks I'm getting and prepared to receive disparaging words. I'm on guard." In the fall of 2008 her 8-year-old daughter felt the backlash over Proposition 8, the measure that bans gay marriage in California. "Some kids said they were yes on Prop 8, and Miles took this very personally," says DeClue. "She was hurt they would think her mom shouldn't be able to marry the person she loves because of being the same sex. Even in L.A. and in very inclusive schools, homophobia comes out." DeClue deals with such negative reactions by bringing up the subject with her daughter, and for the most part believes that Miles and her peers are more open to differences than any generation before. "I think the world will be in good hands when it's their turn to govern," DeClue says confidently.

A new line of research is beginning to approach sexual orientation as much less fixed than previously thought, especially when it comes to women.

Gomez-Barris is also trying to guide her daughter, now 3, and son, 5, through uncharted territory. At first they were confused over what gender to use for Jack, she says. But they came up with calling Halberstam "boy girl," and they love their mother's partner. At her son's school recently, when everyone had to show pictures of their parents, he simply produced three photos. "I have a mama, a papa, and Jack," he told the class.

"My dad is taller than your Jack," one kid said. That, Gomez-Barris says, laughing, was the only fallout.

"Jack is concerned about the future, worried that the kids will face discrimination," Gomez-Barris says, "but I tell him it depends on how we talk to them and their teachers." Then, too, the children are not the only members of Gomez-Barris's world who've had to adjust. When her own mother learned of her new relationship, she was shocked. "Women are our friends, not our lovers," she told her daughter. But Gomez-Barris understood. "Chile, where we come from, is a conservative Catholic country," she says. Eventually her mother came around. "I'm trying to be open-minded and realize that Macarena is a modern woman who has choices," she says now. "Jack is an extraordinary person, and he's very good with my daughter and the children."

Gomez-Barris has had a tougher challenge with some people in her community, from whom she's received the occasional insult and disapproving stare. "When you're in a heterosexual relationship, especially when you have a family with children, the world smiles on you," she says. "I'm having to adjust to the loss of the privileges and acceptance that comes with being in the hetero world, and it's hard at times."

Despite this, Gomez-Barris says she and Halberstam have an incredibly fulfilling relationship. "We're both very fiery. But we work as a team and have good communication. And Jack gives me space to be a mother and an academic," she says. "Jack is the right person for me."

Bridget Falcon, too, feels her efforts have all been worth it. On October 27, 2008, she and April Villa officially married in San Francisco. "It was the best thing we could have done," she says.

"We went through hell, but now we're in heaven." ◖

talking and listening

174 BETWEEN A TALK AND A HARD PLACE I BY DARBY SAXBE

178 "THERE IS A DIFFERENCE BETWEEN BEING AGGRESSIVE
AND BEING ASSERTIVE" I BY DR. PHIL

182 HONEY, I SHRUNK THE ARGUMENT I BY GRETCHEN REYNOLDS

Between a Talk and a Hard Place

She made big plans; her boyfriend made excuses. She pushed; he pulled away. But when Darby Saxbe trained to become a couples therapist, she learned to put down her weapons, lean in—and collaborate on a winning cease-fire.

"Research is me-search."

That's the joke in my psychology department. Among my graduate school classmates, our research interests reveal our insecurities with eerie accuracy. The anxiety specialist is a jittery driver. The quiet one studies shyness. The ADHD researcher switched careers. My work focuses on marriage and health—what could be a better match for the child of divorced doctors? Everyone has emotional demons to battle, but psychologists get to build up a specialized arsenal: statistics, clinical protocols, plenty of jargon.

It was fitting, then, that I started couples therapy training while my own romantic relationship was on the rocks. At the time, my boyfriend, Dan, and I had a continent between us: He'd stayed in New York to pursue his music career after I moved west for grad school, with the understanding that he would join me in Los Angeles when he felt ready. "Ready" turned out to be a hazy concept, one that shifted definitions over the course of a year, while I went through my graduate school paces and wondered how long I should wait. Worse, our conversations about the move devolved into arguments that always started and ended the same way: I would issue my latest ultimatum; he would stall with elliptical nonanswers until he found an excuse to get off the phone ("Uhh, the band's tuning up"). The more I pushed and prodded, the staler our stalemate grew.

Maybe, I thought—just maybe—if I could help unstick a few troubled couples in therapy, I could also pry myself out of a 3,000-mile deadlock.

The first sessions, alas, did not bode well. One client, Amanda*, was convinced that her workaholic husband, Jon*, preferred his job to her. Before my co-therapist and I could even take the couple's history, Amanda was in tears; 20 minutes later, she was still rehashing her anger about a business trip he'd taken two years before. When we finally wrapped up, Jon—who had barely said a word—walked out of the room at arm's length from his wife, as if allergic to her touch.

An hour of watching Amanda lob accusations at her husband left me feeling more than a little bruised myself. It wasn't until after the session, though, that I saw how closely her frustration mirrored mine, and the realization knocked the wind out of me. Dan loved his work as much as Jon did, and I wondered, like Amanda did, whether I

had fallen into second place. I had started making to-do lists for Dan—check out studios in L.A., meet producers, e-mail musicians—that only irritated him. He'd planned a monthlong visit, then canceled after a last-minute gig came up. Whenever we talked about the future, he sounded evasive. Would he grow allergic to me, too?

I fretted that I couldn't help my clients see past their anger when my own relationship lenses were all fogged up, that week's meeting with my couples therapy adviser couldn't come soon enough. "Your couple sounds really polarized," he said, and then explained that polarization happens when the differences that initially draw a couple together become a wedge that divides them. Amanda had been attracted to Jon's ambition, while Jon appreciated Amanda's nurturing. A few years later, his ambition seemed compulsive, and her nurturing felt smothering. We are often drawn to qualities that we lack in ourselves, my adviser said, but when conflicts develop and partners dig in their heels, mild distinctions crystallize into differences that feel insurmountable.

As I continued to see more couples in therapy, I began to find polarities everywhere. It became like a game: Meet a couple, figure out how they're polarized. A buttoned-up lawyer dates a free-spirited writer? They might be polarized around issues of responsibility: how to handle their finances, for example. Every time they disagree on their hot-button topic—money—the conflict refracts onto their images of each other, until the lawyer gets pigeonholed as a miser and the writer as a flake. A social butterfly marries a mellow homebody? In a healthy couple, those differences might balance out: The butterfly learns to enjoy quiet nights, the homebody goes to more parties. But in the fun-house mirror of a souring relationship, the butterfly becomes a needy attention seeker, the homebody a hermit.

As my confidence in couples therapy grew, it was easy to see how Dan and I had gotten polarized around his move to L.A. I'm impatient and optimistic: I tend to jump quickly into new situations and expect luck to sort things out. I couldn't understand why Dan couldn't just relocate already and start setting up gigs. But Dan likes to deliberate, and he needed things to "feel right" before he could book a one-way ticket west. I felt as though he'd never make up his mind; he felt as though I didn't appreciate how hard it would be to uproot his whole life.

And we weren't just split about Dan's move; we were also trapped by how we talked about it. Every unhappy couple may be unhappy in its own way, to paraphrase Tolstoy, but there's an overarching form of polarization that

* Names have been changed.

175

marital researchers, who have studied this beast for decades, call demand-withdraw. It's a polarization not of personalities or values but communication styles. One person takes the role of demander—the one who nags, criticizes, and, yes, makes demands—while the withdrawer ignores, avoids, and generally sticks his head in the sand. The more the demander demands, the more the withdrawer withdraws, and vice versa.

Notice that I said "*his* head in the sand." Researchers have discovered that women are more likely to assume the demanding role and men the withdrawing role. That's true across cultures, races, and age groups. Power is a factor: Men tend to bring more social capital to relationships (earning potential, status, etc.), so they have less to gain from upheaval. Because women often don't have as much negotiating power on issues such as living arrangements, housework, and childcare, they're more likely to desire change in the status quo—which means they also initiate more disputes. When experimenters manipulated whether the topic of a conflict discussion was chosen by the wife or the husband, the demand-withdraw pattern cropped up more when the wife's topic was up for debate.

Another explanation of demand-withdraw centers on men's "autonomic arousal" in the heat of conflict: Their hearts beat faster, their blood pressure rises, and as their fight-or-flight response kicks into high gear, they seek escape. Women are socialized to be more comfortable hashing out issues verbally, so they're left confused by an escaper's exit. If you've ever found yourself fuming at someone on the other side of a slammed door, you may have experienced a demand-withdraw dynamic firsthand.

So how to break the cycle? Simply recognizing it is a big first step. Polarized partners can get so caught up in blaming each other that they fail to acknowledge their own role. Shifting focus from what the other person is doing wrong to where the *system* is going wrong can edit out the mutual maligning that makes polarization so toxic. Couples learn to see the source of their disagreements as existing outside themselves: The problem becomes an "it" rather than a "you."

With my lists and my nagging, I had slid right into the demander role. And Dan's vagueness was a maddening form of withdrawal. Our stances were reinforcing each other: The more I put my foot down about L.A., the more Dan put his foot on the brakes. But finding our polarity—acknowledging I'm a more impulsive decisionmaker than Dan—gave me patience with his vacillations. No matter how much I prodded, he wasn't going to book the next

flight to the West Coast, and I had to make peace with that. The problem wasn't him. It wasn't me, either. We just made decisions differently. In better times, I treasured his thoughtfulness. As I'd been telling my clients for months, it's easier to change the "system"—by changing yourself—than to change your partner.

We started small. One couples therapy technique is to take issues off the table temporarily when they become too loaded—to get a bit of breathing room, to relieve the tension that's choking off a relationship's oxygen, and to stop feeding the demand-withdraw beast. So Dan and I put a moratorium on talking about his move. In the phone calls that followed, we talked about his music, my classmates—anything and everything but the specter of Los Angeles. I felt as though I was talking to a friend again.

Then, a few weeks into our self-imposed hiatus, I broached the Big Move as carefully as I could. "I know this is hard, and we don't want to get into another rut where I'm confronting and you feel attacked," I began.

"So let's talk about when you'll feel ready to come out here. No matter what you say, I'll listen and I won't try to argue with you."

Dan's response floored me. He'd been struggling with the prospect of the move more intensely than I'd ever suspected. And he hadn't been dragging his feet because of doubts about our relationship. It was fear—not an allergic reaction to me—that was holding him back: He felt terrified that if he left his New York contacts behind, he'd never find steady work in L.A.

Couples therapists talk about the "soft" emotions—like fear, shame, and sadness—that can lurk behind the "hard" anger and defensiveness that couples wear into conflict like armor. Getting a glimpse of Dan's softer side, the side that dreaded failure, made me see his perspective more clearly than any of our pre-moratorium arguments ever had. *Empathic joining* is the psychologist's term for when couples share their real feelings instead of sticking to their argumentative guns. By focusing less on scoring points and more on how an issue makes both partners feel, they can dissolve a standoff by finding common emotional ground. After all, Dan didn't like being apart any more than I did. By bonding over our frustration with the distance between

> **If you've ever found yourself fuming at someone on the other side of a slammed door, you may have experienced a demand-withdraw dynamic firsthand.**

us, we could work together to end it.

I wish I could say that, in enlightened couples therapist fashion, I graciously allowed Dan to take all the time he needed to move to L.A. (and, dear reader, it took three long years). It's more accurate to say I learned to temper my nagging, pestering, and cajoling with a little compassion. But once we became aware of our tendency to slip into demand-withdraw, our conversations felt more collaborative. If I got too pushy, I'd take a time-out—and Dan agreed that if he felt attacked, he'd tell me instead of just racing to get off the phone. "The Most Useful Communication Technique of All Time" (*below*) saved us a few times, too.

Since we've settled in L.A., where we share our guacamole-colored house with an old drum kit and a collection of amplifiers, Dan—who's now my husband—and I still argue about everything from politics to dinner plans to baby names. But we've learned how to fight with, not against, each other. Here's an image I like: If conflict creates a tug-of-war, with both partners yanking in opposite directions, imagine leaning toward your mate instead. You might get thrown off balance, but you've also created some slack in the rope. Couples therapy taught me to lean forward instead of back, to shift the balance of power toward the center. That lesson was well worth a little extra me-search. **O**

The Most Useful Communication Technique of All Time

Communication isn't about how much you say but whether each person grasps the other's perspective. If your partner is a reluctant talker, you may be unwittingly fueling his reticence. When he states his case, do you launch a counterattack? Criticize his reasoning? Get upset? If so, he may keep quiet for a reason.

The Most Useful Communication Technique of All Time is deceptively simple, but it works like magic. Next time your partner makes a point, take a moment to digest whatever he is saying. Then say it back to him. Maybe not word for word, but you have to get the gist—and you can't stop trying until your partner agrees you've nailed it. Switch roles and repeat. Once you're not so busy explaining yourself to someone who just doesn't get it, you can look for compromise.

Before I started grad school and officially drank the psychotherapy Kool-Aid, I used to mock this technique as a way to wrap gauze around discord: "I'm hearing that you're a pathetic jerk." "Well, I'm hearing that you're a total loser." But once I tried it, I realized that "I'm hearing…" isn't just psychobabble. It telegraphs the message "I'm listening to you because what you have to tell me is important." And that's the single most important thing couples can say to each other. —*D.S.*

For more information on the couples therapy approach described in this article, visit the Integrative Behavioral Couple Therapy site at ibct.psych.ucla.edu.

Dr. Phil: "There is a difference between being aggressive and being assertive"

• Confronting a rude friend • Helping your grown child through tough times • Speaking out about betrayal • Stopping a boyfriend from overstepping his authority • Learning to loosen up.

Q | I have a friend who often makes cutting remarks to me. Our husbands and children are friends, so avoiding her would likely just alienate me. For a while I thought she was jealous because I have a successful career and she didn't have a job. But she has worked for the past year, and her treatment toward me has worsened. The arrogant things that come out of her mouth leave me at a loss for words, but then later I fixate on what my reply should have been. I spend sleepless nights obsessing over my inability to tell her off. Please help.

Dr. Phil: One thing you need to know about rude people—"mouth bullies," I like to call them—is that they manage by intimidation. They count on you to be nice, to not want to "go there." And the truth is, you *don't* want to get in the gutter with this "friend," because when you roll with pigs, you get muddy.

But telling her off is not your only option. There is a

difference between being aggressive and being assertive. Responding aggressively means you'd protect your rights but step on hers. Behaving assertively means you'd protect your rights but not at the expense of her right to be treated with dignity. That's what you need to do.

But the fact that you lie awake at night obsessing over the right retort tells me your problem is as much with yourself as it is with her. You wouldn't stand by and watch your best friend get bullied, would you? Don't let yourself get pushed around, either. I strongly suggest you have an eyeball-to-eyeball conversation with this woman. If you simply can't bring yourself to do that, tell her how you feel in a letter or a phone call. Here's what you might say:

Script of the Month:
Stop being such a bully

I have something to talk to you about, and I want you to hear me out before you respond. For some reason, you have given yourself permission to act rude, crude, and condescending toward me, and I don't know why. What I do know is that I will not accept it from you for one more day. I can't expect you to change if I don't tell you how I feel, so that's what I'm doing now. You may disagree, and that's okay. But you need to understand that you are going to treat me with dignity or you're not going to treat me any way at all.

I believe that when people show your kind of behavior, it's really based on pain and fear. If that's the case with you, I'm willing to talk to you about the underlying issue or to support you in any way I can. But I am not willing to allow you to continue to abuse me. If you want to think about what I'm saying and respond when you're comfortable, that is fine with me. If you want to respond now—without being abusive—then I'm happy to listen. And if you'd just like to declare this the end of our friendship, then so be it. If that's the case, I recognize it will also affect the relationship between our families, and I'm sorry for that. But our relationship as we have known it is over. My hope is that we can define a new one, but that's up to you. I await your response.

Q | My son and his wife are going through a traumatic time. He lost his dream job in advertising due to cutbacks. His attitude is great, but my daughter-in-law's alternates between limited optimism and quiet desperation. I know she isn't sleeping well. I offered financial help, but how do I offer the right emotional support? Do I speak to them about the potential for depression? I would like to ease their burden as much as I can.

Dr. Phil: Mom, I'm going to give you a sermon here about boundaries. You have to recognize that these are their problems, and you need to let them deal with their issues in whatever way they choose. If they do agree to accept a loan from you, then you have to caution yourself against having expectations. In other words, you shouldn't use the loan as a way to control your son, who is now grown and living on his own and needs to be treated accordingly. I suggest that you set very clear terms on any financial aid you provide, with realistic repayment plans and documents that define the arrangement.

With regard to offering emotional support, I recommend that you speak candidly with your son, sharing your perception that his wife rides a bit of an emotional roller coaster. Recommend that he reach out to get her professional help. Respect that although taking care of his wife is his job and his responsibility, you can offer him advice and support. Once you make your offer or advice known, then the ball is in their court, at which point you need to take a giant step back and allow them to come up with a plan themselves.

Q | My live-in boyfriend has a good friend who regularly cheats on his wife. Every once in a while, his friend schedules a night out that usually ends up with my boyfriend hanging out with him and his latest mistress. They spend the night drinking together and talking about intimate topics like relationships, why men cheat, and why women date married men. I've told my boyfriend that I am uncomfortable with this situation for several reasons: I'm put in a difficult position when we get together with his friend and his friend's wife because I know he's cheating on her; I question my boyfriend because he is essentially condoning his friend's behavior; and I worry about the possibility of my

> The fact is, you are lying by omission. Your boyfriend has put you in a very awkward position, which violates you and your values. And now that you're roped in, your silence makes you part of the conspiracy

boyfriend being influenced by his friend's cheating. Do I have the right to be upset about these nights out? And if so, how can I end them without endangering my own relationship?

Dr. Phil: You write that you feel uncomfortable around your boyfriend's philandering buddy and his unsuspecting wife—well, you should. The fact is, you are lying by omission. Your boyfriend has put you in a very awkward position, which violates you and your values. And now that you're roped in, your silence makes you part of the conspiracy to deceive his wife. Wouldn't it be ironic if this other guy is going home and confiding in his wife that your boyfriend is cheating on you, and neither of you is cluing the other woman in?

I conducted an informal poll about this situation that included my wife, Robin, and a bunch of my producers. Twenty out of 20 people said that you should tell the wife what's going on. It sounds like you instinctively agree with them, so you need to be true to your values and to yourself by stepping up and being a friend to her.

As for your boyfriend, even if he isn't actually cheating, he's guilty by association. Think about it. What does it say about him that he condones his friend's open disrespect and infidelity? What does it say about him that he can go out with his buddy and his mistress and then sit down and have dinner with the guy's wife and play her for a fool? What does it say about him that he puts you in such a position with no consideration for your feelings? The fact that your boyfriend is okay with this guy's behavior should make you question his character and the authenticity of your relationship. You say that you worry about endangering that relationship, but it's a risk you need to take.

Tell him straight up one more time how you feel. You need to confront him, and if he dislikes the fact that you're done with this conspiracy, then that's too bad. The bottom line is that he's a liar, plain and simple. If your boyfriend is not willing to clean up his act, resolve to cut your losses and move on.

Script of the Month:
Refusing to play along in an ugly game

I'm not okay with this on so many levels. That your value system condones your friend's behavior. That you are conspiring to deceive his wife. That you have so little respect for me that you pulled me into this and expect me to lie by omission. I don't want to be part of this deal, and I don't want a boy-

friend who thinks any of this is acceptable. So you need to make this right or we have no future. I fully intend to tell this woman about what's going on when I next see her—I only hope she doesn't have the same news to share with me.

Q | I am a divorced mother with a 16-year-old daughter. I've been involved with a man for the past six years who has been very understanding of my approach to parenting. That changed two months ago, when my daughter had her first date. My boyfriend read her diary and confronted her about its contents (which suggested that she and her date had become intimate), and she strongly defended herself. I feel a diary is private, and that he should have brought the issue to my attention instead of confronting her. He blew up at me for not supporting him, and he won't see us until she apologizes for her "blatant disrespect." She wants him to apologize for violating her privacy. I feel it is unreasonable for him to rest the future of our relationship on the shoulders of a 16-year-old. I'm lost. Do I force my child to apologize, or do I let go of an otherwise functioning relationship?

Dr. Phil: It is your responsibility as a mother to raise your daughter. I assume we agree on that. As for your boyfriend, he has gotten way out of his lane. His six-year tenure in your life does not make him a recognized authority in your daughter's eyes. Nor should it. No matter what his intentions were, this man has demonstrated why a responsible parent should never let an outsider, even one she may love, inject himself into the parenting of her child. His role, if any, is to support you in your parental efforts, and he failed miserably. He should not impose his own value system on your household.

You are right: A private diary is exactly that. It contains your daughter's confidential thoughts, and it is a horrible violation for anyone—let alone some guy that her mom is dating—to read it. His actions indicate poor judgment and a lack of both boundaries and respect for your daughter. That he then took it upon himself to confront her is beyond absurd. That is not his job—it's yours. It is highly disrespectful to you, not to mention condescending.

In other words, your daughter is not the only one who has been severely violated here. And then he had the audacity and insensitivity to hold your relationship hostage by refusing to see the two of you unless she apologizes. You should not force her to say she's sorry. If anybody should do any apologizing here, it is him. Since your daughter's trust has been

> You can't change what you don't acknowledge.

violated, it is important to offer your support. Make it clear that what he did was unacceptable, that you would never disrespect her privacy like that, and that she bears no responsibility for the future of your relationship with him.

The bottom line is that if ignored, his behavior will only get worse, and your daughter will pay the price. In order to salvage this relationship, he would have to acknowledge his transgression to both you and your daughter. I suggest you sit down with him and try the script that follows.

Then it's time for you to deal with the fact that you may have a sexually active 16-year-old. I'm guessing that she lacks the maturity to manage being intimate in a responsible way, so you need to get real with her about how to handle the risks. The two of you need to make some serious decisions about whether she'll abstain from this behavior or, if you think she's likely to continue, use some form of birth control.

Script of the Month:
I'm the parent, not you

You have assumed a victim role here, acting as though you are the offended and violated party. I don't see it that way at all. We need to call time-out and take a step back from this situation until I know that you understand exactly how I feel. I assume that your intentions, however misguided, were good, which is why I'm even bothering to discuss this. Regardless, it is not okay that you violated my daughter's privacy. It is not okay that you took it upon yourself to confront her. It is not okay for you to disrespect me by going directly to her rather than to me. And it is not okay for you to try to manage this situation through intimidation and ultimatums.

You are not my daughter's father. You do not have the history with her to play the role of disciplinarian. You can disagree with me privately, but I will do the parenting and you must support me. If you think I'm crazy, then we can go to an objective third

> The good news: Your marriage sounds healthy and you've admitted that there's an issue you'd like to work on. The even better news is that your problem is treatable: You really can learn to be more spontaneous and fun-loving.

party for input, but that's the deal for now. My daughter's well-being is nonnegotiable, and I will be the one calling the shots. You owe both of us an apology.

Q | Every now and then my husband and I have a "state of our union" talk. In our last one, he gently told me that after 30 years of marriage I've become rigid and not much fun. What hurts is that I know it's true. I've developed a lot of anxieties over the years and stay in my comfort zone to avoid them. I hate being a stick-in-the-mud. How can I change?

Dr. Phil: You already are. The fact that you've had the courage to hear what he said, admit it's true, and ask for help is a huge step forward; you can't change what you don't acknowledge. And I think it is terrific that you and your husband have these talks. So look at all the positives: He feels free to be honest with you, you actually hear what he's saying and recognize its validity, and you want to create some change. Congratulations on many steps in the right direction.

Now you need to figure out the cause of your angst and take steps to reduce it. Recent studies have shown that people with anxiety have a neurological "storm" in their brain. However, therapeutic intervention can often resolve the issue in a matter of weeks or months. I think you would benefit by getting short-term help from a cognitive behavioral therapist, who can assist you in uncovering what you're so fearful about, decide if it's rational, and give you ways to fight it. Medication might also be recommended.

The good news: Your marriage sounds healthy and you've admitted that there's an issue you'd like to work on. The even better news is that your problem is treatable: You really can learn to be more spontaneous and fun-loving. **O**

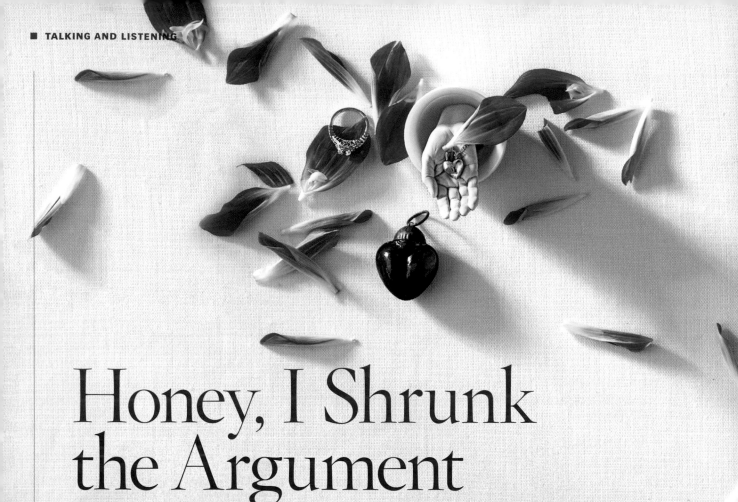

Honey, I Shrunk the Argument

Gretchen Reynolds discovers the art of making a molehill out of a mountain.

L isa Diamond's research associate keeps her voice deliberately neutral as she talks through a microphone to a couple in the next room. The man, Tim, slumped on a couch, and the woman, Stacey, sitting upright on a wing chair, have been wired with monitors that measure their heart rate and respiration, as well as the flow of electrical currents across their skin—all of which are indicators of nervous system activity. An unobtrusive video camera records the couple's every twitch and flitting smile. Earlier, they were shown a series of innocuous photographs of landscapes while their baseline pulse rates and other measurements were recorded. Now they're being asked to argue.

"The source of conflict that Tim chose," the researcher is telling them, "is 'You treat me like you're my mom.'" At this, Stacey, an elegant 30-year-old operations manager for a nonprofit in Salt Lake City, stiffens. Tim, her tall,

lean 29-year-old photographer boyfriend, smiles awkwardly, abashed. With his slouchy T-shirt, clunky black glasses, and floppy hair, he's a study in nerdy chic. He looks at the floor. "Tim, you should explain what you mean by this particular conflict," the researcher continues, "and then both of you try to resolve it. You'll have four minutes."

"Um—" Tim says, by way of starting.

"What do you mean by that?" Stacey cuts in.

And they're off.

For the past year, Diamond, the associate professor of psychology at the University of Utah in whose laboratory Stacey and Tim now snipe, has been studying how couples argue—specifically, studying the measurable changes that occur in their bodies as they fight. It's a tricky business, though not because she has difficulty eliciting spats. (That part is almost comically easy: Just ask each half of the pair to write down a gripe against the other.) The tougher part is getting the couples to *stop* squabbling after the researchers have gathered their data.

And the deepest challenge is teasing out the complex

interplays between wrath and respiration, heartache and heart rate. Diamond is trying to quantify the role the body and nervous system play in relationships and conflict. In the process, she's uncovering lessons—some practical, some poetic—about how small gestures can lessen the damage of big arguments, and about how even a minor reconsideration of what's really happening between you can tamp down, metaphorically and physiologically, all that furious heat.

M en and women typically experience the same relationship very differently," Diamond tells me as we sit in her laboratory watching Tim and Stacey spar. The author of *Sexual Fluidity,* a study of female desire, Diamond is a small woman with darting energy and masses of black hair. "We know from some large epidemiological studies that the long-term health benefits of marriage traditionally have been greater for men than for women," she says. "Presumably this has been because women are often the relationship maintainers. They're the ones putting in much of the work. Men have gotten the benefits of a relationship without as much of the heavy lifting."

In the small room where Tim and Stacey are arguing, the atmosphere has turned icy. "It's not like I wrote down the worst problem I have," Tim is saying, his eyes downcast. "I mean, um, you're bossy."

"Yes, I'm bossy," Stacey snaps back. "I like to control my situation. I offer suggestions. It's not like I'm being a mom. Tell me one time I acted like a mom."

"Um, I don't know," Tim says. "My mind is blank. I... " His voice trails off.

"The classic pattern you see is the demand-withdrawal dynamic," Diamond whispers, referring to a pattern in which the woman makes demands and the man, in response, shuts down. It turns out that each behavior has striking corollaries within the body. "The man usually finds it calming to withdraw from the conflict," Diamond says. His heart rate drops. His breathing slows. Yet, as he pulls away, "the woman watches in growing frustration. She's thinking, *Why won't he talk to me?*" Her heart rate rises. Her breathing becomes shallow and short. "The more he withdraws, the more physiologically aroused she becomes."

If you're the demanding partner in this dynamic, your best response at this point is surprisingly simple: Listen to your heart, literally. Monitor your physiology. If your heart

Step back and take a deep breath. Close your eyes. Calm down.

is racing, your breathing ragged, your eyes ablaze, step back and take a deep breath. Close your eyes. Calm down. This small action can be surprisingly consequential, even profound. "The body is so fundamentally involved in our relationships," Diamond says. "But few of us pay attention to it."

Your own body's cues aren't the only ones worth paying attention to, however. The most important small gesture you can make toward your partner is to empathize. Consider that the very behavior making you nuts—his mumbling and emotional retreat—is calming for him, Diamond says. "It's quite possible that he can't respond in any other way. Our conflict styles develop over a lifetime." So don't raise your voice and demand that he continue engaging in that persistent fight about money or housework or friendships or sex (topics that recur constantly in Diamond's work). Let him withdraw.

Then, when you're calmer, go after him with a smile. "Humor is very important in defusing tension," Diamond says. She describes one couple whose argument in the lab had grown extremely heated. A lab assistant intervened, suggesting they move on to the second chosen topic of conflict. And that topic was, as Diamond recalls, "the neighbor's cow." The two combatants looked at each other, dissolved into giggles, and left, minutes afterward, arm in arm. "We never found out what that source of conflict was supposed to be about," Diamond says. Whatever it was, it didn't make them angry anymore. It made them laugh. It restored their shared affection. "It's always reassuring when we see couples start to laugh."

B ack in the observation room, Tim is squirming on the couch and Stacey's stare is glacial. The lab assistant, directing the interaction toward resolution, suggests that they tell each other something positive.

Tim looks at Stacey and smiles. "I think we have fun most of the time," he says. "We make each other laugh."

Stacey's pursed lips slowly relax. "Well, there was the time you wore that really tight pair of underwear." She smiles, too. "That was funny."

The research associate unhooks both of them from the various machines. They rise, take each other's hands—another important small gesture—and leave.

"It would be interesting to hear the conversations between these couples in the car on the way home," Diamond says. Or maybe that's one small area in which science should leave well enough alone. ◐

family

185 YOU ARE WHAT I EAT I BY MEG GILES

188 THE SNUG LIFE I BY CELIA BARBOUR

190 AN INCONVENIENT YOUTH I BY CINTRA WILSON

196 RASHIDA JONES'S AHA! MOMENT

197 THE GOOD OLD TIMES I BY MARTHA BECK

200 LISA KOGAN TELLS ALL

House Specials

Kenny

Meg's Parents

Kathy with Bird

Meg & husband Dave

Bird

David

Chanterelle

You Are What I Eat

Squash blossoms, steamed asparagus, sliced bananas, fortitude, friendship, kindness, candor, Oreos, and a certain turkey club sandwich. **Meg Giles** lays out her own rules for eating for two.

My daughter is, among other things, a crab-stuffed squash blossom from one of New York's best restaurants, Chanterelle. I ate there the day after I learned I was pregnant, at the insistence of my friend Michael. I suggested that perhaps we should postpone the celebration for a few months, fearing another miscarriage, but Michael responded, as I should have known he would, that we would celebrate now *and* in three months. This is what we do on momentous occasions, he said, we go to Chanterelle. And so, we did.

It was a night of nights: There was the famous sommelier, there was the gracious owner, there was talk of who the baby might be, there was, after all, the food. The four of us ordered nearly everything on the menu. We urged perfect forkfuls of our dishes on each other, each bite a revelation. *Here, you must try this seafood sausage—stop what you are doing, have the steak and potatoes with a dab of the creamed spinach— no, no, taste this halibut in its asparagus corral* (yes, that's right, corral; though we longed for an asparagus *chorale,* a short musical number performed by a local, seasonal vegetable).

My daughter is made of the squash blossom that we shared. She is steak, halibut, the cheese cart, and every dessert they offered; she is a fine meal in Tribeca on a May night; she is Michael's soaring faith in the future, his extravagance, generosity, wit, and she is also this: strawberry soup.

In wine it is called terroir: the peculiarities of the soil, the water, the very angle of the sun, the land that makes a wine distinctly itself. *I am now terroir,* it suddenly occurred to me, *I am someone's terroir.* Pregnancy transpires, somewhat insultingly, without effort (unlike conception, which, for me, required almost heroic effort). The only input I had was what I was eating. The phrase "you are what you eat" leapt to mind, then

Meg with her daughter, Bird, at five months, Brooklyn, 2008.

quickly morphed into "Kid, you are what I eat."

The simplest rubric for eating while pregnant focuses naturally on healthy, fortifying foods, but those guidelines, in their rectitude, have become punitive, shaming, and somewhat alarming, steeped in the language of fear. Pregnant women are now told to beware of deli meat. But I suspect that if a turkey sandwich were going to take down mankind, we'd have disappeared long ago. I wanted my child to be healthy, and more: I also wanted to eat with a mind toward *who* I wanted her to be. If I was, indeed, creating another being, what should be on the ingredient list? Which foods? What qualities? I set about dreaming up a recipe for my kid.

Any child of mine, I decided, should be made of the #2 turkey club sandwich at the Sugar Bowl in Scottsdale, Arizona, my hometown. My father ate lunch at the counter for 20 years every Thursday at 1 P.M., so predictably that they put in his order for the #2 before he sat down. The turkey club, I figure, is our legacy. I put that on the ingredient list.

I thought of the people I wanted her to emulate and decided to eat things that reminded me of them. They, too, were creating my daughter. The recipe drew inspiration from memories (grapefruit from the trees in my childhood backyard, the bread drawer with a sliding metal lid in my great-aunts' house that smelled, deliciously, eternally, of Oreos) and the hope of summoning those who have passed (a sardine sandwich with Kraft coleslaw dressing that my grandfather apparently loved). I even listed ingredients I hate: my friend Carol's peanut butter Christmas cookies, for instance, because they are what she gives (to the great pleasure of everyone else), and I wanted this child to know what it is to be grateful for a gift not because it is perfect but because it is given. I aimed for sensibility (the cheese from a shop in Little Italy that will not permit you to leave unsatisfied, or in under an hour) and the plainly delicious (my husband's spaghetti sauce). She will not have the pleasure of knowing my mother, so I made myself a bowl of banana medallions in orange juice, which she served as dessert when I was a little girl. Then I set about eating.

It was no simple task for me

to get pregnant. When I flinched, certain I would give myself cancer if I tried fertility treatments, my friend Lyle was the one who said to me, "By the time you give yourself cancer, they will have cured it. Ya gotta live now." And so, you can see why my daughter had to be part Lyle. I begged him to make dinner for me, his specialty, an Old Bay shrimp boil. A plate of steamed asparagus. No utensils. He bought lychees on the branch in Chinatown for dessert. I have watched him care for his dying father, I have watched him fall in love, I have watched him work. I wanted my girl to have his fortitude, compassion, verve, the elegance of his mind. She is a meal eaten by hand, she is fluency, she is lychees, she is Lyle.

And she is Kenny, with whom I must have eaten a hundred meals, including an Italian lunch in December. He is, in a man, permission. A hedonist. A grandmother. A diva. After lunch we popped into one lovely store after another, with Kenny plucking things off the shelves, *Here's a book you have to read; here, a toy for the baby*. She is pumpkin ravioli and squid salad from that December lunch, and, I hope, his kindness, his largesse, good taste, zest for life, candor. She is also his finest cherry pie. (Kenny comes from pie people.)

And like wine, she is time. The weather during the months on the vine—how much rain falls, how cold and hot the season—determines what a bottle of wine will ever be. She, too, is made of our personal weather, the events that transpired during her months with me: cupcakes from Lyle's wedding, steak salad from Ian's graduation party, the fruit plate at my husband's grandfather's memorial. She is the burger I shared with David the day a test revealed she might have Down's syndrome, she is a glass of Champagne at a movie premiere. She is the big winter holidays and my favorite rituals, the ones we make up on our own: the wonton soup and orange soda I have at the cheap Chinese joint while planning our Thanksgiving menu, or the coffee we drink across from the high school band playing "Gonna Fly Now" the day the New York City Marathon makes its way through our neighborhood.

Regret found its way into the recipe, as it does. She is the things I wish I hadn't done and many others I failed to do. I'm sorry to report that she is strawberry Pop-Tarts. I never did get to Di Palo to order ricotta and olive oil and talk recipes with everyone at the counter; nor did I actually eat one of Carol's peanut butter balls. When my brother visited, we giddily ate the food of his childhood, Devil Dogs, for breakfast. But my kid is also made from the tension that now clouds our relationship, our strained conversation at dinner over cauliflower and bagna cauda,

I set about dreaming up a recipe for my kid.

because sometimes we gather at a table with people whose lives we can't fathom as surely as they can't fathom ours, but we keep trying. She is heartache and abiding love. She is Devil Dogs.

She is so very many ingredients: candy-striped beets, a hot dog from Shea Stadium, a curried chicken sandwich, black grape raita, chocolate milk, prenatal vitamins, doughnuts, lots of doughnuts, licorice Scottie dogs, peaches and apricots from the farmers' market eaten standing over the sink, bowls of fresh watermelon, pineapple chunks, Earl Grey tea. And so many people: Ana, James, Kathy, Meera, Jack, Megan. My daughter is Coca-Cola, which, to my own surprise, I started drinking again after Cormac McCarthy wrote about the last can on Earth in *The Road,* claiming it as one of life's simplest, greatest pleasures.

Although I could not know it then, the recipe was complete late on a January night, her due date. That meal was shared with my best friends, David and Ian, at a restaurant called Momofuku. Together we slurped salty ramen, then went next door to a café and shared something I can only describe as a Twinkie coffin, a little box of sponge cake, cream, and strawberries. Five hours later, David and Ian were asleep and I was in a car on the West Side Highway, slipping past the Cunard ship afloat in the Hudson, on my way to the hospital. The next day my girl arrived during a brief moment of snow. We named her Bird.

But that is another story and there are too many to tell here, too many ingredients to list. I wrote them down, everything I ate, with whom, why. It seems to me now to have been a way of orienting myself in the face of enormity. I was scared. I needed all the help I could get. Still do. Only now do I see this was a project born of longing for my mom and my fear of being unqualified to raise a child well. It was the only way I could manage to focus or remain hopeful when I was not. It helped me create her, but perhaps it helped me, an unlikely, uncomfortable mother, create myself. I discovered a way of organizing a lifelong conversation, a way of telling her what I value and hope for her.

After all, with food comes story. I can tell her the stories over the many meals I will share with her over the coming years. These are the things you are made of: friends, memory, and pork ramen from the East Village. But this, too, is true: She is everything I ate and still she is a mystery, that unnameable, unknowable ingredient none of us contributed, whatever it is that makes her her. That is a story she will have to tell us. ◐

The Snug Life

After years of squeezing five people into a one-bedroom apartment,
Celia Barbour's family moved to a sprawling old house with as
many bathrooms as inhabitants. Somehow, though, things are still cozy.

The nicest thing I ever did for my single self was to buy an apartment in the West Village. I'd been slumming it for seven years, living in a fifth-floor walk-up tenement, and one day I decided that a proper home was no longer a self-indulgence. I was as real a grown-up as I'd ever be, and deserved a real place.

My lovely one-bedroom apartment had a park out front, trees out back, a working fireplace, and, at 575 square feet, was just big enough for me and my cat, and the occasional dinner party with friends. No sooner had I settled in than I met my husband, Peter, and he moved in. We felt cozy; life was sweet. Sometimes at night, we'd sit on the stoop with two jelly jar glasses of Scotch and watch the people passing by. A year and a half later, George was born, and I dusted off an old baby basket and placed it on the floor beside our bed. When Henry came along 16 months after that, he laid claim to the basket and George was reassigned to our walk-in closet, which Peter, a proficient carpenter, had transformed into a nursery. Then Sidonie was born. Switch-switch-switch: George to a trundle bed (built by Peter) that rolled under our bed, Henry into the closet, the baby girl in the basket. And so we lived, snug as mice, for a very happy little while.

Last year we moved into a house. Built in 1900, it has three stories, eight rooms, and five bathrooms, plus an attic that smells like heat and a basement that smells like mold. It has doors that close and hallways separating one room from another, places to talk privately on the phone and to do yoga in the morning without having my torso straddled by a kid who has suddenly perceived my untapped potential as a hobbyhorse. Our house is not big, at least by contemporary standards, because it has no superfluous rooms devoted to leisure or grandeur—no family room, for example, and no great room cowering beneath a cathedral ceiling. We have just the basic LR, DR, BR, K, study. Which is fine, despite the fact that the kids are growing like corn, because all our rooms are living rooms, by which I mean we live in them all. The only time I find myself wishing for more square footage is when I am overwhelmed by stuff—books, vases, wrapping paper, hand-me-downs waiting to be grown into, chairs—and daydream about building an addition where the flotsam could comfortably reside. Then I think: *Don't be crazy, Celia.* A home is a place to do things, not store things. It's not meant to house your possessions, but your life.

And it turns out that our lives together are quite compact. Yes, during the day we each might spiral off into the wide, wild world—the kids at school studying China or peninsulas, bicycling around the neighborhood or sledding down the hill, Peter and I doggedly pursuing our careers. But back at home, we draw close, this habit of being in each other's presence ingrained. Unconsciously, we collect in the same room, even if we are each doing our own things—the boys building Lego speedboats, Peter replying to e-mails, me reading, Sidonie communicating quietly to her stuffed animals. We may not be interacting with each other at all. But having started out like pieces of a single puzzle nestled together so neatly, we still return to that familiar configuration. As individuals we may be big, but as a family, we are really very small. ◖

During the day, we spiral off into the wide world. But at home, we draw close.

Erin Lopes and her son, Thomas, 9, at their home in Media, Pennsylvania.

An Inconvenient Youth

In Philadelphia, a group of gutsy, sharp-witted, wisecracking mothers (and one honorary dad) are raising kids with autism. From diagnosis (saying the A word) to leaving no treatment untried (avocado, really?) to loving and admiring what can't be "fixed," they're in it together. **Cintra Wilson** is invited to dinner.

I have loved my friend Erin Lopes since seventh grade, despite the fact that she's incredibly smart, hilarious, and looks like Natalie Wood. After working in epidemiology at the California Department of Public Health and earning a master's degree from UC Berkeley, Erin, continuing her trend toward excellence in all things, married Tim, a handsome attorney. They then had a boy and a girl, and bought a two-story house surrounded by trees in a cul-de-sac in suburban Philadelphia, which looks so adorable with its warm yellow lights that when we all pulled into the driveway the first time, I cracked, "Dude, who's your architect? Thomas Kinkade?"

I love Erin's kids, and am frequently rewarded with unidentifiable ceramic creations and fabulous felt-pen portraits. Evelyn, 8, is approximately 45 pounds of eyes, knees, pink plastic jewelry, and dimples. Thomas, who's 9, has such winning movie star looks, I call him Keanu Jr. You perceive that he's wired a little differently only when he talks.

On a recent visit, I walked into the house and gave Thomas a hug. "All that, just because of a cup of coffee!" he said in a cheesy TV announcer voice, rubbing my kiss off—a fantastic non sequitur that charmed my socks off. I am biased, naturally, as his honorary auntie. In 2002 Erin sent her friends an announcement that Thomas had been diagnosed with a form of autism. He doesn't process or express emotion the same way other kids do and often speaks in an unmodulated voice that is a little loud. But just now Thomas was able to encapsulate the dust storm of feelings swirling around my arrival (*Hey! What's all this friendly commotion?*) by quoting a TV ad that mirrored it surprisingly well. It was as if he knew he couldn't squeeze me the juice from a real orange, so he did an intellectual work-around and handed me a glass of Tang—a little prefab emotion.

Tonight, Erin—in between training for a half-marathon and earning a nursing degree—has invited me to a roundtable discussion with eight of her closest friends, a group that has in many ways become a lifeline of support. Most are mothers of autistic children who have connected through the Delaware County Family PDD/Autism Spectrum Support Listserv. These women share the kind of visceral bond I've otherwise seen only in soldiers—they have each other's backs and fight to keep each other's spirits up in what is a daily, ongoing battle to integrate their different kids into the "typical" world.

Every member of Erin's group has gotten that "look": Someone notices their child's autistic behavior and it feels as though they're being judged as bad mothers.

"I get the stares," says Corinda Crowther, a high school English teacher and mother of Max. "Like when your 9-year-old won't get out of the moonbounce at the street fair and you have to climb in after him, pull him out, and watch him tantrum—all the while trying to figure out how to remain calm, secretly wanting to be swallowed up by the asphalt. I can only imagine that the people staring are thinking, *Wow, that mom really screwed up her kid.* When that happens, a part of me dies inside."

One of the most crucial and misunderstood aspects of autism is that it covers a wide range of disabilities. The brain development disorder—or more accurately, autism spectrum disorders (ASDs)—includes autism, Asperger's syndrome, and pervasive developmental disorder not otherwise specified, all of which impair thinking, behavior, language, and the ability to relate to others. Each child on the spectrum is a uniquely scrambled, genetic Rubik's Cube in terms of how his or her disorder manifests, how severe it is, and what medical issues accompany it. Although some autistic kids may respond well to some of the popular treatments, others, for baffling reasons, do not. ASDs affect about one out of 150 children, according to CDC estimates; however, there is no biological test for them (diagnosis involves observing the child's behaviors and skills), and science has yet to find either a conclusive cause or cure.

Everyone at the table has a traumatic memory of receiving the diagnosis. It is the beginning of an intense personal struggle to come to grips with the idea that your child is not perfect—a process that can shake a family to its foundations. At first there's a vast reluctance to admit that autism is the "real" diagnosis. These women have come to call that phase being "in the closet."

As the stories begin to roll out, Heather Haggerty (who recently earned her master's in occupational therapy, in part to help her autistic son, Padraic, 10) raises a fist in the air and declares boldly, "Padraic does not have Asperger's! He simply has autism!"

The group applauds. It's a running joke: Admitting your child "simply has autism" (as opposed to the milder and comparatively glamorous Asperger's syndrome) is similar to introducing yourself at an AA meeting with "Hi, I'm _____ , and I'm an alcoholic."

"There was a moment when I couldn't get that word, *autism,* out of my mouth," says Robert Naseef. "The A word!"

That gets a big laugh. Robert, the lone man here tonight and father of a severely autistic son, Tariq, is revered in this group for his books, including *Special Children, Challenged Parents: The Struggles and Rewards of Raising a Child with a Disability,* and his psychology practice, which is devoted to families with special-needs children. Erin and Tim credit Naseef's counseling with saving their marriage.

"That was a big thing for me, being able to use that word, *autism,*" agrees Margaret Ewing, who works for a center that brings art classes to schools in underprivileged communities. "I've probably only been doing it three, four years. And I have a 12-year-old."

"Welcome!" quips Heather.

Accepting the "A word" requires a learning curve. "You graduate to it," says Erin. "Because this is about: *Let's call it what it is, let's deal with it together.*"

When it comes to dealing with autism, the medical community offers no standard treatment, although certain medications and therapies—including one-on-one applied behavior analysis, which teaches communication and social skills, and floor time, when a parent or facilitator uses play to encourage engagement—may be prescribed to help with symptoms. The only point that's undisputed is that the earlier a child with an ASD receives intervention therapies, the better his or her outcome will be—and the pressure this puts on a parent is nearly unbearable. Any downtime, or financial restraint whatsoever, is a pipeline to constant guilt.

"I used to eat myself alive about how much money or time I was spending with Padraic," says Heather, who has three other children. "You know that if you spend 24 hours a day with this kid, drawing him out of his inwardness, you're going to make a difference. Ninety percent of my self-torture has come from not doing floor time with him because I'm making dinner. I've spent most evenings on the floor of my kitchen in tears.... There's never enough you can do. Ever.

"It's the old proverbial story," she continues. "If a car fell on top of your kid, a mom would be able to lift it off."

"The superhuman kicks in," Erin agrees. "But it's years of trying to lift that car."

"And you can't," says Heather. "And everyone's sitting on top of the car trying to hold it down. That's the way it feels."

"And you get tired," says Corinda.

"Pretty soon you realize the car is on top of you," says Erin.

After a certain amount of sleep deprivation, radical, unproven therapies can start to look reasonable—even promising. Upon hearing a miraculous testimonial from another mother, Corinda and Heather took their boys to a "biomedical treatment" practitioner. Now, when talking about "Dr. Q" (not her name), they both assume the pained expressions people get when looking at their high school yearbook photos. "I can't talk about it with a straight face anymore," laments Heather.

"Dr. Q was $500 initially, then every time you talked to her it was $75 and a trip to the grocery store," groans Corinda.

"She would call you in this flurry in the middle of the night: 'Do you have any avocado oil?! Padraic's not autistic! Something is ravaging him and causing these behaviors! You need to rub avocado oil on his shins every two hours!'" says Heather. "Here's me, brand-new to this whole world. I have a toddler. Padraic's still nonverbal. Very dark place.

"By the end," she continues, "I had to separate 12 egg yolks and put a jar of Grey Poupon in Padraic's bath. I had to slip in at night and put artichokes in his socks. I had to rub down very specific parts of him with yogurt. The poor thing is probably autistic because of what I did to him."

(This is a laugh line, by the way. Autism Mom humor

The mothers (*clockwise from top left*) laugh, cry, and soldier through together: Gerry Arango, Stacey O'Rourke, Heather Haggerty, Margaret Ewing, Erin, and Corinda Crowther.

is delightfully brutal.)

"She told us to put lighter fluid on Max's feet," remembers Corinda. "My brother-in-law, a doctor, said, 'I really don't want you to do that.'"

"Now we'd never do it," says Heather. "But back then, more than anyone else, Dr. Q was giving us hope. Those were the early days. That's when you're really in the dark."

O nce in a while, the blind, hunt-and-peck search for effective cures can yield life-changing results. That's because some of the behavioral problems in these kids are compounded by other medical conditions that can accompany autism. Gastrointestinal problems, for example, are common, which is why dietary changes may improve an autistic child's responsiveness. Thomas and Max also suffer from epilepsy, and as a result, Erin and Corinda have compared extensive notes on medications and lifestyle changes to stop or slow the seizures, which can radically improve a child's development. Occasionally when trying other treatments, there are complete surprises.

"Max didn't talk for a long time," says Corinda. "We assumed it was because of autism. We went to all the best hospitals. Finally we went to the Mayo Clinic when he was 6. We were there 24 hours, and they said, 'Your kid isn't breathing at night. We need to take his tonsils out.' Once they took them out, he started sleeping through the night for the first time. It was *amazing*. Three weeks later, he started talking."

"It was astounding," says Erin, after a moment.

"I still get goose bumps," said Heather.

"Me too," adds Erin's husband, Tim, popping his head into the room.

Would you call it a miracle? I ask.

Everyone nods solemnly.

"That's what it was," says Corinda. "It was his speech therapist who finally told us to go to Mayo. How do you thank her? *Thank you for giving...?*"

For giving your child his voice. Nobody says it; we're all trying not to cry.

The women admit to bouts of depression. "We've all been on 'the cocktail' at one time or another," says Heather, referring to antidepressants. Caring for a child with any disability is challenging, but when the kid can offer a smile or hug, it makes a parent's job a little easier. Children with autism, however, are "blessed" with the tendency to push people away. "My kid bites me. Punches

"I couldn't get that word, *autism,* out of my mouth."

me. When he was little he would rip hair out of my head and chunks out of my skin. He ripped the door off its hinges last summer," says Heather.

Stacey O'Rourke, who works full-time as a pharmaceutical representative, finds the emotional disconnect particularly difficult. Her 4-year-old daughter, Katelyn, is severely autistic and doesn't clearly demonstrate reciprocal love. Stacey's twin girls, age 2, are also worrying her: They don't point, wave, or respond to their names very well. "People say to me, 'Oh, your daughter must really be into Christmas now because she's 4.' No. She has no clue about Christmas. These are constant reminders about how 'not normal' my life and my daughter are. You don't even want to talk to anybody new, so you don't have to explain. It's a continuous grieving process. You go through it every time your kid doesn't reach that next milestone. You realize how far behind you are."

Age 9, the group agrees, is a tough milestone.

"You really think that by 9 they'll be better," says Corinda.

"Because at 9, that is 'the kid you have,'" Erin agrees.

"I used to say when Max was little, 'I hope I never get to that point where I just accept this and move on,'" adds Corinda.

"We all did," Heather affirms.

"Thomas is 9," says Erin. "Am I accepting my son? Am I trying to fix him, or am I embracing him?"

"Am I trying to improve the quality of Padraic's life, or am I trying to improve the quality of mine?" asks Heather.

"At a certain point, I just thought, *Thomas doesn't deserve to be in 40 hours a week of therapy,*" says Erin. "*Thomas deserves a childhood.* Getting stuck in the siren song of finding a cure pulls you out of the necessary work of just being with your kid."

"My daughter's only 4; I'm still in that I-gotta-fix-her mode," Stacey admits.

"That's where you're supposed to be," Robert assures her in his doctorly way.

"That's totally developmentally right in accepting a disability," says his wife and colleague, Cindy Ariel, also a psychologist.

"Never give up," says Margaret.

Although this group of friends has no set meeting schedule (they often gather in twos and threes), when something important comes up they form a roundtable. Tonight that something is Jenny McCarthy.

"Before now, I just don't think I had the wherewithal

to say this," Erin starts in, her voice quavering. "But this mom came up to me at the pool. She was staring at Thomas. He was doing some of his odd things. I just snapped and said, 'He has autism.'"

Tears are now slowly rolling down Erin's face.

"And she said, 'Oh!... But haven't you heard of *Jenny McCarthy?*'"

A chorus of horrified gasps and "Oh my Gods!" ricochets around the dining room.

"Wow. Wow!"

"What did you say then?!"

Erin dabs her eyes. "I think that's the hardest moment, where you're just floored. You're never prepared for it. I said, 'Yeah, I've heard of Jenny McCarthy, and there's a whole other side to autism that I don't think you're probably familiar with.' And I walked away."

There is a beat of silence.

"That was a good answer. Write that one down."

"You were a lot nicer than a lot of us would be."

"I think 'bitch' would have sufficed."

McCarthy's controversial autism group, Generation Rescue (also publicized by her former boyfriend, Jim Carrey), contends—despite solid evidence to the contrary—that vaccines are primarily to blame for the recent rise in cases of autism. (In February 2009 a special federal court set up by Congress ruled that childhood vaccines do not cause autism.) McCarthy also claims that autism can be "reversed" through various regimens and therapies (many of them non–FDA approved and expensive)—her own son, who was diagnosed with autism in 2005, is now, she says, "recovered." For this group of mothers, who have spent the bulk of their children's lives frantically trying every treatment they could get their hands on, McCarthy's ideas can feel like salt in a wound.

"The fact that you *would* do all the things Jenny McCarthy wants you to—but the fact that you *can't*—is the most desperate, hopeless feeling in the entire world," says Heather. "I distinctly remember standing in my front yard. My husband was mad at me because I wanted to try another therapy for Padraic. I said, 'I don't care if I have to live in a cardboard box! I will charge every card that we have and do whatever I have to do for him!' And my husband never fought me again. Now we're in debt up to our ears."

This is another laugh line at the table, because almost

"Dr. Q told us to put lighter fluid on Max's feet."

everyone relates. (Informal marriage counseling is an added benefit the group provides.)

"We would have to mortgage our house if we wanted to try to live up to what Jenny McCarthy has supposedly done for her child," says Stacey.

"What gets me," Erin adds, "is, what if these treatments don't work? What if you do all of it and you still have autism?"

And that leads to a bigger issue—one that really burns this group: the implication that accepting your child's autism is not okay. This attitude is due in part, they feel, to Generation Rescue's dominating and oversimplifying the conversation in America about autism. The simple fact is that not all autistic kids can "recover." "We need to reexamine what it means to be a successful adult," says Erin. "To me, now, a successful adult is a functional adult. We need to give these kids an opportunity to have a shot at meaningful jobs and secondary education. Maybe they'll be bagging groceries, but they'll be paying taxes. They'll be law-abiding citizens. It's not just about the money we'd save, it's about the contributions these kids will make that will benefit everyone. I strongly believe that the energy crisis is eventually going to be solved by an autistic

Heather and her son Padraic, 10. Both have learned to swing between hope and acceptance.

10-year-old boy who is perseverating on batteries. He's got that kind of focus."

At this point, however, society still has a long way to go in terms of tolerating people who behave in unfamiliar ways.

"One thing I've been fearful of is standing in line at the airport with your autistic child, and your kid saying, 'Mom! I've got a bomb!' How the hell am I gonna deal with something like that?" asks Margaret.

I tell her my great-grandmother carried a card in her wallet saying I AM A DIABETIC. I HAVE NOT BEEN DRINKING. If Henry had a card, what would it read?

Margaret exclaims, "'I'm not inappropriate. I'm just autistic.'"

The table erupts in wild cackling.

"You really need a good sense of humor," says Margaret, wiping tears away. "This support group is lifesaving. There's just no other word for it. We laugh a lot. It helps us, doesn't it?"

"It saves me," says Heather.

"It saves me," says Erin.

"Dude, we made it!" Thomas and his rock band performed at the school variety show.

As the evening winds down and everyone starts thinking about leaving, Erin takes a moment to tell a story from their larger online community. A mother of a toddler recently contacted her after receiving an ASD diagnosis, and asked Erin, "If you had to start your path over, what would you do differently?" Erin tells the group, "I wrote her back and said, 'I'd have done less. I would have enjoyed my child more.'

"I'm proud of Thomas," she continues. "I love him, and I love the autism in him. I'm going to help him be the most functional adult that I can, but I love him exactly the way he is. Every family needs to hear that it's not an easy road, but their child, despite the diagnosis, is worth every ounce of their investment because triumph really is possible."

The table discusses various newspaper stories that inspire them—an autistic girl goes to college, an autistic man gets married. With enough care and investment, autistic people may go on to lead normal—and in some cases even extraordinary—lives. But Erin continues: "I worry about a world in which 'cures' can be obtained by some and not others. We need to convey that it's okay to have autism—to the 10-year-old boy who obsessively talks about model trains, to the 16-year-old boy who worries that he's different, or to the 25-year-old woman who can't form relationships—we need to show them: You're one of us. It's okay. We accept you."

A few weeks after the dinner, I get an e-mail Stacey has sent to the group: Her twin girls—2-year-old Julie and Megan—have received a diagnosis on the autism spectrum, though not as severe as Katelyn's. (Parents of a child with an ASD have a 2 to 8 percent chance of a second child also being affected.) "It's a knife in my heart," she writes. "I am scared to death for my daughters' futures, and whether I'll have the resources and ability to help them." But by the time I talk to her on the phone, the other mothers have already come to her aid, especially Heather, who is providing occupational therapy for all three of the girls through her employer. "The emotional support from the group, at least, is a silver lining," Stacey tells me. "These friendships are remarkable."

Erin, too, tells me she's suffered another blow. Thomas's doctor has determined that the seizure disorder will either remain as it is or eventually get worse. "But the same day, as Thomas and I were sitting in the neurology waiting room," she says, "his best friend called. I could hear him shouting, 'Dude, we made it! Our band got into the school variety show!'"

A couple of weeks later, Thomas and his band performed "Enter Sandman," by Metallica, on their school stage. I saw the video, and there he was: a very handsome, slightly aloof little rhythm guitar player in a black T-shirt, occasionally flashing a dazzling, blushing smile into the roaring crowd. As I said, I'm biased, but Thomas rocks. ⬤

Rashida Jones's Aha! Moment

When the actress's mother, Peggy Lipton, was diagnosed with cancer, Jones had a choice: fall into a dark hole or look for the lighter side.

My mother and I are more than best friends; we are partners in crime. After she and my father, Quincy Jones, separated when I was 10 years old, my sister, Kidada, who was 12, went to live with our dad, and I stayed with my mother. Mom is the most unconditionally loving person I will ever know, and she has always supported me on every level. She used to work with me before every audition; she's given me perspective, and she has let me cry when things haven't gone my way—which, when you're an actress, can happen a lot.

In 2002 Mom and I got a chance to act together in a play called *Pitching to the Star,* with her brother, Robert Lipton. The three of us on the same stage—that was such a special experience for me. When the play was over, I went to London for four months. Just a couple of days after I came back, Mom was diagnosed with cancer. At 56, she'd gone in for a routine colonoscopy, and her doctors found a stage III tumor. They recommended surgery and chemo immediately.

The minute the word *cancer* enters your house, everything changes. I felt like a huge anvil had fallen on me. But I knew that action needed to be taken—there were logistics to handle, and my mother needed support. Luckily, both of us now lived in New York, which was a huge blessing.

Chemotherapy is brutal. The goal is pretty much to kill everything in your body without killing you. I wished I could have gone through it for her; I wanted to take the burden off her. Then I figured out a way to help.

I decided my job was to find joyful moments during what could have been a terrifying time for both of us. One time we were in the hospital's chemo suite, waiting for her to be called in for the treatment. There are performers in the waiting room to keep the patients entertained,

and on this day there was a guitarist who was playing Simon and Garfunkel songs. He was so earnest, so sweet... and just not good at all. After he left, we laughed so hard. We had that moment of surrender where I thought, *This is kind of hilarious. I can't believe we're here, but thank God we're here together.* We told dumb jokes all day; at one point, I started calling my mom "Chemosabe." We laughed so much, she almost seemed to forget she was sick. That summer all we did was laugh.

Just because a situation is grim doesn't mean you don't have every right to smile. It isn't about "being strong" and pretending everything's okay; it's about finding joy where you can. My dad has always said, "Approach life with love and not fear." It's such a dynamic way to live.

I know that in life there will be sickness, devastation, disappointments, heartache—it's a given. What's not a given is the way you choose to get through it all. If you look hard enough, you can always find the bright side.

—*As told to Suzan Colón*

The Good Old Times

Shepherding fragile elders can leave a person lost and overwhelmed. **Martha Beck** offers a path back toward sanity.

I once attended a Navajo blessing ceremony, held in a tepee on the red sand of the Sonoran desert. The tepee was set up with great reverence, since to the Navajo, it symbolized the womb from which we all emerge, and the tent poles were "the bones of our grandmother." The word *grandparents* was spoken often and lovingly throughout the ceremony. The group's silver-haired matriarch quietly reigned over the gathering, with everyone else poised to supply her needs. It was a graceful dance of mutual care, with the elderly at the center.

By contrast, our First World way of caring for the elderly is a clumsy, exhausting tarantella. It force-partners isolated caregivers (usually middle-aged women) with decline, disease, dementia, and death. As one woman told me, "Having aging parents simultaneously orphaned me, saddled me

with two insane strangers, and shoved every nightmare about my own future right into my face." I heard many such stories as I researched this subject: Polly nearly bankrupted herself caring for her father, who has Alzheimer's. Brooke has barely slept since her ailing mother-in-law moved in. Jennifer had to testify against her parents in court so they'd be declared "incompetent to drive" before accidentally killing themselves or someone else.

This is what happens when a society forgets something people like the Navajo teach explicitly—that caring for the elderly is a "blessing path" in which the whole community should participate. Although our culture shows no signs of collectively adopting this perspective, there are ways to regain it on a case-by-case basis. If you're one of the 34 million or so Americans who are caring for an older relative, I offer my deep respect, and the following suggestions.

Practical Coping Strategies

As I interviewed people who are known in demographics as "unpaid caregivers," I thought I'd hear a few logistical hints. But that turned out to be like seeking just a few general rules on "how to heal sickness" or "controlling bad emotions." Every aging-parent scenario is unique, and there are precious few generalities that apply. One thing I can say is that you'll have fun with the responsibilities of eldercare if you enjoy running the high hurdles while juggling angry badgers. If not, you might try these techniques.

TRUST YOUR INTUITION ABOUT HOW MUCH CARE IS NEEDED. "There are hundreds of lines between being a little daffy and needing constant supervision," says Polly, describing her father's Alzheimer's. "At first my dad wasn't totally out to lunch; he was just…snacking. Then he definitely went out to lunch, then breakfast, then dinner. I've had to trust my instincts to increase care as he crossed each new line."

Denial is potent and seductive when it comes to dealing with aging. No one wants to acknowledge that a family member is in permanent decline. But when your parent gets really sick, or begins, um, lunching out, you'll feel an uneasy warning from your gut. Pay attention. The sooner you acknowledge the truth—"I must intercede"—the sooner you can begin exploring care options.

PREPARE FOR A LOGISTICAL WILDERNESS. There's no rule book to guide you through the morass of eldercare tasks and demands. Your best source of information is the Internet, where you can e-mail friends and family and research everything from buying walkers to curing constipation. If you're a caregiver and you don't like computers, get over it. Buy a laptop—it will cost far less than the mistakes it will help you avoid—and make some 8-year-old teach you to cruise the Web. Everyone I interviewed, even the technophobes, told me that the Internet was a lifeline in negotiating eldercare obligations.

Online information can prepare you—sort of—for the pragmatic tasks you may encounter: filling out medical paperwork, hiring a care nurse, wrestling the car keys out of a beloved parent's desperate clutches. Many of these duties will be indescribably difficult. But if instincts and information tell you to take a step, take it firmly, without second-guessing, the way you'd lead a frightened horse out of a burning barn. And don't try to manage everything alone.

CREATE YOUR OWN VILLAGE. The Navajo and other traditional cultures understand that there's nothing more soulful than supporting people at the margins of life, those who can't walk fast or talk sense or remember how to use a toilet. They also know that this takes a village.

It really does.

Most eldercare providers in our village-less society end up jury-rigging systems of helpers. The common refrain I heard from people in the trenches? Take notes. Write down every bit of advice you get, from every person who interacts with your family member: doctors, pharmacists, neighbors, hairstylists. Write down these people's contact information. For good or evil, they're your village.

Jennifer has 45 people on her call list should her elderly parents encounter a crisis. Polly rallied support from her parents' church congregation. Not everyone in the village will help care for an elderly person, but a long list gives you multiple possibilities for support.

"No one can tell you what to expect," Anne said to me. "You have to live like a firefighter, ready to call other firefighters to solve whatever problem arises."

Psychological Coping Strategies

Once you've adopted this firefighting mentality about your parent's needs, you'll need a whole new set of strategies like the ones below to deal with the emotional wreckage that piles up along the way.

SURRENDER TO THE EMOTIONAL GRINDER. "The thing that galls me most about caring for my mother," one woman told me, "is that she's the only one who gets a morphine drip." The emotional pain caregivers experience is intense—and unlike the elderly, caregivers are expected to live through it. With every new issue your elderly relative develops, you'll head into the emotional grinder called the grief process: bargaining, anger, sadness, acceptance, repeat.

Grieving, like physical caretaking, differs from case to case. If you had a rough relationship with an aging parent, expect to spend much time in the anger stage. Use this time to clean your emotional closet. Explore the anger with a therapist. Journal it. Process it with friends. Clean the wounds.

On the other hand, if your declining parent was your main source of emotional support, you'll find yourself spending lots of time in sadness. You'll feel as though it's killing you. It won't.

> Just acknowledging that a tough situation is funny makes it tolerable. Cracking up can keep you from, well, cracking up.

As Naomi Shihab Nye wrote, "Before you know kindness / as the deepest thing inside, / you must know sorrow / as the other deepest thing…. / Then it is only kindness / that makes sense anymore…."

As the grieving process scrapes along, you'll learn to offer kindness to everyone: your aging relative, the people of your village, yourself. When you snap under stress and begin to rail at Nana, God, yourself, and the cat, you'll learn to be kind to yourself anyway. At that point, you'll find relief and an unexpected gift: laughter.

NOURISH A SICK SENSE OF HUMOR.

A morbid sense of humor isn't listed in any official guides to eldercare, but to the caregivers I interviewed, it is like oxygen. Take, for example, Meg Federico's memoir *Welcome to the Departure Lounge*. Federico's wry portrayal of her mother's senescence is both sad and hilarious. Without belittling her mother or her stepfather, Walter, both of whom suffered dementia, Federico recounts conversations like this one:

> "I can't seem to find my keys," Walter told Mom. "Say, do you have them?"
>
> "Oh, don't worry about keys, dearest. We don't need them. We can jump out the window and fly home."
>
> "What?" said Walter. "You can fly? I never knew."
>
> "So can you, but you have to take your shoes off."
>
> To Walter's credit, he was not convinced.

Just acknowledging that this is funny makes it tolerable. Cracking up can keep caregivers from, well, cracking up.

"Bill and I are training his dad to 'go toward the light,'" said my friend Anne, whose father-in-law no longer recognizes his family. "Any light we see—lamps, flashlights, the TV—we steer him over there. We figure he can use the practice."

Of course, Anne isn't serious. Not being serious is how she and Bill are surviving. If you can't train your elder to go toward the light, you can make light of the situation. And sometimes, that light becomes splendiferous.

PONDER THE NATURE OF EXISTENCE.

There's nothing like caring for the elderly to help you face your own mortality. Many caregivers told me that their experience was dissolving, through simple drudgery, their fear of death. Pulitzer Prize–winning psychologist Ernest Becker wrote that the denial of death underlies all evils, and that we must drop this denial to live fully. The caregivers I interviewed would agree.

"Fear of death was my biggest obstacle in life," said Polly. "To help my dad, I have to get past it. He's showing me how to die, which is really helping me live."

Other caregivers went further. They said that as they watched the door close on their loved one's physical identity, a door to the metaphysical slowly opened.

"I don't believe in an afterlife, but as my mother died, I truly understood that being dead is no more frightening than being asleep, which I love."

"As my husband's body was failing, he became almost translucent. I went right through my own pain and felt the most intense peace. I can still find that."

"Just before my grandmother died in surgery, I heard her voice saying, 'I'm leaving now, but you'll be fine.' I've been less anxious about everything ever since."

This is why traditional cultures value even the most fragile, disoriented elder, why the Navajo carry "Grandmother's bones" with such reverent attention. Even as you grapple with the logistical and psychological stress of eldercare, there will be moments when you find yourself on the "blessing path." Rather than a long day's journey into night, you'll feel yourself making a long night's journey into day: through fear and confusion to courage and wisdom. Receive this gift, the final one your parents can offer before they take off their shoes, jump out the window, and fly home. ❶

Lisa Kogan Tells All

If you could redo just one moment in your life, what would it be? Our grateful columnist keeps it all in the family.

Mindy Perlmutter was having a birthday party, but this was not just your garden variety, chocolate cake, two kinds of ice cream, balloons, and a piñata type soiree. No, this would be an affair to remember. This would be even more fabulous than Alicia Mittenthal's tie-dye-your-own-pillowcase gala or Daisy Feng's macramé-your-own-bracelet bash. This was to be a build-your-own-terrarium shindig, complete with colored sand and plastic stones and an incredibly classy assortment of glass goldfish bowls. At the time (the time being about 34 years ago), it seemed like a very big deal—I

mean, let's be honest here, it would still be a big deal to go to a party where you get to build your own terrarium...in, you know, a kind of retro, '70s, ironic, hipster way.

So there I sat, looking out the den window, which gave me a clear view to the driveway while I waited for my ride to come spirit me away. Actually, it hadn't been our den since my grandparents returned from their life in Miami Beach and my folks rented a hospital bed to turn the den into my grandmother's bedroom. I loved my grandmother, but I can't say I ever really got to know her. She was the lady who played bingo and walked with a cane and kept a plump red tomato pincushion next to the creaky old foot-pedal-powered Singer sewing machine. I remember that she put up her own pickles and draped strudel dough across the kitchen table, and I know that she learned to reupholster her own furniture and got her first driver's license when she was deep into her 50s, and I'm acutely aware that she spoke to my grandfather in a very stern Yiddish whenever he tried to convince me to watch *The Lawrence Welk Show*. My grandmother endured an awful lot from the man, but no grandchild of hers was going to be forced to watch *Lawrence Welk* so long as she still had breath in her body.

Anyway, the sun was going down and my ride was running late and my grandmother started to talk. I thought she was going to warn me to be careful of something or other, because she was from the generation who believed that pigeons carry polio and she worried a lot, but if she was anxious about anything that night, she didn't show it. "I used to love to go to parties," she told me. She might as well have said that she used to enjoy scaling Mount Everest in flip-flops and a tutu. I was pretty sure I'd heard all the stories from my grandmother's life—and none of them involved a party.

The talk I'd heard was always the same: She and her mother and her five brothers and sisters starving through the bitter Russian winters in a little village whose name sounded like a sneeze. I knew about the malnutrition, the crippling rickets, the father who slaved away for years in Detroit trying to earn enough money to bring his wife and children to America and how when he finally did manage to save enough, the man he entrusted with the job of bringing the family over disappeared with the money (was he killed? did he steal it?), leaving my great-grandfather to start all over again. I'd heard how my great-uncles Sam and Isadore would scrounge through fields looking for anything edible while my grandmother supported everyone with her job as a maid to the butcher's wife, and I knew by heart the story of how she lost that job because the woman caught her taking a sip of milk. I also knew how she met Arthur Levy, the love of her life, who my great-aunt Molly swore looked "exactly like a young Perry Como," and that he died a few weeks after she married him, though she never stopped wearing his ring. I knew that the first son she had with my grandfather had died, and that on a Friday afternoon in 1939, her father, the man who worked so hard to bring the family here, died, too, after being pushed off the roof of a building in an anti-Semitic attack. And, of course, I knew that she worked nonstop to build a better life for her children.

But I realize now that I only knew those stories because they were told to me by other people. The night of Mindy Perlmutter's terrarium party, my grandmother was telling me the things *she* wanted me to know. She talked about dances and boys and a silvery blue dress she'd sewn with her sisters. She told me about a time when all her friends were doubled over with laughter because...well, I'm not really sure what it was they found so funny. There was a honk and the glare of headlights, so I gave my grand-mother a fast peck on the cheek and flew straight out the door. She went into the hospital the next morning, and she never came out.

I sit playing Candy Land with the great-granddaughter Rose Kogan never got to meet. Julia Claire closes her eyes, blows on the dice, and whispers, "C'mon, c'mon, Mama needs a pair of deuces."

I have no idea why my 6-year-old sounds like Edward G. Robinson, but I make a mental note to quit letting her play blackjack with the doormen. She rolls "snake eyes" and becomes my little girl again. "I want a do-over, Mommy."

I start to explain that we don't really get do-overs in this world, that you kind of have to play it as it lays. I believe the parenting books call this a "teachable moment," but my follow-through leaves much to be desired. I hand Jules the dice and say, "Go for it, kid."

The truth is, I want a do-over, too. I have ignored my instincts, I have embraced my neuroses, and there have been more than a few serious lapses in judgment over the years—hell, I once painted my bathroom aubergine. But if I could get just one night back, it would be a chilly October evening when nothing mattered more to me than hanging with my friends in Mindy Perlmutter's basement.

I would have taken off my coat and sat back down, only this time I'd have faced my grandmother instead of the driveway. I would have asked her if the good times outweighed the bad, if there were nights she'd do differently, if she'd ever felt like giving up—or if that was even an option. I never told her how smart and talented and brave and lovely I thought she was. I never heard what was so great about Greer Garson and Walter Pidgeon in *Mrs. Miniver*. I never found out what she did to make her skin so soft and her matzo balls so firm or if she'd have preferred it the other way around. And I never thanked her for being my go-to grandma in the unconditional goodness department.

Julia and I finish the game and say our goodnights. I am eager to return a couple of calls, get her lunch packed for school, and watch the episode of *Mad Men* I've got waiting on our DVR. But my daughter is feeling chatty. "Mommy," she begins, "do you know why the Princess Barbie Musketeers have swords that match their ball gowns?" Before I can answer, she announces, "It's because they're royal squashbucklers." I tell her I'm pretty sure the word is *swashbucklers*, and she tells me she's pretty sure I'm wrong and goes on talking. She doesn't want to let go of the night, and so I nudge away two stuffed poodles and curl up beside her. The calls and the lunch and even Don Draper can wait, because I have learned the hard way that my job is to sit quietly in the dark and listen to whatever my daughter has to say. ◖▮

Breathing Space

KITE KIDS, NATAL, BRAZIL, 2002 | Photograph by Ashton Keiditsch

YOUR LIFE/ YOUR WORLD

make a connection

206 HARMONIC GETAWAY | BY JANE HAMILTON

210 "WILL YOU BE MY SISTER?" | BY EVA LUX BRAUN

213 THE WOMEN IN THE WATER | BY BETTY KINDLEY

216 LISA KOGAN TELLS ALL

218 A SLIM PEACE | BY DINA KRAFT

221 A STITCH IN TIME | BY MERIBAH KNIGHT

226 WHAT ARE THEY THINKING? | BY EUGENE LINDEN

230 THE JOAN SHOW | BY JESSICA WINTER

231 WILD THINGS | BY RICK BASS

Left: Faculty rehearsing in a concert barn at the Apple Hill Center for Chamber Music. *Below, from left:* The quintet—Jennifer Delahunty, Betsy Weinstein, Leslie Brown, Jane Hamilton, Libby Ester.

Harmonic Getaway

Jane Hamilton had no intention of growing, changing, making new friends, or—at 50—going on any more voyages of self-discovery. That was before she and the rest of her rusty quintet took themselves off to a magical, mouse-ridden summer music camp.

In recognition of our approaching 50th birthdays, four college friends and I, all living far away from each other, tossed around several ideas about how best to celebrate the strange accomplishment of having become so old. A spa with a sweat lodge, the pilgrimage to Santiago de Compostela, a crash course in skydiving?

"Why not chamber music camp in New Hampshire?" the violinist in our crowd suggested.

Some of us were dubious. Four out of five of us, musi-cally speaking (cello, violin, string bass, recorder, and piano), are dabblers or bumblers or now-and-againers. In the de-cades since college we've played through our little reper-toire every so often strictly for our own pleasure. If years pass between our private concerts the pieces always sound reassuringly the same: the same errors, the same dips where the instrument isn't in tune, the same omission of a difficult run. And yet, somehow or other the violinist was able to talk us into applying to the camp, which has the ambitiously warmhearted mission of bringing people of all ages and na-tions and skill levels to make joyful noise.

In January of 2007, with July serenely far off, we sent in our applications and our sketchy tapes. A few weeks later we each received enthusiastic letters of acceptance. For some reason, the idea of five 50-year-old rusty dabblers was an excitement to the administration. We couldn't help thinking that they were desperate to fill session three, or the drear winter had gotten to them, or they didn't often get applications from people who weren't also wanting scholarships. We had our initial panic in March, when an e-mail came, sternly instructing us to learn our parts for the Telemann overture that had been assigned to our group. We dutifully ordered the music and tried—we did try—to practice. By the time we were slowly driving up the gravel hill to the camp for ten days of chamber music incarceration, all of us were unsure of the wisdom of the plan. Libby, the bass player, said, "Remind me why we didn't go to a spa?"

We carried our duffels down to our cabin in the woods, which had the unmistakable bitter smell of mouse urine and the more concrete evidence of black sprinkles on the floor. The old pine floors were crudely planed and splintered, the windows, most of which did not open, were smudged, and there was a careless patchwork of drywall. There were the essential five narrow beds, five hooks, five shelves. We noted the great distance between our cabin and the one bathroom. Still, the beautiful meadow and woods, the mountain views, and the dark gray cedar barns did jibe with our sense of what real camp should be, a rustic place of both industry and tranquillity.

We marched down the hill to put our toiletries in our designated swollen wooden cubbies in the damp bathroom. The long, low room was already saturated with the colliding sweetness of various hair products and the ordinary thick odors of communal living. No one said, but I'm sure we were all feeling far too old for this experience. We were taken to the rehearsal barn and shown where to put our instruments and our music. Camp lore has it that in the 1880s the camp had been a sheep farm, and without too much strain I could imagine myself as one among the gang of Hampshires or Dorsets, waiting for my grain, adding my baaing to the chorus, and presumably safely grazing.

After our things were situated in the rehearsal barn, we needed, already, to escape back to the cabin. On our way we walked through the concert barn, where a tall, boyish young man was playing a Handel sonata for violin that had been transcribed for the string bass. It looked as if his instrument had been stitched into his side, as if a large, ungainly, deep-throated girl had attached herself to him, and what else could he do but make her speak tenderly? The notes of the accompanying harpsichord glittered along with the dust motes in the dim post-and-beam space that had one floor-to-ceiling panel of windows. In the distance the Green Mountains were a soft blue in the sunny haze. Jennifer, the cellist, said breathlessly, "I could go home happy right now."

Good idea, I thought—we could all go home happy at this moment! I had come to camp to be a good sport, but I did not really want to be there, I did not want to brush my teeth in the dirty sink in the steamy bathroom, did not want to sleep on the plastic-coated mattress, and I didn't much want to play the bombastic, silly Telemann overture.

Not so many years before, I had dragged my daughter to a wilderness camp in Vermont. She clung to me weeping as I'd tried to say goodbye, and although we later heard from her counselors and knew that all was well, she herself did not send us a single sentence for the month. When it was over, on the way home in the car, across Vermont, New York, Pennsylvania, all the long way across Ohio and Indiana, through the congestion of Gary and Chicago, and finally into Wisconsin, she alternately sobbed and feverishly wrote to her new friends. I couldn't help remembering that feeling I'd had as a girl, the sense that you have left your very heart behind as your parents drive you inexorably toward your bleak town, back to your old gray life. There, it turns out, your family and your friends don't see the person you've become, the person you were meant to be all along, the you who emerged and was acknowledged and treasured at Camp X. What you have left of Camp X, besides the secret knowledge of your best self, is your worn list of addresses, the photographs, the water from the lake in a jar, the sand in an envelope, a few leaves from the tree, songs that matter to you past speech that you will sing to yourself for solace, and private jokes that are the funniest things that have ever been uttered, which no one at home can understand even if they would consider listening to the whole setup. Love, nothing short of love more real than you've ever known, has been seared into your being, and no one can tell this about you at home, and no one cares.

I not only doubted that such a transformation would occur at camp to my nicely fixed 50-year-old self, I fervently hoped nothing of the sort would, not even in the far more mild, somewhat benign form that is appropriate to my age and station. At any level, how tedious that would be, how exhausting, how dull, and, also, how predictable. All I really wanted to do was lie in bed and read, and chamber music camp and the potential attachments were just more interruptions in a lifetime of interruptions.

There were a couple of problems at the start besides the fact that few of the campers seemed interesting, and everyone I didn't already know seemed annoying—just as, no doubt, we seemed to them. On the first morning, right after breakfast, I had to sweep the breezeway and collect trash from the rehearsal barn. There is naturally no camp without announcements after mealtimes, and community-building activities, and jobs. Twenty hours into it the law of camp was clear: The night was for teenagers, the morning for the aged. A few high schoolers sat slumped in their chairs at 9 A.M. while I fluttered around them tidying. I'd paid fifteen hundred dollars to come to a place that was just like home.

After jobs we five dabblers met our coach, an elegant 29-year-old violist from Amsterdam. We played the opening of our Telemann for him. He looked stunned. And then he put his chin down and laughed softly into his chest. We are strong and impervious so of course this did not affect us, not at all. We could see the bubble over his handsome head: *Oh my God*. We could see him mustering his reserves, trying to remember the creed of the camp, that he was supposed to be positive and nurturing. Some of us have serious intonation problems, some of us cannot count, some of us are afflicted by nerves when we play for anyone other than ourselves, some of us suffer from all of those troubles, but it must be said that none of us lacked courage during the first session.

That night, in the dark, dark cabin with the thick spattering of stars in the heavens through the windows, and the blanket of quiet all around us, a mouse ran across Leslie's face. She screamed and leaped from the wafer that was her mattress. I suppose if we'd been able to look down upon such a scene from a great height we right away would have found it funny that a small, soft, white-bellied creature with dewy and soulful eyes who was scampering like the wind with claws had struck horror and revulsion in those who have great intelligence and massive body weight, relatively speaking. We were repulsed down to our marrow. We did not want to try to go back to sleep—how could we sleep? Leslie, who, after the scream, was of remarkably good cheer,

Summer sonata: Apple Hill's rehearsal barn and auditorium.

said that it had actually been an extraordinary experience, but she did think, in spite of the thrill, that she'd go up to the barn to read for a while. (While she was sitting in the rehearsal room, another mouse ran over her foot.) At any rate, we did then try to find the situation comic rather than fearsome and gross in the extreme as we lay awake waiting for it and its siblings to return. The next day I went to the hardware store and got the sonar devices that plug in to the wall, two of them, even though one will do for a medium-size room, and also I purchased four traps, which we set out with the relish of explorers in the territories. We began to look forward to checking the lines to see what had come in.

In those first days I had little interest in slogging through the preliminaries of friendship, I suppose because I know enough people at this stage and have more than enough e-mail correspondents, and because, as I said, I wanted most of all to be reading a novel. But I began to feel, in spite of myself, a general, vague affection for the group. It was very nice to bathe while the Brahms Serenade from upstairs in the concert barn steamed with the water through the showerhead, and one afternoon when a group of teenagers was playing the Ravel String Quartet, rain began to fall, a soft sheet down the long windows, which seemed to seal us into the gorgeousness of the moment. There was nothing better than drinking a cup of tea on the porch in the morning while inside the barn the A, taken up by the violin, and passed to the other strings and the woodwinds, gathered force, the note swelling out into the open air and down the hillside. I did love the fact that all of us, the witty, the shy, the old, the super-talented, the plodders, were held under the same spell.

Even before I gave myself up to camp, there were plenty of scenes, several a day in fact, that seemed well worth the price of admission. We were growing fond of our valiant coach, and in our small rehearsal room—Betsy on the harpsichord, Jennifer on the cello, Leslie, violin tucked under her chin looking worried, Libby on the bass trying to keep us in time and in tune, and I, toodling on the recorder—we now and again managed to transcend our limitations and actually come together to make music, what felt like the real sublime thing. The night the faculty gave a concert, we sat

Libby said, "Remind me why we didn't go to a spa?"

up in the balcony of the barn looking down on the Bruckner String Quintet that went on for 45 riveting minutes. We were close enough to read their impossible sheet music on the stands and see the smallest flickering smiles between them, signs of private jokes, or assurances, or maybe gratitude. The second violist was wearing green flip-flops with daisies, and before an entrance she'd quick wrap her foot around the leg of her chair, her red toenails flashing. The music and the friendship between them seemed a kind of improbable physics, a profound and effortless labor.

As a girl I had been prone to rapture, but I am no longer in thrall to it as I once was. I don't remember when that part of me that responds intensely began to retreat, but I can feel how much it isn't there anymore. It seems wrong to call this middle-aged absence, this flatness, serenity, but perhaps that's what it is. The faculty concert wasn't an ecstatic event for me, but it was nonetheless a great privilege to be so close to the miracle of the music as it was being made. It's possible that without the high pitch of rapture an experience itself is more pure, that without so much rattling emotion there is room for clarity. In any case, we 50s, as they called us at camp, are well past the ambition of youth, and also past the point of having a future of failure. In the usual inevitable ways, we've already failed—failed ourselves, our spouses, our children—and we know we only have more failure to look forward to. Failure, *c'est nous*. And so, in that dusty room with the passionate, difficult Bruckner, we, without ambition and with so much already done, were free in a way a 20-year-old could not imagine.

By the fifth day I was no longer anxiously trying to find time to read my book. The people, as is their irritating habit, were proving, damn them, to be fascinating and irresistible. There was the cellist camper from New York, who'd spent her girlhood in her bedroom playing along with a recording of Dvořák's Piano Quintet in A Major and was finally, at age 40, playing the piece with live musicians, this after surviving two complicated back surgeries and not practicing for years. The dazzling 18-year-old Israeli pianist had learned to speak English by listening to rap music and thus was someone you would not want your children to encounter. His playing was fierce and mature. The twin girls with Pre-Raphaelite hair were equally charming and brilliant, and while they played tangos one night after dinner with day lilies tucked behind their ears,

We could see the bubble over our coach's handsome head: *Oh my God.*

one on the violin, the other on the piano, a bat swooped back and forth above them. A 16-year-old violinist from Brooklyn was alternating, in her spare time, between *Catch-22* and the then just-released last Harry Potter book. The Navy captain and doctor who works for the FDA and is an expert in infectious diseases, and who practices his clarinet every day for two to four hours before work, who at first seemed standoffish (or was that us?) turned out to be warm and engaging and, incidentally, a terrific musician. The Irish girls, the couple from Turkey, the three from Cyprus, the three from Burma, the shy high school senior from Fort Wayne, all of them wormed their way into our affections.

The final concert, the big performance all of our practice was leading to, was a butchery and a preview of hell. The error I made in the first measure was so critical we had to stop the piece and begin again, and the second time I did not get it right either. I could not catch my breath, I had too much air, I could not stop trembling, my fingers were wet, I hit my recorder on the stand while it was in my mouth and hurt my tooth, and my face was aboil. And yet, when we took our bows the whole place went crazy, everyone cheering wildly, clapping and stomping their feet. What a fantastic camp! What a bunch of glorious if maybe deranged enthusiasts! Afterward one of the coaches said, "Your performance had everything in it—and I mean everything." A camper said, "You played really a lot of notes!" We retired to a cabin the size of my kitchen table where 25 people crowded in and around the bed to drink. Soon I had forgotten my disgrace. Later we joined the teenagers, who didn't seem to mind, and danced in the barn long after every last mouse was caught.

I didn't cry or sniffle leaving camp even though I loved the place and enjoyed the characters and revered the principles of the institution. At my half-century mark my love for the people was far more general than my former girlish passion for each of her fellow campers. At chamber music camp I loved the spectacular array of the personalities, the whole bizarre and astonishing fact of the human spectrum. I loved all the musicians for their love of chamber music, and I loved best being able to leave them and go home. At 50 it's a solace to know that you have been in the path of rapture, and that it will be there, that great pool of beauty, whether or not you're there to feel it. ◘

Eva Lux Braun (*left*), 81, and Miriam Brach, 79, in Brooklyn in 2008, 64 years after their first meeting en route to Auschwitz. "Without Eva, I would not have made it," says Brach.

"Will You Be My Sister?"

In the horror of the Holocaust, Eva Lux Braun saved another girl's life—
and a remarkable friendship was born.

Miriam Rappaport and I had a lot in common: We were both teenagers from comfortable middle-class homes in Kassa, Hungary; we had blonde hair and blue eyes; and we were Jews. In the eyes of the Third Reich, this last fact was unpardonable. It is why they forced us to wear yellow stars. It is why in the spring of 1944 the police ordered our families to leave our homes and report to an old factory an hour away, along with the rest of the region's Jewish population. When my family arrived, we saw thousands of people living in terrible conditions, sleeping on straw mats, with nothing but a suitcase each, the clothes on their backs, and whatever dignity they had left. Miriam was sitting on the mat next to mine. The first thing I said to her was, "What are we doing here?" We did not know that this factory, where bricks were once made, was a halfway house to Auschwitz.

She was 15, I was 16½. At night we would lie on our mats, talking about school, friends, and all the other things we missed. We didn't want to admit it to ourselves, but we knew our former lives were over. Only hope and faith sustained us. "It shouldn't get worse, it should only get better," our parents told us. "The important thing is that we are together."

After three weeks, in late May, the police herded us onto cattle cars. In the madness, I lost track of Miriam.

We didn't know where the train was going. On the third day someone looked out through a crack and said, "We just crossed the Polish border." Eventually we stopped. There were a lot of SS officers and emaciated men in striped pajamas. Black smoke and a terrible smell filled the air. A sign read AUSCHWITZ-BIRKENAU.

As we exited the train, a tall, handsome German officer directed men to the right, women to the left. Then the women were divided again. My mother and little sister Susie went with the older women and small children; my younger sister Vera and I with the young, healthy girls. Vera was taller and sturdier than I, and I remember how the officer put his hands on her shoulders and murmured, "strong." (Later, another prisoner whispered to me that he was Josef Mengele, the Angel of Death.) Everyone was screaming for their loved ones. "Take care of your sister!" my mother cried out to me. "Stay together!"

One of the men in striped pajamas seemed to be in a position of authority. Pointing to the chimneys, I asked him, "What is that smoke?"

He said very nonchalantly, "They are liquidating another camp. Your family is going there, to be gassed and put in the crematorium."

Shocked, I asked, "Why can't you lie? I want to hear a lie, not the truth."

"Concentrate on living," he replied. "Forget everything that was before."

I can't begin to describe our terror as Vera and I were lined up with the other young women and taken to the showers. Our heads were shaved and we were stripped and disinfected as the guards smirked at our nakedness. We were given discarded clothes, herded to quarantine, and six weeks later, led to permanent barracks in an adjoining camp. As Vera and I stood in line for our meager food—thin soup and a piece of hard, dry bread—a girl approached us. It was Miriam! We were thrilled to find each other again, but clearly she was frightened, desperate, and alone. It was common for girls to bond together in the concentration camps for support; there was even a name for it: *lager-schwester*. "Eva," she said, "will you be my camp sister?"

From then on, the three of us were inseparable. We were together when they tattooed our forearms; at the quarry where we loaded rocks into wheelbarrows; and at night, in our hard bunks, unable to sleep. We were kicked and beaten, called swine, whores—names I'd never heard before. When Vera and Miriam refused to eat because they didn't want to live anymore, I made them eat. When they cried at night, I comforted them. When they refused to work, I urged them on so they wouldn't get beaten. Every five minutes we were told that the only way out of Auschwitz

We were together when they tattooed our forearms; at the quarry where we loaded rocks into wheelbarrows; and at night, in our hard bunks, unable to sleep.

was through the chimneys. I knew my mother and sister had left that way, but I prayed my father was still alive. My dream that Vera and I would see him again kept me going.

One day the elder of the camp block said the guards needed 200 girls to work at a factory in Germany. They assembled us and divided us into two groups. For the first time in nine months, Vera and Miriam were separated from me. Everyone was ordered to strip. When the guard led my group to the showers, and when hot water, not gas, came out of the pipes, I knew that I was leaving Auschwitz and that my sisters were condemned to death.

After the shower we were herded back into the anteroom. The other group was still there, naked and shivering. Miriam and Vera were holding each other, sobbing. There was a bench between us and an SS officer with a rifle and a dog. On the floor lay a hose. Suddenly the guard was called away, leaving us unwatched.

Many times I've wondered what made me do it—despair, the will to help my sisters survive, the courage to resist. I toppled over the bench, picked up the hose and began to spray the other group. "Get wet! Everybody get wet!" I cried. When the guard came back he couldn't tell which group was which. He demanded to know who had done this, but miraculously, nobody turned me in. Fortunately, we were needed for the German war effort or they would have killed us all. By the time he had regrouped us, Miriam and Vera were with me.

We spent the winter of 1945 in Germany marching from one factory to another. With no coats, and in shoes held together with string, dozens of Jewish prisoners walked for miles through the snow. Our numbers dwindled. Several times, when Miriam and Vera wanted to give up, I forced them to continue—anyone who sat down was shot. At Salzwedel concentration camp, a French POW told us that the end was near and urged us to hold on. That night, American tanks entered the camp, but we were too frail to celebrate.

After several weeks in a transient camp in Germany, Miriam and I parted ways. She hugged me tightly and cried and thanked me for taking care of her. She returned to our hometown, while Vera and I traveled to Budapest, where we had an uncle, finally ending up back in Kassa;

> Many times I've wondered what made me do it— despair, the will to help my sisters survive, the courage to resist.

the city had been annexed by Czechoslovakia and renamed Kosice. Miriam was no longer there. Vera went to live in a boarding school in Bratislava, and I stayed in Kosice for a few years, working as a cashier in a stationery store, hoping against hope that my father would return. He never did.

One day, while visiting family in Nitra, I was reunited with a distant relative named Eli Braun, whose family had survived the war by assuming Christian identities. Eli and I became engaged. He had relatives in Williamsburg, Brooklyn, where Vera had landed two years earlier. In January 1950, Eli and I arrived in Williamsburg. A few days later, I was leaving my apartment building when I saw a young woman walking down the street. She was heavier than I remembered and wore a blonde *sheitel,* or wig, but there was no doubt: It was Miriam. We ran to each other, tears of joy streaking our faces, and embraced. She told me she was married to another survivor, Sam Brach, who had lost his parents and nine siblings in the Holocaust, and they had a daughter.

"Where do you live?" I asked.

"Right here!" Miriam said, and pointed across the street.

There is a saying from the Talmud, "...anyone who preserves a single life is as though he preserves the whole of mankind." Miriam acknowledged that by saving her, I had saved the children she would someday have. We lived across the street from each other for two years, and our families spent Sundays together; her daughters would sprawl on my floor, watching *Lassie* with my son. They often asked us about the war, but we didn't like to talk about it. We tried so hard not to remember. Today Vera is in poor health, and Miriam, a widow, lives near me. Neither of us likes to speak of those dark ages, but I feel it is my mission to talk about that time. I tell my story to high school children in New York City and to visitors at Yad Vashem, the Holocaust History Museum in Jerusalem, where I have volunteered as a guide. My rabbi says that nothing is coincidence; everything is preordained. So I must have been meant to cross paths with Miriam, not just once, but twice; to survive where six million died; to live to bear witness, while I still can.   —*As told to Dana White*

The Women in the Water

Battling a deadly riptide, **Betty Kindley** thought all was lost—until two rescuers appeared in the waves.

I believe that things happen and we don't understand why, and perhaps we never will. Yet there must be a purpose, a reason that McKenzie Perry and Kary Hodge were on the same beach on that day, at that time, and that they both had the courage and the will to risk their lives for me, a stranger. Their heroism taught me that a chance encounter can not only change a life; it can sometimes save a life.

It was June 2006. Six friends and I had driven from Asheville, North Carolina, to Charleston, South Carolina, to spend a few days with our friend Judy Davidson, who had grown up with us and retired to the shore. She was a former schoolteacher, attractive, kind, and upbeat. Everyone loved her. On Sunday morning, we debated going to church but decided to go shelling on Sullivan's Island instead. We arrived at about 10 A.M. There had been storms all week off the coast, and just as we entered the water, thunder rumbled in the distance.

Judy, her husband, Bobby, our friend Maureen, and I entered a calm ocean and waded in up to our waists. They walked out onto a sandbar while I stayed behind at a deep tide pool, feeling for sand dollars with my toes. Instead I found a small, perfect conch and a sea urchin. *How odd,* I thought. In all my years of shelling, I'd never found either of these. I went back to the beach, showed my treasures to the rest of the girls, and put them in my bag.

I went back into the ocean again and joined Maureen on the sandbar. Bobby and Judy were playing in the water about 15 feet away; he was bouncing her on his knees the way a parent bounces a child. Suddenly, Judy, still in his arms, yelled to us, "Bobby says he feels a strong current." Maureen and I also felt the current tugging at our legs, and I said, "We'd better go back." As we started wading toward shore, Bobby let out a bloodcurdling scream for help. I turned to see a huge wave hanging over them, like an enormous paw, and Bobby desperately trying to throw Judy shoreward. I rushed to them thinking, *I'll take Judy's hand, and Bobby and I will walk her out of the water.*

Instead all three of us were sucked into the giant wave. It churned us around as if we were in a washing machine. Through the clear water I watched the current sucking sand out to sea and Bobby on his hands and knees, clawing his way out, as if he'd fallen on a speeding treadmill. The sandbar was breaking apart beneath us. Bobby and Maureen managed to fight their way to safety, but I was focusing on Judy, who couldn't swim. The ocean floor disappeared and the monster wave carried us both out toward the sea. Summoning my high school lifeguard training, I wrapped my arms around Judy's chest and neck and tried to swim toward shore, but it was impossible. I didn't want us to waste our energy battling the current, so I decided that the best thing to do was simply go with it.

The current pulled us out, farther and farther, as towering waves crashed over us. Judy couldn't tread water, and the waves made floating impossible. I knew how to kick and go over the waves, but she didn't. Judy kept going under. A wave would wash her out of my arms, I'd swim to her, dive down, and pull her back up. For what seemed like an eternity, we struggled. She never panicked—she called out for help only once—but I talked to her nonstop: "Let me hold you up. It's going to be okay." The day before, we'd seen dozens of windsurfers and Jet Skis on the water, but now I saw nothing. I learned later that on the beach, some men had rushed into the water but were turned back by the colossal surf. Someone even tried to launch a catamaran, but it broke apart in the violent waves.

Out at sea, I whispered a brief prayer: "God help us."

When Judy stopped moving, I wasn't sure what had happened. I held her face out of the water and grasped her swimsuit strap, keeping her with me.

As a wave lifted us up, I saw for the first time how far we were from shore, and my heart sank. I couldn't imagine getting back in, we were so far out. Yet I couldn't leave her. I thought surely a boat would come soon. *This is really happening,* I thought. *I might not make it.*

Suddenly, I heard a woman's voice: "Where are you?"

I jerked my head in the voice's direction, astounded. I never expected anyone to swim out. Ships, boats, yes. But not this.

"Over here!" I yelled. For 20 minutes we called back and forth to each other until a young woman swam up to me. "My name's McKenzie," she gasped. She circled me, afraid that I was going to latch onto her the way a drowning person tends to. I didn't, so she said, "Swim this way."

"Can you help me with her?" I asked.

"Who?" McKenzie asked. She hadn't seen Judy through the waves. "Is she okay?"

"No," I said. "I think she's gone."

> The ocean floor disappeared and the monster wave carried us both out toward the sea.

McKenzie swam to Judy and confirmed that she was. Then she said, "If you're going to make it, you're going to have to leave her."

She gave me permission to let Judy go. Still, McKenzie had to pry my hand off Judy's swimsuit strap. I had never been so tired. McKenzie turned me on my back, and I swam using the elementary backstroke, just as I'd been taught as a girl. All I can remember is looking up at the sky.

Unbelievably, another young woman appeared out of the waves; she said her name was Kary. "Do you need help?"

Using the Sullivan's Island lighthouse as a landmark, they guided and pulled me to shore, one on each side of me. As we swam against the current, they'd tap me on the shoulder and say, "We're here. Don't worry. We're here." When I'd stop from exhaustion, they'd tread water beside me and encourage me on again.

We were almost at the beach when a fire department Jet Ski appeared. I was pulled up onto it, and McKenzie and Kary held on to the sides as it took us to shore.

In the chaos of the following hours, I lost track of my two rescuers. When I think back, the scenes flip by like a slideshow: My friends' stunned faces after I told them what had happened, Bobby's grief; giving statements at the town hall; the long drive back to Judy and Bobby's house; the lunch I couldn't eat. I took one of Judy's sleeping pills, and my friends put me to bed. The next day I woke up distraught, but determined to know who those young women were, to find them and thank them.

Four days later, Judy was laid to rest in Asheville. The day of the funeral, I called the Sullivan's Island fire department on the hunch that it might have the women's names and numbers. I was right. I called Kary Hodge right away; when she answered, I said through my tears, "You saved my life. And I love you and thank you so much." Kary said she had been on the beach that day with her husband, Josh, a naval submarine officer. She was 28, a breast cancer survivor who had been training for a tri-

I never expected anyone to swim out. Ships, boats, yes. But not this.

athlon to get her strength back. She, too, saw Bobby's desperation. At first she thought it was a shark and raced into the water, afraid that a child was in danger.

The number they'd given me for McKenzie was incorrect, and I scoured the Internet without success. Finally, three weeks later, I wrote a letter to the local paper thanking everyone who had helped and asking for assistance in finding McKenzie. The town manager called to inform me that McKenzie Perry was the daughter of a lawyer in Charleston.

When I called her, McKenzie told me she was 20, a prelaw student who lived with her parents near the beach. She was supposed to go surfing that day, but the water was too rough, so she was working on her tan instead. She saw my friends screaming for help, and heard Bobby yelling that his wife and a friend were caught in a riptide. She was familiar with the currents and had a general idea of where to enter the water. She dove in without hesitation.

Both of these women received awards from the Carnegie Hero Fund Commission, established in 1904 to honor those who risk their lives to help others. I went to Charleston to see McKenzie receive her award, and a few months later, Kary and Josh visited me in Asheville. We all talk regularly to this day. I'm a substitute high school teacher in Asheville, and I've shared our story with my students, especially the girls. "Never give up," I tell them. "McKenzie and Kary didn't." They are extraordinary, beautiful young women, and not a day goes by that I don't thank God for them.

And not a day goes by that I don't think of Judy. She was a true friend, the kind who made me want to be a better person. I put the shell and the sea urchin shell I found that day in a glass vase I keep in my living room, a reminder that I lost a wonderful friend but that I gained two more. Adrift in a vast, merciless ocean, I was not alone. ❶

Lisa Kogan Tells All

Sure, Bogie had Bacall, but our highly impressionable columnist had tuna salad mixed with little green olives, Joy mixed with Aqua Net, and a fantastic tribe of women who taught her everything she knows about girl power.

There are a few things I'm not particularly good at. Now, before you think I'm being coy or self-deprecating or anything else that it's not okay to be these days, I'll just say that there are a number of areas in which I excel. For one thing, I possess an almost encyclopedic ability to remember every detail of every TV show that ran during the 1970s. Sure, Paul Krugman won a Nobel Prize for integrating the previously disparate fields of international trade and economic globalization, but let's not kid ourselves, he's never going to be able to tell you that it was Miyoshi Umeki who played Mrs. Livingston on *The Courtship of Eddie's Father*. Lest you think this is my only talent, let me add that I'm also exceptionally gifted at finding lost Legos, and I was once instrumental in getting a squirrel out of the house, which may not seem like much, but talk to me after you've used your loofah mitt to shoo a large panicky rodent from the bathroom to the front lawn while dressed in nothing more than a towel and shower cap. Believe me when I say you feel pretty damn triumphant.

Anyway, those are the things I'm good at. The list of what I'm not good at is a work in progress, but I'd definitely place men right near the top. I am not now, nor have I ever been, particularly good at men. I like them, I even keep one around the apartment in case of emergencies (that would be Johannes, father of my 6-year-old, protector against future squirrel invasions), but I can't pretend that I'm totally at ease with them—at least not in the same way I am with women.

It seems to me that there are women who are women's women and women who are men's women. Lauren Bacall always struck me as a real man's woman. Glamorous, seductive, but pretty no-nonsense at the same time—the kind of dame who could smoke, shoot pool, drink everybody under the table, and still get up early to go fly-fishing without ever once chipping her nail polish. Bacall gave as good as she got, and what she got was Humphrey Bogart.

But she's not the only one of the girls who was one of the boys. Ava Gardner, Myrna Loy, Katharine Hepburn, Marlene Dietrich, Shirley MacLaine, Rosalind Russell, Angelina Jolie, any one of them could probably call your bluff in a high-stakes game of Texas Hold'em or change a flat tire without batting an eyelash or grab a rifle and go off skeet shooting.

I don't know what a skeet is or why anyone would want to shoot it. I don't know how to gut a catfish or loosen a lug nut, or flirt in a way that doesn't lead a guy to wonder if I might need to be institutionalized.

In my heart, I'm Lauren Bacall throwing Bogie the perfect *To Have and Have Not* exit line, "You know how to whistle, don't you, Steve? You just put your lips together and...blow." But in my apartment, I'm still me and the exit line is more like "You know how to take the garbage out, don't you, Johannes? You just separate the recyclables and...go."

I blame my mother. I have decided that it's her fault my comfort zone is ruled by women for two simple reasons: (1) It is both easy and convenient to blame one's mother, and as a single working mother myself, I'm forever searching for ease and convenience...hence my freezer full of White Castle microwavable cheeseburgers. And (2) because my mother, along with her friends, always made the company of women look so incredibly appealing.

How many times did I see Helen or Ruby, Beverly or Renee, Naomi or Lilo and later Myrna use that old "giving the hostess a hand" excuse so they could disappear into the camaraderie of the kitchen—where they always seemed happiest to me, where they didn't have to look gorgeous, where they could pick at leftovers and polish off their Blue Nun and bitch without disclaimers, where they'd kick off their shoes and begin the postparty process of transferring all the stuff in big plastic Tupperware containers into slightly less big plastic Tupperware containers.

All of them smelled really, really good— like Wind Song, or Jean Naté, or Joy, or Aqua Net, with perhaps just a soupçon of brisket.

The kitchen was their avocado green or harvest gold or white Formica sanctuary, and my favorite thing was to listen in to the blasts of laughter that punctuated every crazy contradiction, savored secret, or funny story as one by one, these lovely and amazing forces of nature would take a seat at the table until it was time to round up their husbands and head for home.

I loved those nights and I still love those women. Barbara Capalongo had a thing for Elvis Presley and the cheapest vanilla ice cream she could find— the kind that came studded with tiny crystals of frost. She chopped up little green pimento-stuffed olives and put them in her tuna salad—the most glamorous touch imaginable to me. Cyvia Snyder liked Danish Modern design and had her own membership card to the Museum of Modern Art in New York City. Sheila Abrams wore bell bottoms and eyeliner and taught me how to knit. And all of them smelled really, really good—like Wind Song, or Jean Naté, or Joy, or White Shoulders, or Aqua Net, with perhaps just a soupçon of brisket.

There is no room for a kitchen table in my kitchen... because here in the Big Apple, everything's a trade-off; I now have my very own membership card to the Museum of Modern Art, but I somehow ended up with a kitchen that only has room for three forks and a dish towel. Still, every few weeks or so, my girlfriends and I leave our various husbands and boyfriends and God-knows-what-to-call-this-but-we're-sort-of-together-at-the-moment relationships behind and settle in at my putative kitchen table to refuel our spirits or eat something we shouldn't, or both.

Inevitably one of us will announce that she's not doing what she set out to do with her life and the room will go quiet for a couple of seconds. Someone will refill the glasses, someone will clear the dishes, someone will crack a joke about setting out to get her PhD and her dry cleaning—guess which thing got accomplished, someone else will pin it on her mother (see previous column), but we'll all know exactly what our friend is mourning. And sooner or later, we'll break open the Pepperidge Farm Entertaining Cookie Collection box and come up with an inventory of her many assets. We will get high on hope and possibility and espresso. We will be the strong community of women I had no idea I needed so much until my own daughter was born. And there she'll be, Julia Claire, swiping a Mint Milano, ducking under the table, and listening to us laugh. ◐

Left: Suad Zeid, a Palestinian (*center*), swaps diet tactics with Israeli group mates Arlene Harel (*left*) and Suzanne Sapir. *Right*: Two chefs—Palestinian Rida Astteeyr (*left*) and Israeli Zion Abu-Hazera—teach healthy cooking.

A Slim Peace

In the most unlikely of weight loss groups, 14 women—Israelis and Palestinians—drop pounds, lose inches, and together gain immeasurable humanity. Dina Kraft sits in.

I want to feel comfortable with my body."

"I want to feel more confident."

"I want to lose weight."

Suha Khoury reads aloud from slips of paper that have been written on and tucked into a plastic cup by the women now sitting in a circle on name-tagged chairs. They've gathered in a school classroom, festooned with student artwork, for the first meeting of a ten-session weight loss group. Strangers still, they cast their eyes downward, offering only shy, brief exchanges.

Khoury, the group dietitian, continues pulling slips of paper from the cup, reading each woman's goals in staccato succession. Then she gets to one note and takes a breath: "I want to get to know Palestinians." An attendee shifts in her seat, another clenches her jaw.

The fact that these 14 Israeli and Palestinian women have shown up at a school in Jerusalem to support one another—in the everyday fight for slimmer bodies—is in some ways unthinkable. Outside this room, their two peoples are engaged in a much bigger war—one that has been raging for nearly a century, with no end in sight.

The women are part of Slim Peace, a program started by Yael Luttwak, a 36-year-old American filmmaker who is also a citizen of Israel and now lives in London. Using the common denominator of weight—and women's near-universal anguish over it—as a way to bridge deep political, cultural, and religious divides, the project's sixth group will meet for ten two-hour sessions. The idea came to Luttwak about a decade ago when historic peace efforts between Israel and the Palestinians completely collapsed. At the time she had managed to drop a few pounds through Weight Watchers and remembers thinking, *Ariel Sharon is very overweight, and Arafat is not thin either. If they lost weight together, maybe they'd be in a better mood and make better decisions.*

It took six years for Luttwak to organize the first group of women, and they became the subject of her 2007 documentary, *A Slim Peace*. Supported by the Charities Advisory Trust in London, the program selects candidates (through word of mouth and slimpeace.org) based on interviews to determine whether they are open and expressive, and asks them to pay a nominal fee of about $50. To date, the groups have combined women who often reside only blocks away from each other but nevertheless live in entirely separate worlds. "I've been struck by what little opportunity they have even to speak with one another before we bring them together—and by how, within just a few hours, they find similarities," Luttwak says. "It's always heartbreaking and hopeful for me."

For their initial meeting in October 2008, the women of group six navigate the narrow streets and alleyways of Jerusalem to Prophets Street, near the de facto seam between the traditionally Arab east side where the majority of Palestinians live and the predominantly Jewish Israeli western neighborhoods. Most of the participants live in Jerusalem, although in other groups some have traveled from the West Bank—where the Palestinians must obtain special permits to cross through Israeli roadblocks. As they near their destination, the women follow a milky limestone wall, push open a heavy green iron gate, and enter a cloistered garden oasis on the grounds of a private school. There, amid purple bougainvillea and tangerine trees where Lawrence of Arabia once sipped afternoon tea, they find refuge.

After writing down their goals for the course, they play a quick icebreaker game, standing shoulder to shoulder and tossing a ball to one another as they call out their names. Khoury, who is codirector of Slim Peace and fluent in English and Hebrew as well as her native Arabic, always works with an Israeli facilitator. "This is not a Palestinian program. It's not an Israeli program. It's a program by women and for women," Khoury says, reminding them that they are now on neutral ground.

Next she instructs everyone to jot down a story that relates to food and tell it to the person sitting next to her; that woman will then share it with the group. "'I eat when I'm anxious. Especially chocolate,'" says Pearl Landsman, 62, an Israeli artist and holistic healer, relaying the words of Palestinian Hadil Mussa.

Mussa's dark brown eyes are fixed firmly on the floor as Landsman speaks for her. When she looks up around the circle, women nod and send her encouraging smiles. She smiles back.

Khoury then gives a talk about the value of whole grains and the challenges of social eating. Both societies, she says, suffer from rising rates of obesity. In the Palestinian diet, whole-fat dairy products, shawarma, and oriental sweets tend to be fattening. For Israeli women, high-calorie snacks and heavy family meals over the Sabbath can add on the pounds. But like women everywhere, this group is dealing with issues that cut deeper than calorie control. "Especially for the Palestinians, there is social pressure now to be thin, and many women are devastated," says Khoury. "Some are getting verbal abuse from their husbands or are on the verge of divorce because they cannot lose weight."

Leaving the first meeting, Shoshana Aharoni, 62, a soft-spoken retired nursery school teacher whose parents both lost family in the Holocaust, stumbles on a step and bruises her leg. Three of the Palestinian women rush to assist her. "They took me home in their car—to come to a Jewish neighborhood, no less—and it was hard to say goodbye," Aharoni says later. "Here they were, three Palestinian women, and I thought on the one hand I should feel afraid of them. It was a very special experience."

Such simple but profound moments punctuate the sessions as they unfold with weekly weigh-ins (accompanied by collective groans) and the turning in of food diaries for

Left: Sue Freedman, an Israeli, with Makarem Awad, a Palestinian, who lost 17 pounds. *Right (from left)*: Daniele Tobelem, Yael Shalem (both Israeli), and Suad Zeid admire a cut cucumber.

Khoury's feedback. Mussa decides to cut out all sweets. Pearl Koelewyn, 53, an Orthodox Jew and mother of five, stops using cream in her coffee. In the name of increasing activity levels—and with 10,000 steps a day suggested as a goal—the women have also been given pedometers, which end up becoming a running (if only!) joke.

It's December 3, 2008, the seventh session. And the women are agitated. The day before, just a few blocks away, a Palestinian man was stabbed—a grim reminder of the violence that plagues the city. Jaffa Road, which runs parallel to Prophets Street, has seen its share of exploding buses. And terrorists have started plowing bulldozers into cars and pedestrians as a weapon of attack.

Once settled in the cocoon of their classroom, the women relax. By now they are greeting each other with warm hellos, standing closer together and clasping each other's hands as they inquire about work, health, and children. At one point, sitting down in a circle again, they discuss the relationship each had with food as a girl. Koelewyn speaks about her overweight mother, who took diet pills, making her a "nervous wreck, which she took out on me." Koelewyn blames her mother's behavior for some of her own poor habits, like waiting to eat until she is starving and then tearing into food.

Landsman, the holistic healer, who is known in the group for her warmth and quick smile, says she was sickly as a young child and had no appetite. "But by age 10 I was obese."

Suddenly her low, velvety voice seems to sink an octave: "I have no memories of food," she says. "I am a rape survivor, from my father."

The room falls silent.

"Most of my issues with food are about protection," she continues.

Many of the women have tears in their eyes as they embrace her afterward and ask how she made it through.

As the group gathers for the final session in late January of 2009, they can't ignore the political tensions. During the five-week break to observe the Muslim, Christian, and Jewish holidays, war has erupted in Gaza, leaving three Israeli and hundreds of Palestinian civilians dead.

Walking down the path to the school entrance, Koelewyn mentions to another woman that her son was among the Israeli soldiers in the ground invasion of Gaza. The woman, Mis'sada Jaber, a 26-year-old Palestinian, is silent.

Inside, as they take their seats, Khoury tries to ease the tension. "We are experiencing a very painful war, and despite that, you are all here today—a real testament to what we are doing." Lifting some of the heaviness in the room, Landsman pulls out a bag of unbuttered popcorn and passes it around as "preventive medicine." Eventually the charged conversation segues into the swapping of strategies for healthy eating: Have fruit before the ice cream; don't arrive hungry to social events; try chopsticks; eat with your nondominant hand; use small plates. For this last meeting, the women have been asked to come with a symbol of hope. They take turns placing their objects in the center of their circle. Makarem Awad, 49, a Palestinian who works for a UN agency, carefully adds her pearl earrings to the pile of objects, saying softly, "They grow out of the darkness." Selma Braier, 49, an Israeli, plunks down her pedometer, with a toast: "Here's to hopes of reaching 10,000 steps a day." Everyone laughs.

As she has with the other groups she's led, Khoury notes with pleasure how the women have unclenched their fists and begun to see through stereotypes to their own value and shared humanity. "One comes up with beautiful conclusions in the end," she says: *I am more valuable than I thought. I need to dedicate more time to taking care of myself. And 'The other' is not as threatening as I've been led to believe.*

When it's time to part, congratulations are given to the women who have lost weight, like Awad (almost 18 pounds) and Mussa (22 pounds), and encouraging words are offered to those who have not. There are hugs, whisperings of good luck, and promises to meet again. Awad is committed to joining a gym. Maureen Rajuan, 59, and two of the Palestinian women make plans to go power walking together.

"What I notice," says Slim Peace founder Luttwak, who hopes to start hundreds of groups—including some in the United States—"is that even if they don't stay in touch, they are forever changed by virtue of having met. They cannot go back as easily and demonize each other. They've become human beings." ◑

Veronica Grant shows the group exercises that can be done at home.

A Stitch in Time

The grandmother she hardly knew had created miracles with fabric; her mother found sewing a bore. Curious about where she fit, **Meribah Knight** picks up the thread.

The author's grandmother, Hortence Lasky, in 1958, fitting her daughter's watered-silk graduation dress.

I t never struck me as odd that my Jewish grandmother sewed and embroidered a Christmas stocking for me. Instead I marveled at the perfect placement and lettering of my oddball name: Meribah. I ran my fingers over the stocking's fleecy-soft details, admiring the painstakingly perfect tree decorated with multicolored glass balls, lit candles, and yellow thread tinsel, meticulously embroidered by my grandmother Hortence's hand.

When I was 7, about a year after my grandmother's passing, I discovered her sewing kit, tucked in a dark corner of our guest bedroom. Inside the wicker basket, spools of thread were stacked in rainbow order one atop the other, and needles lined the thick green felt, from small to big to small, like the pipes of a church organ. Bobbins, scissors, thimbles, and measuring tape each lived in their own pocket.

Without a clue or a purpose, I began experimenting. I threaded needles, rearranged the spools, sorted buttons by color and size, then sewed them in the air. This entertained me for hours.

Yet the kit remained a mystery. In our house the lifting of hems and reattaching of buttons were left to tailors. To my mother, sewing was a bore, an activity that was beneath her. Instead, she spent her days crafting plotlines for her novels. My grandmother, however, had put her whole heart into making not just my stocking but also

■

221

the quilt I had for the cold winter months and the patchwork placemats I ate my morning oatmeal on. I wanted to know what had inspired her to make these things, and if there were lessons in it for me.

Twenty years later, I was still searching for answers. I had learned the basics of sewing and had grown to love it, but something was missing. If my grandmother had been around, I could have asked her what sewing meant to her, and why she had taken the time and the care.

Luckily, Isabelle Troyer, the 101-year-old last remaining member of my grandmother's sewing group, was willing to help. She said I could visit anytime. So I drove, from Chicago to Indianapolis, in search of her stories.

It was the end of April, and spring had arrived in Indiana. Blossoms exploded from dogwood trees, and the scent of lilacs drifted through the neighborhood. A faded picket fence encircled Isabelle's house.

Hunched over a walker, Isabelle greeted me at the back door. A silver barrette gathered her hair in a neat swirl atop her head—a style she has worn for more than 70 years. We sat at her kitchen table, where everything she needed for our conversation was within arm's length: books, family photos, a large magnifying glass, a scrapbook of obituaries, and a black rotary telephone. The smell of freshly made toast and Isabelle's favorite instant coffee hung in the air.

They'd called themselves the Tuesdays, she said, because every week at 2 o'clock on their namesake day, they met carrying wicker baskets full of buttons, needles, and darning thread. Isabelle told me that the week's hostess would provide hot coffee, soft couches, and decadent dessert. One member, Elaine Thomas, had a penchant for sweets that resembled her own sense of style—pink and puffy. My grandmother was more reserved, Isabelle said. She preferred to make a cinnamon crumb cake. Once the desserts had been arranged and the coffee brewed, the baskets would come out and the mending would begin.

The Tuesdays had formed officially in 1941, when the United States entered World War II and the women's spouses departed. Dottie's husband, Bob, was shipped off to serve in the army's intelligence agency. Elaine's husband, Lowell, a doctor, was sent away as a medic. The women needed each other, Isabelle said. By the time my

The group had grown to a dozen housewives. For a few hours every week, the ladies ruled their own kingdom.

mother was born, in 1944, the group had grown to a dozen Indianapolis housewives. Their weekly commitment continued when the men came home and the children went off to school. For a few hours every week, the ladies ruled their own kingdom.

As they gathered to mend torn shirts and reattach buttons, they'd yak about politics and literature and neighborhood gossip. None of them worked, but all held college degrees, unusual for women of that era. They were members of the League of Women Voters and the Shakespeare society. "We were like a family in a way," Isabelle said.

In time, the camaraderie grew into something more like life support. Without the Tuesdays, Isabelle might not have survived the unexpected death of her 19-month-old son, or the car accident that left her other son a paraplegic at the age of 16. Helen would have had to suffer alone when her son was stabbed to death inside his home. After she discovered his body at the foot of his staircase, the women took care of her, and listened when she told them the reason for his murder: a hate crime against his homosexuality.

Six hours later, Isabelle's stories were still coming. Listening to her, I realized that although my grandmother had died before I was old enough to hold a needle, the visit had given me the answer I was looking for. Buttons and darning were the least of it. Sewing animated the spirit of the group. It had brought the Tuesdays to life.

The opening photo is from June 6, 1958, the day of my mother's graduation from eighth grade. She stares impatiently into the camera, her black hair and pale face punctuated by cherry red lips. My grandmother's hands are up my mother's skirt making last-minute adjustments to a dress she'd sewn for the occasion. My mother had high hopes that this dress would be the evening's sensation. She loved the way its skirt puffed up like freshly beaten egg whites. She had read *Gone with the Wind* three times that year, and this was her bid to be the Jewish Scarlett O'Hara. There was no pattern for the dress, just my mother's direction: princess style, please, with poufy sleeves. It was made out of white watered silk, a fabric chosen for its delicate, tissue-like weightlessness.

For my mother, coming of age in Indianapolis felt like asphyxiation by normalcy. Fidel Castro, the 32-year-old revolutionary, had come down from the hills to overthrow

U.S.–backed Cuban dictator Fulgencio Batista. Castro's good looks and charisma sent my mother, an incurable romantic, into a whirlwind romance with revolution. Kenya's Mau Mau uprisings were in full swing; Elvis had heeded Uncle Sam's call, and a new product—pantyhose—was about to infiltrate the top drawers of women everywhere.

In her world there was little time for sewing and even less desire. She fantasized about make-out sessions with Che Guevara in South American jungles; she became infatuated with Nick and Nora Charles from Dashiell Hammett's novel *The Thin Man.* Nick, a retired private detective, and Nora, a wealthy society woman, spent their life eating cold duck, solving crimes, and downing cocktails. "That is what I expected to be doing," my mother told me. "They never had any children, they never cooked a meal, and they drank a lot of martinis. They had this adventurous life with incredible sophistication. Sewing to me did not mean sophistication."

So instead of settling into a weekly coffee klatch when she became a young married woman, my mother found herself gripping the railings of a 30-foot sailboat in the first of two transatlantic crossings. There she was, far away from her landlocked reveries, smack in the middle of the Atlantic Ocean with no one but my father. She, Nora, amid thumping waves and whipping winds, had finally found her Nick. Thoughts of crocheted toilet-tissue covers remained back on shore.

Knight's grandmother Hortence, in the 1970s.

Ten years after I first stumbled upon the sewing kit and somewhere between beepers and Nike Air Maxes, tradition had fallen out of favor, needlepoint was not cool, and home economics was the least popular class in my high school. But at 15, I had taken my trial-and-error period as a seamstress about as far as it could go, so I signed up. "That course still exists?" my mother said when I told her about it. "What about photography?" "Yes it does," I replied, ignoring the photography comment. "And I am planning on taking it."

The classroom was a concrete, windowless box tucked away in the armpit of my high school, right above the

Buttons and darning were the least of it. Sewing animated the spirit of the group. It brought the Tuesdays to life.

daycare center for teen mothers. While other girls tore up the soccer fields or ran time trials at local track meets, my afternoons were spent hunched over cutting tables and vibrating sewing machines as aromas of baking cakes and simmering tomato sauce drifted over from the cooking class next door.

From this course came pajama bottoms, a two-piece pantsuit made from champagne-colored raw silk, a pink flamingo Hawaiian shirt for my mother, and an appetite to stitch anything I could get my hands on. For a teen with a meager $11 a week allowance, doing it myself was a kind of defiance. I didn't have to rely on the mall.

When I made a pair of silk pants or reworked a jewel-encrusted '60s top for a school dance, it was as though I had supernatural powers. "You made that?" people would ask. "I can't believe it." They acted as if the clothing they wore every day magically appeared, via stork or steamship, into the store and onto the rack. "I just cut it and sewed it," I would say. "No big deal."

It actually felt like a very big deal. I could make anything I wanted to wear—all I needed was a ride to Jo-Ann fabrics and enough money to buy a few yards of material. My mother had spent her youth trying to escape a mundane Midwestern life of crocheting and cream of mushroom casseroles; I never had that sense of stultifying convention. I was brought up in Cambridge, Massachusetts, the liberal fulcrum of the East. Our block parties consisted of dishes like gazpacho and couscous salad. But I still needed to defy something. Some people listened to punk rock. Some people sailed across oceans. I sewed.

When I moved to Manhattan to attend college, my Singer—a gift for my 16th birthday—came with me. I was in love with New York, but the notion of spreading out four yards of fabric meant removing all the furniture in the apartment, so the sewing machine migrated to the top of my refrigerator. Years passed without a stitch. If it hadn't been for the depression that overtook me six years later, I might never have made my way back to sewing. I had struggled with depression in the past, but the sadness took hold of me with a fierceness I'd never before encountered. Days, weeks, months— I'm not sure, they all ran together— were spent on my couch, cocooned in a thick heavy cotton comforter. I was living in Brooklyn and working as a free-lance fashion editor. I hated everything about my job.

Then one day, as if it were a pang of hunger, I got the urge to sew. I unwrapped myself from my comforter, retrieved the box from atop the fridge, and took out my sewing machine. I was worried. Did I even remember how to thread the thing?

The first garment I sewed was a gray wool pleated jumper. I remember pressing the pleats so carefully they took on an accordion-like quality. The second item was a plaid wool shift dress. I had no pattern for either, but that didn't matter. Instead I got a roll of butcher paper and created my own designs with a measuring tape, a plastic ruler, and a pair of scissors.

I may not have been able to figure out how to get from point A to point B in my professional and personal life, but I knew if I could take three yards of fabric, cut it, pin it, and sew it into a dress, then that day would be better than the one before.

Like everyone else's, my life is often dominated by the computer. Wake up, check e-mail, click to a new window, read *The New York Times,* click to a new window, check the weather, click to a new window, check Facebook, click to a new window, Twitter. At a certain point my eyes glaze over, and this is when I pull out my needlepoint or a few yards of fabric. This is when my hands must touch something besides a mouse.

My grandmother would have said the Tuesdays got her out of the house and connected with the world. I say sewing keeps me in the house and unplugged from the world. It immerses me in the pleasure of actually making something, and reminds me that not everything is made up of pixels. With the passing of my depression, sewing took on an almost sacred role in my life. It quieted my mind and engaged my hands. And it introduced me to a like-minded community.

I first heard about the Renegade Craft Fair the year it was in Brooklyn. I went to it wearing my favorite plaid shirt with a vintage denim skirt I had shortened and cinched at the waist. On the inside of my right wrist was a freshly inked tattoo of my middle name, Grace. I wasn't quite sure what to expect from the day's outing, but from what I'd been told I was sure to find other tattooed ladies who were heavily into crafts.

After sewing alone for so long, the thought of finding a few crafting com-

> Sewing immerses me in the pleasure of making something, and reminds me that not everything is made up of pixels.

The Tuesdays in the late '50s (*right*): Hortence (*top row, second from left*) and Isabelle Troyer (*bottom row, third from left*). *Below*: The author and the mobile she made for her niece.

rades sounded like a welcome idea. I had heard of a "DIY generation" on the rise. I assumed that included me, but I had always felt so isolated that an entire generation of similarly inclined women seemed unimaginable. But as I zigzagged through the tents at the fair I began to see flyers—like the Sublime Stitching company's "This ain't your gramma's embroidery!"—and it felt familiar. I realized that what I was doing—and had been doing since I was 15 years old—fit into something much bigger. I had suddenly become we. Many of us had mothers or grandmothers who crafted. That is how we began, but now we wanted to define the tradition on our own terms.

When my niece, Luella Grace, was born, my first thought was: *Is she healthy? My second thought was: What can I make for her?* First came a pair of embroidered onesies. Then, as Christmas rolled around, I knew exactly what I wanted to make next. I was 26, still using the stocking my grandmother had made for me, and thought it would be cool to stitch a similar version for Lulu. I called my mother to tell her the idea, but she was one step ahead of me. "I already got Lulu a stocking," she said, brimming with excitement. "I bought it from L.L. Bean and they were able to embroider her name on it and everything." I was crushed, though I didn't show it. I would have to find something else to make little Lulu for her first Jewish Christmas. So I decided on a mobile.

Using my father's band saw, I cut and sanded two arcing pieces of wood and coated them in thick white paint. From there I sewed and stuffed five birds, all in different sizes and fabrics, and used clear monofilament thread to hang them from the wood frame so they looked as though they were flying. At least there would be something handmade for Lulu's first holiday.

When we all came down the stairs Christmas morning, the mobile—next to Lulu—was the showstopper. My brother and his wife loved it. "It will go perfectly in the nursery," my brother said. And little Lulu gazed at it, mesmerized by the floating birds. Even Hanzo, the dog, sat under it for a good hour.

Next year I will make my niece a stocking. It will be fleecy-soft, have *Lulu* stitched across the top, and (I hope) be as exquisite as the one my grandmother made for me—the workmanship perfected through decades with the Tuesdays. It will hang right next to ours, and maybe one day it will inspire Lulu to ask her Aunt Meribah just how she made it. And I will show her. ◖

Experts now believe that animals share "human" feelings like compassion, love—even embarrassment.

What Are They Thinking?

From playing practical jokes to manipulating currency to performing amazing acts of heroism, our planetmates are a funnier, shrewder, kindlier, more altruistic, and more empathetic bunch than most of us realize. Eugene Linden reveals what the experts have found. You take it from there.

Thirty years ago, at a now defunct marine park in Palos Verdes, California, a baby orca took ill. The illness itself was nothing noteworthy, but what happened afterward had a profound impact on all who witnessed it.

The staff had used a forklift and stretcher to hoist the 420-pound infant out of the main tank for emergency medical care. In a remarkable act of trust, the baby's parents, Orky and Corky, patiently watched the proceedings from the other side of the tank. The trouble began when the keepers tried to return the baby to the tank. The forklift operator, lacking a clear line of sight, halted the stretcher a few feet above the water, just beyond the grasp of the keepers who were waiting below. As the keepers struggled to reach and release the orca, it began throwing up—which, as trainer Gail Laule recalls, made for a desperate situation.

Orky, the father, then did something he'd never been trained to do. He swam beneath his baby, let a keeper stand on his head, and, using the awesome power of his flukes, held himself steady so the keeper could reach the latch on the stretcher and let the baby slip into the water. Not only did he seem to realize that the humans were trying to help; he appeared to understand that he could *help* them help.

In December 2005, a female humpback whale did Orky one better—by acknowledging the help. While swimming in the Pacific near San Francisco, the whale found herself entangled in a web of crab traps and lines. A team of divers assembled by Marin County's Marine Mammal Center spent an hour working to free the 50-ton animal. Like Orky, she seemed to realize that they were there to help. And when they succeeded, she swam around them, gently nudging each diver as though saying thank you.

After nearly 40 years of writing about wild animals, I'm still astonished by their "humanity." And sometimes I just have to laugh at their humanness. Wildlife researcher Charlie Russell and his partner, Maureen Enns, were working in the Russian Far East when a mother grizzly bear apparently decided she could trust them to look after her two cubs. Despite the fact that hundreds of grizzlies are killed by hunters and poachers in the area each year, the mother, named Brandy, deputized the humans for daycare duty while she did her foraging. And like many a human parent who's confessed to sneaking away in order to avoid a scene, Brandy cleverly waited until the cubs were distracted before making a quick exit.

These anecdotes are just stories, of course; they're not scientific in the way that strictly controlled studies are. I've come to realize, though, that credible stories can tell us what animals are like in ways that strictly controlled studies cannot. I spent years writing about animal intelligence before it dawned on me that I might convey a fuller picture of the animal mind and—yes—soul by complementing studies with insights I'd collected from hundreds of scientists, zookeepers, and field observers. These days, after years of frustrating attempts to test elusive abilities such as intelligence or language, even behavioral scientists are more willing to consider observation and anecdote as guides.

The picture that emerges when you look at animals this way is a far cry from the simplistic wind-up-toy model of old—a model that presented animals as virtual automatons, sleepwalking through life. In addition to indications of intelligence, there are strong suggestions of animal capacity for emotions and states of mind that most people would identify as human. And once you begin to see these capacities in animals, it becomes impossible to believe that the natural world is an us-and-them proposition.

Humans, it turns out, don't hold the patent on characteristics that "humanity" comprises: humor, generosity, love, even empathy—a trait that, in the animal kingdom, is far rarer than love because it requires the emotionally sophisticated act of understanding another's plight. (I'm thinking of a female chimp at the Dallas Zoo consoling a zookeeper who had lost her daughter. Or Sophi, an elephant at the Indianapolis Zoo, who, after watching a keeper struggle to push a cart up a hill, walked over and began pushing the cart herself.)

Understanding another's plight requires consciousness. In its simplest form, consciousness means that we recognize ourselves as separate from other creatures. It's a tremendously powerful evolutionary development—and it doesn't just lead to empathy. If you are aware of yourself as distinct from others, you can understand that others might know something that you don't. You can also understand that *you* might know things others don't—which is the basis of trickery and subterfuge, not to mention a good prank.

In children, this awareness doesn't emerge until sometime between 3 and 4 years of age. The old view was that in animals it never emerges, but in that case, how to explain the game witnessed by Suzan Murray, chief veterinarian of the National Zoo, when, as a veterinary student, she was doing research on chimps in Tanzania's Gombe National Park?

In the late afternoon when the young chimps were playing, Murray would sometimes see an adolescent sneak up behind one of the alpha males and proceed to make rude gestures to another adolescent. The offended youth would respond with a threat, and the alpha male, thinking the threat was directed at him—a huge breach of etiquette in chimp-world—would become enraged at the poor dupe. The prank suggests that the chimp was intentionally manipulating the big male.

Like Wall Street types, some animals are savvy enough to game the system. Spock, a dolphin at another now defunct marine park in California, discovered that if he brought stray pieces of paper to his trainer, he would be rewarded with treats. But the trainer, Jim Mullen, wasn't always around when Spock found a piece of paper. Perhaps this is why Spock started hoarding, collecting pieces and wedging them against an outflow pipe, demonstrating an admirable thrift and an understanding of the basic principles of paper money and banking.

Chantek, an orangutan raised in a lab as part of a language experiment at the University of Tennessee at Chattanooga, stumbled upon the concept of inflation during his off hours. Part of his day involved doing simple chores, for which he was paid in poker chips. Eventually he figured that he could extend the supply of chips simply by breaking them in half. When Lyn Miles, the scientist in charge of the experiment, switched to metal washers to thwart the scheme, Chantek moved on to counterfeiting—collecting pieces of aluminum foil and rolling them into crude circles to look like washers. Countless other stories suggest that animals are quick studies when it comes to estimating the value humans put on various objects—itself a sophisticated ability—and are not above cheating when they can get away with it. (Once, when asked to share some grapes with me, Chantek gave me the stem and kept the grapes for himself.)

> Humans, it turns out, don't hold the patent on characteristics that "humanity" comprises: humor, generosity, love, even empathy.

While conniving is complex, love is simple. Because reproduction is a fundamental drive, common sense tells us that nature would make producing offspring a positive experience. That's the perspective of biological anthropologist Helen Fisher, PhD, who notes that chemicals in the brain produce the feelings associated with love (and lust, and long-term attachment) not just in humans but in a broad range of species. Obsessed with the object of your affection? That's probably because an elevated level of dopamine has driven down your serotonin levels, which in turn permits obsessive thinking. Similar chemistry is at work in elephants, lions, beavers, and a host of other creatures. To be sure, humans are the most eloquent animals when it comes to reflecting on feelings of love, but the neurobiology of the feelings themselves is widely shared.

Intelligence may be widely shared as well—and of all the things I've learned about animals over the years, this has been perhaps the biggest surprise. I'm not alone in that broadening of perspective. "I was something of a snob about where to look for animal intelligence," admits Karen Pryor, a behavioral biologist, "but over the years I've seen animals do things they're not 'supposed to' be able to do." Forty years ago, Pryor caused a stir when she demonstrated that a dolphin could invent its own tricks. Now she's gotten dogs to do the same.

The late zoologist Donald Griffin, a pioneer in the study of animal intelligence, would not be surprised. He always believed that some degree of awareness was present in many animals. For the sake of argument, let's say Griffin was right. If consciousness is broadly spread throughout the animal kingdom—if animals share to some degree the abilities and feelings that combine to make us human—what does that mean?

It shouldn't make a difference in how we treat animals—no creature need pass an awareness test to justify its existence—but, of course, it does. Once you've heard enough stories about the intelligence and valor of pigs (like Priscilla, who towed a struggling boy safely to shore in a Texas lake; or Harley de Swine, a Vietnamese pot-bellied pig who literally ran to work, such was his enthusiasm for helping head-injury patients at a medical facility in California), it's hard to keep eating pork. I should know: I gave it up, even though it was my favorite meat. The short, miserable life on a typical hog farm is bad enough, but the possibility that pigs might be aware of their situation is intolerable.

We tend to treat animals as commodities (useful for food, clothing, labor, research and experimentation, etc.) or as personalities (remember *Free Willy?*). Yet the evidence of animal awareness suggests a third choice: that animals are fellow participants in an unfolding evolutionary drama. We humans want to believe that we are special. The idea that we're intrinsically different from other animals gives us, among other things, the moral justification for treating those animals as so much stuff. But nature has no stake in any particular species, including humans. And if natural selection can produce identical shapes in animals with utterly different ancestries (witness the pangolin and anteater), perhaps it has also produced similar emotional states and mental tools in humans and, say, crows.

This perspective allows us to appreciate that other creatures besides ourselves might have a sense of humor, pride, even honor. And, we can hope, appreciation might lead to recognition of our deep bonds. We can see ourselves as the lone species capable of thought in a landscape otherwise populated with wind-up toys. Or we can embrace the idea of a world filled with many sentient beings, some of whom can scheme and joke, and some who would cooperate with humans to save their babies. Acknowledging consciousness in other species might be inconvenient for us comfort-seeking omnivores (it requires treating animals with respect—particularly the ones we eat), but I know which world I would rather inhabit. ◐

The Joan Show

A wily little kitten brings big change to Jessica Winter's household.

My husband saw her first, on a cold December afternoon. The veterinary clinic down the street from our apartment sometimes parks stray kittens in its front window; a scrawny calico, with fur like dandelion fluff, was mewling at him through the glass, as if he were an errant teenager who'd just plowed his bicycle into her parked car. He called me; I hustled over. When I picked her up, her body relaxed instantly, as if she'd been rigid with anticipation a long time and now could finally breathe easy. She hooked her tiny white paws over my shoulder and snuggled close. She purred dreamily. She sighed a little kitten sigh. Half an hour later, she was in our apartment.

The feline brain, it is thought, can't imagine the future and prepare accordingly—it lacks the cortical real estate to create cunning plots and plan checkmate maneuvers. Yet two and a half years later, that moment at the clinic remains the one and only time I have ever gotten a hug from my cat. First impressions to the contrary, Joan—my husband named her Joan, as in Didion, "for her poise and figure"—does not like being cuddled. When she submits to petting, it is often in the wriggly, distressed manner of a small child surrendering to the attentions of a grizzled old aunt with an ashtray kiss.

If an important part of pet ownership is the ability to "read" your cat or dog or bunny or pot-bellied pig, I began in abject failure. In fact, failure has touched much of my tenure as Joan's co-guardian. I failed to teach her to fetch. I failed to convince her that the couch is not a potato that needs peeling. I failed to sell her on her water bowl. (Faucets only.)

I can't change Joan, or even slightly modify her. Instead, she has changed me. I never used to sob at ASPCA ads, or avoid movies with animals (because *what if one of the animals gets hurt?!?)*, or try to make friends with every dog I pass on the street. And it never occurred to me before that I could love another creature so much without expecting reciprocation. I must be content to admire Joan slightly from afar, as one might admire a famous actor or athlete. The upside is that I have year-round tickets (excellent seats, too) for *The Joan Show*: *Matrix*-style spinning leaps through the air at a dangled dish towel; *Spider-Man* vertical sprints along our living room walls; heroic combat-crawl missions into my parents' garden, from which she emerges with voles attached to her claws like finger puppets.

And once in a while she'll curl up beside us at bedtime, or offer a friendly headbutt. Maybe I'll come home from work and she'll trot up the hall to greet me, cooing like a turtle dove. Or maybe I'll be crying over something stupid and she'll place a comforting paw on my knee. Come to think of it, she does that dainty paw-pat every time, and it always makes me laugh through my tears. ◐

Joan at her Brooklyn home in 2007.

Born free: Zebras grazing in Kenya's Rift Valley.

Wild Things

What's the best way to deal with untamed animals?
Rick Bass makes the case for keeping our paws to ourselves.

There are Canada geese that live on golf courses, and Canada geese that flare wildly at the sight of a single truck traveling down the road. There are bears that ride motorcycles in the circus, and bears that live far back in the forest and run from even the scent of a human being.

Humans, too, possess varying degrees of the wild and the domestic. I'm lucky. I get to live at the edge of wild country, and from time to time on my quiet walks into the wilderness, I glimpse traces—a track, even a flash of fur—of the animals that simply will not tolerate mankind.

Wild animals behave differently from domestic ones, having not been sculpted by the overheavy hand of man. I'm thinking of the black rhinos of Namibia, which have been pushed to the edge of an environment so severe that finally they are safe, in country so uninhabitable that people cannot survive it long enough to pursue them. Or the last grizzlies of Montana, the last wolverine, last lynx, last redband trout—animals that have not learned to accept man in the last two million eyeblink-years and show no real signs of doing so in the next two million.

These are not the animals whose edges have been sanded off by contact with humans. They are not the ones whose spiritual and physical integrity we've interfered with: the raccoons that learn to prefer the garbage can in the alley or the dog food on the porch to the crunch of freshly caught crayfish from a stream in an old forest; the grass carp that gorge on the lush abundance of vegetation fed by the fertilizer rolling off emerald golf courses, fertilizer laden with heavy metals that ultimately kill the carp, and kill the animals that eat the carp. Everything wild we touch becomes less wild, then dies, and usually without the dignity of doing so within its own system of grace and logic.

If people were ever to vanish from the Earth, wild animals would survive. But if the wild animals vanish, I think our odds go way down. We need these animals. I just don't know how to prove this. And I often fear that by the time we have the proof, it will be too late.

Although they haven't learned to accept us, wild animals are being forced, at an ever-accelerating pace—at warp speed, really—to react to us. It's not news that as humans we're a kind of super-predator. (There is no species or population so large that we cannot cause it to fail utterly, before our onslaught, our hunger; the term "too big to fail" does not apply.) But now researchers at the University of California at Santa Cruz have completed a study, a meta-analysis of various species, that quantifies just how outrageous are our effects on the wild animals of the world.

It turns out that we are drastically accelerating evolution in the animals we prey on, causing them to become smaller (and therefore less appealing—or usable—as prey). The researchers, tracking the rate of change by a unit of measurement called a Darwin, have found that we are speeding up evolution by 300 percent.

From limpets to salmon to bighorn rams, we are erasing the largest of entire species, one by one and million by million. Nature—at that 3x pace—is selecting for the meek, the unbold, the shy, the secretive; for the slender little fish that slip through the trawl, rather than the fat, tasty ones; for the rams with tiny horns rather than the old battle-battered males with the spectacular full curl. It's as if such creatures must now hide their formerly uncompromising magnificence. And as the mature and dramatically visible animals vanish before the colossus of our hunger, the survivors are breeding at ever-younger ages, resulting in fewer—and smaller—offspring, sending populations closer to collapse. Harvested populations are averaging a 20 percent reduction in body size from previous generations, and the age of first reproduction is a whopping 25 percent earlier, reports Chris Darimont, PhD, lead author of the study.

In this downsizing of the grand, this unprecedented disruption of the way the world works, the wildest of the wild animals are vanishing.

I'm not saying that cows and sheep and pigs and chickens and dogs and cats are unworthy. I'm saying I don't want a world without bighorn rams and rhinos and zebras, and I believe that the places they need in which to *be* bighorn rams and rhinos and zebras are likely the anchors that keep so much else in place, whether we know and appreciate it or not.

Not that wild country, and the wild things borne up out of that country, should have to be utilitarian to survive. These beautiful creatures, and the beautiful landscapes that sustain them—and that they in turn, with their living and dying, sustain—possess a value and a virtue regardless of our dwindling connection to them. But it seems that there is a virtue and a wisdom in keeping some things beyond our reach: that the protection of wildness itself is imperative.

I think of us as teetering on a steep slope, having vaulted momentarily to the top, where we stand on the shoulders of giants. And now everywhere we turn, looking down, the world over which we scrambled to get to this supreme vantage is becoming smaller.

Maybe we could accept a world of smaller limpets. Maybe even a world without pandas. But as we shrink and diminish and lessen what we touch, we make our position at the top ever more precarious. We have touched, and are consuming, everything.

The world is very old, and we are so new. I like the feeling of awe—what the late writer Wallace Stegner called "the birth of awe"—in beholding wild country not yet reduced by man. I like to remember that it is wild country that gives rise to wild animals; and that the marvelous specificity of wild animals reminds us to wake up, to let our senses be inflamed by every scent and sound and sight and taste and touch of the world. I like to remember that we are not here forever, and not here alone, and that the respect with which we behold the wild world matters, if anything does. ◐

> I like to remember that we are not here forever, and not here alone.

getting through it

234 "I WILL NEVER KNOW WHY" I BY SUSAN KLEBOLD

239 THE HARD-TIMES COMPANION I BY MARIE HOWE

241 MUFFIN MANIFESTO I BY SUZAN COLÓN

243 THE LONGEST NIGHT I BY JO ANN BEARD

245 JULIANNA MARGULIES'S AHA! MOMENT

246 "WHY DIDN'T THEY STOP HIM?" I BY PHOEBE ZERWICK

256 SEND, RECEIVE I BY KRISTY DAVIS

258 OPRAH TALKS TO JAY-Z

Susan and Dylan Klebold celebrating Dylan's fifth birthday, September 1986.

"I Will Never Know Why"

More than a decade after Dylan Klebold took part in the massacre at Columbine High School, his mother, Susan Klebold, finally talks: about the horror of that day, the agony that followed, and her search for answers in the terrible place where murder and suicide meet.

Since the day her son participated in the most devastating high school shooting America has ever seen, I have wanted to sit down with Susan Klebold to ask her the questions we've all wanted to ask—starting with "How did you not see it coming?" and ending with "How did you survive?" Over the years, Susan has politely declined interview requests, but several months ago she finally agreed to break her silence and write about her experience for O. Even now, many questions about Columbine remain. But what Susan writes here adds a chilling new perspective. This is her story. —Oprah

Just after noon on Tuesday, April 20, 1999, I was preparing to leave my downtown Denver office for a meeting when I noticed the red message light flashing on my phone. I worked for the state of Colorado, administering training programs for people with disabilities; my meeting was about student scholarships, and I figured the message might be a last-minute cancellation. But it was my husband, calling from his home office. His voice was breathless and ragged, and his words stopped my heart. "Susan—this is an emergency! Call me back immediately!"

The level of pain in his voice could mean only one thing: Something had happened to one of our sons. In the seconds that passed as I picked up the phone and dialed our house, panic swelled within me; it felt as though millions of tiny needles were pricking my skin. My heart pounded in my ears. My hands began shaking. I tried to orient myself. One of my boys was at school and the other was at work. It was the lunch hour. Had there been a car accident?

When my husband picked up the phone, he shouted, "Listen to the television!"—then held out the receiver so I could hear. I couldn't understand the words being broadcast, but the fact that whatever had happened was big enough to be on TV filled me with terror. Were we at war? Was our country under nuclear attack? "What's happening?" I shrieked.

He came back on the line and poured out what he'd just learned during a distraught call from a close friend of our 17-year-old son, Dylan: There was some kind of shooting at the high school...gunmen in black trenchcoats were firing at people...the friend knew all the kids who wore trenchcoats, and all were accounted for except Dylan and his friend Eric...and Dylan and Eric hadn't been in class that morning...and no one knew where they were.

My husband had told himself that if he found the coat, Dylan couldn't be involved. He'd torn the house apart, looking everywhere. No coat. When there was nowhere left to look, somehow he knew the truth. It was like staring at one of those computer-generated 3-D pictures when the abstract pattern suddenly comes into focus as a recognizable image.

I barely got enough air in my lungs to say, "I'm coming home." We hung up without saying goodbye.

My office was 26 miles from our house. All I could think as I drove was that Dylan was in danger. With every cell in my body, I felt his importance to me, and I knew I would never recover if anything happened to him. I seesawed between impossible possibilities, all of them sending me into paroxysms of fear. Maybe no one knew where Dylan was because he'd been shot himself. Maybe he was lying in the school somewhere injured or dead. Maybe he was being held hostage. Maybe he was trapped and couldn't get word to us. Maybe it was some kind of prank and no one was hurt. How could we think for even a second that Dylan could shoot someone? Shame on us for even considering the idea. Dylan was a gentle, sensible kid. No one in our family had ever owned a gun. How in the world could he be part of something like this?

Yet no matter how hard I wanted to believe that he wasn't, I couldn't dismiss the possibility. My husband had noticed something tight in Dylan's voice earlier that week; I had heard it myself just that morning. I knew that Dylan disliked his school. And that he'd spent much of the past few days with Eric Harris—who hadn't been to our house for months but who'd suddenly stayed over one night that weekend. If Eric was missing now, too, then I couldn't deny that the two of them might be involved in something bad together. More than a year earlier, they had broken into a van parked on a country road near our house. They'd been arrested and had completed a juvenile diversion program that involved counseling, community service, and classes. Their theft had shown that under each other's influence they could be impulsive and unscrupulous. Could they also—no matter how unbelievable it seemed—be violent?

When I got home my husband told me the police were on their way. I had so much adrenaline in my system that even as I was changing out of my work clothes, I was racing from room to room. I felt such an urgency to be ready for whatever might happen next. I called my sister. As I told her what was going on, I was overcome by horror, and I started to cry. Moments after I hung up the phone, my 20-year-old son walked in and lifted me like a rag doll in his arms while I sobbed into a dish towel. Then my husband shouted from the front hallway, "They're here!"

Members of a SWAT team in dark uniforms with bulletproof vests had arrived. I thought they were coming to help us or to get our assistance in helping Dylan; if Dylan did have a gun, maybe they were hoping we could persuade him to put it down. But it seemed that in the SWAT team's eyes, we were suspects ourselves. Years later I would learn that many of their actions that day were intended to protect us; fearing that we would hurt ourselves or that our home might have been rigged with explosives, they told us we had to leave the house. For the rest of the afternoon, we stayed outside, sitting on the sidewalk or pacing up and down our brick walk. When we needed to use the bathroom, two armed guards escorted us inside and waited by the door.

I do not remember how or when, but sometime that day it was confirmed that Dylan and Eric were indeed perpetrators in a massacre at the school. I was in shock and barely grasped what was happening, but I could hear the television through the open windows. News coverage announced a growing tally of victims. Helicopters began circling overhead to capture a killer's family on film. Cars lined the road and onlookers gawked to get a better view.

Though others were suffering, my thoughts focused on the safety of my own child. With every moment that passed, the likelihood of seeing Dylan as I knew him diminished. I asked the police over and over, "What's happening? Where's Dylan? Is he okay?" Late in the afternoon someone finally told me that he was dead but not how he died. We were told to evacuate for a few days so authorities could search our home; we found shelter in the basement of a family member's house. After a sleepless night, I learned that Dylan and

Eric had killed 12 students and one teacher, and injured 24 others, before taking their own lives.

As a young child, Dylan made parenting easy. From the time he was a toddler, he had a remarkable attention span and sense of order. He spent hours focused on puzzles and interlocking toys. He loved origami and Legos. By third grade, when he entered a gifted program at school, he had become his father's most devoted chess partner. He and his brother acted out feats of heroism in our backyard. He played Little League baseball. No matter what he did, he was driven to win—and was very hard on himself when he lost.

His adolescence was less joyful than his childhood. As he grew, he became extremely shy and uncomfortable when he was the center of attention, and would hide or act silly if we tried to take his picture. By junior high, it was evident that he no longer liked school; worse, his passion for learning was gone. In high school, he held a job and participated as a sound technician in school productions, but his grades were only fair. He hung out with friends, slept late when he could, spent time in his room, talked on the phone, and played video games on a computer he built. In his junior year, he stunned us by hacking into the school's computer system with a friend (a violation for which he was expelled), but the low point of that year was his arrest. After the arrest, we kept him away from Eric for several weeks, and as time passed he seemed to distance himself from Eric of his own accord. I took this as a good sign.

By Dylan's senior year, he had grown tall and thin. His hair was long and scraggly; under his baseball cap, it stuck out like a clown wig. He'd been accepted at four colleges and had decided to go to the University of Arizona, but he'd never regained his love of learning. He was quiet. He grew irritated when we critiqued his driving, asked him to help around the house, or suggested that he get a haircut. In the last few months of senior year, he was pensive, as if he were thinking about the challenges of growing older. One day in April I said, "You seem so quiet lately—are you okay?" He said he was "just tired." Another time I asked if he wanted to talk about going away to college. I told him that if he didn't feel ready, he could stay home and go to a community college. He said, "I definitely want to go away." If that was a reference to anything more than leaving home for college, it never occurred to me.

Early on April 20, I was getting dressed for work when I heard Dylan bound down the stairs and open the front door. Wondering why he was in such a hurry when he

Dylan, 17, at Susan's 50th birthday party, three weeks before the shooting.

could have slept another 20 minutes, I poked my head out of the bedroom. "Dyl?" All he said was "Bye." The front door slammed, and his car sped down the driveway. His voice had sounded sharp. I figured he was mad because he'd had to get up early to give someone a lift to class. I had no idea that I had just heard his voice for the last time.

It took about six months for the sheriff's department to begin sharing some of the evidence explaining what happened that day. For those six months, Dylan's friends and family were in denial. We didn't know that he and Eric had assembled an arsenal of explosives and guns. We believed his participation in the massacre was accidental or that he had been coerced. We believed that he did not intend to hurt anyone. One friend was sure that Dylan had been tricked at the last minute into using live ammunition. None of us could accept that he was capable of doing what he did.

These thoughts may seem foolish in light of what we now know, but they reflect what we believed to be true about Dylan. Yes, he had filled notebook pages with his private thoughts and feelings, repeatedly expressing profound alienation. But we'd never seen those notebooks. And yes, he'd written a school paper about a man in a black trenchcoat who brutally murders nine students. But we'd never seen that paper. (Although it had alarmed his English teacher enough to bring it to our attention, when we asked to see the paper at a parent-teacher conference, she didn't have it with her. Nor did she describe the contents beyond calling them "disturbing." At the conference— where we discussed many things, including books in the curriculum, Gen X versus Gen Y learners, and the '60s folk song "Four Strong Winds"—we agreed that she would show the paper to Dylan's guidance counselor; if he thought it was a problem, one of them would contact me. I never heard from them.) We didn't see the paper, or Dylan's other writings, until the police showed them to us six months after the tragedy.

In the weeks and months that followed the killings, I was nearly insane with sorrow for the suffering my son had caused, and with grief for the child I had lost. Much of the time, I felt that I could not breathe, and I often wished that I would die. I got lost while driving. When I returned to work part-time in late May, I'd sit through meetings without the slightest idea of what was being said. Entire conversations slipped from memory. I cried at inappropriate times, embarrassing those around me. Once, I saw a dead pigeon in a parking lot and nearly became hysterical. I mistrusted everything—especially my own judgment.

Seeing pictures of the devastation and the weeping survivors was more than I could bear. I avoided all news coverage in order to function. I was obsessed with thoughts of the innocent children and the teacher who suffered because of Dylan's cruelty. I grieved for the other families, even though we had never met. Some had lost loved ones, while others were coping with severe, debilitating injuries and psychological trauma. It was impossible to believe that someone I had raised could cause so much suffering. The discovery that it could have been worse—that if their plan had worked, Dylan and Eric would have blown up the whole school—only increased the agony.

But while I perceived myself to be a victim of the tragedy, I didn't have the comfort of being perceived that way by most of the community. I was widely viewed as a perpetrator or at least an accomplice since I was the person who had raised a "monster." In one newspaper survey, 83 percent of respondents said that the parents' failure to teach Dylan and Eric proper values played a major part in the Columbine killings. If I turned on the radio, I heard angry voices condemning us for Dylan's actions. Our elected officials stated publicly that bad parenting was the cause of the massacre.

Through all of this, I felt extreme humiliation. For months I refused to use my last name in public. I avoided eye contact when I walked. Dylan was a product of my life's work, but his final actions implied that he had never been taught the fundamentals of right and wrong. There was no way to atone for my son's behavior.

Those of us who cared for Dylan felt responsible for his death. We thought, *If I had been a better (mother, father, brother, friend, aunt, uncle, cousin), I would have known this was coming.* We perceived his

actions to be our failure. I tried to identify a pivotal event in his upbringing that could account for his anger. Had I been too strict? Not strict enough? Had I pushed too hard, or not hard enough? In the days before he died, I had hugged him and told him how much I loved him. I held his scratchy face between my palms and told him that he was a wonderful person and that I was proud of him. Had he felt pressured by this? Did he feel that he could not live up to my expectations?

I longed to talk to Dylan one last time and ask him what he had been thinking. I spoke to him in my thoughts and prayed for understanding. I concluded that he must not have loved me, because love would have prevented him from doing what he did. And though at moments I was angry with him, mostly I thought that I was the one who needed his forgiveness because I'd failed to see that he needed help.

Since the tragedy, I have been through many hours of therapy. I have enjoyed the devotion and kindness of friends, neighbors, coworkers, family members, and strangers. I also received an unexpected blessing. On a few occasions I was contacted by the parents of some of the children killed at the school. These courageous individuals asked to meet privately so we could talk. Their compassion helped me survive.

Still, Dylan's participation in the massacre was impossible for me to accept until I began to connect it to his own death. Once I saw his journals, it was clear to me that Dylan entered the school with the intention of dying there. And so, in order to understand what he might have been thinking, I started to learn all I could about suicide.

Suicide is the end result of a complex mix of pathology, character, and circumstance that produces severe emotional distress. This distress is so great that it impairs one's ability to think and act rationally. From the writings Dylan left behind, criminal psychologists have concluded that he was depressed and suicidal. When I first saw copied pages of these writings, they broke my heart. I'd had no inkling of the battle Dylan was waging in his mind. As early as two years before the shootings, he wrote about ending his life. In one poem, he wrote, "Revenge is sorrow / death is a reprieve / life is a punishment / others' achievements are tormentations / people are alike / I am different." He wrote about his longing for love and his near obsession with a girl who apparently did not know he existed. He wrote, "Earth, humanity, HERE. that's mostly what I think about. I hate it. I want to be

> My husband had noticed something tight in Dylan's voice.

free...free... I thought it would have been time by now. the pain multiplies infinitely. Never stops. (yet?) i'm here, STILL alone, still in pain...."

Among the items police found in his room were two half-empty bottles of Saint-John's-wort, an herb believed to elevate mood and combat mild depression. I asked one of Dylan's friends if he knew that Dylan had been taking it. Dylan told him he hoped it would increase his "motivation."

Each year there are approximately 33,000 suicides in the United States. (In Colorado, suicide is the second leading cause of death for people ages 15 to 34.) And it is estimated that 1 to 2 percent of suicides involve the killing of an additional person or people. I will never know why Dylan was part of that small percentage. I will never be able to explain or excuse what he did. No humiliating experience at school could justify such a disproportionate reaction. Nor can I say how powerfully he was influenced by a friend. I don't know how much control he had over his choices at the time of his death, what factors pushed him to commit murder, and why he did not end his pain alone. In talking with other suicide survivors and attempters, however, I think I have some idea why he didn't ask for help.

I believe that Dylan did not want to talk about his thoughts because he was ashamed of having them. He was accustomed to handling his own problems, and he perceived his inability to do so as a weakness. People considering suicide sometimes feel that the world would be better off without them, and their reasons for wanting to die make sense to them. They are too ill to see the irrationality of their thinking. I believe it frightened Dylan to encounter something he did not know how to manage, since he had always taken pride in his self-reliance. I believe he tried to push his negative thoughts away, not realizing that bringing them out in the open was a way to conquer them.

In raising Dylan, I taught him how to protect himself from a host of dangers: lightning, snake bites, head injuries, skin cancer, smoking, drinking, sexually transmitted diseases, drug addiction, reckless driving, even carbon monoxide poisoning. It never occurred to me that the gravest danger—to him and, as it turned out, to so many others—might come from within. Most of us do not see suicidal thinking as the health threat that it is. We are not trained to identify it in others, to help others appropriately, or to respond in a healthy way if we have these feelings ourselves.

In loving memory of Dylan, I support

I was nearly insane with sorrow for the suffering he'd caused.

suicide research and encourage responsible prevention and awareness practices as well as support for survivors. I hope that someday everyone will recognize the warning signs of suicide—including feelings of hopelessness, withdrawal, pessimism, and other signs of serious depression—as easily as we recognize the warning signs of cancer. I hope we will get over our fear of talking about suicide. I hope we will teach our children that most suicidal teens telegraph their intentions to their friends, whether through verbal statements, notes, or a preoccupation with death. I hope we come to understand the link between suicidal behavior and violent behavior, and realize that dealing with the former may help us prevent the latter. (According to the U.S. Secret Service Safe School Initiative, 78 percent of school attackers have a history of suicide attempts or suicidal thoughts.) But we must remember that warning signs may not always tell the story. No one saw that Dylan was depressed. He did not speak of death, give away possessions, or say that the world would be better off without him. And we should also remember that even if someone is exhibiting signs of suicide risk, it may not always be possible to prevent tragedy. Some who commit suicide or murder-suicide are—like Eric Harris—already receiving psychiatric care.

If my research has taught me one thing, it's this: Anyone can be touched by suicide. But for those who are feeling suicidal or who have lost someone to suicide, help is available—through resources provided by nonprofits like the American Foundation for Suicide Prevention, and the American Association of Suicidology. (If you are having persistent thoughts about suicide, call the national suicide prevention lifeline at 800-273-8255 to speak with a counselor. And if you are dealing with the loss of a loved one to suicide, know that National Survivors of Suicide Day is November 21, with more than 150 conferences scheduled across the United States and around the world.)

For the rest of my life, I will be haunted by the horror and anguish Dylan caused. I cannot look at a child in a grocery store or on the street without thinking about how my son's schoolmates spent the last moments of their lives. Dylan changed everything I believed about myself, about God, about family, and about love. I think I believed that if I loved someone as deeply as I loved him, I would know if he were in trouble. My maternal instincts would keep him safe. But I didn't know. And my instincts weren't enough. And the fact that I never saw tragedy coming is still almost inconceivable to me. I only hope my story can help those who can still be helped. I hope that, by reading of my experience, someone will see what I missed. ❶

economy basics simple

steel knife and a steel fork with
Ma had a tin cup and Pa
rie had a little

LAURA INGALLS WILDER
Little House on the Prairie

BY GARTH WILLIAMS

The Hard-Times Companion

Inspired by the trials and triumphs of a resilient pioneer family, Marie Howe
and her daughter find the joyful rhythm in a pared-down life.

T summer of 2008 my 8-year-old daughter and I returned to New York City after I didn't get the very lucrative job I'd hoped for in another city. Let's go home, honey, I said, and downsize into simplicity. And so we came back to our tiny fifth-floor walk-up apartment in the West Village, gave away or stored a lot of our stuff, and resettled into a space the size of a very small houseboat. Within two months the economy began to wobble and then falter.

It seemed a good time to read the series I'd known as the Little House on the Prairie books, written by Laura Ingalls Wilder. I'd never read them as a child, had only glimpsed the TV series, and autumn was upon us. We sat on the couch under the lamplight, the book in my lap, my daughter leaning against me, warm and fresh from a shower. Through our two front windows: the worn red bricks of the 19th-century buildings across the street, and beyond them, the gleaming Empire State Building shining over the darkened city.

From our white couch each night we accompanied Ma and Pa as they moved their children, Laura, Mary, and Carrie, from a log cabin at the edge of the Big Woods in Wisconsin on to Kansas, into Indian territory, and still farther on to Plum Creek, where they spent that winter in a dugout sod house in a hill. With every move Pa built another cabin, another set of beds, fashioned the stable, and set his traps or plowed his field. And Ma unpacked their few clothes, set up the stove and the kitchen, settled the girls, and finally unpacked her single luxury, a china shepherdess statue, and set her on a high shelf—and the family began again.

By December I'd lost half my retirement savings, as

had many of my friends, but I still had the job I'd returned to and was growing ever more grateful for it. The Ingalls family had moved three times, lost their good dog Jack, and suffered through a long bout of scarlet fever that had left Mary blind. Heat, hunger, grasshoppers. Pa worked the field, hunted when he could; Ma made supper, and the girls did their daily chores: fetching water, making the beds, setting and clearing the table, washing dishes. Page after page, they worked, then settled down to stitch quilt squares and study. If the chores had the feel of a regular metronome, the rhythm of their daily life seemed like a quiet song.

It was several weeks of reading before I noticed how the uncomplaining dignity of those people was slowly entering us. My daughter and I, almost unconsciously, began to slow down when we were at home. She began to read her schoolbooks out loud to me as I cooked dinner. (I cooked dinner! We are New Yorkers, used to eating out or ordering in.) And we started to refer to our housework as chores. Okay, honey, I'd say in the morning, before you leave for school we need to do the chores. And without a word of the usual resistance, she'd wash out the breakfast dishes as I straightened our three small rooms. At night, I, who'd always hated housework, experienced a deep satisfaction putting every single dish away—as Ma did. Sometimes I'd stand in the hall looking in—as if the tiny kitchen were the world, ordered, clean, and, in the little table-lamp light, lovely.

It was a cold winter in New York, bitter cold, stinging cold. The economic downturn had become a recession. Every week brought more news of layoffs and cutbacks. Day after day that February we pulled on layers to go to school and work, then scarves and hats and mittens, and we bent into the wind as we walked toward the river. The Ingallses by that time were living in a shack—blizzards blew across the prairie so hard and thick they couldn't see out their small windows for days. The girls woke up to their quilts coated with ice. They were starving and weak and broke. Pa checked and fed the animals, Ma made dinner, be it only potatoes, and the girls cleaned up, tended the baby. My own salary was frozen and threatened. I lay awake at night, a single mother, wondering what I would do if..., tossing and waking with worry.

One night I heard my daughter quietly crying in the loft where she sleeps. What is it, honey? I called out. Mom, she called back, I can give away some of my things

Sometimes I'd stand in the hall looking in—as if the tiny kitchen were the world, ordered, clean, and, in the little table-lamp light, lovely.

to other kids who need them. And for my birthday, you don't have to get me any presents. What in the world? I went in, climbed the ladder, and asked what she was so worried about. The economy, she said, the word sounding odd and overlarge in her voice. (Of course she must have heard the phone calls and conversation.) What could I say? Look at Laura, and Ma and Pa and Mary, I said; they live simply, and they are happy. We are okay, and we will be okay. You don't have to worry. And she put her head down on her pillow.

We began to cook rice and beans twice a week and invite neighbors in our building over for tacos. We joined the church across the street and met more neighbors. We'd never given expensive gifts at the holidays, but this year we made them all—embroidering pillowcases and knitting long bumpy scarves. And when things felt hard—trudging up the five flights carrying heavy bags, or stomping through a cold night, blocks from home, my daughter would say, It's not so bad, it's not what Laura had to do.

The Ingalls family did survive that long winter (although I was so worried they wouldn't I read ahead one night while my daughter slept). Throughout the unrelenting hardship, the politeness and care that family showed each other never wavered; their daily tasks seemed to keep them steady and sane. And one day Laura heard a new sound—the wind they call the Chinook, the warm wind, blowing across the prairie. Ma opened the cabin door to the coming spring.

As the American winter melted into May, we had only one and a half more books to read in the series. We went slowly. We didn't want them to end. Laura was older now, a teacher, and a man we both liked was courting her. We sat on the couch and read a chapter on a Saturday morning. And through our two front windows came that light that always astonishes in its brightness. Spring in New York.

And then, with a rush of warm wind, summer came. I wrote this with the two windows wide open; through them, as in every summer, the various, vibrant sounds of the city: honking, sirens, the constant and real emergencies—and, as in every summer, the sound of jackhammers, someone banging a hammer, a shout, someone sawing, someone building something. ◐

Muffin Manifesto

When the economy slowed, she started baking for the fun of it, but her friends reacted as if she were setting feminism back 30 years. Suzan Colón starts a banana-walnut revolution.

hen in doubt, bake. That's always been my answer to uncertainty, maybe ever since I slid that first tin of chocolate cake mix into my Easy-Bake oven as my mother wondered aloud how she was going to pay the phone bill. The more things change, the more they stay the same; last year my 401(k) evaporated, my husband's stock reports looked like Ponzi schemes, and as many of our friends were laid off as were employed. I had to make the switch from staff to freelance in a shrinking job market, and soon the only growth industry I knew of was the incessant baking going on at our house.

For me, baking is better (and cheaper) than therapy. It gives me something to do with my hands besides wring them nervously. It makes the house smell great—I'm convinced that warm bread is the original aromatherapy— and it yields tangible results. Baking is a form of meditation, as I learned from Edward Espe Brown, a Zen Buddhist priest who wrote *The Tassajara Bread Book*. Mindfulness is essential; one wrong measure (was that a quarter or half teaspoon of baking powder? or was it baking soda?) really can make the cookie crumble.

My baked good of choice during this Chicken Little year has been muffins. Bread takes patience, which I've been short on, and cookies give me the sugar blues. But muffins are an ideal marriage of the two: light and fluffy, a little sweet but not too, and versatile. They work for breakfast, a teatime snack, or dessert. My husband likes to take them to work for a midmorning holdover until lunch, so I started baking them for him.

Out came the muffin tins and the recipe books. I started with an old standby, banana walnut. It's the perfect solution to any overripe bananas that might otherwise be thrown away (horrors! the waste!); in fact, the spottier they get, the sweeter the muffin will be. The tenderness of the cake and the firmness of the walnuts make an excellent match, and the result is a rich, moist muffin that doesn't taste nearly as healthy as it is. I then moved on to applesauce muffins laced with cinnamon and, feeling a little bold one gray Sunday afternoon, I test-drove pear-ginger muffins. On a day when I had no fresh fruit in the house, my baking Yoda, Ed Espe Brown, supplied an imaginative recipe using dried fruit. ("Best muffins ever!!" read the text message from my husband.)

Baking muffins for him gave me an outlet for my anxiety and made him happy. With practice, I gained the satisfaction of getting good at something when everything else was going to hell. My only mistake was talking about it.

The first muffin oppressors were a group of women I worked with years ago and have dinner with once a month. One wrote a book about traveling through the jungles of Costa Rica; another blogs about Spanish wines; the third styles celebrities for fashion shoots. I was the last of us to get married, so the question of whether I'm still experiencing wedded bliss comes up every time we get together. They're always thrilled to hear that the honeymoon isn't over, but they nearly dropped their iPhones right into their iCocktails when I mentioned the muffins.

"You're doing what?" asked one.

Baking muffins, I said. For Nathan.

"How's that book coming?" sniped another.

"Wow," said the third, looking particularly unwowed. "You're a really good wife, aren't you?" Ah, the Good Wife—June Cleaver of *Leave It to Beaver*, the scapegoat of the Equal Rights Amendment. I'd forgotten that her crest was two rolling pins under a muffin tin.

It wasn't just my women friends who had something to say about me and my muffins. Even an open-minded male friend chortled when I mentioned the dried fruit recipe. "Oh," he said after a moment, "you weren't kidding." This even though I'd taken the precaution of talking about my book first.

I don't remember any antimuffin diatribes in Gloria Steinem's *Revolution from Within*. In *The Feminine Mystique*, Betty Friedan didn't mention baked goods as being particularly dangerous to women's advancement; apparently she even liked to munch on them while having debates with her friends. Pundits have announced that feminism is dead—in this post–*Sex and the City* world, 20-something girls seem to have no use for it—so I thought it was safe to bake muffins again.

Or was all this derision due to the muffin's lowly position in the pastry hierarchy? Would I have gotten kudos instead of sneers if I said I'd learned how to whip up a mean poisson cru?

In hindsight, maybe I should have explained the reasons behind my muffin-baking spree. In a time of tremendous anxiety, when suddenly we all had so many questions, there was something simple I could do that yielded positive results almost instantly: Hunker down and make food. For me, that meant baking—something comforting, sweet, small, and warm. Something that could be shared, like the little chocolate cake that gave my mother a moment's distraction from worrying about that phone bill. Something that, when eaten alone in the afternoon with a cup of tea, could make me feel like everything would be okay.

So let my friends sneer. Let them laugh. Let 'em eat cake! Baking muffins doesn't make me a work-shirking antifeminist Good Wife. It makes me happy. ◗

The Longest Night

Jo Ann Beard takes her beloved friend on a final journey.

Something happened to her while she was eating, or right afterward. She began turning in circles and couldn't stop. In my kitchen, in my car, and then in an examining room at the vet's office. I sat on the floor with her while the vet stood leaning against the wall, watching us. I was crying, but he ignored that.

"You indicated once," he said, looking through the file, "that we should let you know when it might be time."

It wasn't time.

"It looks like a brain abnormality, something that's grown, or shifted. We might wait a day or so to see what happens. But if this doesn't stop..." He paused.

"Sheba, stop," I said, and held her. She looked like Lady from *Lady and the Tramp,* only old; she was 15.

It was like putting your hand on a spinning top; as soon as I let go, she began turning again. We used to call her Top Dog, because she liked to sleep stretched out on our old black Lab, her head settled on his head, both of their eyes closed. Once, many years ago, the Lab had gotten carefully to his feet, made his way to the kitchen where my husband was cooking, and accepted a treat, all without disturbing the sleeping puppy draped over his neck.

The Lab lived to be 15, too. The marriage, 14.

I took my hands away to button my jacket, and she turned blindly for a moment on the gleaming linoleum, then bumped into the single leg of the examining table.

"It might be time," the vet said, putting his foot out to stop her. Except for those neon running shoes, he was completely nondescript, like an actor you aren't sure why is in the movie until the very end, when he turns out to be the killer.

At home, it didn't get any better or any worse, Sheba following herself, nose to tail, around and around in a circle while I tried as best I could to keep her steady. My neighbor came over for a few minutes and watched, her eyes round and nervous. "This doesn't look hopeful," the neighbor finally said.

It was dark by then, and I was kneeling on my living room floor in lamplight, holding her and then letting her turn, holding her and then letting her turn. It was winter, but the neighbor was wearing flip-flops.

"Aren't your feet cold?" I asked her.

"Yes," she said, and went home.

We were used to being alone. Our house was small and dark, set into a hillside, but we had a stone fireplace and built-in bookshelves and a screened porch overlooking a blue lake, our own dock, certain seabirds that didn't seem like they belonged there, so we chased them away each morning, or rather one of us did, while the other stood on a giant ornate piece of driftwood and drank coffee in her sunglasses, even though nobody needed sunglasses in Ithaca.

We had brought more or less nothing from our previous life—a few pictures, some ceramic bowls, a Turkish rug that we hardly noticed in our old, big Iowa house but that became in the new house a focal point, the last remnant of what used to be. Sheba began urinating on it sometime around midnight, in a series of dark rings overlapping and intersecting one another. By 1 o'clock it was my turn, and I ran to the bathroom and came back to find her spun into a corner and stuck there, bumping against the baseboard.

Turning and turning in the widening gyre.

"Sheba," I said.

The falcon cannot hear the falconer.

"Sheba," I said, holding her face in my hands. She looked back blindly and I saw suddenly that the vet was right, something had grown or shifted, blocking her in there all alone.

I always knew I'd have to live without her someday, I just didn't know it would be tomorrow. *Things fall apart.* Here in the safe silence of Ithaca, I had forgotten that.

So we stayed awake all of her last night, waiting for the vet's office to open, in the living room on the Turkish rug, in the kitchen next to her food bowl, and finally on the bed, pushed into the corner, my body between her and the edge. At some point I couldn't help it and let my eyes close, and when I did, it felt like I was turning, too, our lives unraveling like a skein of yarn stretched from Ithaca back to Iowa. I see my husband patting his chest and holding out his arms, Sheba jumping into them. I see the Lab, wearing her like a bonnet on his head. I see her running under the seabirds as they fly along the shore. Don't leave yet, I say to my husband, who leaves. "Don't leave yet," I say aloud in the darkness of the bedroom.

She used to sleep at the foot of the bed, and at first light, first twitch, would crawl sleepily up to my pillow, so that when I opened my eyes she was what I saw. The aging dog-actress face: still the dark eyes, still the long glamorous ears. Don't leave yet. If I let go of her she moves in wider and wider circles, getting close to the edge. *Come back, little Sheba.* We're both close to the edge now, peering over it into the great metaphorical beyond.

And then dawn arrives, and then it's 8, and I begin to move forward, into it, without thinking. I carry her down to the water and let her stand on the shore, the birds wheeling and making their noises. In Iowa she ran into a cornfield once and didn't come out for a long time, and when she did she seemed thoughtful. The Lab once went on a garbage run and afterward threw up what looked like a whole birthday cake, candles and all.

I carry her back up the hill and the neighbor runs out of her house, half dressed for work, and opens the car door for me.

"Is it time?" she asks me.

"Not yet," I tell her.

All the way across town, driving and holding Sheba in the passenger seat with one hand, I think to myself, *Don't think.* All the way from Iowa to Ithaca, 800 miles, she stood in the backseat on the rolled-up rug, her chin on my shoulder, and watched the landscape roll by. I feel her humming against my hand, trying to turn and then we're turning, we're in the parking lot, we're here.

It's time. ❶

> All the way across town, driving and holding Sheba in the passenger seat with one hand, I think to myself, *Don't think.*

Julianna Margulies's Aha! Moment

It took an exhausting night, complete with crying baby, for the actress to understand in an instant what her mother had been telling her for decades.

I went back to work when my son, Kieran, was 5½ months old. In my business, we work 17, 18 hours a day, and I was exhausted. And when you're tired, your emotional self sings the loudest, so you don't always think clearly.

One night Kieran woke up at 2; my husband was away, and I had a 6 A.M. call time to be on set. I didn't know what was wrong with him—maybe gas pains—but whatever it was, this baby was not happy. I worked myself into a complete state of anxiety about how I wasn't going to get enough sleep, how I was going to be late for work, how I'd be tired when I got there...all of which only made things worse. And just then, I heard my mother's voice in my head saying what she'd always told me: *Honey, this is only a moment; it's not the rest of your life.*

When you're young, you tend not to listen to your parents. Then you become a parent yourself and you think, *Ohhhh, so that's what she meant.* I never really understood what she was talking about until that night. It was so poignant, because I got it in one second.

I immediately calmed down. As I held Kieran, I thought, *What's the worst that can happen? So I'll have bags under my eyes; that's what makeup people are for.* As I relaxed, so did the baby, and at last I could put him down and go back to bed. Was I tired when I went to work after three

hours of sleep? Sure. But I got through the day.

At any given moment, we're usually thinking about what has happened in the past or what's going to happen in the future. I'll be in the middle of a scene at work and think, *Oh my God, I didn't tell the nanny she needs to come early tomorrow!* I constantly have to reel myself in because I'm a doer, and I'm always thinking about what's next on my list. We're always being reminded to stay in the present moment, but when that present moment is a stressful one, you think it's going to last forever. My mother's saying put things in perspective for me in a remarkable way, because it made me realize that all moments pass quickly, the good ones as well as the bad. I became cognizant of that the night I sat there, tired, holding my crying baby: *Before I can blink an eye, he's going to be 14 and not letting me into his room!*

Since that night, I say to myself at least once a day: *This is just a moment; it's not the rest of your life.* I say it to my niece, who's 19 and isn't sure what she wants to do with her life; when she's 30, she'll wish she had just enjoyed being 19. I tell it to my friends who are having babies. I say, "Enjoy all of it, even the stressful things, because you'll never have that time with them again." What people say is true: You *should* live in the present. Instead of making difficult times hard, make them loving. Knowing that this is just one moment, whatever kind of moment it is, is a more peaceful way to live. *—As told to Suzan Colón*

245

It was inside Vernetta Cockerham's old house in Jonesville, North Carolina, that her estranged husband attacked her and her daughter. "It was absolute torture what he did," she says.

"Why Didn't They Stop Him?"

Vernetta Cockerham did everything by the book. She took her abusive husband to court. Got a protective order. Reported his violations to the police. Yet in the end, none of that was enough to prevent the worst tragedy she could imagine. Why aren't the laws against domestic violence enforced? Phoebe Zerwick investigates.

Vernetta Cockerham woke up on November 19, 2002, feeling at peace for the first time since she could remember. After months of living in terror of her estranged husband's violence, knowing he would kill her if he could, she'd gone to sleep the night before relieved beyond words by the thought of his finally being arrested. Today she could fully focus on her children. Her oldest, Candice, had an appointment with an army recruiter. Cockerham was so proud of her daughter, the way she made friends easily even though she was one of the few African-American students in her rural North Carolina high school. And now, at 17, Candice wanted to serve her country.

Cockerham loaded her three kids into the Explorer and dropped off 6-year-old Rashieq at school, just down the street from where they lived. Their home, an old yellow farmhouse, had belonged to her grandmother and stood right in the center of Jonesville, within plain view of the town hall and the police station.

She drove the baby, Dominiq, almost 9 months old, to daycare, then left Candice at the library to copy a few documents for her interview. Cockerham had one more stop that morning. She needed to call the department of social services because someone—and she was sure it was her husband—had filed an anonymous child-neglect complaint against her. That man would stop at nothing. But at least now that he was in jail, he wouldn't be showing up everywhere she went to slam her around and threaten her, or digging holes near the house and telling her they would be the family's graves. She made the call from a friend's place and went back to the library. But Candice had already headed home.

As Cockerham pulled up to the house, she noticed the front door—it wasn't like her daughter to leave it ajar that way, especially with all that had been going on.

And then in a horrifying instant she saw them: her husband's keys, dangling in the lock.

She was barely through the door when he lunged at her with a knife.

"I killed her," she heard him say as if in slow motion. "And I'm going to kill you."

She reached for the knife, grabbing it by the blade.

There was no pain. Only terror.

"Candice!" she screamed. "Candice!"

He lunged again and Cockerham took cover behind a heavy three-tiered plant stand. It toppled, the glass shelves crashing and knocking the knife from her husband's hand.

She felt a shard of glass slice into her head and the warmth of her blood dripping down her back. Just before she blacked out, she felt his hands around her throat.

When Cockerham came to, she thought she heard Candice's voice calling for her, as if rousing her from a deep sleep.

"Ma, get up. Get up."

But she didn't see her daughter anywhere. The front door was closed now, and as Cockerham struggled with the dead bolt, she caught sight of her fingers—cut so badly, bone showed through the flesh. The lock gave and Cockerham ran, stumbling in the morning chill, across the street and through the vacant lot facing her house to the police station. There she collapsed in the doorway, her throat slashed and bleeding heavily. Drifting in and out of consciousness, she pleaded for someone to help her daughter. Chief Robbie Coe held a towel to her neck, trying to stanch the bleeding. "I know who did it, but *you* need to tell me who did it," he told her. But Cockerham had only one thing on her mind: *Where are my kids?*

Coe sent two officers, Scotty Vestal and Tim Lee Gwyn, to the house, where they waited for backup. Another officer found Candice's body in the downstairs bedroom. Heavy duct tape covered her mouth and nose. She'd been beaten and suffocated; an electrical cord was tied around her neck and reinforced with a layer of tape. Her hands and feet had been bound. And her jeans were pulled down around her knees, leaving her half naked.

The police had not arrested Cockerham's husband, Richard

Cockerham's grandmother, Marie Edmonds, raised her and has always stood by her side.

Ellerbee. And despite everything she'd done to protect herself and her family from a crime like this, the unbearable tragedy had happened anyway. "It was absolute torture what he did," she says.

Like every state, North Carolina has stringent laws to protect women and their children from domestic violence. The process often begins with a woman filing for an emergency protective order, which can be obtained without a lawyer from a local court (it requires filling out paperwork and is usually issued by a judge on the strength of the complaint). Protective orders (also called restraining orders) vary from state to state but typically forbid an abusive partner to come within a certain distance of the victim and may make other restrictions, like prohibiting phone calls or e-mail. In North Carolina, the emergency order remains in effect until a hearing takes place (usually within ten days), at which time both sides are allowed to present evidence. The judge then decides whether to grant a final order, which lasts up to a year.

If police find probable cause that an order has been violated—even something as simple as driving past the victim's house—most states have laws that call for an arrest. However, a study published in 2000 in *Criminal Justice and Behavior,* based on Massachusetts records and studies in other states, suggests that as many as 60 to 80 percent of restraining orders are not enforced. Furthermore, a 2000 U.S. Department of Justice study found that officers made arrests in only 47 percent of cases in which the victim reported being raped—even fewer when the complaint was assault (36 percent) or stalking (29 percent). In California a 2005 report by the state attorney general's office found widespread hesitation among police and prosecutors to enforce restraining orders—with dangerous consequences. "For the victim," the report concluded, "there is a loss of faith in the system and reluctance to report new violations, even as these violations grow in seriousness. For the batterer, there is a sense of empowerment to commit new violations and more violent crimes." When the rules call for mandatory arrest, says Kristian Miccio, an associate professor of criminal law and procedure at the University of Denver's Sturm College of Law, "and they don't enforce it, you have the illusion of protection, which is worse than not having it at all."

Vernetta Cockerham is living that

> "I go over it every day, and every day I say to myself, *You did everything you were supposed to do by law.*"

painful truth. When she took out a protective order against her husband in October 2002, she believed fully in the power of the law to keep her safe. And repeatedly she reported Ellerbee's violations to the police. But even when they arrested him, he was released on bond. "I go over it every day," she says, "and every day I say to myself, *You did everything you were supposed to do by law.*"

Now she's trying to change the system. On November 18, 2004, almost exactly two years after Candice's murder and her own near death, Cockerham sued the town of Jonesville and its police department for failing to enforce the restraining order that was in place to protect them. It's been an exhausting legal battle, leaving some of the facts in dispute—including the promise she says the police made to arrest her husband the night before the bloodshed. Cockerham's resolve is steely, but when she describes the crowd of teenagers who lined the street for Candice's funeral, she still breaks down and weeps.

Cockerham is a slender woman with high cheekbones, a wide smile, and today, a thick scar that runs down the left side of her neck, from jaw to collarbone. Despite what she's been through, she laughs easily and walks with a skip in her step. At 41, she could easily pass for 25.

She was born in 1969 in Paterson, New Jersey, the youngest of three girls. Her paternal grandmother, Marie Edmonds, stepped in early to raise the sisters because their parents were unable to provide a stable home. When it was time for Cockerham to go to school, her grandmother moved the children to her home in Jonesville, a town of about 1,500 in the northwest corner of North Carolina. The family could trace its roots there at least five generations back. Just about every other house on their winding street belonged to an aunt, uncle, or distant cousin.

Edmonds worked the third shift at a nursing home and raised her grandchildren the old-fashioned way. She canned vegetables, washed clothes by hand, made sure everyone went to church on Sundays. And she taught Cockerham how to fend for herself.

When Cockerham turned 14, she moved to Newark, New Jersey, hoping to get to know her mother; then she went to live in Paterson with her father and enrolled in high school. The summer before her sophomore year, she became a math tutor, and one of her students was a linebacker named Kevin Baker. He was three years older,

Cockerham's daughter, Candice (*in photo*), was 17 when she was murdered by her stepfather. Her ashes are kept on the shelf near the family Bible.

almost 18, but he and Cockerham fell for each other. By the middle of that school year, she was pregnant.

After having the baby—Candice—in Jonesville, Cockerham joined Baker in Paterson and married him. His sister was dating a family friend, a hardworking carpenter named Richard Ellerbee. It was Ellerbee who told Cockerham that her husband was cheating on her. Grateful to Ellerbee, 13 years her senior, for letting her know, she soon found herself confiding in him.

Cockerham and Baker divorced. She finished school and got a job in the records room of the Paterson Police Department. But when Candice was 6, Cockerham decided she'd rather raise her daughter in Jonesville. Back home, she found her own place, and juggled two jobs. She had the early-morning shift at a Shoney's restaurant, bringing Candice with her when she opened the place at 4:30 A.M., then taking her to school during her break. When that shift was over, she'd go work at a state prison near Yadkinville, about a half hour away.

Ellerbee kept in touch with her, and in 1993, when Cockerham was 24, he called. He was desperate to leave Paterson. Could he visit? Soon enough he was job-hunting in Jonesville and making plans to settle there. She found that she liked having him around.

It's hard to say when their love, if that's what it was,

tipped into something dark and frightening. At first she felt needed, and that appealed to her. But soon she started noticing he didn't like being told what to do. She also noticed how controlling he was. "Having to ask him, not tell him, what I was doing," she says, "became an issue for me."

Cockerham never wanted children with Ellerbee. After a difficult birth with Candice, she believed she couldn't conceive again, but in 1995 she found herself pregnant with Rashieq, who was born in May of the following year. Around that time, she says, she tried to pull back from a sexual relationship with Ellerbee. But he was a large, heavy man, more than six feet tall, and at 5'7" and only 140 pounds, she was unable to stop him from doing as he pleased. "I didn't know what to do," she says. "It was as if the more I drew myself away, the more aggressive he would become."

Feeling miserable and trapped, she threw herself into her church. "It'll work out," her grandmother assured her. "And you got to do right by the kids." In August 1999, however, during a routine argument, Ellerbee grabbed her purse, hit her in the face with an open hand, choked her, and threw her to the ground. Cockerham got a protective order, but after he threatened her, she dropped it.

Cockerham's son Dominiq, 7 (*far left*), was a baby when his sister was murdered. Her older child, Rashieq, 13, helps his mother stay strong.

By the summer of 2001 she was pregnant with her third child, and Ellerbee insisted that they marry. Her pastor, who had counseled the couple, was wary of Ellerbee's interest in her assets and refused to conduct the ceremony. Cockerham hoped Ellerbee would drop the idea. But one day he offered to drive her to the grocery store, and headed toward the county courthouse instead. They were married there December 1, 2001. "I knew something wasn't right, but I did not know how to get out of it," Cockerham recalls. "I just wanted the family life to work. I wanted the father figure. I wanted the normalcy." During the ceremony, she says, "I cried the entire time. I never said a word. He spoke for me."

Dominiq was born February 26, 2002, and by summer Cockerham found herself always on edge, waiting for her husband to explode. On the Fourth of July, he did. Cockerham had packed a picnic for the family and piled the baby's stroller and other belongings by the front door.

"I'm not going," Ellerbee said.

"What do you mean?"

Instead of arguing in front of the kids, they went outside and sat in his silver Chevy Blazer. As they continued fighting, she saw him glance at Rashieq's baseball bat in the backseat.

"I know you're not going to hit me with that baseball bat," she said.

He reached behind him, grabbed the bat, and swung, hitting her on the back of her head. As much as it hurt, at least the children hadn't seen their father strike her. Ellerbee walked back into the house. Worried he might do something to the kids, Cockerham followed him through the door and up the stairs, motioning to Candice to get the boys outside. When Cockerham reached the second floor, her husband threw her onto the bed and held a pillow over her face.

"I'm your God," he said, his voice so smooth it terrified her, "and I can take your breath away when I get ready."

It was her breaking point.

That night, the police came and arrested Ellerbee, charging him with felony assault with a deadly weapon. Released on a $1,000 bond, he moved out of the house, at some point getting a room at the Holiday Inn off the interstate near the outskirts of town.

For Cockerham, having Ellerbee gone was almost worse than having him at home, because she never knew where he was or when he would turn up. All summer he followed her around town. He'd call and leave her messages. "I saw you at the Food Lion," he'd say, only to delete the message remotely with the codes he still had to the voicemail. He tampered with the fuse box and the gas tank outside the house. He left more messages.

In September Ellerbee pleaded guilty to reduced charges of misdemeanor assault with a deadly weapon and assault on a female and was put on three-year probation, on the condition that he not harm or threaten Cockerham. She agreed to the reduced charges because she didn't think the felony would stick—a view shared by Chad Brown, the assistant district attorney in Yadkin County who prosecuted the case. Brown thought the probation, which required Ellerbee to go to jail for 120 days if he harassed or hurt Cockerham again, would be strong enough to keep her and her children safe. The judge, Mitchell McLean, made a point of asking the clerk to note on the docket sheet that if Ellerbee violated his probation, McLean wanted to hear the case himself.

But the stalking continued. Cockerham couldn't sleep. She couldn't eat. She called the police, the sheriff, her domestic violence caseworkers. At the same time, Ellerbee also began complaining about his wife showing up at his house. "She came in a couple of times. He came in a couple of times," says Jonesville police chief Robbie Coe, who left the department in 2004. "It appeared to be a normal domestic situation, just fussing back and forth."

Most days Cockerham would check in with the Weyerhaeuser lumber plant where Ellerbee worked to make sure he was there and it was safe to leave the house. She started carrying a nine-millimeter pistol her father had given her years earlier. But as the weeks turned into months, she only felt more afraid.

One day in October, she was at the local phone company when he showed up and yelled across the parking lot, "I'm gonna get you. I will kill you before this is all over."

Again, she went to the authorities. On October 10, Ellerbee was charged with communicating threats, but as before, released on a $1,000 bond. Cockerham knew the laws by now, and took out an emergency protective order. This time she meant business. On top of the conditions for his probation, Ellerbee was ordered to stay away from the children's school and daycare center, and keep a 250-foot distance from Cockerham. "The defendant shall not assault, threaten, abuse, follow, harass (by telephone, visiting the home or workplace, or other means), or interfere with the plaintiff," the order read. "A law enforcement officer shall arrest the defendant if the officer has probable cause to believe the defendant has violated this provision."

Cockerham got a job as an assistant manager at the Quiznos sub shop in Elkin, a town across the Yadkin River, in the next county. The order applied there, too, but on November 2, Ellerbee showed up during her shift. Through the window, she could see him pacing, motioning to her to come outside. Cockerham called the Elkin police, but they didn't have a copy of her protective order—nor could she find hers, which she thought she'd put in the car—and they said there was nothing they could do. Not wanting to endanger the others in the shop, Cockerham went out to meet her husband.

He grabbed her by the shoulder, half dragged her to her Explorer, and demanded that she drive him to the one-story brick house he'd rented in Elkin. Terrified, she got into the car. He kept his hand on the steering wheel the whole time, telling her where to turn. At the house, Cockerham screamed at the top of her lungs for help, but no one responded. Ellerbee opened her car door and tried to pull her out. Cockerham took her chance, reached for the pistol under the seat, and hit him on the forehead, hard, with the butt end. But he snatched the gun, she says, threw it on the pavement, then yanked her from the car. After wrestling her to the ground, he slammed her head against the gravel and dirt. Cockerham heard him call the police from his cell phone.

He had set her up perfectly. She was at his house, with her Explorer, and she had a gun. That day Cockerham was charged with assault, while Ellerbee went free. She spent the weekend in jail, with her hair and bits of gravel matted to a throbbing wound on her forehead.

Monday morning, Tom Langan, an assistant district attorney in Surry County, which has jurisdiction in Elkin, took one look at the wound on Cockerham's forehead and knew right away that police had charged the wrong person. He was furious. "In speaking to her, it became obvious to me that she was the victim," Langan says. "This did not seem like something that would go away unless someone went to prison for a long time. Or someone died."

In 1994 Congress passed the Violence Against Women Act, which set aside more than $300 million in 2008 for training law enforcement and victims' services. And to some extent, the effort has been successful. According to the U.S. Department of Justice, the number of women killed by their boyfriends, husbands, or ex-husbands dropped by almost 26 percent (from 1,587 to 1,181) between 1976 and 2005, the last year for which there are statistics, while the number of men killed by intimate partners fell by 75 percent (to 329). Nevertheless, the Justice Department estimates that more than 1.8 million women a year are raped, assaulted, or stalked by an intimate partner, and 30 percent of female homicide victims are murdered by one.

A great deal has been written about how victims become paralyzed by abuse—one reason that only about 20 percent of those who have been assaulted, raped, or stalked by an intimate partner obtain a protective order, according to the data available. But the failure of authorities to adequately respond to women like Vernetta Cockerham is also key to explaining why domestic violence remains so deadly. And that is due, in large part, to the fact that many police officers and court officials essentially don't understand the psychological dynamic of abuse, says Evan Stark, PhD, a professor of public health at Rutgers University and author of *Coercive Control: How Men Entrap Women in Personal Life*. Police often react to each infraction as an isolated incident, for example, when it is the accumulation of small abusive acts—both physical and emotional—that wears a woman down and emboldens the batterer. Even when a batterer is arrested, Stark says, he rarely spends time in jail, because most assaults are relatively minor: a blackened eye, a bruised arm. (In fact, the most calculating batterers figure out how to game the system—filing charges against their spouse, or reporting her to social workers, knowing that the threat of losing her children is more chilling than any beating. And in the presence of authorities, these abusers often appear calm, while the victim is hysterical. Often *she* ends up being the one blamed.) "Essentially one of the most dramatic forms of oppression in our society is transformed into a second-class misdemeanor," Stark says. "What kind of indignity should women be allowed to suffer before the community takes notice?"

Jessica Lenahan is still trying to make her voice heard. During her marriage to Simon Gonzales, he was never physically violent to her, or to the three girls they were raising in Castle Rock, Colorado. But if the breakfast biscuits were overcooked, he'd hurl them in the trash. If the socks weren't folded the way he liked them, he'd empty the drawers and demand that she redo the laundry. Occasionally, he'd cut off her access to their bank accounts. At one point, he tried to hang himself in the garage, in front of their daughters. The couple separated in 1999, but he continued to terrorize the family by stalking Lenahan and hiding in the closet of the girls' bedroom. On May 21, 1999, Lenahan got a court order that required him to stay 100 yards away.

A month later, on the afternoon of June 22, she discovered her daughters—ages 7, 9, and 10—missing from the front yard. She immediately called the police to alert them that the restraining order was being violated; they told her to wait and see if the kids were returned by 10. It wasn't until 8:30 P.M. that she was finally able to speak to Gonzales on his cell phone. He said he had the girls at an amusement park in Denver, about 30 miles away. Frantic, she called the police again and pleaded with them to find her husband and rescue her children. But they kept telling her to phone back later. Lenahan called the police several more times before going down to the station about 1:00 in the morning to submit an incident report.

At 3:20 A.M., Simon Gonzales drove up to the police station and opened fire with a semiautomatic handgun. The police shot him dead, and when they went to his truck, found the bodies of the three girls in the backseat. "I was so angry," says Lenahan now. "I believed the police would do their job." After the murders, she sued the town of Castle Rock and appealed her case as far as she could, alleging that the police had violated her 14th Amendment right to due process. In 2005 the U.S. Supreme Court heard the case, *Castle Rock v. Gonzales,* ruling that the arrest laws left room for police discretion and that she had no constitutional right to have her restraining order enforced. Justice Antonin Scalia wrote for the majority: "We do not believe that these provisions of Colorado law truly made enforcement of restraining orders *mandatory*. A well-established tradition of police discretion has long coexisted with apparently mandatory arrest statutes."

Many advocates worry that the decision has weakened victim protection, even though it didn't strike down mandatory arrest laws. "The cops I meet around the country say, 'Castle Rock means we don't have to enforce these orders,'" notes Marcus Bruning, supervising deputy with the St. Louis County sheriff's office in Duluth,

Minnesota, who trains police nationally to recognize abuse—teaching them, for example, that although it's frustrating when a woman repeatedly returns home to her batterer, that is a sign of his power and control.

Lenahan has gone on to file a petition with the Inter-American Commission on Human Rights, which is part of the Organization of American States, in the hopes of bringing attention to the system's failures. Her struggle fills Vernetta Cockerham with misgivings. "I have an unbelievable fear that my case will end up like Jessica's," Cockerham says.

After the incident in Elkin, Ellerbee was charged with felony assault and violating the emergency protective order; the charges against Cockerham were ultimately dropped. Meanwhile, domestic violence workers had been telling her to take the children to a shelter. But the closest one was in Elkin, in plain view of the road, with no real security or surveillance, and Cockerham felt safer at home with the police station less than 70 yards away. She was also hopeful about her next hearing, scheduled for Tuesday, November 12, at which a judge would rule on extending the emergency protective order. Ellerbee now faced charges in two counties—assault in Surry and communicating threats in Yadkin. She felt confident the judge would revoke his probation and send him to jail, and that safety was just a few days away.

But after spending the weekend before the hearing out of town, she came home to find a large boot print in the fine dust that covered her porch chair—and another one on the railing of the upstairs balcony. Ellerbee had broken in through a window while she was gone. The lock on the file cabinet where she kept her valuables was broken and inside was a note on a torn piece of notebook paper. "I will kill you," it said in Ellerbee's block print. "You will die."

The November 12 hearing was postponed a day while Ellerbee was booked in Surry County on the assault charges and released on a $3,000 bond. The case was supposed to be heard by McLean, the original judge in the July assault case. But, perhaps because of an oversight, a new judge, Jeanie Houston, presided. (The court record is unclear regarding this matter; both McLean and Houston declined to comment.) The assistant district attorney prosecuting Ellerbee was new to the case, too.

Houston found that Ellerbee posed a threat to Cockerham and the children, sufficient evidence to extend the protective order for a year. But the judge did not find that he'd violated his probation, in spite of a recommendation from his probation officer that it be revoked.

When Cockerham realized that Ellerbee wasn't going to jail, she became hysterical.

"He's going to take my life," she screamed at the court. "What else can I do?"

Two states away, in Louisville, Kentucky, Jerry J. Bowles, a circuit judge in Jefferson County, runs a very different court—an example of reform efforts being made in various places around the country to improve protection for domestic abuse victims. In Louisville, social workers help judges prepare for cases, and the same judges stay with a case—for years if needed—until it's resolved. Court officials, police, and social workers also meet to review domestic homicides to figure out how the system failed. And a local company developed the nation's first automated system to notify victims when an assailant is released from jail or prison. When it comes to protective orders, Bowles is a strong believer in enforcement—"not only mandatory arrest but sanctions," he says. "I have people serving six months in jail for not completing treatment." As a result, none of the cases that have come before him in the past 13 years has resulted in a murder.

One morning last January, he arrived early for court, wearing cowboy boots under his robes. He took his seat high up on the bench, behind a protective shield of heavy plastic. There were 32 domestic violence cases on the day's docket—mostly women seeking protection. One had been raped by her husband, another beaten, a third stabbed with a corkscrew. A nursing assistant in her 40s sat quietly at the plaintiff's table. The father of her two sons drinks too

Jessica Lenahan's three daughters were killed after being abducted by her estranged husband—despite a restraining order. Her case went to the Supreme Court.

much, she explained to the judge; she wants out, but he threatens to kill her if she ever leaves. Recently they argued over money, and he pushed her against a chest of drawers.

"It never should have got as far as it did," the man told Bowles. "Yes, I did threaten her. But I'm not a real threat to her. I've got two kids by this lady. I'm not going to do something to hurt my kids."

Bowles issued the protective order. "There's only one reason we threaten people," he told the man sternly. "We want them to think we have the ability to hurt them if they don't do what we want."

After the November 13 hearing, Ellerbee's threats took a darker turn. Cockerham began seeing him in the empty lot across the street from her house with a shovel and wheelbarrow, digging. Then came his voice on her answering machine: "You and the kids will be in those graves and no one will ever know."

Cockerham called Police Chief Coe. He was one of the few who had never dismissed her fears, and she wanted him to hear Ellerbee's words. Coe came to her house, and she showed him the two freshly dug holes just 30 feet from her driveway, one as deep as an adult-sized grave, the second smaller and shallower.

When Coe saw the graves, he says, he put his department of nine officers on alert. According to Coe's deposition, he told Lieutenant Tim Lee Gwyn, "We need to keep a closer watch on what's going on with these people because it could escalate." Still, Ellerbee was not arrested. The protective order gave police the authority to make an arrest without a warrant. Yet because police hadn't actually seen Ellerbee digging the graves, Coe told Cockerham to get a warrant from a magistrate.

Monday morning, November 18, Ellerbee showed up at the Magic Kingdom daycare center, another clear violation of the protective order. Cockerham says she went straight to the police station to report it. Again she was told to obtain an arrest warrant, this time by Scotty Vestal. Cockerham drove 16 miles to the county courthouse and got one.

Later that day, Cockerham stopped Vestal on the street near the station and pointed out Ellerbee's silver Blazer following close behind her. Vestal took off after it in an effort to identify the driver, but Ellerbee eluded him. In his deposition, Vestal said he called Gwyn, who was his supervisor, for help. Gwyn, too, was unable to locate the Blazer. The officers (who are both named in the suit) never turned on their sirens or sent out a general bulletin to law enforcement in the region to find Ellerbee.

As dusk fell late that afternoon, Cockerham says she called the police department and asked Vestal and Gwyn

to meet her down the road outside her father's house. She had a copy of the protective order with her and wanted to make sure the officers understood that a violation required them to make an arrest. While the three were talking in the front yard, Ellerbee drove by, slowly, as if taunting them, according to Cockerham, and the two officers got in their cars. She says they told her that they would get him and not to worry. She watched as they followed her husband's Blazer out of sight.

But that conversation—central to Cockerham's lawsuit—is in dispute. Vestal and Gwyn say they met Cockerham there just after the silver Blazer slipped away from them near the police station, not later. They say they never saw Ellerbee drive by the house—and never promised to arrest him.

"Lieutenant Gwyn did tell me that they did see him come by there and that they went after him and couldn't find him," Chief Coe stated in his deposition. The next morning was the day of the murder.

The last memory Cockerham has of Ellerbee is of his hands around her neck.

According to police reports, a neighbor saw him running down the street carrying a paper bag. He went to a convenience store in town and then drove north, headed for New Jersey. On November 22, three days after the murder, he bought a gas can at a Kmart store, filled it at a gas station, walked to a gazebo in Eastside Park in a historic section of Paterson, and set himself on fire.

Two young men saw the smoke and flames. Police found the smoldering body of an unidentified black male.

That was the same day Cockerham left the hospital, where she'd been since the attack, to attend her daughter's funeral, her hands and head still bandaged. Her injuries were so severe that at first the doctors hadn't told her about Candice's death. When the surgeon finally gave her the bad news, he warned her not to scream or cry or do anything that might rupture the sutures in her neck. "There's no words for that," she says. "To lose a child and not be able to cry. You can't scream. You can't holler. You can't yell."

In the hospital, Cockerham was put under police guard, which lasted until Ellerbee's remains were identified through dental records. But even then, Cockerham had a hard time believing her ordeal was over. Any relief she felt turned into anxiety about her boys. She was desperate to see them and hold them close again. But the Yadkin County department of social services had taken them into protective custody. "Their reasoning was if I got into that relationship with Richard, I was subject to getting into another," says Cockerham. "They told me I had my kids in a war zone. I was very offended."

Cockerham hired attorney Loretta Biggs to help get her children back. Biggs, who had just returned to private practice after a year on the North Carolina Court of Appeals, could not fathom why Cockerham's boys hadn't been returned to her. The more Biggs learned about the case, the more she came to believe that the system had seriously betrayed her client. "I think she was perceived as not being worthy of protection, and I just do not understand it," Biggs says.

Once Cockerham regained her footing, she began to get angry. Overwhelmingly angry. After reading up on the law, she filed her suit. While the Supreme Court had ruled in the Castle Rock case that police have discretion to enforce (or not enforce) an order, and that Jessica Lenahan hadn't been entitled to personal protection, Cockerham's case argues that she *was* entitled to protection, because police had promised it to her. Cockerham's lawyers, Harvey and Harold Kennedy, have won two appeals. In 2006 the North Carolina Court of Appeals ruled that Cockerham had the right to proceed with the case. Two years later the court ruled that she could also seek punitive damages. Lawyers for the police department have countered that Cockerham is partly responsible for her daughter's death because she did not move to a shelter or take other precautions to protect her. And Cockerham expects attacks against her credibility at the trial.

In preparation for a court date in February 2010, the Kennedys showed her crime scene photos she had never seen, including a blown-up color photograph of her daughter's body bound in gray duct tape. The image left her shaken for days, but she says it has only strengthened her resolve to remain steadfast, and to help other battered women. Working with the North Carolina Coalition Against Domestic Violence, she recently helped lobby for legislation to bolster the state's arrest laws.

It was raining one day in the winter of 2008 when Cockerham visited her old street. She hasn't lived there since 2005, when she lost the house to foreclosure. The police station has moved to newer quarters, but the library and school are still within sight of the porch where she used to stand and listen for the morning bell to ring as she watched her children walk to class.

Today she and her two boys live in an apartment in Winston-Salem about 40 miles away, depending on social security benefits of about $800 a month. The nightmares that once made her call out in her sleep have mostly subsided. Dominiq, now 7, knows his father and sister are dead but is too young to remember. Rashieq, who just turned 13, has Ellerbee's features—"his face, his walk, his hands; he's the spitting image," Cockerham says. Every time she looks at her beloved son, she realizes she is able to forgive his father a little more.

Candice's ashes rest in the living room, on a rickety bookshelf with the family Bible and a stack of yearbooks. Some days Cockerham drapes one of Candice's favorite knit caps over the wooden urn. It makes her feel as though her daughter is still with her, close by. "I wanted so much for her," she says. ◖

In July 2009, Vernetta Cockerham settled with the Jonesville Police Department for $430,000. She is now advocating for improved sevices for domestic violence victims in Yadkin County.

Where to Get Help

October is **National Domestic Violence Awareness Month.** If you'd like to give money or time to a group that assists victims—or if you need help yourself—here is a list of organizations:

FOR IMMEDIATE ASSISTANCE

National Domestic Violence Hotline (800-799-7233): Open 24 hours a day, 365 days a year, this line is a resource for safety information and can connect any caller with shelters and protection advocates in her area.

VINE (vinelink.com): Active in 47 states, vinelink.com allows women to search for an offender in custody by name or identification number, then register to be alerted if the offender has been released or transferred, or has escaped.

Women's Law (womenslaw. org): This site has state-by-state legal information and resources for victims, as well as advice on how to leave an abusive situation, gather evidence of abuse, and prepare for court.

FINANCIAL AND MEDICAL RESOURCES

Amy's Courage Fund (nnedv. org/projects): The fund gives emergency financial assistance to women trying to escape a domestic abuse situation. Grants are available for up to $2,000.

Education and Job Training Assistance Fund (nnedv.org/ projects): Grants from The Allstate Foundation help domestic violence victims enter and stay in the work force. The money (up to $1,000) can be used for classes, clothes, computers, and other resources.

Face to Face (800-842-4546): This program provides free plastic and reconstructive surgery to victims who've sustained injuries to the face, head, or neck.

Give Back a Smile (800-773-4227): Front teeth damaged by a violent partner or spouse are repaired pro bono.

Send, Receive

Their loss was too devastating to talk about. So **Kristy Davis** and her father found a different way to communicate.

fter my mom died, we bought home electronics.

My father sat across from me in a restaurant booth. Here was a man I hardly recognized: vulnerable. Two days before, cancer had killed my mom in the bedroom they shared for almost 30 years.

"So how's school going?" he asked.

"Fine," I said.

"You know, your mother wanted you to go."

"I know, Dad."

"You know, she was happy that you..."

"I know, Dad."

I've since heard my father compared to early Paul Newman characters like Cool Hand Luke, a prisoner whose bulletproof resolve leads to trouble. But if my dad—a retired air force colonel, devoted Christian, and family patriarch—has a flaw, it's one we share. Or, as Luke put it, "What we've got here is a failure to communicate."

Because we couldn't talk about God, politics, or her, we went to Best Buy. We trolled the fluorescent aisles, browsing among shiny objects. It smelled like plastic. It sounded like static, an incipient white noise holding hostage otherwise erratic thoughts.

Talking about operating systems counts as a conversation between my father and me. The man owns his own power generator, fiber-optic flashlight, and solar-powered radio. I've had my gearhead phases, too: rock climbing, photography, and lighting design equipment. We are a lot alike. We are completely opposite. I'm Apple, he's PC.

While we've always been gadget crazed, the high-tech spree began after the hospital sent her home to die under hospice care. My father upgraded every possible device to provide comfort and to make life easier. But the week preceding the funeral was an all-out electronics binge.

My dad bought two additional keyboards (one collapsible, one hardwired) for his newly acquired laptop, a wireless mouse and a wireless modem to connect our portables along with his desktop to the printer. We had a lot of work to do, a funeral to plan. We needed all systems up and running. This we threw ourselves into with zealotry fit for presidential elections. Every hour brought something else we needed: USB cables, another modem, better software, photo paper, ink cartridges.

My older sister arrived with a PowerPoint presentation featuring family photographs set to music—a Hawaiian ukulele player's rendition of "Over the Rainbow." We bought an LCD projector to display the slideshow. We could have borrowed one, but all projectors were not created equal, we knew.

I drove an hour south to buy a mini disc player to record the service. It wasn't enough to turn on an analog tape recorder. We needed top-quality sound, good enough for a movie, but burnable to CD.

We spent a lot of time getting these devices to work. While my brothers transported family members, and my sisters went to the morgue, my dad and I saw to all things technical. We hardly had time for condolences.

When visitors arrived, we made them watch the PowerPoint presentation, thereby determining the proper focus for any given square feet of distance, from projector to screen.

"Computer stuff," my older brother said, when someone asked our whereabouts. "They're in there doing computer stuff."

I used to think the digital binge was about my shortcomings. I couldn't help my mother as she sat keening with pain. I stared at the white wall bawling until my sister (a nurse who was doing all the work anyway) mercifully asked me to get something from the other room. But I could set up the laptop near her bed, just in case she wanted to do any typing.

For my father, it was typical "dad response." He could buy stuff and figure it out. He could get wireless Internet for a family full of laptops. Had we wanted the funeral to be like a Broadway show, he would've rented the theater.

And the funeral went off without a hitch. But our penchant for circuitry didn't end there. We bought more to dull the ache: a large-screen television that told us who was calling through its connection to the phone, a light box for seasonal affective disorder, a clock that projected time onto the bedroom ceiling.

Sometimes materialism quells sorrow. My electronics purchases were funded in part with money from my mother's life-insurance policy. After the cash ran out, I felt better—it was never a fair trade from the start. How could it be?

Lately, though, I've come to wonder what prevented us from confronting the magnitude of our loss. This behavior was such an obvious if unconscious retreat. We flicked the off switch in our grief box. Why couldn't we look each other in the eye and say, "The person who loved us most and whom we loved most is *gone*. I have no more mother/I have no more wife."

Maybe sharing a bathetic moment of understanding would have felt cheap. Even more, I wonder if we would have told the truth instead of obscuring each other with saccharine sayings and a dose of God.

And what is the truth? That death changed us, that our bond felt tenuous.

These days, spending time together has to be enough. Whether we're having a silent drive or an awkward meal, language is bound to struggle.

But recently we've begun exchanging e-mails. My father wrote—and this is something I've never heard him say—"Always remember; my love for you is not conditional.... I love you because you are my lovely daughter, and nothing can ever change that."

At the moment of crisis, we are workers in a hive, busy little bees. We are documentarians, resurrecting the dead in high-definition sound. They say funerals are for the living. But death, too, is all *about* the living. ◖

Walking through the Marcy housing project in Bedford-Stuyvesant, Brooklyn, where Jay-Z grew up.

THE _O_ INTERVIEW

Oprah Talks to Jay-Z

At 13 he was selling crack. By 30 he was a hip-hop legend—having gone, in his words, "from grams to Grammys." Now Jay-Z charts his escape from the hard-knock life, describes the reunion that healed the wounds of his childhood—and even reveals the standing Sunday date he has with what's her name.

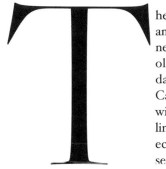

The first time the hip-hop artist and record executive Jay-Z witnessed a murder, he was 9 years old. It was 1978, and in those days, he was known as Shawn Carter—a quiet kid who lived with his mother and three siblings in a sprawling housing project in the Bedford-Stuyvesant section of Brooklyn.

"That was my apartment right there—5C," Jay-Z told me one afternoon in August of 2009 as we strolled the sidewalks of the Marcy Houses. "Navigating this place was life-or-death." He wasn't exaggerating; as the crack epidemic took hold in the 1980s, 13-year-old Jay-Z began selling drugs. His father had abandoned the family when Jay-Z was 11. And like many of his friends, he found his role models in the neighborhood dealers. "On the streets, you had to operate with integrity," he told me. "If you broke your word to someone, he wasn't going to take you to court—he was going to deal with you himself. So it was here in the projects that I learned loyalty."

It was in the projects, too, that he began rapping. Around the neighborhood Shawn became known as Jazzy—a reference, he says, to the way he carried himself: "like an older guy, like an older spirit." He gained a local following after he started selling his own records out of his car. And in 1996—disenchanted with the small-time label that finally signed him—he launched his own label, Roc-A-Fella Records. Later that year, *Reasonable Doubt* hit stores nationwide, and Jay-Z (the play on Jazzy he'd adopted after that name started to feel "too glittery") was on his way.

Since then, Jay-Z has released ten solo studio albums (the most recent, *The Blueprint 3,* debuted in September 2009). He has sold more than 30 million records, won ten Grammys, and built a business empire that includes the Rocawear clothing line and Roc Nation entertainment company. In 2004 he became a part owner of the NBA's New Jersey Nets.

In December 2009 he turned 40, and in recent years his focus has been on more than just his career. In 2003 he reconciled with his father, Adnes Reeves, shortly before Reeves's death. That same year, he began to put his wealth to good use, founding the Shawn Carter Scholarship Fund for disadvantaged and formerly incarcerated youth who hope to attend college (though Jay-Z never did time himself, in 2001 he pleaded guilty to stabbing a record executive at a Manhattan nightclub and was sentenced to three years' probation). In 2006 he teamed up with the United Nations to raise awareness of the worldwide water short-

age. And in 2008, after six years of dating, he married the singer Beyoncé Knowles.

After our walk through the Marcy projects, Jay-Z and I visit a three-story row house a few blocks away. The house used to belong to his grandmother, and until he was 5 years old, Jay-Z lived here with his parents, three siblings, and extended family. As we sit on the front stoop chatting (the same spot where, Jay-Z says, he spent long summer evenings "just chillin' "), the passersby who spot him form a crowd on the sidewalk; several boys climb the iron fence that surrounds the property. "Is that really Jay-Z?" one boy says to another. "Yep—and he's from here," the other responds.

Sitting on this stoop, it's stunning to think about how far Jay-Z has come. Not only is he an entirely self-made man, he's found his great success doing exactly what he loves. He is thoughtful and intelligent, a reader and a seeker. And in between telling me how he survived life on the streets, how a scolding from his mother helped him fall in love, and even how he and Beyoncé managed to keep their wedding small and private, he explains why he cares so much about connecting with kids who remind him of him—kids he hopes will point to his photo and say, "I can make it, too."

OPRAH: We all carry memories that are triggered when we return to a childhood home. What are your fondest memories from here?

JAY-Z: Outside in front is where I learned to ride a bike. I learned to ride a ten-speed when I was 4 or 5. My uncle gave me the bike, hand-me-down, and everyone used to stare at me riding up and down this block.

OPRAH: You could ride a ten-speed when you were 5?

JAY-Z: I was too short to reach the pedals, so I put my legs through the V of the frame. I was famous. The little kid who could ride the ten-speed.

OPRAH: Wow. That's one great memory. Any others?

JAY-Z: The boat. For some reason there was an abandoned boat on this block. We used to play on that boat all the time, every day.

OPRAH: You know, I also grew up poor, but rural poor is different. Did you feel poor?

JAY-Z: Not at all. Probably the first time was in school when I couldn't get the newest sneakers. We didn't have elaborate meals, but we didn't go without. We ate a lot of chicken. You know, 'cause chicken's cheap. We had so much chicken—chicken backs, chicken everything. To this day, I can only eat small pieces or else I feel funny.

OPRAH: That's too much chicken in a lifetime. So when you were 5, your family moved to the Marcy projects—and then your father left when you were 11. When you look

back at that, what did your 11-year-old self feel?

JAY-Z: Anger. At the whole situation. Because when you're growing up, your dad is your superhero. Once you've let yourself fall that in love with someone, once you put him on such a high pedestal and he lets you down, you never want to experience that pain again. So I remember just being really quiet and really cold. Never wanting to let myself get close to someone like that again. I carried that feeling throughout my life, until my father and I met up before he died.

OPRAH: Wow. I've never heard a man phrase it that way. You know, I've done many shows about divorce, and the real crime is when the kids aren't told. They just wake up one day and their dad is gone. Did that happen to you?

JAY-Z: We were told our parents would separate, but the reasons weren't explained. My mom prepared us more than he did. I don't think he was ready for that level of discussion and emotion. He was a guy who was pretty detached from his feelings.

OPRAH: Did you wonder why he left?

JAY-Z: I summed it up that they weren't getting along. There was a lot of arguing.

OPRAH: And did you know you were angry?

JAY-Z: Yeah. I also felt protective of my mom. I remember telling her, "Don't worry, when I get big, I'm going to take care of this." I felt like I had to step up. I was 11 years old, right? But I felt I had to make the situation better.

OPRAH: How did that change you?

JAY-Z: It made me not express my feelings as much. I was already a shy kid, and it made me a little reclusive. But it also made me independent. And stronger. It was a weird juxtaposition.

OPRAH: I've read that when you were 12, you shot your brother in the shoulder. Did your father's leaving have anything to do with that? Did it turn you into the kind of angry kid who would end up shooting his brother?

JAY-Z: Yes—and my brother was dealing with a lot of demons.

OPRAH: How old was he?

JAY-Z: About 16. He was doing a lot of drugs. He was taking stuff from our family. I was the youngest, but I felt like I needed to protect everybody.

OPRAH: Was it a dysfunctional household?

JAY-Z: Looking back, I guess it was quite dysfunctional. But I didn't have that feeling until I got into my early teen years, when we were living in the Marcy projects. That's when crack hit my neighborhood hard and I started getting into mischief.

OPRAH: How were you in school? I've heard that when you were in sixth grade, you tested at a 12th-grade level.

JAY-Z: I was bored and distracted.

OPRAH: Did you like anything about school?

1. Jay-Z accepting the Global Leadership Award for his efforts to bring clean water to the world, 2008. 2. Performing in support of Barack Obama with Sean Combs, record executive Kevin Liles, Mary J. Blige, and Beyoncé Knowles, 2008. 3. Young Shawn Carter in grade school. 4. At a New York film premiere with Beyoncé, 2008. 5. Announcing his joint purchase of the New Jersey Nets, 2004. 6. At a school near Durban, South Africa, to which he donated a water pump, 2006.

JAY-Z: I loved English.

OPRAH: I know you love to read now. Were books part of your childhood?

JAY-Z: No. I don't remember that.

OPRAH: And I thought we had so much in common!

JAY-Z: I just daydreamed a lot.

OPRAH: What about?

JAY-Z: Performing or playing baseball and basketball. I took my mind out of my environment, to the point where I wasn't paying attention to what was happening around me. I still do that now.

OPRAH: You didn't listen in class, you didn't read books—and you still tested as a 12th grader. You must have a naturally high IQ.

JAY-Z: Or I'm an idiot savant.

OPRAH: So when did you start rapping?

JAY-Z: I probably started around 9—but I was just playing around.

"No one aspires to be a drug dealer. You don't want to bring trouble to your mother's door."

OPRAH: Were the rappers in your neighborhood your role models?

JAY-Z: The drug dealers were my role models. Rappers weren't successful yet. I remember the first time I saw the Sugarhill Gang on *Soul Train.* I was 11 or 12. I was like, "What's going on? How did those guys get on national TV?" And then, when I was a little older, a rapper from the neighborhood got a record deal. I was shocked. "They're giving you *money* to do that?" Because by this time, the music had taken hold of the entire neighborhood. Just like crack had before, now this music had taken hold. Everyone was either DJ-ing or rapping.

OPRAH: And rapping came naturally for you?

JAY-Z: It was a gift. I had a notebook full of material. It was just a makeshift thing—someone found some papers, put a paper clip on them, and made me a notebook.

OPRAH: Please tell me you still have that notebook.

JAY-Z: I wish.

OPRAH: When did you realize that rapping was a career

possibility—after you saw Sugarhill on TV?

JAY-Z: Yeah—but I still didn't really think it was a possibility for me. It wasn't until Jaz got a contract that I was like, "Wow, this stuff is going to happen." [Jonathan Burks, a.k.a. Jaz-O or Jaz, was Jay-Z's musical mentor.] And Jaz went to London to make an album, and took me with him. I was a kid from Marcy projects, and I spent two months in a London flat.

OPRAH: So tell me how you got into the drug dealing.

JAY-Z: It was natural....

OPRAH: Because drug dealers were your role models. There wasn't a teacher or a lawyer or a nurse or a doctor or an accountant in the neighborhood?

JAY-Z: Well, we were living in Marcy by then, so, no. And if anyone did become something like that, they moved out. They never came back to share the wisdom of how they made it. If anyone made it, you never knew it. That's why I've always said that if I became successful, I'd come back here, grab somebody, and show him how it can be done.

OPRAH: So you didn't have even one positive black role model?

JAY-Z: Just my mom. She worked two jobs and did whatever she had to do for us.

OPRAH: Did you aspire to be a drug dealer?

JAY-Z: Well, no. No one aspires to be a drug dealer. You don't want to bring trouble to your mother's door, even though that's what you're doing. You aspire to the lifestyle you see around you. You see the green BMW, the prettiest car you've ever seen. You see the trappings of drug dealing, and it draws you in.

OPRAH: How old were you when you got involved?

JAY-Z: Maybe 13.

OPRAH: Did you realize it could cost you your life?

JAY-Z: In my mind, that wasn't risking a lot. You think, *If I'm living like this, I'll risk anything to get more. What's the worst that could happen?*

OPRAH: You could die.

JAY-Z: Yes, but you don't think about that.

OPRAH: Were you seeing people get shot?

JAY-Z: Definitely—I saw a guy get shot when I was 9. And he wasn't even a bad guy. His name was Benny. He was the guy who would take us to play baseball. We always believed he could have made it to the majors. He was that good. Some guy was chasing him—and then I heard a shot and saw him on the floor.

OPRAH: So by the time you were 13, this was a way of life.

> "I started seeing people go to jail and get killed, and the light slowly came on. I was like, "This life has no good ending.""

nobody knowing how to shoot.

OPRAH: What happened in each situation?

JAY-Z: It was one situation, three shots.

OPRAH: So he *was* a bad shot.

JAY-Z: Well, no one really practices shooting a TEC-9 machine gun, right? And when you're a kid, with little bony arms—no wonder nobody could aim.

OPRAH: Getting shot like that would be a wake-up call for the average guy. But you continued in the drug world.

JAY-Z: You want to shoot back. Well, maybe not everyone, but I did. I was angry.

OPRAH: Did you go home and get a gun?

JAY-Z: Yeah. But the guy and I were actually friends.

OPRAH: This is also where we differ! I don't shoot at my friends. Did you ever make up with him?

JAY-Z: You can't. You can agree not to shoot at each other, but you can't be friends after that—unless the guy is your brother.

OPRAH: You were able to make up with your brother after you shot him?

JAY-Z: Yeah.

OPRAH: So even after you went to London with Jaz, you stayed in the drug world?

JAY-Z: Right. Before I went, I spent a week making sure everything would be cool for when I came back. I was preparing to come back to the streets because I always had a fear that this music thing wouldn't be successful. And since Jaz's album didn't work out, I did end up back on the streets. The same record label tried to sign me, but Jaz was the one who'd brought me in, and I felt that signing wouldn't be loyal to him. So I told them no. I didn't want to be involved with those record guys. They weren't stand-up people.

OPRAH: It's ironic that you, a drug dealer, couldn't trust the guys in the record business, as if they had no integrity!

JAY-Z: Exactly.

OPRAH: How do you define integrity?

JAY-Z: As doing the right thing.

Did the lifestyle frighten you?

JAY-Z: No. It was normal. And at some point, you become addicted to the feeling. The uncertainty and adrenaline and danger of that lifestyle.

OPRAH: This is where we differ. Because I'd be very scared! Weren't you shot at three times—within six feet—and you lived to talk about it?

JAY-Z: That was divine intervention. Divine intervention, and

OPRAH: **So there's honor among thieves and drug dealers.**

JAY-Z: I never understood that saying. Because thieves, you know—

OPRAH: **They're thieves.**

JAY-Z: They're thieves.

OPRAH: **You can't trust them.**

JAY-Z: Right. But in the streets there's a certain respect level. If two drug dealers make it to a certain level, they show a certain respect when they see each other. It's bad business for them to be warring.

OPRAH: **Meaning there's a hierarchy on the streets.**

JAY-Z: Of course.

OPRAH: **Well, how did you decide to leave the streets for good? How did you decide you could let it go?**

JAY-Z: I started seeing people go to jail and get killed, and the light slowly came on. I was like, "This life has no good ending."

OPRAH: **That is so fascinating to me. Because what crack did to the community—drug dealers were a part of that. When you were dealing, did you not see yourself as a part of the problem?**

JAY-Z: Later. Looking back. Not while I was in it. I didn't know the effect it was having on the community. We used to say all the time, "Man, her life is all messed up—she used to be so cute. She was fine six months ago. Look at her, she's finished." But you never thought you contributed to that.

OPRAH: **How is that possible?**

JAY-Z: You're just in it. So deep in it, and so young, that that type of introspection never happens. It's just living. And it's fast.

OPRAH: **Looking back on that time, do you have regrets?**

JAY-Z: Well, any person is responsible for the knowledge that they know, right? So of course I do—now, knowing. But at the time I had no knowledge of it.

OPRAH: **It was just a way of life. A way of survival.**

JAY-Z: To be honest, I can't even say that. At that point it was beyond survival. I was successful. It wasn't like I was doing it to feed my family anymore. I was buying cars and jewelry and things like that. I had become addicted to the lifestyle.

OPRAH: **So how old were you when you realized that the life had no good ending?**

JAY-Z: Around 20. I'd been trying to transition from the streets to the music business, but I would make demos and then quit for six months. And I started

to realize that I couldn't be successful until I let the street life go. My mom always taught me—you know, little boys listen to their moms too much—that whatever you put into something is what you're going to get out of it. I had to fully let go of what I was doing before for the music to be successful. That was a leap of faith for me. I said, "I have to give this everything."

OPRAH: **Did you feel that in some kind of passionate way— like it was a calling?**

JAY-Z: Yes—and that first album, *Reasonable Doubt,* is my favorite, because all the emotions and experiences of 26 years came out in it. That was the record I had 26 years to make.

OPRAH: **I just got that in a way I never have before. *Reasonable Doubt* is 26 years packed into one record— and that can never happen again. That's why it's your definitive album. Aha moment! So is it harder to make each successive album?**

JAY-Z: It's harder for me to write music that everyone can relate to, because I don't live a typical life anymore.

OPRAH: **That's true. That's true. So here we are, talking on a Sunday afternoon. If you weren't sitting here with me, what would you be doing?**

JAY-Z: I'm gonna get killed for this, but I'll tell you anyway. There's a great pizza spot we go to every Sunday. It's our tradition. It's a small place in Brooklyn, you can bring your own wine, and there are candles there. It's a nice date.

OPRAH: **And I guess you would be there with what's her name.**

JAY-Z: Yeah. [*Laughs*]

OPRAH: **Do you and Beyoncé have a pact that you just won't talk about each other?**

JAY-Z: Yeah. When you're a public person, you have to keep some things to yourself, or else people will just—

OPRAH: **Eat it up. I know. But can I ask how in the world you kept your wedding a secret?**

JAY-Z: Late planning!

OPRAH: **How many people knew?**

JAY-Z: Very few. The sad part is that we offended some. But people who love you understand. Because at the end of the day, it's your day.

OPRAH: **How small was the wedding?**

JAY-Z: Very small. Maybe 30 people.

OPRAH: **And how has marriage changed you?**

JAY-Z: Let me just say this: Reconnecting with my father changed me more than anything. Because it allowed me to let people in.

OPRAH: **Let's talk about that.**

> "My mom always taught me that whatever you put into something is what you're going to get out of it."

At Jay-Z's grandmother's Brooklyn home, where he lived with his extended family until the age of 5.

JAY-Z: Well, I always had that wall up. And whenever someone got close to me, I would shut down.

OPRAH: **So how did you get back in touch with your father?**

JAY-Z: My mom set up a meeting. And now I realize why—it makes all the sense in the world. I remember very distinctly that I had a conversation with her in my kitchen. I was saying, "You know, Ma, I've really been trying to look inward, and maybe I'm just not meant to fall in love like other people do." She just looked at me like, "Hush up, boy."

OPRAH: **Wow.**

JAY-Z: And I guess from that point, she figured out what was wrong with me, and she planned a meeting between me and my father. I was like, "Ma, I'm a grown man. I

don't need a dad now."

OPRAH: **You didn't feel a hole in your soul?**

JAY-Z: I never looked at that. I guess I didn't want to deal with it. Because, you know, once I looked, I'd have to do something about it. And I guess I still had too much resentment and anger.

OPRAH: **In one of your songs, you wrote that you weren't sure if your father even remembered your birthday is in December.**

JAY-Z: I believed that. When I was a kid, I once waited for him on a bench. He never showed up. Even as an adult, that affected me. So when my mom set up this meeting, I told her he wouldn't come—and the first time, he didn't.

At that point, I was really done, but Mom pushed for another meeting, because she's just a beautiful soul.

OPRAH: **The second time, your father showed up.**

JAY-Z: He showed up. And I gave him the real conversation. I told him how I felt the day he left. He was saying stuff like "Man, you knew where I was." I'm like, "I was a kid! Do you realize how wrong you were? It was your responsibility to see me." He finally accepted that.

OPRAH: **Where had he been?**

JAY-Z: At his mom's house ten minutes away from me. That was the sad part.

OPRAH: **Was there any explanation he could have offered that would have satisfied you?**

JAY-Z: Yes—and that's why we were able to mend our relationship.

OPRAH: **What was his reason?**

JAY-Z: When I was 9 years old, my dad's brother got stabbed, and my dad went looking for the guy who did it. People would call in the middle of the night and tell him, "So-and-so is out here." So my dad would get up, get his gun, and go outside to look for the guy. After a while, my mom was like, "Hey, this is your family now. You can't do that." But this was my dad's baby brother. And my dad was in so much pain that he started using drugs and became a different person. So I understand that the trauma of the event, coupled with the drugs, caused him to lose his soul.

OPRAH: **When you saw him again, had he come back to himself?**

JAY-Z: He was broken. He had a bad liver, and he knew that if he continued drinking, it would kill him. But he didn't stop.

OPRAH: **How soon after you saw him did he die?**

JAY-Z: A couple of months. I got him an apartment, I was buying furniture. And he passed away.

OPRAH: **Did you instantly make peace with him during that conversation?**

JAY-Z: Pretty much. I felt lighter.

OPRAH: **The conversation freed you in ways that you hadn't been free before?**

JAY-Z: One hundred percent.

OPRAH: **Did it open the door for you to have a life with love in it?**

JAY-Z: Absolutely.

OPRAH: **One reason I wanted to talk to you is that I see a common thread between our lives—except that I never shot at anybody and I never—**

JAY-Z: Got shot at. Those little things.

OPRAH: **Little things like that. But the**

> "I always had that wall up. And whenever someone got close to me, I would shut down."

biggest common thread is that we've both become successful by being ourselves.

JAY-Z: There's nothing worse than becoming successful as someone else.

OPRAH: **So what's your personal creed?**

JAY-Z: Be true to yourself—and keep things simple. People complicate things.

OPRAH: **My creed is that intention creates reality.**

JAY-Z: Now I'm having an aha moment! That's true.

OPRAH: **What's the basis of your spiritual belief?**

JAY-Z: I believe in karma: What you do to others comes back to you.

OPRAH: **But don't you think we're responsible only for what we know? Otherwise, you'd be facing karma for every person you sold drugs to.**

JAY-Z: As a kid, I didn't know any better. But now, if I were to act as if what I did wasn't bad, that would be irresponsible. And I'd have to bear the weight of that.

OPRAH: **Maya Angelou always says, "When you know better, you do better." Do you still think back on that time in your life?**

JAY-Z: All the time. When you make music, you're constantly on the psychiatrist's couch, so to speak. That's an outlet for me. Because I'm not normally a talkative person. I don't have conversations like this for no reason.

OPRAH: **Speaking of conversations, when I met you a few years ago, we discussed our disagreement over the use of the N word and misogynist lyrics in rap music. Do you believe that using the N word is necessary?**

JAY-Z: Nothing is necessary. It's just become part of the way we communicate. My generation hasn't had the same experience with that word that generations of people before us had. We weren't so close to the pain. So in our way, we have disarmed the word. We have taken the fire pin out of the grenade.

OPRAH: **I was once at a Jay-Z concert, and there was a moment when everybody—including white people—was screaming the N word. I gotta tell you, it didn't make me feel good.**

JAY-Z: That's understandable.

OPRAH: **But it didn't seem to affect you. You were having a good time up there onstage.**

JAY-Z: I believe that a speaker's intention is what gives a word its power. And if we eliminate the N word, other words would just take its place.

You know, hip-hop has done so much for race relations, even with its ignorance—which, by the way, we do have to take some responsibility for.

But even without directly taking on race, we've changed things just by being who we are. It's difficult to teach racism in the home when your kid loves Jay-Z. It's hard to say, "That guy is beneath you" when your kid idolizes that guy.

OPRAH: I'll give you that. But when I hear the N word, I still think about every black man who was lynched—and the N word was the last thing he heard. So we'll just have to disagree about this.

JAY-Z: It's a generational thing.

OPRAH: Okay. Just the other day, an elderly person reminded me that we all need to have more fun. Because in the end, it's not about how much work you've done. So what gives you pleasure?

JAY-Z: Seeing people around me happy. Here's a story. The first time I went to Capri, Italy, I had some spaghetti. It was simple, but it was prepared in such a fresh way that I immediately called my friends to come and share it with me. They took a plane, a train, and a boat just so we could enjoy the food together. That made me totally happy.

OPRAH: I wish I was on your friend list! But let's continue: Who loves you?

JAY-Z: Everyone loves me, and I love everyone! [*Laughs*]

OPRAH: I know you're joking when you say that, but it's true. Everybody loves you. Everybody also says how smart you are.

JAY-Z: That's crazy.

OPRAH: You don't think you're smart?

JAY-Z: I'm a thinker. I figure things out. I don't have a high level of education, but I'm practical—and I have good instincts.

OPRAH: Are you a good businessman?

JAY-Z: Yes, because when I promise something, I deliver it—and I expect the same from others.

OPRAH: That's great. Now let's move on to another topic: your support of Barack Obama during his campaign. Did you believe he would become president?

JAY-Z: At a certain point, yes. Before he announced he was running, I met him and we had dinner. I was like, "Man, this guy is special." Certain people just glow. I also know Bill Clinton. But I was willing to put that friendship at risk to support Obama, because Obama represents hope around the world. I would rather lose on the side of hope than win on the side of the favorite.

OPRAH: Did you lose the Clintons' friendship?

JAY-Z: No. Bill understood. We're cool.

> "When you make music, you're constantly on the psychiatrist's couch, so to speak. That's an outlet for me."

OPRAH: You were there during Obama's inauguration. What did you feel?

JAY-Z: Euphoria. At one point, this white lady was in the hotel elevator with me and my friend Ty Ty, and she turned to Ty Ty and fixed his tie. It was such a small thing, but everyone had this feeling of—

OPRAH: Connection. On another day, she might have been scared of Ty Ty.

JAY-Z: Exactly. There was a feeling of hope.

OPRAH: Did Obama's victory change the way black men are perceived?

JAY-Z: Yes. It also changed the way the world sees America. America is supposed to be the land of the free and home of the brave, so how is it possible to have 43 presidents of the same background?

OPRAH: Was there a shift in the rap community?

JAY-Z: The election of Barack Obama sent a strong message. Afterward I said, "The day that Barack Obama became president, the gangsta became less relevant." I meant that in a positive way. I meant that we grew up without accountants and lawyers as role models, but now we see something different. There's something else for us to aspire to.

OPRAH: At 40, are you proud of the man you've become?

JAY-Z: Very—but I've still got some growing to do.

OPRAH: What do you know for sure?

JAY-Z: I know that there's a higher being: The One, or whatever you want to call it. There has to be, for everything to work so perfectly in the human body, and for the world to work the way it does.

OPRAH: What makes you most proud?

JAY-Z: Taking care of my family. That's every little boy's dream, right? To buy Mom a house.

OPRAH: Many of the little boys who grew up in the Marcy projects are either in jail or dead. Why do you think you got to grow up and buy your mom a house?

JAY-Z: There's the gift, there's the spirit, and there's the work—all three have to come together. If one of those things is off, it can stop you from becoming who you were meant to be.

OPRAH: Is there anything else you still want to do?

JAY-Z: I want to represent hip-hop culture positively. No one in my family is wanting for a meal right now, so that part is done. Rap is what took me out of my situation, and now I must care for it. I have to leave it as I found it—or better—for the next generation of kids. Then maybe they can change their situation like I did. ◑

giving back

268 THE GIFT | BY BONNIE ROCHMAN

276 BLOOD BROTHER | BY HELEN ROGAN

278 OPRAH TALKS TO MICHELLE OBAMA

289 MARCIA GAY HARDEN'S AHA! MOMENT

290 $100 AND A DREAM | BY GERALDINE BROOKS

293 GIVING WITHOUT BORDERS | BY SARA CORBETT

296 GOOD TITHINGS | BY A.J. JACOBS

298 SISTER STREET | BY LIZ BRODY

307 MISSIONS ACCOMPLISHED | BY KATIE ARNOLD-RATLIFF

311 "THAT WAS AN AHA MOMENT FOR ME—TO EXPERIENCE
HOW A 'SMALL' ACT CAN HAVE A HUGE IMPACT" | BY OPRAH

Lynn Page with four-week-old Ashtyn, at home in Norfolk, Virginia, December 2008.

The Gift

Even when Lynn Page felt she'd lost everything, she still had something invaluable to give. **Bonnie Rochman** tells the story of a mother's devotion and the little-known network of medical miracle workers that's quietly helping the babies who need help most.

Lynn Page was 37, and a pediatric psychologist—old enough for things to go badly with her pregnancy, and informed enough to know it. So during her first ultrasound, when the doctor's face suddenly fell and he told her she could get dressed, her heart was hammering as she asked, "What's wrong?"

This was November 2006. Lynn was alone at the appointment. She and her husband, Chris, live in Norfolk, Virginia, but Chris, a 19-year navy man and chief petty officer on the submarine USS *Boise,* was underwater somewhere in the Pacific. When Lynn had learned she was expecting, she'd sent off a package to his next port, in Japan: licorice, M&M's, and a dad's guide to pregnancy called *My Boys Can Swim!*

If the doctor was about to give her horrible news, she wanted Chris with her.

But the doctor surprised her. "There's nothing wrong," he said. "There's just three."

Three! Lynn didn't know what to say. Triplets was a possibility she'd never considered. Twins, sure; she's a twin herself, and there were others in her family, on both sides. No one in her family had ever given birth to triplets, though. As the doctor began describing how hard it would be to carry three babies in one body, Lynn tried to keep her shock from turning to panic. There was scant hope that she would carry a full 40 weeks. Triplets are more likely to be delivered around 32 weeks and are at greater risk for serious health complications.

Despite the risks, though, Lynn and Chris convinced themselves that everything would be all right. Maybe it was a necessary defense mechanism, or maybe willful naïveté, but they decided to be optimistic. In mid-February, the navy sent Chris home to be with Lynn. Lynn started shopping, cautiously picking out onesies. And at an appointment on March 5, when she was just past 20 weeks, it seemed their optimism was well-founded. "You're doing great," the doctor said.

But before two weeks had passed, Lynn began having back pain. She went straight to Portsmouth Naval Medical Center, where she discovered that the pain was actually contractions. Five days later, on March 22, 2007, her water broke. She was 23 weeks pregnant, barely halfway there.

Seth and Rowan, brother and sister, were born first. Within 24 hours, both died, of "extreme prematurity," yet Lynn and Chris hardly had time to grieve. They had a third baby—Reese Magdelyn—to worry about.

In her work, Lynn treated children with serious medical conditions, and had often counseled families whose infants had landed in neonatal intensive care units. She had helped parents deal with the stress, the high highs and low lows. It was different when it was your own child, though.

Reese weighed one pound, four ounces. Head to toe, she measured just over 11 inches. Her arms were the circumference of a tube of penne pasta. When Lynn was released from the hospital on March 23, Reese stayed. When Lynn went back to work on April 2, Reese was still there. The Pages had no idea when they'd be able to bring their daughter home to their little white house with its green shutters and picket fence.

When a baby is born so early, there isn't much a parent can do—a truth that Lynn relearned each day when she went to the hospital to sit beside Reese. She couldn't pick her up. She couldn't rock her and cup her head in the palm of her hand. She couldn't kiss her forehead or whisper in her ear. She couldn't cradle her to her chest and feed her. But she could make sure that the milk her body was making would be ready and waiting for Reese to be fed.

From the moment she learned she was carrying triplets, Lynn knew there was a good chance the babies would have to fight for their lives. And she knew she could increase their odds by breastfeeding. Reese wasn't strong enough to nurse now, but the doctors believed she would be someday. So from the day Reese was born, Lynn began pumping breast milk. Wherever she went, she lugged her pump; it was like another appendage. A woman who pumps is said to be expressing her milk. For Lynn, it was one of the few physical ways she could express her love.

Though about 74 percent of American mothers start off breastfeeding, only about 12 percent are still nursing exclusively by the time their child is six months old, despite position statements from every major pediatric, family health, and public health organization that babies do best if they're fed only breast milk for six months and continue to nurse until at least their first birthday.

Human milk for human babies—that's how lactation experts sum it up. Although babies can and do thrive on formula, most formula is derived from cow's milk, and then—to make it resemble the composition of human milk—augmented with corn syrup, sugar, vitamins, minerals, and vegetable oils. But no amount of laboratory tinkering has yielded a way to infuse formula with the unique and potent cocktail of hormones, human growth factors, digestive enzymes, and antibodies that human milk conveys.

Because breast milk is composed of white blood cells that fight infection and stimulate the immune system, babies who receive human milk gain extra protection against illnesses such as pneumonia and staph infections. Premature babies in particular, prone as they are to infection, benefit from breast milk's immunological properties. Breastfed babies have fewer ear and respiratory tract infections, and less diarrhea. Studies indicate that they're less likely to get certain childhood cancers. They have a lower risk of developing diabetes, allergies, and possibly heart disease later in life. Some research even suggests that they can wind up with higher IQs.

When it works, human lactation is as automatic and easy as breathing, yet it's a finely calibrated physiological feat. The milk that a new mother produces in the first days after giving birth—a thick, protein-packed substance called

> Reese weighed one pound, four ounces. Head to toe, she measured just over 11 inches. Her arms were the circumference of a tube of penne pasta.

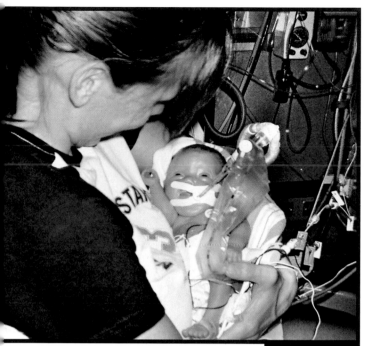

colostrum—is typically present from about the fourth month of pregnancy. About three days after delivery, colostrum transitions to mature milk, which is higher in water, lactose, and fat content. And over the course of every subsequent feeding, that milk will transform itself again and again: At the start of each meal, it will be thin and watery; by the end, it will be rich and creamy. One more neat trick: As soon as the milk glands empty, the body gets to work refilling them. Demand creates supply—and the body doesn't care at all if a machine is the thing doing the demanding.

Still, pumping your breasts is nothing like nursing. Instead of the tug of a baby's mouth, there is strong mechanical suction from two plastic cones that screw onto plastic bottles. When you nurse, the warmth of the baby tucked against you, skin to skin, stimulates the release of the feel-good hormone oxytocin, which helps trigger milk flow. When you pump, all you get is the whine and wheeze of a motor.

Reese had arrived so early that Lynn hadn't even unpacked her pump from its box. While she set it up the first time, Chris had to read her the instructions. Within the first weeks of her daughter's life, though, she fell into a routine. Every day, every three or four hours around the clock, at home, at the hospital, at work, Lynn pumped for Reese. Without the aid of a crying baby to rouse her, without even needing an alarm clock, she woke every night at 2 A.M. to sit and pump in the old-fashioned upholstered wing chair that had belonged to Chris's grandmother. In the still of the night, she'd phone the hospital. Always the same question: "How's Reese doing?" The nurses knew to expect her call.

Even though breast milk is easy to digest, Reese was so premature that her stomach couldn't handle it. Instead, she was given, intravenously, a liquid that looks like yellow Kool-Aid and contains carbohydrates, electrolytes, protein, fats, vitamins, and minerals. Only on rare occasions were the nurses able to give her tiny amounts of Lynn's milk, through a tube inserted directly into her stomach or intestines.

When she was a month old, Reese developed necrotizing enterocolitis—a condition that causes portions of the intestines to die—and underwent surgery to remove withered sections of her intestine. But as the weeks passed after the surgery, she began getting stronger. When she was two months old and weighed three pounds, Lynn got to hold her for the first time. By June she had gained more weight. She was looking at her toys and using her pacifier and figuring out how to keep the doctors in line. When they came to do a procedure, she'd make as if to cry, then relax when they backed off. The doctor who'd once called her a little pistol was right.

All the while, Lynn kept pumping, stockpiling her milk for the day when Reese would be strong enough to digest it. Get up, shower, pump. Eat breakfast, go to work, pump. Head to the hospital, see Reese, pump. The more, the better. It was a gift for her daughter, but it helped Lynn, too. It was a way to prepare for the future, for when Reese would come home. She had already passed a billion hurdles; it was just a matter of being patient.

At the hospital, there were two pumping rooms near the intensive care nursery: the lavender room and the yellow room. Both were furnished with gliders that moved back and forth in a soothing one-two beat. Lynn would sink into a glider, thumb through parenting magazines, think about Reese, and pump.

The nurses were incredulous. They'd never seen a woman pump so much for so long. One day a lactation consultant mentioned that with so much milk, Lynn might consider donating some.

Donating? Lynn barely paid attention. Why would she donate her milk? Reese would need every drop of it herself someday soon.

The concept of sharing mothers' milk is hardly new. Throughout most of history, wet nurses filled in for mothers who couldn't breastfeed or who chose not to. (The prophet Muhammad had a wet nurse. So did Napoleon, Alice Roosevelt, and Luciano Pavarotti. After the future King George IV was born, in 1762, his wet nurse, Mrs. Scott, became a minor celebrity.)

In the United States, the practice of using surrogate nursers died out in the early 1900s, when formula became popular. But even then doctors were aware that breastfed babies were hardier than those who got formula. In 1911, a Boston physician opened a facility where poor mothers who were nursing their own babies were paid to pump milk for other infants. It was, effectively, the country's first human milk bank.

By the 1980s, there were about 30 milk banks in the United States, all of them not-for-profit. The banks were the answer for mothers whose health issues (prior breast surgery, diabetes, pituitary gland or thyroid problems) hindered milk production, or whose milk had been tainted by medical treatments. They were ideal for mothers whose milk supply was stifled by the stress of premature birth.

Then AIDS arrived, and suddenly bodily fluids were terrifying. The AIDS virus was deadly, and it could be transmitted through breast milk. Milk banks started closing; before long, fewer than ten remained.

In 1985, the Human Milk Banking Association of North America (HMBANA) was founded to establish safety standards for processing donor milk, and before long, all the banks that had stayed open were doing what dairy farmers had been doing for decades: pasteurizing. The process kills bacteria and viruses, and that safeguard, coupled with scores of scientific studies affirming the benefits of breast milk, reinvigorated interest in donor milk banking.

Today HMBANA comprises ten nonprofit banks in the United States (and one in Vancouver), each primarily serving a designated section of the country. In 2007 these banks distributed nearly 1.2 million ounces of milk—both to hospitals and to women like Sheila Reigner, in Pennsylvania, who can't nurse because she's undergoing chemotherapy for breast cancer, and Marianna Manley, in Indiana, who can't produce enough milk for her quintuplets.

That 1.2 million ounces is roughly double the amount the banks were distributing a decade ago, and as more hospitals embrace donor milk, demand is bound to keep increasing. Each year approximately 60,000 VLBW babies (very low birthweight—less than 1,500 grams) are born in the U.S., and on average, some 51,000 survive. These are exactly the babies who stand to benefit most

from breast milk. Yet Audelio Rivera, MD, president of the Mothers' Milk Bank at Austin, has prepared a mathematical model showing that if every surviving baby were given breast milk, milk banks would need to supply more than 8.9 million ounces to compensate for what the babies' mothers couldn't provide themselves.

To collect that much milk, banks would likely have to do extensive public outreach; today they operate quietly, with little or no marketing budgets. Few people even know of their existence; even those in the business of caring for critically ill infants aren't necessarily aware that this resource is out there. Soon after her baby died at a hospital in North Carolina, a woman named Nancy Woodyard returned to collect the milk she'd pumped and take it to a milk bank—only to find that someone on the staff had already thrown it away.

Every ounce of milk Lynn pumped was another ounce she and Chris had to safely store. After they filled their kitchen freezer, they invested in a chest freezer. After that was full, they commandeered the freezer of Chris's old friend Matt, who had been best man at their wedding. After that was full, they went on Craigslist and found an upright freezer, its sides dented and its beige paint chipped but its motor intact. When the woman selling it heard what it was to be used for, she dropped the price from $25 to $20. Sold.

Meanwhile, Reese seemed to be doing better. At the

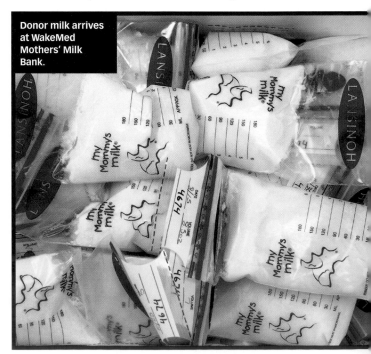

Donor milk arrives at WakeMed Mothers' Milk Bank.

end of June, her breathing tube was removed, and suddenly Lynn was able to hold her every day. Reese smiled. And cried. Without the breathing tube blocking the sound, Lynn and Chris finally got to *hear* her cry. But two weeks after the tube came out, it had to go back in as Reese began getting weaker.

Still, the milk kept coming. Though Lynn poured some into ice cube trays, most went into two-ounce containers she and Chris had once used to serve Jell-O shots at a party. They'd bought the containers at Costco, where the smallest quantity available was 2,000. They figured they'd never use them all. Now they were running out.

O n weekdays, two nurses and a technician work in the WakeMed Mothers' Milk Bank in Raleigh, North Carolina. Crammed into 650 square feet of space, the bank is attached to the department of neonatology on the third floor of a nondescript seven-story brick and glass structure, the main building on the WakeMed hospital system's main campus. With two rooms the size of walk-in closets (one a tiny lab where milk is pasteurized; the other, a storage area where it's kept frozen), and a slightly larger administrative space that was carved out of physician sleeping quarters, the bank manages to serve the entire East Coast, from Maine to Florida and west to Tennessee.

When frozen donor milk arrives via an overnight FedEx flight, it's quickly unpacked and sorted according to the month it was pumped (frozen breast milk is good for up to a year), then returned to a freezer to await processing. When a technician is ready to pasteurize a batch, she selects milk from three to five mothers (the milk is mixed to balance its nutritional profile). In the lab, the milk is thawed, mingled in a flask, and cultured for bacteria. It's poured into glass bottles (two-ounce containers for new preemies, eight-ounce for older babies), then pasteurized in a water bath for 30 minutes at about 145 degrees Fahrenheit, a process that kills any bad things that may be lurking in the milk while retaining most of the good ones. Next, the bottles are plunged into an ice bath, another culture is taken, and the bottles are sealed and placed in a holding freezer until the cultures have returned from the hospital lab. If the milk is "clean," it's moved into the dispensing freezer, where it might sit for

> Lynn woke every night at 2 A.M. and phoned the hospital. "How's Reese doing?" The nurses knew to expect her call.

a day to a week, depending on demand.

Each bottle of milk is labeled with a batch number. Each batch is keyed to a record of which donors contributed. (For legal purposes, records are kept for 21 years, though there has never been a lawsuit involving donor breast milk.)

Although the banks are not-for-profit, they charge recipients up to $4.50 an ounce, to cover costs. Those costs begin with donor screening; at WakeMed, potential donors are first interviewed by phone, then asked to complete a 49-part questionnaire. Question No. 5: In the past five years, have you ever used recreational drugs such as marijuana, cocaine, LSD, ecstasy, or amphetamines? No. 7: Please describe your daily intake of caffeine. No. 21: Have you had an accidental needle stick, or exposure to someone's blood? The banks also cover the cost of donor blood tests, the cost of processing and storing the milk, and the cost of shipping it (which involves dry ice, Styrofoam, and cardboard boxes or coolers labeled HUMAN DONOR MILK).

At any given time, the WakeMed bank has about 135 donors. Most are mothers of healthy infants who happen to have an abundance of milk. But some are mothers whose babies have died, and for these women, donating breast milk can be therapeutic. Giving away their babies' milk so another infant might survive can help a grieving mother make some sense of catastrophe.

O n October 11, 2007, Lynn made her usual 2 A.M. phone call. Reese's lungs had always been compromised due to her extreme prematurity, but more recently, things had gotten worse. Her liver had become enlarged and begun to press on her lungs, which made it hard for them to expand, which made it hard for her to breathe properly, which made it hard for oxygen to get to her heart. That night, though, she seemed to be holding steady. Everything is fine, the nurse reported. Reassured, Lynn finished pumping, climbed back into bed, and curled up against Chris. A couple of hours later, the telephone jolted them awake. *We need you to come in, a nurse said.*

Reese's heart rate had slowed so dangerously that doctors had had to resuscitate her. She'd survived six and a half months after the death of her brother and sister, but now her system was collapsing. At the hospital, the attending doctor told Lynn and Chris there was nothing more anyone could do. Lynn and Chris talked it over. They decided they wouldn't withdraw treatment but wouldn't ask for heroic measures, either. As Chris went to tell the doctor, Lynn glanced up at the heart monitor just in time to see the numbers drop again.

At 6:30 A.M., Reese died in Lynn's arms, with Chris by her side. *We let her go,* is how Lynn still thinks of it today.

Reese had lived 203 days, every one of them in the hospital. Lynn had gotten to hold her maybe two dozen times. Now she and Chris stayed with her, holding her once more. For the first time, there were no wires or monitors or IV lines.

By 9 A.M., Lynn's breasts were throbbing, painfully full. She'd skipped her early morning pumping session to be with Reese, and now Reese was gone, and still, here was this milk, this force of life that wouldn't be denied. "I need to pump," she said, even though it seemed surreal. She headed for one of the pumping rooms, sat down in the nursing glider, and let the milk come.

Later that day, back at home, she and Chris would sit and stare at each other. They would make arrangements to cremate Reese, as they'd done with Seth and Rowan, not wanting to leave their babies behind should the navy ever decide to transfer Chris. After Seth and Rowan died, Lynn had found tiny porcelain urns in the shape of baby shoes, laced with satin ribbon and sprinkled with a delicate floral pattern across the toe. They would have to order another shoe, for Reese.

But for now, Lynn pumped. And at some point she turned, overwhelmed, to a nurse. "What am I going to do with all this milk?"

Premature babies aren't the only humans who stand to gain from breast milk. Children with severe allergies, people recovering from organ transplants, and patients with autoimmune diseases sometimes drink donor milk because its proteins, fats, and carbohydrates are easily tolerated and its immunological properties help protect against infection.

Research suggests that breast milk may even have the potential to kill cancer cells. Several studies in Europe and Asia have investigated a complex called HAMLET—an acro-

> But for now, Lynn pumped. And at some point she turned, overwhelmed, to a nurse. "What am I going to do with all this milk?"

nym for human alpha-lactalbumin made lethal to tumor cells—that's found in human milk. In the mid-1990s, Swedish researchers discovered that purified HAMLET, when mixed with cultures that contained either healthy or cancerous cells, destroyed the tumor cells but left the healthy cells unharmed. A preliminary human study—involving fewer than a dozen bladder cancer patients who were injected with HAMLET—showed promising results, though there's no evidence to suggest that simply drinking breast milk can kill tumor cells. Nevertheless, some adults with cancer have used it as part of their disease-fighting regimen.

Although milk banks would love to provide milk to every person that would benefit, donors are ultimately the ones controlling the supply. One month, stores may be up on the West Coast and lagging far behind on the East Coast; the next month, the opposite may be true. The banks serve as backup for one another. When one is low, a group e-mail will go out: "Got milk?" Milk bank administrators are routinely forced to triage, which they do following HM-BANA guidelines.

Desperately sick premature infants, it is agreed, need donor milk more than healthy full-term babies. Babies, in general, stand to benefit more than toddlers. But as is the case with most any set of guidelines, there is room for interpretation. In California, Wesley Forslund-Mooers was suddenly left without a source of breast milk after a stroke killed his mother when he was only three days old. He was a perfectly healthy baby—you could argue that he didn't *need* the milk—but no one at the donor bank in San Jose was going to refuse him.

The day after Reese died, Lynn called WakeMed Mothers' Milk Bank.

"We lost our daughter," she told Sue Evans, the lactation consultant who answered the phone. "We've got a lot of milk."

"We'd love to have it," Sue said. "We'll send you coolers so you can ship it."

Ship it? How could they ship it? The milk was part of their connection to Reese. And there was so much of it. All those days and nights of pumping. It had to get there safely. It had to stay frozen. They couldn't ship it. They would have to deliver it themselves.

It was pouring rain the morning that Lynn loaded

milk into coolers. Chris wheeled the freezers out of the garage and up the ramp of a rented trailer they'd hitched to the back of their Ford Escape. It was hard work. The freezers were packed full; for weeks he'd been using phone books to weight down the chest freezer's lid. As he hooked up a generator to keep the milk frozen, he couldn't tell the difference between the rain and his sweat.

Lynn, Chris, and Ashtyn; the ceramic shoes on the windowsill hold the ashes of triplets Rowan, Seth, and Reese.

They swung by their friend Matt's house to empty his freezer. Then to the hospital, where the neonatal nurses had been storing the last of the milk. Finally, with the freezers and two coolers lashed tight, they headed south to Raleigh. Two hundred miles to think about Reese.

When they arrived at WakeMed, Sue Evans met them at the portico, started opening the freezers, and said, "Oh my."

Never had one family shown up with so much milk. The freezers held 7,260 ounces.

It had been only two weeks since Reese died. It had hurt to pack the milk up, and now it hurt to unload it. Lynn and Chris were silent as they worked, thinking about Reese, and how she was here but now she wasn't, how it was so hard to believe that they had lost her and that they were giving away what was supposed to have been hers.

They helped the nurses stack the milk on hospital carts. All those plastic bags and Costco containers and frozen bricks of opaque ivory. Some of the milk went back to the first week of Reese's life. Of the vast quantity Lynn pumped, Reese had been able to take in only about ten ounces, less than a small coffee at Starbucks.

Handing over the last bit felt like a goodbye, as if they were letting go, again, of Reese herself. Lynn was crying and the nurses were crying, and Sue Evans kept hugging her and thanking her. Sue hadn't understood why Lynn and Chris wanted to drive seven hours round-trip, but now she got it.

"If anyone asks," Lynn said, "tell them we did this out of love for our babies."

It took four nurses three hours to catalog the milk.

On the west coast of Florida, Laura Oursler gave Lynn's milk to her son, Keegan, who was born with a neurological condition that left him unable to eat normally.

In Orlando, Lisa Vratanina gave Lynn's milk to her son, Thomas, whom she adopted two years ago when she was 48.

In Maine, Julie and John Montemurno gave Lynn's milk to their son, Gabriel, after he was delivered by emergency C-section ten weeks early and Julie was unable to pump.

In all, Lynn's milk was sent to 16 infants, two young children, and six hospitals. It nourished a lot of babies.

In the fall of 2008, at Portsmouth Naval Medical Center, where Reese spent her entire life, Lynn got ready to do it all again.

"Do you want the lights dimmed?" a nurse asked.

"I don't care."

"Would you like the birth filmed?"

"No!"

"Do you want a mirror so you can watch your baby being born?"

"I don't think so."

On November 14, 2008 at 1:04 A.M., Ashtyn Grace Page was born. She weighed seven pounds, six ounces. She had her father's nose and mouth, her mother's long, graceful fingers, and a swath of black hair. She was a healthy, full-term baby.

Within an hour of her birth, Ashtyn's pink O of a mouth gaped wide and latched onto her mother's breast.

It was such an odd sensation, this tugging and pulling that was so foreign but so welcome. Because until then, despite pumping more than 56 gallons of milk, Lynn Page had never nursed a baby. ⬤

To donate milk or learn more about milk banks, go to hmbana.org, the Web site of the Human Milk Banking Association of North America.

Blood Brother

Albert Fischer started donating pints of his O-positive when Truman was president, and has continued to do so every 56 days—for 58 years.
By Helen Rogan

On a sunny fall morning, a clutch of TV camera crews and reporters stands chatting at the door of a country club in Woodbury, Long Island. They're all waiting for Albert Fischer, the man of the hour, to drive up in his car with the license plate O BLOOD. Fischer is being celebrated today for an extraordinary feat: The pint that he's about to donate will bring his lifetime total to 40 gallons of whole blood.

Fischer walks slowly through the door and into the throng. At "75 plus," as he likes to say, he's stooped and stiff from years of back problems. But, smiling in his neat slacks and dark blue American Legion shirt and patiently answering the reporters' questions, he is clearly eager to get on with the routine he's undertaken about six times a year for 58 years. Asked how he's feeling, he says, with a sidelong grin, "I'm overwhelmed! But I'm glad to get to this part of my blood-donating life."

Centuries ago, sick people were bled, deliberately, in the belief that it might save their lives. These days we know better: The need for blood is limitless. Every two seconds, someone in the United States requires blood; more than 38,000 donations are needed every day of the year. Since blood cannot be made synthetically, it has to come from people's generosity. Processed into its components—red cells, platelets, and plasma—one pint can help as many as three people. But the shelf life is limited: for regular red blood cells, it's just 42 days. And only 5 percent of those who are eligible donate.

Sitting and drinking coffee in a diner the week before the big event, Fischer told his story. "When I started, I wasn't going for a record," he said. While working and attending textile school in South Carolina, he decided to participate in a blood drive at the First Baptist Church in Union. He liked the feeling of doing something good, so he gave blood a second time. That got him hooked. Since then, he has given every 56 days—except for one disappointing New Year's Day many years ago. "I was so mad because they were closed!" In the old days, before records were computerized, he could even get away with sneaking in a few extra donations.

Fischer is not the type to sit around. He served in the Coast Guard during the Korean War; on a blind date at the Brooklyn Navy Yard Officers' Club, he met a pretty young woman named Myrna. He proposed that very evening. Married, with a young child, Fischer was in constant motion. He became a successful textile salesman, spent, by his estimation, "300 nights a year" betting on horses at the track, and played a lot of golf. On weekends he was a lifeguard and took his wife to parties at the American Legion. "I had a busy schedule," he says, letting out a raspy chuckle. He started working as a printer, going to work for the police department, and it wasn't until his wife became disabled after an operation 17 years ago that he slowed down.

He's still happily working—in a print shop—but now he goes home after work and catches *Jeopardy!* with his wife. On weekends they might sit at the shore watching the boats or check out the tee-off at a golf tournament. He still bets on the horses, but over the phone, and goes by the American Legion from time to

time "for the comradeship." And then there's the blood, every 56 days without fail.

Ask him why he keeps on donating, and Fischer will shrug and say simply, "Look—I want to help people. And it doesn't hurt me. When I was a salesman, driving the whole metropolitan area, I'd come home and say, 'I've had a terrible day, but you know, I gave blood, and that perks me up.' People are living because I gave blood." At a rate of three people per pint, he's helped about 1,000 people over the years.

He cheerfully allows that he's always been competitive. Years ago, he recalls, "feeling very expansive, I said to the phlebotomist, 'What's the record around here? I've got 80 pints!' She called over a little old lady and said, 'Mary, how many pints have you given?' She says, 'This is my 136th.' It made me feel so small…."

As if his regular service weren't enough, Fischer learned his O-positive blood is Code 96. That means it lacks a particular combination of antigens, which makes it especially useful for specialized cases: transplants, people who have been transfused so often that they reject regular blood, and fragile babies.

When Ronald Reagan was shot, Fischer arranged for two receipts to go to him. Was there a thank-you note? Nope, but never mind. Still, he gets a kick out of what he calls "the notoriety," the blizzard of citations, certificates, and plaques, and he proudly mentions that he was named one of President George H.W. Bush's Points of Light.

You'd think by now that Fischer would have made it into the *Guinness World Records,* but he's behind the current recordholder, Englishman Anthony Davis, and Maurice Wood in St. Louis, who is just a few pints ahead. He and Wood have talked; neither one is about to give up. Fischer's keeping an eye on Wood, who recently moved into an assisted living residence, so who knows?

On this bright morning at the country club, the technicians fuss over Fischer as the TV cameras roll and a spry jazz combo plays. The other donors smile at him as they leave with their gifts—small pots of chrysanthemums, Glen Campbell CDs. None of the local politicians he's been hoping for have shown up, but Fischer seems content, telling stories and savoring the moment. How much longer will he keep on giving? "Until I drop." He adds wryly, "After this, no more big events. Fifty gallons? Do the math…."

For now, he's planning to take the rest of the day off, maybe do some chores for his wife. But he'll be back when it's time. ◐

THE *O* INTERVIEW

Oprah Talks to Michelle Obama

Our First Lady on the surprises of life in the White House ("If you want pie, there's pie! If something breaks, it's fixed. In an hour")…the rules she's laid down for Malia and Sasha ("I want the kids to be treated like children, not little princesses")…her decorating philosophy ("You've got to be able to make a fort with the sofa pillows")…and how she hopes to use "one of the best jobs in the world" to help women transform their lives.

On the second floor of the White House, the Yellow Oval Room—which is part of the First Family's private residence—offers a stunning view of the nation's capital. The Washington Monument stretches into the heavens. The Lincoln Memorial sits above the glassy water of the Reflecting Pool. In the distance, you can see the U.S. Capitol, where the world's attention was focused on January 20, 2009, as millions gathered to witness an event many had thought would never happen. This room is where I interviewed First Lady Michelle Obama in February of 2009, and as I gazed out the windows and took in the view, I was struck by the immense legacy she and her family have inherited. I felt the weight of history, and I understood what she means when she says, as she often does, "This is not about us."

Yet for all the majesty of the White House, the First Lady has infused it with a palpable ease; her presence makes the place feel open and approachable. When we

In the Jacqueline Kennedy Garden, on the White House grounds, February 17, 2009.

In the East
Colonnade,
which looks out
on the Jacqueline
Kennedy Garden.

sit down to talk, she seems as relaxed as she did when I first interviewed her and her husband in their Chicago apartment in 2004. "This room has the best light in the house," she tells me as we settle in, shoes off, on a comfortable sofa. "And there's pie here, too. The pie in the White House is dangerously good."

The Obamas packed up their belongings in Chicago and headed for Washington in early January 2009 so then 10-year-old Malia and 7-year-old Sasha could get started at their new school. A few weeks later, Michelle and her mother, Marian Robinson, began settling the family into their new home. When I returned to Chicago after the inauguration, I spent the weekend thinking, *What are the Obamas doing now?* Later, when I was looking for some cough syrup in my medicine cabinet, I suddenly thought, *Michelle never has to go out to buy cough syrup again!* For the First Lady and her family, it's a whole new reality. As we talk, she tells me how they're adjusting—and what she's planning to do in her awesome new role.

OPRAH: I had heart palpitations coming through the White House gate, recognizing that this really is now your home. It's the White House, and it's your home.

MICHELLE OBAMA: And it's a beautiful home. When you go out and come back, especially at night, with all the white lights on—it's just beautiful. We feel privileged, and we feel a responsibility to make it feel like the people's house. We have the good fortune of being able to sleep here, but this house belongs to America.

OPRAH: Your saying that makes me feel different than I've ever felt about the White House. When you say that, I actually do now, for the first time, think, *Yeah, it is the people's house.* How did you come to understand that so clearly?

MICHELLE: Well, I had some time to think about it, because we ran for so long....

OPRAH: The longest run anybody's ever seen.

MICHELLE: Right. And at some point, you start thinking about what living here would really mean. I've taken Barack's mantra: This isn't about us. There's so much history here that no one family can claim this space as their own.

OPRAH: So when did it hit you?

MICHELLE: I don't think it has. Everything's been moving at the speed of light. The whole process of transitioning here, the inauguration, all the protocol, seeing to it that

"We have the good fortune of being able to sleep here, but this house belongs to America."

the girls are doing well—I've really just been trying to make sure everything gets done.

OPRAH: I can't imagine what the inauguration was like for you. For me, it felt like a moment in time that had been coming since time began.

MICHELLE: I definitely sensed that, standing on the Capitol steps. But I would love to see a tape of what was going on down on the Mall. Because when you hear from people who were there, they talk about the emotions and the calm and the fact that you had more than a million people descending on this very small city with no incident, all love—I long to know that feeling as well.

OPRAH: What was your prayer the night before you moved into the White House?

MICHELLE: That we stay whole as a family through this process. And when Barack and I talked, he said that he wanted to get through the day with everyone intact, everyone who attended—he said he would feel good when every last visitor left safely. And fortunately that happened.

OPRAH: Every last visitor. Every train. Every bus. There were so many people. And all of them had their eyes on you. Were you in your body?

MICHELLE: Oh, I was in it. And it was pretty cold.

OPRAH: One of my favorite, favorite moments was during the parade—the two of you getting out of the car and walking, and your arms are linked and your head is sort of on his shoulder. I loved that. But I wondered about the conversation before you got out. Did you just suddenly say, "Look, we're going to walk for a while now"?

MICHELLE: We were trying to see if the girls wanted to get out. They were like, "No"—they wanted to stay in the car. And while we were out, they were partying in there—when we got back in, they had the music blaring. But Barack and I felt that walking outside was a natural extension of the campaign: *Okay, we can't come over to you, we can't hug you—can't do that—but we can be out here waving.* Of course, then there was a point where we felt like, *Whoa, three blocks is long.* My feet started hurting.

OPRAH: How did your feet feel at the seventh ball that night?

MICHELLE: What a good workout, right? I just remembered that even though it was the seventh ball for me, it was the first ball for everyone there. I thought about that during the parade, too. I thought, *I'm going to stand here and cheer for every last person, because this is why they came—to walk in front of the president of the United States.*

OPRAH: **Weren't you freezing?**

MICHELLE: I was a little cube of ice. My coat had layers, but from the legs down, I was cold. I would have loved to be wearing a pair of warm, toasty boots.

OPRAH: **But your shoes looked good! So after the inauguration, what was your first weekend in the White House like?**

MICHELLE: Well, we still had family here, so it was almost like a wedding. A huge, very complicated wedding. The last visitors didn't leave until Sunday. And then the first Monday was kind of weird. You know: *Now we live here, and Barack is getting up and going to work, and it's just us. This is our home now.* But the kids didn't act any differently.

OPRAH: **They didn't?**

MICHELLE: No. They have been so steady and rock solid that I pinch myself sometimes. Sometimes I pinch them—*are you real?* Because they've adjusted so well. And that was always my concern: How are they going to do? How is this going to be for these little precious girls who were doing just fine in Chicago and had a happy life? But once I saw them thriving—not just living, but thriving, happy, excited about their day and very much focused on their world—that's when I was able to breathe.

OPRAH: **And how are *you* adjusting to everything? What are your days like?**

MICHELLE: My day is structured so that I'm usually not working until 10 or 10:30. That gives me time to get the girls out of the house. My mom is taking them to school because it's less of a scene for her. With all the security involved, it's a more normal experience for them when I don't go.

OPRAH: **What do people at school call you? First Lady? Mrs. Obama?**

MICHELLE: When I introduce myself, I usually say, "Hi, I'm Michelle—Malia and Sasha's mom." And then when you sit down with another parent and have a conversation, all the titles melt away anyway, and you're just talking about your kids. But to get back to your question, after I see the girls off, I usually work until 3 or 4. Then they're back and we start in on homework. Then Dad comes home and we all have dinner. That's the beauty of living above the office: Barack is home every day. The four of us sit down to eat as a family. We haven't had that kind of normalcy for years. And now I can just pop over to his office, which sometimes I'll do if I know he's

> ## "I can just pop over to his office and say hi, which I'll do if I know he's having a particularly frustrating day."

having a particularly frustrating day.

OPRAH: **You pop over to the Oval Office?**

MICHELLE: Yes. I'll just pop over and say hi. And all of this—this being together as a family—is what has made the transition here easy. We have each other, in a really fundamental way.

OPRAH: **What are weekends like?**

MICHELLE: We're still getting the kids' activities schedule straight. They're trying to figure out what they want to do. Sasha has played basketball—

OPRAH: **She's coming up in the basketball tradition.**

MICHELLE: I know, Barack's losing his mind. I was like, "Settle *down*—don't act too excited, or she will not want to do it."

OPRAH: **And how is your mother doing? I am so impressed with her. We had a conversation right before you moved, and she said she was going to make sure you all had your dinners as a family—but that she would not be at the table.**

MICHELLE: I know.

OPRAH: **When I asked her why, she said, "Because that's Michelle's family."**

MICHELLE: My mother has some really wise approaches to family. But there are times when we're like, "Mom, come down here."

OPRAH: **She originally wanted her own apartment.**

MICHELLE: And I told her, "You can live right here and never even see us if you don't want to!"

OPRAH: **She told me that the reason she decided to live here is that she didn't want you and the president to have to pay for her to have her own place.**

MICHELLE: Oh, that's good. We're cheap, for sure. And I bet she said so!

OPRAH: **But there *is* a lot of room here.**

MICHELLE: Plenty of room. There are many times when she drops off the kids, we hang out and talk and catch up, and then she's like, "I'm going home." And she walks upstairs.

OPRAH: **Like she's going across town. So she's adjusting well to living in Washington?**

MICHELLE: Yes. She's made friends, she's had visitors, she's been to the Kennedy Center more than I have. She was actually so busy one weekend that she forgot to check my schedule. Then she thought, *Well, maybe Michelle's going to need me Sunday.* And I said, "Actually, yeah, the first state dinner is Sunday. But we'll get a babysitter.

1. Viewing portraits in the East Colonnade.
2. Fresh flowers fill the rooms of the White House. 3. The south portico, part of the First Family's private residence. 4. Arriving in Indianapolis for a campaign event, May 2008.
5. On the Truman Balcony, outside the Yellow Oval Room. 6. At home in Chicago, October 2006. 7. Touring the White House grounds.
8. Sharing a moment in Indiana, May 2008.

Don't worry." [*Laughter.*] Pretty soon she's going to come up to me and say, "You know, I can't pick those kids up, I've got so much going on."

OPRAH: What's it like to walk into a world where you have so many people available to handle your every need? You've gone from doing everything, managing your whole household, getting the kids off to school, picking up your own cough syrup...

MICHELLE: Going to Target...

OPRAH: Going to Target—and now you walk into this world...

MICHELLE: Where, if you want pie, there's pie. If something breaks, it's fixed. In an hour. Look, I appreciate it.

OPRAH: How many people are on the staff?

MICHELLE: There are about 95 people who manage the residence. But I want it to feel like home, so it's important for me to get to know the people we work with, to be able to joke with them and tease them.

OPRAH: Before you moved in, you said you wanted the girls to keep making their own beds and doing chores. Is the staff on board with that?

MICHELLE: It took a second. At first they were like, "Are you sure?" But if these girls don't learn how to make a bed or clean a room, what are they going to do when they go to college? It can't be foreign to them to be part of a working household. So in the first few days, I gathered my East Wing team and the residence staff—the folks who clean the chandeliers, the people in the kitchen, everyone—and thanked them for helping us transition through the move. Then I talked about our vision for this house: that it would be filled with life, that we'd have people in and out, that the kids would roam around. I want the kids to be treated like children, not little princesses. I told everyone that they should make their beds, they should clean their plates, they should act respectfully—and that if anyone on the staff sees differently, they should come to me. So the girls help set the table, they help bring the food out, they work with the butler staff, and they're in the kitchen laughing and making their toast in the morning. And everyone has adjusted to the rules. Now I joke with the staff: "Don't spoil them—spoil Mom!"

OPRAH: You can handle it!

MICHELLE: I can handle it.

OPRAH: There's a solidness about the girls—a real groundedness—that speaks to the great work you've done as a mother. What are you most proud of in terms of raising them?

> "My happiness is tied to how I feel about myself. I want my girls to see a mother who takes care of herself."

MICHELLE: It's that: that they're so steady. And that they're kind—to each other, and to other children. It's important to me that they have empathy. I want them to be able to think, *Well, I could see how that person feels and why that would hurt.* And to make decisions not just based on their own needs but on what's going on around them.

OPRAH: How are they with each other?

MICHELLE: There's genuine love and affection. I'm big on the idea that their sister is all each of them has. Even when they argue, I want them to act with respect. I say, "Do you know how painful it is for a mother to watch her two children, who she loves equally, arguing?" I say, "You don't see it much, but the one or two times you've seen Dad and me disagree, you started falling apart." And they get it.

OPRAH: Are there fewer arguments between you and the president now that you don't have to fix things around the house?

MICHELLE: Absolutely. That was kind of a growth point in our marriage that I've talked about before—the stress of needing help, and then finally realizing that the help doesn't necessarily have to come from your husband. It can come from anywhere.

OPRAH: You seemed to grow together over the course of the campaign. The connection between the two of you seemed to intensify.

MICHELLE: When you work on something really hard together and enjoy the successes and challenges with each other, and then get through it not just whole but stronger—you realize how very blessed you are, how much love you have together. So, yes, I think we've grown. But not just me and Barack. It's the girls, too. And even our whole extended family.

OPRAH: And how have you managed to stay in touch with family and friends?

MICHELLE: That's the thing about being the First Lady: You try to catch your friends up on what's happening in your life, and they're like, "We know—we read it in the paper."

OPRAH: "We saw it in the *Tribune.*"

MICHELLE: So we get to see friends—we've been back to Chicago—but I think people will wind up coming here to visit us because...

OPRAH: It's hard to travel when you're First Lady.

MICHELLE: It is. You know, you asked me when it hit me that all this was really happening. I'll tell you when it hit

In the White House, "we want approachable comfort," the First Lady says.

me. There was a moment before our first visit to the White House, when we came to meet the Bushes. I had flown in early to visit a school, and then I went back to the airport so Barack and I could ride to the White House together. As we drove up, my Secret Service agent said, "There's the president-elect's motorcade." And there were like 20 cars! There was everything in that motorcade except the caboose! Now I tease Barack: "You've got the

horse and carriage, the dogsled, the airplane, the bike..."
OPRAH: And the kids know he's home when they hear his helicopter landing.
MICHELLE: Once someone on my staff e-mailed to tell me that the president was on his way. But you could already hear the helicopter, so it was like, well, no kidding.
OPRAH: "Dad's home!"
MICHELLE: The girls don't move. I'm like, "You want to

see Daddy landing in the helicopter?" "No, that's okay. We already saw it."

OPRAH: Is living in the White House fun?

MICHELLE: There's fun every day. I have one of the best jobs in the world. Because I don't have to fix the economy, thank goodness. Yet I get to go say hello to the people who make this government work, who hold us up and who will still be here after we're gone. I get to go read to kids. We're also working on a wonderful new garden project.

OPRAH: Will kids get to visit the garden?

MICHELLE: We want to use it as a point of education, to talk about health and how delicious it is to eat fresh food, and how you can take that food and make it part of a healthy diet. You know, the tomato that's from your garden tastes very different from one that isn't. And peas—what is it like to eat peas in season? So we want the White House to be a place of education and awareness. And hopefully kids will be interested because there are kids living here. We're even putting a swing set on the South Lawn.

OPRAH: So Dad can look out from the Oval Office and see the girls.

MICHELLE: Yes—though I hope the swing set won't be just for the Obama girls. I want the staff to feel that they can bring their children to the place where they work and let them feel connected to what their parents do.

OPRAH: It's wonderful that you want to be so inclusive. But do you get privacy when you need it?

MICHELLE: Absolutely—as much as we need. This is our home, and everyone treats it that way. There is a great deal of respect and decorum around the residence.

OPRAH: How will the decorating style change?

MICHELLE: It will reflect our family. I want comfortable sofas, I want art that reflects contemporary and traditional, I want to bring in new American artisans.

OPRAH: You want more than just a few plates on the walls. You want pieces that are inclusive of American culture.

MICHELLE: Right. And we want approachable comfort.

OPRAH: So you can take off your shoes.

MICHELLE: And you've got to be able

to make a fort with the sofa pillows! Everything must be fort-worthy.

OPRAH: Okay, shifting gears now. How are you a different woman today than you were when Barack Obama announced his candidacy in 2007?

MICHELLE: I'm more optimistic. More hopeful. It comes from traveling all over America and connecting with so many different people. And this was long before anyone thought Barack had a chance. This was the kindness of strangers. I think we should all have to get to know one another around kitchen tables. It changed me. It's helped me to give other people the benefit of the doubt.

OPRAH: What did you see that changed you?

MICHELLE: I saw our shared values. We fundamentally want the same things for ourselves and for each other. We want our kids to be safe and to grow up with some resources and aspire to a slightly better life than ours. No one's looking for a handout. People just want fairness and opportunity.

OPRAH: That's so good to hear. Because you know what? We live in an *American Idol* culture where it seems like everyone just wants to be in the spotlight.

MICHELLE: That's not the America I saw. People value their communities. They're rooting for one another. Even in places where I thought people wouldn't accept or relate to me, I always walked out feeling like, *Wow— that was fun.* That changed me. And it helped prepare me for this. Because I think if you're going to be First Lady, you have to believe in the possibility of what this country stands for. You have to see it in action and know what you're working toward.

OPRAH: That's so interesting—and it all came from sitting around kitchen tables. Speaking of which, did you change your diet during the campaign?

MICHELLE: When we first started running, my big concern was making sure we ate well on the road. So we started looking at our diet, trying to eliminate junk, getting seasonal fruits and vegetables that were grown locally. We walked the kids through reading labels. We talked about why one juice might be better than another juice.

OPRAH: What foods did you give up?

MICHELLE: Things with artificial ingredients. That's a tough change for

> "We fundamentally want the same things for ourselves and for each other. We want our kids to be safe and to grow up with some resources and aspire to a slightly better life than ours."

a lot of families, though, because so many foods aren't real anymore. But lots of people don't have access to a farmers' market, or can't afford to shop at one, so this is a bigger issue. It's *really* big, because changing your diet makes such a difference. I've seen it in my own family. We have more energy now. And I caught only one cold during the last year of the campaign, even after shaking millions of hands!

OPRAH: On the campaign trail, weren't people offering you every kind of food imaginable?

MICHELLE: Yes, and a lot of times, I'd eat it. Hey, I love pie. I love a good candy bar. And sometimes when you're working so hard, the only thing you have is that candy bar and those potato chips. But if I went home to a balanced diet, then those days wouldn't kill me. I feel the same about the girls. If they're eating healthy most times, I don't panic when they get popcorn at the movies. I don't want them freaking out about food.

OPRAH: That's right. In addition to eating well, do you work out?

MICHELLE: Yes. There's a small gym here that has everything we need. I work out about four or five days a week—and Barack does six. He's a workout zealot.

OPRAH: Well, you look better than ever—despite the rumors that you've got a baby bump.

MICHELLE: [*Laughter.*] I know—I was like, "*Baby* bump? As hard as I work on my abs?!"

OPRAH: By the way, nobody would be happier if you were pregnant than Gayle King. Out of nowhere, she'll tell me, "Oh God, I really hope Michelle gets pregnant—and that it's a boy!"

MICHELLE: [*More laughter.*] Here's the scoop: Not pregnant. And not planning on it.

OPRAH: Not pregnant.

MICHELLE: Not pregnant.

OPRAH: Okay, so that's settled. Back to exercise. You do treadmill?

MICHELLE: I do treadmill, I do weights—

OPRAH: I think anyone who saw you on the cover of *Vogue* knows you do weights. Those arms!

MICHELLE: I also do some jump rope, some kickboxing—and I'd like to take up Pilates, if I could figure out whether there's time. After I had Malia, I began to prioritize exercise because I realized that my happiness is tied to how I

> "Work-family balance isn't just a policy conversation; it's about changing the expectations of who we have to be as women and parents."

feel about myself. I want my girls to see a mother who takes care of herself, even if that means I have to get up at 4:30 so I can do a workout.

OPRAH: When you first told me that a few years ago, I was like, "*You get up at 4:30 to work out?*"

MICHELLE: Well, I just started thinking, if I had to get up to go to work, I'd get up and go to work. If I had to get up to take care of my kids, I'd get up to do that. But when it comes to yourself, then it's suddenly, *Oh, I can't get up at 4:30.* So I had to change that. If I don't exercise, I won't feel good. I'll get depressed. Of course, it's easier to do it here, because I have much more support now. But I always think about women who don't have support. That's why work-family balance isn't just a policy conversation; it's about changing the expectations of who we have to be as women and parents.

OPRAH: What you mentioned earlier is key: We have to ask for help. You can't do it all. It's impossible.

MICHELLE: That's a conversation I'd love for us to have as a society. How do we set expectations that are attainable?

OPRAH: And how do we change the perception of what women should be able to handle? Parents have always needed help—but our generation decided that women should somehow do everything. Yet for thousands and thousands of years, parents had kids so that the kids could help them!

MICHELLE: And we once lived in small enough communities where people could help each other. Families were together. That's how I grew up. My grandmother lived around the corner, my grandfather lived two blocks away, they each lived with aunts and uncles. My paternal grandparents lived maybe ten blocks away. It was rare to see a family where one person was trying to cook, clean, watch the kids, do it all. You always had a community. But nowadays people have to move away from their community just to find a job. And then they're leaving their support base. So we have to acknowledge that that's going on and ask what it does to the family structure and what it means in terms of how we have to reengineer support.

OPRAH: Your saying that out loud is so powerful for women. And liberating. You're a mighty force. You know, I've wondered: Do you feel the glare of the fishbowl?

MICHELLE: I don't pay attention to it. There isn't a bigger fishbowl, but I don't own the glare.

■

OPRAH: **Now that your husband is president, everybody has an opinion about what he should or should not be doing. How do you handle that? I sometimes get offended—and I'm not the one who is married to him!**

MICHELLE: We live in the experience that we're actually having. In just a few weeks, my husband got a stimulus bill passed and made some amazing policy changes that will affect people's lives in a fundamentally positive way. I'm so proud of him. That's the reality. Everything else is just what comes with the territory. The people who disagree with Barack don't dislike him; they just disagree. That's what democracy is about. But at some point, you've got to make a decision and move forward, and your hope is that people will give you the benefit of the doubt that you're making decisions based on what you think is best for the country.

OPRAH: **Gayle once interviewed you for her radio show and was blown away by something you said: that your husband has never disappointed you. Gayle was like, "I can't believe that!"**

MICHELLE: Barack is a human being with flaws. And I can rattle down all the flaws and tease him about them every day, but those flaws are not fundamental. They don't hit upon things that are intolerable to me. In terms of his core values, he has never disappointed me. He is a very consistent person—which is why I knew unequivocally that he would be a phenomenal president. He is steady. Has he made me mad? Yes. Does he sometimes do things that I don't like? Absolutely.

OPRAH: **That's called marriage.**

MICHELLE: But as a human being, he has never disappointed. And I would hope he could say the same thing about me. Ask him!

OPRAH: **I will. First chance I get. Has your love deepened during this whole process?**

MICHELLE: Absolutely. I don't lose sight of the fact that

> "Barack is a very consistent person—which is why I knew unequivocally that he would be a phenomenal president."

he's the president, but first and foremost he's my husband, my friend, and the father of my children. That didn't change with his hand on the Lincoln Bible. But it doesn't mean I don't appreciate the gravity of what he's doing. The way I can honor that is by working by his side and adding value to what he's doing in any way that I can. That's my part in this. That's why I'm out there trying to be an aid and a support to his vision and his values. I am supporting the president of the United States.

OPRAH: **It seems that every woman I speak to—black, white, older, younger—says the same thing about you: "She's just like us." People feel an affection for you that I find so touching.**

MICHELLE: I've always thought that what I owe the American people is to let them see who I am so there are no surprises. I don't want to be anyone but Michelle Obama. And I want people to know what they're getting.

OPRAH: **What I see in you is a confidence that comes from such an authentic place. A reporter who interviewed me ten years after she'd first met me said, "Gee, you're the same person—but it feels like you've become more of yourself." When do you think you got to be this much of yourself?**

MICHELLE: I think in my 40s, I started feeling very comfortable in my own skin. Motherhood helps, marriage helps—those learning curves that force you to be better. And my hope is that my 50s will hone that. I never consider myself a finished project.

OPRAH: **So what do you know for sure, Michelle Obama?**

MICHELLE: I know that all I can do is be the best me that I can. And live life with some gusto. Giving back is a big part of that. How am I going to share this experience with the American people? I'm always thinking about that. **O**

Marcia Gay Harden's Aha! Moment

It was the winter of her discontent: She had no money, no acting parts, and no snow boots. Then a stranger let her know (rather bluntly) just how much she had to be grateful for.

About 25 years ago, I got off the bus from Washington, D.C., to start my career as an actress in New York City. As I lugged my suitcase behind me, I thought, *Look out, here I come!* But four months later, I still had no acting jobs. And no matter where you come from, no matter your education or training, you are not prepared for this city. I lived in a fourth-floor walk-up apartment with a bedroom the size of a bathroom; you could fit a single bed, a dresser, and not much else. Every morning I got up at 6 so I could stand in the Actors' Equity line. I'd get a number so I could come back at lunchtime and audition, and then I'd go to whatever temp job I had.

Winter came, and I had never seen such snow. There were huge, slushy puddles at every corner, and you'd have to leap to get from the street to the sidewalk. One day I was slogging along in this mess—I had a fever, I was wearing sneakers, my feet were wet, I wasn't getting cast in any shows—and I started to cry. We're not talking pretty crying, either—this was snotty crying, with gulping sobs.

In the middle of 57th and Broadway, a man who looked to be homeless came up and said, "Whatchoo crying for, lady?"

He and I continued across the street to the sidewalk, where we finished our conversation.

"I have a cold (*sob, sob*), I hardly have any money, my feet are wet (*sob, gulp*), I want to be an actress and (*snuffle, sob*) nobody's casting me...."

And he said, "You got a job, lady?"

"Yes," I said, sniffling.

"You got a home, lady?"

"Yes..."

"You got a family that loves you?"

"Yes."

"Then quit your crying," he said, "and get to work."

He didn't say it in a mean way. In fact, he could have passed me by. But in that moment he cared. He helped me snap out of my self-pity and be grateful for the opportunities I had had. I've tried to share this lesson with young people just starting out, but if I tell them to quit their crying, they reply, "That's easy for *you* to say." They don't believe I struggled, too. But that man was different. Today I work with Help USA, a group that assists people who are homeless because of poverty, domestic violence, or war-induced trauma. I never realized until now that this may be my way of giving back to a person whose name I never learned, of bringing the story full circle. That man had enough compassion for a dorky out-of-towner to tell me to believe in myself and to always be grateful for what I have. He didn't say that exactly, but that's what I heard. It's a lesson I'm happy to relearn every day.

—*As told to Suzan Colón*

$100 and a Dream

How to turn a modest gift into a dynamic little nonprofit, 36 scholarships, dozens of changed lives, and counting… Geraldine Brooks reports.

The letter from Texas had taken a couple of months to find its way to my desk in Cairo. Inside was a $100 bill and a brief note.

Every so often in journalism, something you write touches readers, and they feel moved to help. Usually, I was delighted when that happened, but this time my reaction was weary and ungenerous.

Getting the money to the intended recipient wasn't going to be easy. It meant another trip into violence and danger. For a minute or two, I thought about sending the money back to Texas.

In December of 1987, a Palestinian teenager stoned my car as I drove alone through the West Bank. I was new in my job as *The Wall Street Journal*'s Mideast correspondent, and my editor had asked me to get an interview with one of the youths involved in the uprising that had suddenly erupted in Israel's occupied territories. So I jumped from my damaged car and chased after the boy, whose face was wrapped in a red-checked headscarf. We ended up spending the afternoon together in the crumbling four-room, raw-concrete hovel he shared with 12 younger siblings, and I subsequently wrote an article about an intelligent 15-year-old named Raed who wanted to be a doctor but knew there was no hope of such a future for a boy in his circumstances. Instead, he was willing to die, fighting with stones.

A hundred dollars was more than Raed's father, a laborer, earned in a month. It was sent by an ophthalmologist in Austin, along with a note asking me to pass it on to Raed and "let him know that if he wants to be a doctor, I'm prepared to help him"—a few scribbled words that promised a future to a boy who hadn't expected to have one.

So in April of 1988, I returned to the West Bank camp and made my way through trash-strewn alleys in search of Raed, who had refused to give me his last name. Finally, I learned that he had been arrested by the Israelis for throwing a Molotov cocktail at an army patrol and was in jail, awaiting trial. Unexpectedly, his father, a Hebrew-speaking moderate who worked on Israeli building sites and advocated Israeli-Palestinian reconciliation, had also been arrested in a routine security sweep. He was being held without charge in a desert prison while the family, deprived of its only breadwinner, subsisted on handouts. I gave the $100 to Raed's mother, Rahme, who shared the crowded living quarters with her husband's second wife, Fatin. Rahme kissed the bill, and the two women called down God's blessings on the doctor in faraway Texas.

Rex Repass knew what it was to struggle to achieve an education. Raised in an underprivileged family in Dallas, he'd worked his way through college at the University of Texas, then joined the navy as a way to get to medical school. In 1988 he was 45, with a prosperous practice, a beautiful home, a private plane. His wife, Kathleen, had recently given birth to their first child. Repass read the *Journal* to keep track of his stock portfolio, but he was also keenly interested in foreign events. Almost a year after he sent me his letter, he came to Jerusalem himself, to volunteer for several weeks in a Palestinian eye hospital. While he was there, he met Raed's family, paid for food, medicine, and a lawyer for Raed, and renewed his pledge to fund Raed's education when he got out of jail.

A little over four years later, in 1993, I learned that Raed had finally been released from prison. I'd left Cairo by then, and was covering the Mideast from London. When I traveled to the West Bank that spring, I found Raed working 16-hour days in a Palestinian

sweatshop, making plastic sandals and sleeping on the factory floor. I arranged to meet him there on his one day off, and then I set about calling Repass, to tell him that Raed was at last in a position to accept his help. In Austin, a receptionist answered my call. When I asked to speak to the doctor, there was a moment's silence on the other end of the line. "I'm sorry, but Dr. Repass died a year and a half ago."

He had taken his Beechcraft Bonanza up for a short flight on a sunny afternoon. The plane fell out of the sky, and neither the Federal Aviation Administration inspectors nor the private investigators Kathleen hired had been able to figure out why.

As I struggled to break the news to Raed, I realized that I wasn't capable of dashing the hopes I'd raised by bringing Repass into his life. After my husband and I talked it over, we decided to pay for Raed's education ourselves.

It took him a year to catch up on his high school studies, but in 1994 Raed was admitted to Bethlehem University. At 21, he felt too old for medical school, so he decided to study education instead. In 1998 he graduated with honors. I was there for his commencement, perched in the stands between Rahme and Fatin. I thought about Dr. Rex, and I hoped he'd be pleased by what his $100 bill had accomplished. I didn't know then that the yield on Repass's spontaneous act of generosity was about to be amplified many times over.

In February of 1999, I wrote an article for *The Washington Post Magazine* about Raed's long journey to his college graduation. Within days of its publication, out of the blue I got a call from a Palestinian-American Quaker, who introduced himself as a retired educator. "You're Australian and you're Jewish, and yet you helped that boy," he said. "I as a Palestinian want to help, too."

Fahim Qubain and his wife, Nancy, proceeded to set up the Hope Fund (thehopefund.org), a tiny nonprofit they ran from their kitchen table in Lexington, Virginia. Their mission was to find young Palestinian refugees, like Raed, who were academically gifted but whose poverty made higher education an unreachable dream. By trial and error, Qubain, then a passionate and persuasive 85-year-old, hit on a successful formula for helping the maximum number of students despite operating with a very small donor base. His first breakthrough was to convince Roanoke

> A hundred dollars was more than Raed's father earned in a month. It had been sent by an ophthalmologist in Austin.

College in Salem, Virginia, to share his vision and provide two four-year scholarships in 2001. He then asked Amideast, a long-established nonprofit devoted to increasing educational cooperation between the United States and the Arab world, to identify gifted students. He used his own money, plus small donations, to pay for the students' travel, medical insurance, and whatever else they needed, whether it was a warm winter coat or a desk lamp.

One of the first two scholarship recipients was Hanan Dahche, one of 11 children of a lathe operator, who was living in the Ein el-Hilweh refugee camp in Lebanon. When told of her chance to go to college in America, she at first asked if the scholarship could be transferred to her older brother. But the Hope Fund is committed to educating equal numbers of young women and men, and Hanan's parents were eventually persuaded to let her go. Two years into her degree, she was spending her summers at NASA, designing advanced composites for radiation shields. On graduation, she obtained further scholarships and is now completing a PhD in biochemistry at Virginia Tech. She hopes to teach at the American University of Beirut.

The other scholarship recipient in 2001 was Khaled El-Nemr, the oldest of six children whose father, a tailor, could barely support his Beirut family because of diabetes. Khaled, too, won further scholarships and is now completing a PhD in materials science engineering at the University of Alabama in Huntsville.

The success of these first two students eventually made it easier for the Qubains to persuade other colleges to join their mission. They now have 16 partnering colleges, and some are offering multiple scholarships. The Hope Fund has ten graduates, many returning students in the United States, and seven more just starting in the fall.

Each student arrives with his or her own story of hardships overcome. Hiba Assi, one of six girls in an impoverished family in Lebanon's Beqaa Valley, never believed she would have a chance to go to college. A sibling had won a UN scholarship for higher education, and the program's rule was that only one scholarship could be awarded per family, no matter the other siblings' academic achieve-

ment. Nevertheless, Hiba worked hard at her studies and hoped for another miraculous kind of aid. It came in the form of a Hope Fund scholarship to Washington and Lee University in Lexington, Virginia. But just days before she was to leave, the rockets of the 2006 war between Israel and Hezbollah began falling. The Qubains, expecting to meet Hiba's flight, lost track of her and feared she had been killed. Instead, with her family, she risked heavily bombed roads to escape across the border to Syria, where the U.S. embassy in Damascus quickly issued her visa just days before classes were to start. She has excelled in college as a physics and math major, with a special interest in quantum dense coding.

In the fall of 2007, Yahia Abu Hashem missed what would have been his freshman year at Roanoke when Israel and Egypt closed the crossing points from Gaza in retaliation for Hamas attacks. He had recently lost his best friend to an Israeli rocket while walking by his side in Gaza. The college extended the scholarship for a year, but Gaza remained sealed. As time ran out, Yahia, desperate, camped by the crossing point into Egypt, waiting for three days and nights until he got the chance to risk making a run across the border. He arrived in Virginia sunburned and exhausted, just in time to enroll in computer science and business.

Manal Zaher despaired of even finishing high school because of her family's poverty. "Whenever I read about a genius scientist, my passion for science would jump all over the place and I imagined myself doing something great," she says. Then, as reality set in, she would weep and her mother would try to comfort her, telling her not to abandon hope. Manal secured a place in a UN–run high school and went on to attend Bryn Mawr. During her last summer break, she returned to her former school, bringing donated lab equipment, and ran a summer school for other refugees with big dreams.

As for Raed, the former angry stone-thrower, I last saw him in Sydney in 2004. He was there on business, an executive for a Saudi firm whose mission is to advise Arab students on programs available at universities overseas. He was married, with a family and a home in Jeddah, Saudi Arabia. No longer confined by razor wire and stunted hopes, he regularly traveled all over the world. And that's a pretty good return on $100. ❶

> When told of her chance to go to college in America, she at first asked if the scholarship could be transferred to her older brother. Two years into her degree, she was spending her summers at NASA.

Brooks, with Batwa children in Uganda, believes that small gestures make a big difference.

Giving Without Borders

Traveling the world donating clothing, wheelchairs, books, and chickens (when he's not laying bricks, building wells, and planting trees), Barton Brooks is a one-man international aid organization. By Sara Corbett

If you were to go traveling with Barton Brooks, there are a lot of things you might do. You might go for an elephant ride in Laos or take a long hike through a pretty Ugandan farm valley. You might go to the beach in Dubai or spin prayer wheels in a Tibetan village, or maybe just wander awestruck around the Taj Mahal until you figured you'd seen enough to go home happy and fulfilled. But this is exactly when Brooks—the kind of traveler who seems perpetually awestruck and often punctuates a meaningful moment by calling out, "This is a-*maaaay*-zing!"—will start looking for something better and more hands-on to do, like shopping for hens with a Cambodian granny or digging a toilet for a Kenyan school under a blazing midday sun.

At 38, Brooks is what you might call a professional helper. Simply put, he spends most of his time doing the two things about which he is most enthusiastic: traveling and volunteering. Getting to this point involved swapping a career as a real estate broker in New York for a bare-bones, itinerant existence, which he says is far more fulfilling than making money ever was. "I felt lost for a long time," he says. "I had a bit of wanderlust and somehow never felt like I was home." But four years ago, inspired by an exuberant and needy group of kids he'd met out-

> Getting to this point involved swapping a career as a real estate broker in New York for a bare-bones, itinerant existence, which he says is far more fulfilling than making money ever was.

side a temple while vacationing in Cambodia, he left his job and launched a grassroots organization called Global Colors, a deliberately small outfit with a deliberately simple purpose: connecting people who could use some help with others interested in helping. Most of the actual work gets done by Brooks himself, fueled by small donations made via his Web site (globalcolors.org), but he happily encourages fellow travelers either to meet up with him on the road, or to take a few days out of their vacation time to engage in his particular form of international volunteerism, which he calls Guerrilla Aid. "Those guys who go out and drop 10,000 pounds of grain out of the back of a military plane over Sudan? That's fine, but it's not what I can do," he says. "So why not do what I can do?"

Brooks, it turns out, can do a lot of things—not because he is any handier than the rest of us but because he is perhaps more willing. He carries a little Canon point-and-shoot camera with him everywhere, uploading pictures and videos for the many people who follow him online. When a couple he met in Kathmandu last winter introduced him to the 40 orphans they'd taken in off the street who were sleeping on the concrete floors of their three-bedroom home, Brooks introduced the 40 orphans—laughing and tumbling around, all the while shoeless and subsisting on rice—to his online friends. "If you show happiness that needs help, people respond better," he remarks. "Rather than saying, 'Look at how sad they all are—everyone's hungry,' I say, 'Hey, I've got these amazing, joyful kids. Let's help meet their needs.'" Thanks to the instant nature of Internet donations, he spent the next two weeks buying bunk beds for the children and kitchen supplies, as well as installing a water tank and an awning for the sun-scorched roof.

Anybody can do Guerrilla Aid, according to Brooks. It is simply a matter of showing up somewhere and offering some small bit of your time and energy. "If you're on vacation in Cancún, there are three orphanages within driving distance," he says. "Why don't you make that part of your spring break? Go in, do something, get out." Guerrilla Aid is about fitting yourself into the culture you're visiting, he adds, noting that he never plans a project in advance but rather arrives in a new place and starts by asking questions and listening. "You don't just show up and say, 'Here's me and here's a present from the U.S.,'" he explains. "You say, 'What do you need? What can I help you create?' And then with them, you create what they want. You are building upon their idea, not some idea of your own."

Over the past several years—while traveling on a budget of about $20 per day, with breaks in the United States—Brooks has given away clothing, wheelchairs, bikes, water jugs, and chickens. ("Chickens are kind of a universal theme," he says. "Almost everybody is better off with a new chicken.") In rural India, he passed out notebooks and pens to schoolchildren. He laid bricks at a temple restoration project in Nepal. In Mozambique, leading a group of volunteers, he built a well and planted saplings on a deforested patch of land. He has given milk cows to Masai widows in Kenya, added books to a library in Laos, planted vegetable gardens in Senegal, and hauled firewood in Ethiopia. One time, arriving on foot in a rugged and hilly part of southern Uganda, he held a fund drive to buy thumb pianos for members of a pygmy tribe who'd been forced to sell their traditional instruments in order to afford food. Brooks's blog posts to his own tribe

"If you're on vacation in Cancún, there are three orphanages within driving distance. Why don't you make [helping them] part of your spring break?"

of supporters at home usually reflect his irreverent humor ("Is my butt looking better? Because with all of this hill climbing, there's got to be something that comes out of this...."), wide-open heart ("Okay, I'm crying again!"), and unswerving focus on whatever is left on his to-do list. "We're still a bit short on chickens, cows, and dresses," he wrote from the pygmy village last winter, "but all in all we're well on our way."

His work, however, is not without its hazards. He's been stranded on an empty stretch of the Mekong River after the boat he was traveling on broke down. He's had dysentery and bug bites, and every once in a while sees a snake he wishes he hadn't. While riding a motorbike on a rural road in Uganda, Brooks came around a blind corner and was hit head-on by a truck. He broke his right shoulder, lacerated his face, and shattered his left arm and several bones in his left leg; after passing several hours splayed in pain on the side of the road, he was rescued by a passerby and driven to a clinic two hours away. He spent seven or so months recovering in hospitals in Kampala and New York, where he had his eighth surgery.

But somehow it's all worth it. One of Brooks's videos from his time with Uganda's Batwa people shows him meeting a white-bearded old man named Kilembe, who was living alone in a straw hut, unable to walk and with very little food. Asked what he most needed, the man said he'd like to live in the nearby village so he wouldn't feel so isolated. "Okay," Brooks said brightly, as if discussing what to make for breakfast, "so we just need to build him a house?" Over the next two weeks, assisted by villagers, Brooks built a thatched-roof mud hut for Kilembe, a communal chicken coop he then filled with chickens, and a beehive colony to help the villagers establish a source of income. After finishing intensive physical therapy, Brooks planned to be back in Uganda by Christmas of 2009 to check up on Kilembe in his new home before continuing on with a round-the-world Guerrilla Aid odyssey meant to promote the idea that small gestures can make a big difference. And that the rewards are entirely mutual.

"Honestly," Brooks declared one day in the winter of 2008, while videotaping the lush hillsides and Batwa villagers using pickaxes to clear land for the coop, "I am the luckiest man on the planet." ◘

Good Tithings

The Bible tells us to tithe. It never adds: "Thou shalt not whine about it." A.J. Jacobs discovers the pleasure inside the pain.

There are many practices from biblical times that are best left in the past. Stoning adulterers comes to mind. As does sacrificing oxen.

But let me tell you about one dusty Middle Eastern custom that deserves a comeback: tithing. For those who skipped Sunday school, tithing is the practice of giving 10 percent of your annual income to the needy. You donate one out of every ten dollars (or shekels or sheep) to the orphans, the widows, the destitute, or the temple high priests. Granted, some folks in 21st-century America still tithe (devout Mormons, for instance, are expected to cough up 10 percent). But the practice has largely gone the way of pharaohs and women named Bathsheba. Which isn't surprising. Tithing is hard as hell, especially in these lean times.

I first learned about tithing a few years ago. At the time, I was trying to follow every rule in the Bible—a journey I chronicled in a book. The Bible told me to tithe. So I tithed.

When I told my wife, Julie, about my plan to tithe, she fretted. In general, she's much more magnanimous than I am. She's a sucker for those charities that send you free sheets of return-address labels with little cartoons of a Rollerblading Ziggy, along with a heartbreaking brochure about lymphoma. I tell her it's emotional blackmail. She ignores me and mails them checks.

But even for Julie 10 percent is high, especially with the ridiculously expensive prospect of raising children in New York City. Julie asked whether I could count my literary agent's fee as a tithe. She was only half-joking.

"Can you at least do 10 percent after taxes?" she said.

That night I called a friend who's a Lutheran pastor. "You shouldn't get too legalistic," he said. "Give what you can. And then give some more. It should feel like a sacrifice."

I studied my Bible for insight. It seems that in the time of ancient Israel—before the Romans took over—no one paid taxes per se. The tithes were the taxes. And the tithing system was as complicated as any 1040 form. The farmers gave to the priests, the temple-keepers, the temple itself, the poor, the widows, and the orphans. So I decided that after-tax tithing was probably okay.

I calculated 10 percent of my projected salary. It wasn't a huge number—but that was precisely the problem. If I were making $10 million a year and had to give away $1 million, that would have been easier.

Although many modern tithers give to their church, I decided to go directly to the needy. I spent hours browsing the Web site charitynavigator.org. It's sort of a Michelin guide to aid organizations. (Even this leads to coveting—they list the salaries of these charity CEOs, and some break half a million.)

I settled on several organizations focusing on children and widows, two groups the Bible says are always in need. One was called Feed the Children, another Save Darfur.

The giving was painful. I mean, 10 percent? That would have an impact on our lives. Vacations would need to be scaled back, new furniture would have to wait. It was a huge amount. When I pressed "send" on the donations, my palms got wet, my heart rate spiked.

But it was a pain mixed with pleasure. When the confirmation e-mails pinged in, I felt good. There's a haunting line from the movie *Chariots of Fire*. It's spoken by Ian Charleson, who plays a deeply religious sprinter in the 1924 Olympics. He says: "When I run, I feel His pleasure." And as I gave away money, I think I might have felt God's pleasure. Which is odd. Because I'm agnostic. I don't know if there's a God or not, but still I felt some higher sense of purpose. It was like a cozy ember that started at the back of my neck and slowly spread its warmth through my skull. I felt like I was doing something I should have done all my life.

That feeling of pleasure when giving—scientists call it the warm-glow effect—isn't strong enough to get most Americans to cough up 10 percent, though. According to the Roper Center for Public Opinion Research, the average American donates about 3 percent of his or her salary to charity. Low-income workers are the most openhanded set, donating an average of 4.5 percent. (Of course, there are many exceedingly generous high-income people. Angelina Jolie has said she gives away a third of her income. The pastor Rick Warren reverse tithes—he gives away 90 percent of his profits from his megaselling books.)

I must confess that I haven't tithed every year since. I'm a quasi tither. In 2009 I donated about 7 percent of my income. Tithing for me is a goal that I want to meet but sometimes don't. (I will, however, be tithing the writer's fee for this article. How can I not?)

I've developed some strategies to help make tithing easier. The key is to make it concrete. Try thinking in terms of time. Every ten minutes of work, you are essentially doing one minute of volunteering for the needy. Six times an hour you're doing a mitzvah! Since I'm a writer, I also tell myself this: One out of every ten words belongs to someone deserving. In that previous sentence, it was the word *deserving*.

I also try to remember what I teach my sons. Sharing is caring, I always tell them. If my son had two lollipops in his pocket, and a friend asked for one, I'd tell him to fish one out of his pocket and hand it over. It's the proper thing to do. I should practice what I preach.

Finally, I try to think of tithing as a sort of cosmic 10 percent tip. Scientists say that gratitude is like a psychological wonder drug. And by tithing, I'm saying thank you to the universe—or to God or to fate or to whatever you believe in—for allowing me to be alive. I want to acknowledge how lucky I am to have food, a roof, a bed, a warm shower, and a father who didn't sacrifice me on top of a mountain. That deserves a donation to the Big Tip Jar in the sky, don't you think? ◘

> As I gave away money, I think I might have felt God's pleasure. Which is odd. Because I'm agnostic.

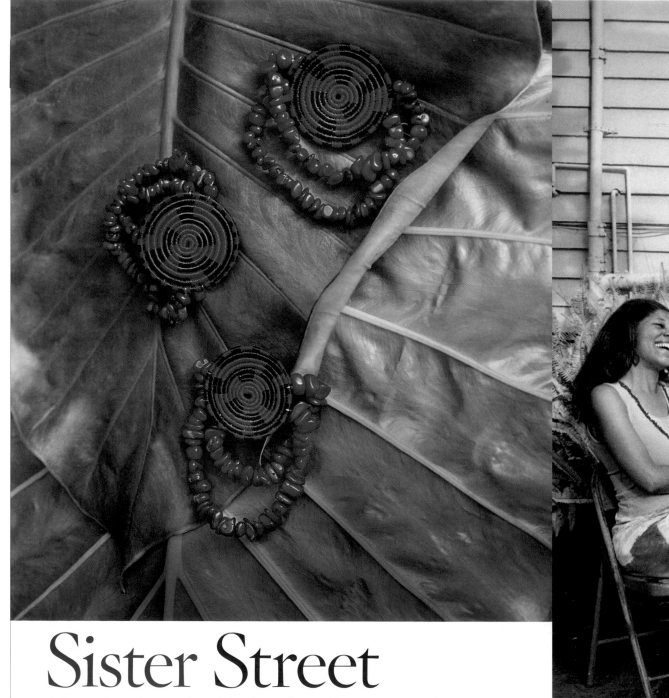

Sister Street

A levee breaks, and suddenly artists all over New Orleans are forced to rebuild their lives. Half a world away in Rwanda, survivors still fight every day to move beyond the genocide that wiped out nearly one million people. Now women from both countries are making friends, money, and the ultimate fashion statement. Introducing a brand-new *O* Bracelet! By Liz Brody

FRIENDSHIP BRACELETS After a day of making jewelry together, two visitors from Rwanda bond over a joke with their hosts in New Orleans. *Back row, from left:* Stella Jones, Asante Salaam, Brigitte Nyampinga (from Rwanda), Beatriz Soco Ocampo. *Front row:* Chanell Gautreaux, Rukiya Brown, Cely Tapplette-Pedescleaux, Janet Nkubana (also from Rwanda), and Ausettua Amor Amenkum.

On a muggy Saturday morning in May 2009, 24 women showed up at the Stella Jones Gallery in downtown New Orleans. They were African-Americans mostly, from girls barely out of their teens to "been there, honey" grandmothers, almost all dressed in tennis shoes and jeans topped off with a bossy pair of earrings. Some came family-style—small clans of mothers, daughters, cousins, aunts—while others arrived arm in arm as teams of friends; all of them artists, carrying bag lunches and cups of take-out coffee, ready for a day of work and gab.

Inside the gallery, the women greeted one another and went off to find jewelry needles—thin wires with a flexible loop at the end—which they'd be using to thread beads with all day. Then they took their places at long folding tables set with bowls and cardboard egg cartons full of round turquoise beads and glittering citrine crystals, bone tiles of zebra-striped batik and nuggets of blazing-red coral. As the conversation jumped between their two favorite topics—food and men—the women sorted through the bowls and egg cartons, picking out beads as though at a buffet.

Stella Jones herself was dressed in trusty straightforward solids, blouse over slacks, silvery Avia sneakers, and, of course, the earrings—$2 white metal hoops. To create this gathering, she had recruited artists from all over the city. Four years post-Katrina, many of the women were still living in temporary homes. Half of them were jobless. But on this day they had a triple purpose—to earn a little money, to welcome two honored guests, and to help make something special: *O Bracelets*.

If you own an *O Bracelet*, thank you: Our four previous editions were crafted by East African women who, for their labor, earned up to 12 times their average daily wage—money that has put food on their tables, sent their kids to school, and paid for the installation of clean water systems in eight villages. Now with the fifth edition, we decided, along with our partner Fair Winds Trading, not only to continue our work in Africa but to extend the project to women in our own country. We chose New Orleans for our home base because, with its rich history, love of jazz,

and carnival traditions, it is in many ways the most African city in America.

We also chose a design with two distinct parts to reflect both groups of women coming together: Each bracelet has a patterned disk that sits on the wrist like a watch face, and a beaded band. Stella is managing the beading process in New Orleans, while the disks have been woven by 250 women in Rwanda under the direction of one of today's guests, Janet Nkubana. A champion of improving life for rural African women, Janet has come to Stella's gallery along with a young Rwandan weaver she's trained, Brigitte Nyampinga. They're here to hand off the disks in person and spend a week making bracelets with the local beaders—some of whom are also painters, quilters, sculptors, and textile artists, and one of whom, Rukiya Brown, makes dolls. (See oprah.com/omagextras to read more about the artists.)

Dressed in a billowy shift from Cameroon covered with a chunky jumble of beads and silver, Rukiya has arrived looking more African than the Africans. As it turns out, most of the women in the room have never been to Africa, which is why several say this project is perfect for them. In fact, much more than the prospect of earning some extra money, what moved them to participate was the chance to connect to their roots—to something that can't be ripped away by a storm.

At one point, as she works, Rukiya looks down at the gallery's concrete floor, which has been signed and drawn on by visitors. Under her feet someone has written: "Keep showing us who we are—and who we can be."

The daughter of sharecroppers, Stella Jones grew up in Houston sleeping three to a bed. Every Sunday she and her six brothers and sisters would pile into the family's green Chevy and arrive at church smelling like gasoline because the car was so old it had a hole in the floor.

As a young woman, Stella worked her way through a pharmacy degree ("Whites were not ready to accept me as a pharmacist—they threw the medicine back through the window," she says matter-of-factly), followed by a master's degree in public health and an MD at Texas Tech. Along the way, she married and had two children. She moved to New Orleans in 1976 when she started her ob-gyn residency at the sprawling old Charity

Many of the women were homeless, jobless. But they had a purpose— to help make something special.

TWO COUNTRIES, ONE WORLD *Clockwise from top,* New Orleans: Rukiya, a doll artist (*left*), and Brigitte outside Rukiya's apartment in the Treme, center of the city's African-American culture. When they met, the two women discovered they had endured similar tragedies. Rwanda: Janet (*right*) with her sister Joy Ndungutse (*left*) at their Gahaya Links training center, where 250 women—including Brigitte (*center*)—learned to weave the disks used in our new O Bracelet. New Orleans: Stella Jones, who transformed her gallery into a jewelry-making center.

FAMILY TIES *Above,* Rwanda: Brigitte and her children (*from left*), Diane, 13, Divine, 8, and Eric, 14. "We go without food two or three days a week," Diane says, "but we're used to it." Brigitte hopes the bracelets will get her family back on its feet. *Left,* New Orleans: Ausettua dances in her handmade Mardi Gras suit.

Hospital—such a medical abyss, she says, "they not only had RANDO procedures (Residents Ain't Never Done One), but they also had SANSO (Staff Ain't Never Seen One)." The pace at Charity was intense. It was nothing for Stella to deliver 30 babies in a day—you could tell how many by the number of times she'd rolled up the cuffs on her scrubs, since between births there was no time to change.

The work didn't ease when she opened her own practice on Tulane Avenue, which mainly served disadvantaged black women—often there was a line out the door, and they came to her not just for medical treatment but for help with all their problems. Though by now Stella and her husband had four children, and she was busier than ever, she loved treating her patients. But over the years, the difficulty of their lives began to wear her

down—especially the violence they lived with as New Orleans's crime rate spiked in the mid-1990s and the city became known as the murder capital of America.

"There are days that you don't forget," Stella says. "And I will never forget the day in 1995—I'd been up all night with a difficult delivery, and my nurse met me at the door and said, 'You're not going to believe who's in room 3.' It was the mother of a boy who'd just been killed. I thought, *Well, fine, I can handle that.* But then she said, 'Let me tell you who's in room 4.' I asked who, and she said Mrs. So-and-So. 'It was her son who did the killing.' And I just stood there, thinking, *Nothing has changed. It's time for me to go.*"

After attending to the two women and all her other patients that day, Stella took her degrees down off the wall, stashed them in the back of her banged-up gray Toyota Corolla, and drove away.

The next year, she opened the Stella Jones Gallery. When Katrina destroyed her home—a stately white-brick, five-bedroom that's still gaping and gutted—the gallery survived. In New Orleans, it is *the* place to buy African-American art. And after the Rwandans show up, it is the place to bead.

When Janet Nkubana arrives in New Orleans, she has part one of the bracelet project with her: 1,000 patterned disks made of tightly coiled sisal wound with rayon thread (Rwandan silk was deemed too fragile for daily wear). The other 7,000—the women intend to make 8,000 O Bracelets—are headed this way, too, soon to be shipped from Rwanda. The disks are traditionally used there as tops to milk jugs—milk being a cherished part of the Rwandan diet. When Janet was a girl, she says, her mother used to send her off on a day's walk to find cattle farmers who'd let her fetch water or clean up cow dung—whatever work they needed—in exchange for a jug of milk. The jugs were made of dried gourds; if dropped, they broke. "Sometimes on the way back, you'd stumble," she says. "And then you'd just sit down in the middle of the road and cry because the milk was spilled." She laughs. "Yes, we had that saying, too."

Janet, a Rwandan, grew up in a refugee camp in Uganda—was actually born on the way to the camp in 1963 as her parents fled their country during a wave of ethnic violence against the Tutsi minority. The contrast between her life at 45 and her "humble beginnings" (which she refers to as fondly as if they were beloved pets) never fails to inspire her. What the family of 12 had to eat—which wasn't enough—they shared from a single saucepan. The only privacy in their drafty hut was afforded by her mother's dress, which she would unwrap from her body at night and hang as a curtain to separate herself and her husband from the ten children. But when Janet was 13, she got on a bus in her first pair of shoes and headed, courtesy of a scholarship, to one of Uganda's best boarding schools. And although the "rich men's children" teased her there, she was a quick study to a better life.

In 1994, when she heard about the genocide going on in Rwanda—100 days during which the country's Hutu ethnic majority killed nearly a million people, mostly Tutsis—Janet was 30, working in a restaurant in Kampala, and raising four children. She'd been through Idi Amin's brutality and now found herself struggling in her marriage. Not only could her husband be violent, but he was also having an affair with the babysitter. "When I found out, I was hot beyond talking," she says. She packed her bags to go "home"—

Painters, sculptors, quilters, textile artists, and a dollmaker—today, they're all beaders.

back to Rwanda, the homeland she'd never seen. She was tired of being a refugee.

Soon she was living in Kigali, Rwanda's capital, which the genocide had turned into a city of desperation; the killing was over, but you could still trip over a skull or a body on the street. Janet got a job managing a rundown hotel, and began scrounging food for the hungry women who constantly came asking for help. "It was so hard to see these women begging, to see them suffer with no dignity," she says. "But then, instead of empty hands, they started coming with baskets they had woven." To encourage them, Janet opened a little shop in the hotel to sell their goods. Her older sister, Joy Ndungutse, quickly saw the potential and said, "Come, let's run a business."

With the sort of drive that could move the equator, the sisters started a small venture they called Gahaya Links and built it into a weaving cooperative of nearly 4,000 women, most of them living in tiny villages, many of them Hutus and Tutsis working side by side. Today the company sells its products to Macy's and Starbucks (in partnership with Fair Winds Trading, which helps develop markets for the world's poorest artisans). It is the kind of business Rwanda's president, Paul Kagame, believes is essential for his country's future. He sees enterprise as the key to moving beyond the need for foreign aid—and knows full well just how enterprising Rwandan women can be. Fifty-six percent of Rwanda's parliament and 37 percent of its cabinet are women—"and not just as figureheads, but making decisions," he says. "Women have proved that they are just as capable as men, and in many cases, they are doing much better."

At the gallery, surrounded by boldly colorful paintings, Janet helps the New Orleans women strategize on how to get their 8,000 bracelets finished on time. Of the five designs, they decide to focus on the red-and-black one first, and start diving into the bowls of coral. As everyone strings and beads, pushing the squeezable loop of their needles through the small holes, Janet describes her favorite comfort food: matoke, a mashed plantain dish. Which leads to Rukiya Brown's secret banana pudding recipe—which leads to everyone passing around a bag of Hershey's Kisses.

As the women work, passersby in business suits peer in and ask what's going on.

■

In April 1994, 15-year-old Brigitte Nyampinga huddled in a church along with thousands of other terrified Tutsis, waiting to die.

When a neighbor arrived at the church saying that Brigitte's father and older brother had been killed, she told herself it wasn't true, trying to buy a little credit until her heart could afford to pay. But what happened afterward was something she could never have prepared for.

On April 15, the church flew apart in an explosion of grenades and gunfire. When the killing stopped, Brigitte's mother, two sisters, and two brothers lay strewn among the pews and Bibles, somewhere in the human discard. "I couldn't really have any feeling," she says. "I was almost dead."

At the Red Cross Hospital—where one of the attackers took her, promising to kill her later—she lay in bed with a machete wound to the shoulder. Hutu militia came and murdered patients randomly. Even worse, for Brigitte, were their menacing threats of rape. A machete was one thing, but the idea of a Hutu driving his hate into her like a stake in the ground, boring through the only thing she had left, her dignity—that was unbearable.

A Hutu woman on staff took a kind eye to Brigitte, and convinced two watchmen to lock her in a storage room so she'd be safe. But the first night, the men let themselves in with clear intentions. *Ndabyanze—I refuse*—she kept telling them. They beat her with machetes, then took her by the legs. "To me," she says, "that was the end of my world."

The Hutu woman, seeing her mistake, arranged an escape over the hospital's barbed wire fence. But outside, there was no safe place for a Tutsi girl. After a few days, Brigitte found a prayer meeting. It was there that a neighbor who had participated in the attack on the church spotted her. He forced her home with him, into his bed, and kept her as a sex slave. Within weeks she was pregnant. She was alive, but what did that mean, she asked herself, if you went to church only to be murdered, or to the hospital just to get raped?

When Brigitte told her story to the women at Stella's gallery, with Janet translating, the tide of warmth that washed out from them almost capsized her. It was the Rwandan women's first night in town, and Stella had

"It was so hard to see these women begging with no dignity. But then, instead of empty hands, they started to bring baskets they'd woven."

summoned her artists for a welcoming party, commanding: "Show them the love!"

And the women did, gathering around Brigitte, taking her hands, touching her face. Although she's 30, her skin is as smooth as a girl's—as if, upon meeting up with the machete blade 15 years ago, her body closed for business, just stopped aging in its tracks. And when she tearfully explained that she'd lost every member of her family, the group, without seeming to move, surrounded her and took hold.

"You have family now," said Rose Bratcher, a painter, walking up to hug her.

"You're so beautiful," added Herreast Harrison, one of the city's well-known beaders, taking Brigitte's face in her hands.

Stella came forward with two fancy umbrellas—a New Orleans tradition—and handed one to each of the guests, declaring, "We're all under the same umbrella."

And soon Ausettua Amor Amenkum, the gravelly voiced leader of an Africa-influenced dance company, had everyone in a circle clapping and chanting: "We say Ashe, we say Ashe because there is power in sisters being together. We thank you, Brigitte, for coming."

Wandering through the gallery after the welcome festivities ebbed, Brigitte and Janet stopped in one of the small side rooms, where they were captivated by a two-foot mannequin-like figure behind glass. The piece is called *Unforgivable Blackness:* a young, pitch-dark woman with big lips, high cheekbones, and wild explosions of hair, wearing a ruffled, lacy white wedding dress, her eyes closed in a way that suggests an uneasy vulnerability. It is one of Rukiya's dolls.

Rukiya Brown, who had just turned 57, has been making dolls since she was a girl in Chicago. She comes from a large family—eight brothers and sisters by four different fathers—and was raised by a mother who worked as a maid and switched price stickers at the supermarket because it was the only way she could afford to put meat on the table. The family moved to New Orleans when Rukiya was 15. That year, despite her mother's salvos about not falling for the first man who "showed his teeth," Rukiya ended up dating just such a man and eventually got pregnant. People said her boyfriend was "too fast" for her, and she found out just how fast he was when she caught him sneaking off to see his twin babies—same age as Rukiya's daughter—and their mother, another girl in another housing project.

Still, Rukiya married him and they moved to England after he joined the air force. She pulled herself together there, working in promotions for the base, studying textiles and design in London. But he'd had one too many affairs, and when she got back to New Orleans in 1995, she decided she was done with him, and got busy making dolls.

Rukiya met Stella at the New Orleans Jazz Fest in 2002. "She had a booth and was selling her dolls, and I was just awed by them," Stella says. (She has since given Rukiya two gallery shows, and Rukiya still can't believe it. "I had no idea I was an artist.")

Stella met Janet the morning of the welcome party. Within minutes, they'd sized each other up with a flash of kindred-spirit recognition. Aside from having defied expectations professionally, they're both proud of the children they've raised. (Stella reeled off the occupations of her four—corporate attorney, foreign-service generalist in the state department, pediatric dentist, Wall Street bond trader—and Janet quickly countered: eldest daughter going into her second year at the Harvard Kennedy School, first-born son a music DJ at a radio station, the younger three at home, excelling or else.) The two women also share an unquestioned commitment to help-

ing their sisters—the Rukiyas and Brigittes of the world.

Janet met Brigitte last year in Kinyinya, a community built by the Rwandan government for the most severely psychologically traumatized genocide victims. Janet had gone there to volunteer and found Brigitte and her three children—all the result of rape—making do in a mud-brick shelter. Janet has big dreams for Brigitte. She taught her to weave baskets and disks for O Bracelets. But migraines and depression—which have plagued Brigitte since the genocide—sometimes make it hard for her to work. As a result, two to three days a week, she and her children go without food.

At O bracelet central, there have been a series of problems: First the stretchy cord was too thick to thread through the holes in some of the beads. Then the sumptuous red of the coral turned out to travel—onto one's wrist! (Fair Winds Trading had to find different cord, and then replacement beads—no-bleed red glass.) And finally, what kind of knot is best to secure the beaded bands? (An overhand knot is the strongest but, because of the bead placement, not feasible. It will have to be a half-hitch. Make that three half-hitches.)

One day, to give everyone a break from beading, Rukiya invites Janet and Brigitte to please come over to her place if they'd like to see more dolls. A few days later,

The O Bracelet
How to lend a hand and decorate your wrist.

Each bracelet has been around the world—the first thread woven in Rwanda and the last knot tied in New Orleans. The bracelet-makers on both continents are using their earnings to rebuild their lives. "The women are very grateful," says Stella Jones, the gallery owner who is overseeing the New Orleans group. "For some of them, this is their only source of income."

All the disks are rayon thread woven over sisal. *Clockwise from top left:* **1.** Red and black Czech glass beads, $42. **2.** Brown Indian

bone beads, $35. **3.** Black-and-white-batik bone beads, $35.
TO ORDER: Visit macys.com/obracelet. As part of a continued commitment to assisting the women of Rwanda, Macy's is helping make these bracelets available and will receive no profit on their sale. At the time of this printing, all three bracelets are available for purchase.

Special thanks to Georgia Wilson, owner of The Bead Shop in New Orleans, whose group of artists also helped make bracelets.

seven or eight of the New Orleans women escort their Rwandan guests to Rukiya's apartment in a clapboard house with peeling pink paint, a 20-minute walk from the gallery. Rukiya doesn't have a doorbell, so the women holler for her, then settle on the stoop, swapping stories and telling jokes.

Rukiya opens the door, lets Brigitte and Janet in, and leads them through the apartment. Dolls are everywhere—standing on shelves, ledges, and windowsills, propped in corners, hanging from the wall. The latest figures are made in honor of the women of Congo, who are being gruesomely raped in a drawn-out ethnic war that originally spilled over from the Rwandan genocide.

Brigitte asks why the Congo dolls have shards of mirror for eyes.

"To show that if it can happen to them, it can happen to you," Rukiya says, motioning her to sit on the couch.

"What pain, what sorrows, do you have in your life that have driven you?" Brigitte asks, looking around.

"I, too, was raped," Rukiya says, leaning closer. "Many, many times. There was no baby, but it was still a violation. And I was 13, 14. And I didn't talk about it to anyone for 30 years."

"How many were there?" Brigitte asks.

"Ten. And afterward, everywhere I went, people would say, 'Oh, there's that girl that got a train pulled on her.' It got to a point where I just would not feel anything."

"Even to this year, I don't have any desire," Brigitte says, looking down at her hands. "I can flirt with a man, but once he crosses the line, I become someone else. All I want to do is bite him—and if I had a knife, I'd cut him. I'm only 30, and I would like to be in love someday, but I can't."

"That's me, too. And it was hard to share affection with my kids," says Rukiya, whose son is serving a ten-year prison sentence for dealing drugs, while her daughter ended up going to San Jose State and becoming a child therapist.

Everyone in the car hugs, arms encircling arms, until it's hard to tell where one woman begins and another ends.

"It's still very hard for me to accept my children," Brigitte admits. "I love them, but I don't have the heart to be their mother. Sometimes I'll take the food I'm cooking and throw it away because I'm just angry."

"We may have to go through more pain than other people," Rukiya says. "But out of making dolls, I find a peace. All of us have a gift that God gives us. And you, Brigitte, are a weaver."

Before the week is over, many of the New Orleans women offer their hospitality. At the homes of Herreast Harrison and Joyce Montana, Brigitte and Janet get a glimpse of a local African-American tradition: the handmade costumes worn on Mardi Gras. The "suits," as they are known, are stunning cascades of wildly colored feathers and bravura beading that take a whole year to design and fabricate, usually involving a full family effort. The way the women describe it, when you step into a suit to join the parade, you are transformed. You become your heritage. You reach deep into your African roots.

Brigitte and Janet are deeply moved by what has been lost in New Orleans. Both are overwhelmed by seeing street after street of rotting, abandoned houses and patches of dirt where libraries and schools once stood. One afternoon, driving through the Lower Ninth Ward with a few of their hosts, the car stops where the levee broke. The women look up at the street sign.

Sister Street.

"When I am here, I don't feel like I'm an African," Janet suddenly says. "I feel like I am one of you."

Everyone in the car hugs, arms encircling arms, until it's hard to tell where one woman begins and another ends. Because what started as a project to make bracelets has turned into something more—the creation of a band of sisters. ◨

Missions
Accomplished

In 2008 we met 80 women hoping to get some big ideas off
the ground. Within one year, three of those ideas had taken flight.
World, prepare to be changed. Katie Arnold-Ratliff reports.

A t *O,* we may be all about the aha moment, but until 2008's Women Rule! conference in New York City (featured in our November 2008 issue), we'd never seen so many of them happening at once. The 80 women having the insights were those who'd won our Women Rule! contest—cocreated with the White House Project, a nonprofit organization that gives women the training they need to advance in business, politics, and media. Chosen from more than 3,000 entrants, all were self-starters with one thing in common: the idea for an innovative project that hadn't yet taken shape. The women immersed themselves in three days of workshops, lectures, and coaching on everything from fund-raising to public speaking, and at the end, the scrimmage for business cards and e-mail addresses turned into a full-contact sport. Marie Wilson, the White House Project's president (and cofounder of Take Our Daughters to Work Day), understands the power of female networking. "At the conference," she says, "we gave the women the tools to push their ideas forward—and that's important—but the energy and encouragement they got from each other was the kicker for me. And it is every time." After one year, three participants told us how that energy put them over the top.

Raolat Abdulai

27, Clarksville, Maryland

HER PROJECT:
A free holistic medical clinic

HER WOMEN RULE! TAKEAWAY:
Always be ready to rethink the plan.

When it comes to healthcare, something revolutionary is happening in Washington, D.C.—and not on Capitol Hill. Just beyond the double doors of Howard University Hospital, in the city's LeDroit Park neighborhood, a brand-new clinic is providing free health and social services to uninsured patients, all thanks to a fourth-year medical student named Raolat Abdulai.

"I'm going to come there and make a difference," Abdulai had written in her application to Howard University College of Medicine, where she was accepted in 2006. Born in Nigeria (her family moved to Maryland when she was 5), she devised a plan to open the student-run clinic during her second year of med school. She wanted it to provide comprehensive services to patients lacking insurance—including assistance with mental health issues, housing, food, and transportation—and also give future doctors practice in delivering holistic, compassionate care. Her professors were enthusiastic, and Abdulai quickly assembled a planning committee of fellow medical students from Howard, Georgetown, and George Washington universities; together, she imagined, they would organize the jointly run clinic.

But even scheduling a meeting with the time-pressed students from all three schools proved nearly impossible. Between the logistical challenges and a lack of funding, Abdulai's project had all but flatlined when she won a place at Women Rule!, where she says she learned two valuable skills: the ability to write a business plan and the art of adaptation. "One of the speakers told us, 'If you have a plan that isn't working, shift your approach. Even if it's not how you originally envisioned getting there, it's going to help you reach the finish line.'"

After the conference, Abdulai decided to pare down her volunteer pool. Instead of reaching out to three schools for students, she narrowed her focus to Howard. She contacted the school's alumni for donations, and in addition received $30,000 from the Association of American Medical Colleges Caring for Community Grant program. Once the money was in place, she enlisted the help of a few Howard MBA students to wrangle the financials. Finally, after finding a site in the hospital's outpatient center, an attending physician to supervise all patient care, and two dozen willing volunteers, Abdulai opened her clinic in June 2009.

It was a meteoric accomplishment, especially on top of going to medical school. But bafflingly, after all that hard work—the planning, the passion, the effort—the patients didn't come. "I was so disappointed," Abdulai says. "We thought everything was fine, and then it just... it just didn't work." That's when she remembered the "stay flexible" message. And she realized that the clinic's location, in the depths of the hospital, was too out-of-the-way for the patients it was meant to serve—primarily walk-ins. So she moved it just off the hospital's main 5th Street entrance.

Today patients fill the spacious waiting area. When one arrives, medical students take her history before her case is presented to the attending physician. Each patient is also assessed for social needs and connected with health insurance, housing, and food services. A medical student follows up after she leaves.

Patient feedback has been so positive that Abdulai is already considering ways to expand. Howard medical students are lining up to participate. "If it wasn't for the conference," says Abdulai, who has decided to pursue internal medicine, "I'd probably still be running in place." ◑

single lawn mower, along with a schedule of everyone's turn to use it. This was the idea that got Micki Krimmel, an energetic Internet consultant, fired up to start a new Web site: neighborgoods.net.

By no means limited to lawn mowers (though there is currently one available to borrow in Austin if you're interested), NeighborGoods has everything from computer printers to concertinas, which members in the same locale can borrow, rent, sell, or give away to one another. (For example, while you might lend your ladder to anyone in your network, you'd probably offer your favorite boots only to friends, and you'd likely charge money for the use of your car.) The site keeps track of each exchange and alerts users when a requested item becomes available.

Founder of the popular Mickipedia blog and video series—a rollicking catalog of her thoughts on life, politics, and her Roller Derby team—Krimmel conceived her idea after working for the company behind Al Gore's Oscar-winning 2006 documentary *An Inconvenient Truth.* Charged with creating a social-networking campaign for the film, she came to understand the transformative power of viral word of mouth. "We were always talking about building communities, and having a smaller footprint. Instead of getting rid of stuff, I thought, *Why not share it?"*

Yet despite her extensive consulting experience, when it came to starting a site from scratch, she says, "I felt like I was jumping headfirst into an unknown world." Krimmel's first hurdle involved securing financial underwriting. "I was spending so much time thinking about partners and investment, it was overwhelming," she says.

But then she attended Women Rule!, where she met scores of other women dealing with similar roadblocks: "I remember thinking, *Instead of focusing on what I don't have, I can focus on what I do have."* Shortly after she returned home, one of her consulting clients decided to invest in NeighborGoods and gave her what she needed to get the project off the ground. The site launched its trial run in July 2009.

Eventually, members will be charged a small fee to help cover NeighborGoods' administrative costs, but for now the site is free. "The environmental and financial benefits of sharing are obvious," says Krimmel. "Really what I hope this does is bring people together. Ideally, by sharing things like power tools and camping gear, we can regain the sense of local community we seem to have lost." ◖

Micki Krimmel
31, Los Angeles

HER PROJECT:
A green, online swap meet

HER WOMEN RULE! TAKEAWAY:
When lacking resources,
look within yourself.

Picture a suburb full of lawn mowers, one per garage. Each machine is sturdy, dependable, a sizable investment, and—given the energy required to manufacture, store, package, and ship it—quite the carbon culprit, especially since most lawn mowers see action only once every week or two. Now picture the same neighborhood with just a

Lea Webb

29, Binghamton, New York

HER PROJECT:
A grocery store in an
underserved neighborhood

HER WOMEN RULE! TAKEAWAY:
If you're out of options, rally the troops.

It may be only one block long, but Pearne Street—located in Binghamton's North Side—offers a crash course in the socioeconomic challenges facing the area. The crumbling Victorian homes, apartment buildings in disrepair, and trash-strewn lots give way to Binghamton Plaza, where one of the neighborhood's two grocery stores used to stand. Now the plaza is almost empty except for a Kmart, and there's nowhere to buy fresh food for more than a mile in each direction. A dispiriting sight, to say the least—unless you're accompanied by City Councilwoman Lea Webb. The first African-American to hold office in Broome County, Webb knows how to look past the problems to see the potential. She points out municipal notices posted on the derelict houses: Thanks to her efforts, the city will be addressing these eyesores. That vacant lot? It's slated to become a community garden. And the abandoned McDonald's in the plaza? This is her biggest coup yet. The structure—empty for a decade and surrounded by cracked asphalt—will soon be torn down to make way for the neighborhood's first grocery store in more than 15 years.

A lifelong resident of the city, Webb understands firsthand the frustrations of having to take a taxi or public transportation to buy fresh food. But it was in 2006 at a community meeting that a warm, intense woman named Mrs. Marshall—affectionately known in the neighborhood as Grandma—stood up and said something that galvanized her: "She told me she didn't want to see any more old women struggling to get off the bus with their groceries," Webb says. That was the moment Webb put the cause at the top of her to-do list.

At first she made only stuttering progress as she waded through miles of bureaucratic red tape, while organizing a weekly farmers' market as a stopgap solution. But as the months wore on, Webb grew discouraged. How would she obtain a site, funding, approval from the city—or even advice? Despite her loyal supporters and iron will, the project stalled.

Then she won a spot at Women Rule! and met Libby Cook, president of Philanthropiece (a foundation that supports local service projects) and cofounder of Wild Oats Markets, the second largest natural foods chain in North America. Cook, who counseled some of the participants at the conference, offered Webb guidance for months afterward. Webb also took home a valuable lesson from Marie Wilson: "She said, 'Bring people into your project who have something to gain from its success,'" Webb recalls. "It was so simple—and so smart."

Once home, she picked up the phone. It wasn't hard to find people who would benefit from the grocery project. "It meant jobs at the store, and jobs for those constructing it. It meant healthier residents. It meant other stores being willing to develop nearby. It meant money staying right here in this neighborhood," says Webb. She called Binghamton University professors, Broome County officials, community groups, local charities, the mayor, and a state assemblyperson. Her outreach efforts eventually caught the attention of New York state senator Malcolm Smith. "Government, community, church, the private sector—Lea's got them all behind her," he says. "That's not easy to do. There's always one missing." Impressed by her crusade, Smith pledged $150,000 of state money toward the old McDonald's demolition and the clearing of the site.

Finally, the whole thing came together. With input from one of Cook's contacts, Webb chose a vendor—the Save-a-Lot grocery chain, which agreed to meet all of Webb's criteria (they must hire locally, pay at least a few dollars above minimum wage, provide employee benefits, and address the area's ethnically diverse food needs). With environmental inspections under way, the store is expected to open this year. "At the groundbreaking," Webb says, "I'm going to have tears in my eyes." ◐

O thanks the White House Project staff as well as American Express, which funded the training program, for making Women Rule! possible. To learn more about the 77 other Women Rule! alumnae who are also changing the world, visit thewhitehouseproject.org/womenrule.

WHAT I KNOW FOR SURE: OPRAH

"That was an aha moment for me—to experience how a 'small' act can have a huge impact."

I'm one of the blessed ones. I get paid—highly—for being myself and for doing what I most enjoy: sharing ideas with other people. I live a big life. But in reality it's the small things that fill me up. I sliced a fresh peach today that was so sweet, so succulent, so divinely peachy that even as I was eating it I thought, *There are no words to adequately describe this peach—one has to taste it to understand the true definition of peachiness.* I closed my eyes, the better to feel the flavor. Even that wasn't enough, though, so I saved the last two bites to share with Stedman, to see if he affirmed my assessment of best peach ever. He took the first bite and said, "Mmm, mmm, mmm…this peach reminds me of childhood." And so that small thing got bigger, as all things do when shared in a spirit of appreciation.

The summer of 2009 while I was visiting the Oprah Winfrey Leadership Academy in South Africa, four seventh graders came to my little house on campus to escort me to their dorm for a surprise. When I walked into the recreation area, there stood the entire class: 63 girls, all in uniform, many with musical instruments, others prepared to recite a poem and then sing a song they'd composed to thank me for the opportunities they've been given at the school. No fanfare, no stage. Just me, the school's resident mother, and Gayle's two children, William and Kirby, listening to the girls pour out their appreciation.

Of course, I cried.

And when they finished, I said, "Girls, I've received many awards and accolades, but nothing have I felt more deeply than what you did here on your own today."

One child said, "Mum Oprah, we didn't know what to give you, so we decided to give you ourselves. This is from our hearts."

That was an aha moment for me—to experience how a "small" act can actually have a huge impact.

The largesse of their efforts to show their gratitude—to secretly compose, rehearse, and perform their own song and poetry—is the sweetest gift. I'll treasure it forever.

What I know for sure: Any act of appreciation affirms our connection to each other. Validates us. Expands who we are in the world. Deepens our spirit. And can turn an ordinary moment into an extraordinary peachy and praiseful day.

Oprah

Breathing Space

EARTH SHADOW AT DAWN FROM MOUNT TAMALPAIS STATE PARK, CALIFORNIA, 2001 | Photograph by Galen Rowell

ABOUT THE CONTRIBUTORS

UWEM AKPAN is a Jesuit priest living in Nigeria. His collection of short stories is *Say You're One of Them* (Little, Brown).

KATIE ARNOLD-RATLIFF is an assistant editor at *O*. Her forthcoming novel is *Bright Before Us* (Tin House Press).

CELIA BARBOUR is *O*'s contributing food editor.

KIM BARNES is the author of the novel *A Country Called Home* (Knopf).

NAOMI BARR is a research editor at *O*.

RICK BASS is a writer whose works include *The Wild Marsh* (Houghton Mifflin Harcourt).

JO ANN BEARD is the author of the autobiographical essay collection *The Boys of My Youth* (Little, Brown).

MARTHA BECK writes a monthly column for *O*. She is a life coach and has written six books, including *Steering by Starlight* (Rodale).

BETSY BERNE's novel is *Bad Timing* (Villard). She has written for *The New Yorker, Vogue,* and *The New York Times.*

AMY BLOOM is a psychotherapist and novelist. Her books include the bestsellers *Where the God of Love Hangs Out* and *Away* (both Random House). She is a writer-in-residence at Wesleyan University.

ALAIN DE BOTTON has written six nonfiction books, including *The Architecture of Happiness* and *The Pleasures and Sorrows of Work* (both Pantheon). He is the founder of the School of Life, a London-based educational center that helps students find meaningful livelihoods.

EVA LUX BRAUN is a Holocaust survivor who shares her message of hope in schools in the New York City area.

POLLY BREWSTER is a freelance writer, blogger, and web developer. She lives in Brooklyn, New York.

LIZ BRODY is a freelance writer and a blogger for shine.yahoo.com.

GERALDINE BROOKS won the 2006 Pulitzer Prize for her novel *March*. Her most recent historical novel is *People of the Book* (both Penguin).

FARAI CHIDEYA is piloting *Pop and Politics*, a syndicated public radio show.

SUZAN COLÓN is an *O* contributing writer and the author of the memoir *Cherries in Winter* (Doubleday).

SARA CORBETT is a contributing writer for *The New York Times Magazine*.

KELLY CORRIGAN is the author of *The New York Times* bestseller *The Middle Place*. Her latest work is *Lift* (both Voice), a meditation on parenting.

KRISTY DAVIS is an associate editor at *O*. She is currently at work on a collection of short stories.

JUNOT DÍAZ's novel *The Brief Wondrous Life of Oscar Wao* (Riverhead) won the Pulitzer Prize in 2008.

ANNE DRANITSARIS, PhD, is a Toronto-based psychotherapist and consultant who designs and administers personality assessments.

MARY DUENWALD is a deputy editor for *The New York Times* Op-Ed page.

GILLIAN FASSEL is a writer based in San Antonio, Texas.

MARY A. FISCHER is an investigative reporter who has written for *GQ, Men's Journal,* and *Elle.*

HELEN FISHER, PhD, is a biological anthropologist at Rutgers University. Her latest book is *Why Him? Why Her? How to Find and Keep Lasting Love* (Henry Holt).

RAJMOHAN GANDHI is the author of *Gandhi: The Man, His People, and the Empire* (University of California Press). He is a research professor at the Center for South Asian and Middle Eastern Studies at the University of Illinois at Urbana-Champaign.

MEG GILES lives in Brooklyn, New York, with her husband and two daughters. She is currently writing a book about family.

ALLISON GLOCK is a contributor to *ESPN The Magazine* and author of the memoir *Beauty Before Comfort* (Knopf).

TIMOTHY GOWER is a journalist and co-author of *The Sugar Fix: The High-Fructose Fallout That is Making You Fat and Sick* (Pocket Books).

BOB GREENE is a bestselling author, exercise physiologist, certified personal trainer, and founder of thebestlife.com.

JANE HAMILTON is the author of the novels *Laura Rider's Masterpiece* (Grand Central), *A Map of the World*, and *The Book of Ruth* (both Anchor).

SARI HARRAR is a freelance writer based in Bucks County, Pennsylvania. Her articles about medicine and science have appeared in *Reader's Digest, Good Housekeeping,* and *Women's Health.*

JOHN HASTINGS is a health writer and editor living in New York.

JESSICA HELFAND is the author of *Scrapbooks: An American History* (Yale University Press).

ROBIN MARANTZ HENIG is a freelance science writer in New York.

PAM HOUSTON is a frequent contributor to *O*'s Reading Room section and the director of creative writing at the University of California, Davis. Her books include *Sight Hound* (Norton) and *A Little More About Me* (Washington Square).

MARIE HOWE is an award-winning poet and the author of *The Good Thief* (Persea), *What the Living Do,* and The *Kingdom of Ordinary Time* (both Norton). She teaches poetry at Sarah Lawrence College.

A.J. JACOBS has written *The Guinea Pig Diaries: My Life as an Experiment* and *A Year of Living Biblically* (both Simon & Schuster). He is the editor-at-large at *Esquire*.

DAVID L. KATZ, MD, is director of the Yale-Griffin Prevention Research Center and president of the nonprofit organization Turn the Tide Foundation, Inc.

BETTY KINDLEY retired from full-time teaching in 2008.

SUSAN KLEBOLD lives in Colorado. She supports suicide research and encourages prevention and awareness practices.

MERIBAH KNIGHT is a Chicago-based writer.

LISA KOGAN is *O*'s writer-at-large and the author of *Someone Will be With You Shortly: Notes from a Perfectly Imperfect Life* (HarperStudio).

DINA KRAFT is a freelance journalist based in Israel.

ANNE LAMOTT is the author of *Imperfect Birds, Traveling Mercies,* and *Bird by Bird* (all Riverhead).

MARK LEYNER is the co-author of *The New York Times* bestsellers *Why Do Men Have Nipples?* and *Why Do Men Fall Asleep After Having Sex?* (both Three Rivers Press).

EUGENE LINDEN is a senior writer at *Time* and a leading expert on animal intelligence, the environment, and man's relationship with nature.

CAITLIN MACY is the author of the story collection *Spoiled* (Random House).

JOANN MANSON, MD, is the author of *Hot Flashes, Hormones, and Your Health* (McGraw-Hill).

CRYSTAL MARTIN is an assistant editor at *O*.

PHILLIP C. MCGRAW, PHD, hosts the daily television talk show, *Dr. Phil.* He is the author of six best-selling books, including *Real Life* (Free Press). He writes a monthly column for *O*.

CAROL MITHERS is a freelance journalist in Los Angeles. Her work has appeared in *The New York Times* and *The Los Angeles Times.*

VALERIE MONROE, *O*'s beauty director, is the author of *In the Weather of the Heart,* a memoir.

SUZE ORMAN, host of CNBC's *The Suze Orman Show,* is the author of several books on personal finance, including *2009 Action Plan: Keeping Your Money Safe & Sound* (Spiegel & Grau). She writes a monthly column for *O*.

MICHELE OWENS blogs at gardenrant.com and is the author of *Eat the Yard* (Rodale), due out in 2011.

NOELLE OXENHANDLER is the author of the memoir *The Wishing Year: A House, a Man, My Soul* (Random House).

MEHMET OZ, MD, is the host of *The Dr. Oz Show* and a daily Sirius XM radio show. He is vice-chair and professor of surgery at Columbia University and directs the Cardiovascular Institute and Complementary Medicine Program at New York Presbyterian Hospital.

SARAH REISTAD-LONG is a writer in New York City. She is the co-author of the forthcoming *The Big New York Sandwich Book* (Running Press).

GRETCHEN REYNOLDS is a fitness columnist for *The New York Times Magazine* and a frequent contributor to *O.* She lives in Santa Fe.

BONNIE ROCHMAN is a staff writer at *The News & Observer* in Raleigh, North Carolina.

HELEN ROGAN is a writer whose work has appeared in *The New York Times* and *The Wall Street Journal.* She lives in Brooklyn, New York.

PETERO SABUNE is the Protestant chaplain at Sing Sing Correctional Facility in Ossining, New York.

DARBY SAXBE, PHD, is a psychologist whose research focuses on stress, health, and relationships.

SAÏD SAYRAFIEZADEH is the author of the memoir *When Skateboards Will Be Free* (The Dial Press).

HEATHER SELLERS is an English professor at Hope College in Holland, Michigan. Her latest book is *You Don't Look Like Anyone I Know* (Riverhead).

SARAH BOWEN SHEA is the co-author of *Run Like a Mother: How to Get Moving—and Not Lose Your Family, Job, or Sanity* (Andrews McMeel Publishing). She lives in Portland, Oregon.

MARISA SILVER is the author of a collection of short stories, *Alone with You* (Simon & Schuster).

ELIZABETH STROUT's latest novel, *Olive Kitteridge* (Random House), won the 2009 Pulitzer Prize for fiction. She teaches at the MFA program at Queen's University in Charlotte, North Carolina.

CINTRA WILSON is the author of three books, including *Caligula for Presidency* (Bloomsbury USA) and *Colors Insulting to Nature* (HarperPerennial). She writes the Critical Shopper column for *The New York Times.*

JESSICA WINTER is a senior editor at *O*.

SELENE YEAGER is a health and fitness writer and a certified personal trainer. She is the author of *Ride Your Way Lean* (Rodale).

PHOEBE ZERWICK is an investigative journalist who lives in North Carolina. She is a former reporter for the *Winston-Salem Journal.*

JESS ZIMMERMAN is a journalist who lives near Washington, D.C.

PHOTO CREDITS

INDEX

A

acupuncture, 142
addiction
    in the neighborhood, 258-266
    overcoming, 101-103
adoption, 64-65
aggressive, 178-179
aging, 59, 62-63, 77, 197-199
    and muscle loss, 25
    turning 50, 206-209
Aha! Moments
    Anika Noni Rose, 73
    Julianna Margulies, 245
    Marcia Gay Harden, 289
    Rashida Jones, 196
Alzheimer's, 198
anger, 113, 159-161, 260, 262
animals
    human effect on wild, 231-232
    intelligence of, 227-229
anxiety, 60, 72, 242
    physical symptoms of, 60-61
arguing
    gestures when, 183
    respectfully, 284
assertive, 178
autism, 190-195
    autism spectrum disorders (ASDs),
    191, 195
    Generation Rescue, 194

B

baking to relieve anxiety, 242
Baldwin, Alec, 137
beauty, perception of, 56-57, 58-59
Beyoncé, 263
bicycle, 99
big world, 100
blood, donating, 276-277
blood pressure, 37
blood sugar, 38
BMI (body mass index), 24, 25
bone density, 38
brains, differences in male and female, 158
breastfeeding, 270-275
breast milk, 270-275
    and AIDS, 272
    as cancer-fighting regimen, 274
    donating, 271-275
    pumping, 271-274
Breathing Space, 150-151, 202-203, 312-313
budget
    A 10-Step Money-Saving Plan, 44
    Organics: When are they worth it?, 44

cooking with a shrinking, 42
bulimic, 14

C

calling, 110-111, 115, 116, 144-145, 148, 263
camaraderie of women, 216-217, 222
cancer, 196, 256
    finding joyful moments during treat-
    ment of, 196
cell phones, 39
change, 101, 104, 113-114
    accepting, 114, 181
    and the Dalai Lama, 114
    fear of, 113-114, 177
    Rat Park, 101-103
cheating, 179-180
children
    and eating healthier, 10, 43
    Feeding Active Kids: Don't Sweat the
    Sugar, 43
    picky eater, 10
cholesterol, 37
cognitive-behavioral therapy, 61, 181
college, scholarships for going to, 259, 292
Columbine, 234-238
    Susan Klebold, 234-238
communication, 12, 176, 177, 256-257
    in marriage, 162, 181
    The Most Useful Communication
    Technique of All Time, 177
    styles of, 176
    via email, 257
confidence, 72, 88
    Who Am I Meant to Be? (quiz), 118-120
conflict, 182
    demand-withdrawal dynamic, 176, 177,
    183
    polarization, 175-176
    using humor to resolve, 183
connected feeling, 100
cooking
    and involving children, 43
    A 10-Step Money-Saving Plan, 44-45
    A 10-Step Time-Saving Plan, 42-44

D

Dalai Lama, 114
dance lessons, 154-155
dating, 105
    after divorce, 163-165, 167
death, 256-257, 262, 274
debt, 78, 122
    living without, 78
decision-making, 105

DeGeneres, Ellen, 82-88
depression, 76, 78, 193, 224, 237
    and menopause, 50
    and posture, 26
determination, 116-117
diabetes, 11, 25
    blood sugar, 39
    visceral fat and, 25
diet plans, 22, 23
    choosing the best, 22
    exercise and, 23
domestic violence, 246-255
    Where to Get Help, 255
donating, 293-295. See also help, tithing,
volunteering.
    breast milk, 271-275
    via the Internet, 295
dopamine, 33
downsizing
    at home, 74-81, 239-240
    at work, 239

E

eat healthier, 10, 12, 18, 19, 34, 41-45, 286,
287
    cost of, 21, 41
    planned menus 30 days in advance, 10
    Pritikin Family Program, 11, 12
    10 rules for eating right, 20-21
    You really are what you eat, 21
eating
    disorders, 16
    emotional, 11
    and planning, 19, 21
    restrictive, 17
    on the run, 21
    slow the pace of, 21
    "Weekend Effect" and, 19
elderly
    building support for, 198
    caring for the, 197-198
    Navajo, respect for the, 197, 198, 199
    using humor when caring for the, 199
emotion, expressing, 87
empathy, 284
estrogen, 49-53
exercise, 12, 17, 22-23, 24-25, 95, 287
    Bob Greene's "Back to Business" Plan, 34
    excuses, 29
    and lowering blood pressure, 37
    and posture, 26-27
    sticking to it, 33
    to strengthen bones, 38
    while watching TV, 28

F

Fair Winds Trading, 300, 303, 305
family, 10-12, 41-45, 188-189, 221-225, 239-240, 256-257, 287, 304
    appreciating, 200-201
    sisters, 306
    sit down to dinner, 21, 42, 44, 282
    A 10-Step Money-Saving Plan, 44-45
    A 10-Step Time-Saving Plan, 42-44
    fat, 13-17, 24-25
    being, 13
    A Few More Ways to Help Your Family Fight Fat, 12
    around the midsection, 24-25
    fat acceptance movement, 15, 16, 17
    how the body stores, 25
    normal-weight person but too much, 25
    omental, 38
    and public health guidelines, 24
    visceral, 25
fear, 73, 177
    of death, 199
    of failure, 67-69
Fey, Tina, 133-139
FICO score, 90
financial security, 89-91
    autopilot, 90
finding yourself, 112-113, 115-116
    dealing with anger, 113
    Who Am I Meant to Be? (quiz), 118-120
find joyful moments, 196
fitness level as predictor of mortality
    risk, 25
food
    addiction, 33, 35
    diaries, 18, 19
    grow your own, 45
    photographing, 18, 19
    as reward, 11
friendship, 56, 57, 77, 113, 195, 210-212
fruits, 20
    grow your own, 45, 46-47
    Organics: When are they worth it?, 44
    USDA recommended servings of produce a day, 20

G

Gandhi, Mahatma 146-147
garden, 46-47, 286
    organic, 79
gay marriage, 88, 172
gender roles, 169, 170, 172
genocide in Rwanda, 298, 303
goals, 12, 67-69
    career, 104
    financial, 90
    shifting, 78

grandmother, 221-223, 225
gratitude, 289, 297, 311
grief process, 198
grocery shopping, 42
    ethnic markets, 45
    farmers' markets, 45

H

happiness, 142
    pudding, 98
healing, 142
heart disease, 25, 38, 39
    resting heart rate, 37
help, 142, 305. See also scholarships.
    asking for, 141-143, 160, 161, 287
    Guerrilla Aid, 295
    Where to Get Help, 255
heritage, 64, 65, 221-225
heroism, 213-215
Holocaust, 210-212
    camp sisters, 211, 212
homosexuality, 83, 84, 166-172
    acknowledging, 86
hormone therapy, 49-53
    Should I Take Hormones or Not?, 53
humor, 133-139
    improv, 136, 137
    in resolving conflict, 183
    using in caring for the elderly, 199
    using to deal with autism, 195

I

independent, 260
integrity, 259, 262
Internet
    donating via, 295
    to find experts, 32
    using as a tool for caregivers, 198
Internet Web sites
    accuquote.com, 91
    acefitness.org, 32
    charitynavigator.org, 297
    eatwild.com, 45
    foodnews.org, 44
    healthychildren.org, 32
    healthywomen.org, 32
    ibct.psych.ucla.edu, 177
    macys.com/obracelet, 305
    match.com, 95, 164, 165
    neighborgoods.net, 309
    nlm.nih.gov/medlineplus, 32
    nnedv.org/projects, 255
    nrcs.usda.gov/partners/for_homeowners, 45
    nutritiondetectives.com, 21
    oprah.com/omagextras, 300
    plentyoffish.com, 95

    power-surge.com, 32
    resolve.org, 32
    selectquote.com, 91
    suzeorman.com, 91
    thehopefund.org, 291
    vinelink.com, 255
    webmd.com, 32
    weekendgardner.net, 45
    womenshealth.gov, 32
    womenheart.org, 32
    womenslaw.org, 255
    yourdiseaserisk.com, 32

J

Jay-Z, 258-266
    Shawn Carter Scholarship Fund, 259
job loss, dealing with, 179
jobs, 67-69, 76
just-in-case, 70-72
    hoarding, 71, 72
    and weight gain, 71
just in time, 70-72
    clutter, 72
    confidence, 72
    and money, 71
    and weight loss, 71

L

lifestyle strategies, 70-72
    collector, 76
    living in excess, 71, 72
    pursue intrinsic values, 78
    "voluntary simplicity," 74-81
love, 16, 71, 72, 87, 143, 265, 270, 275
    and legal documents, 91
    romantic, 162
    and sex, 158
    unconditional, 16, 196, 257
    yourself, 113

M

marriage, 105, 116, 162, 181, 288
    roles in, 167
    sex in, 104
    staying in, 159-161
mastering one thing, 67-69
McCain, John, 134
McGraw, Phillip C. (Dr. Phil), 104, 105, 178, 179, 180, 181
    Script of the Month, 179, 180, 181
menopause, 49-53
    "bioidentical," 49, 51
    and depression, 50
    Should I Take Hormones or Not?, 53
money, 71, 78, 81, 121-123, 167, 239
    investing, 91
    saving, 90

Morgan, Tracy, 137
mortgage, paying off, 91
muffins, 241-242
music,
       hip-hop, 265
       rap, 261
music camp, 206-209

N

New Orleans, 298-306

O

The O Interviews
       Ellen DeGeneres, 82-88
       Jay-Z, 258-266
       Michelle Obama, 278-288
       Tina Fey, 133-139
Obama, Barack, 65, 96, 134, 266
Obama, Michelle, 45, 278-288
O Bracelets, 298-306
       The O Bracelet, 305
       to order, macys.com/obracelet, 305
O Power List, 124-132
       Anna Deavere Smith, 125
       Ann E. Dunwoody, 129
       Donna Brazile, 127
       Lateefah Simon, 127
       Lauren Ambrose, 128
       Lilly Ledbetter, 129
       Mayda del Valle, 130
       Melanie Sloan, 132
       Shirley Ann Jackson, 131
       Venus Williams, 126
Oprah Winfrey Leadership Academy in
       South Africa, 311
Organics: When are they worth it?, 44
Orman, Suze, 89-91, 121-123
osteoporosis, 38, 50
overweight and fitness level, 25
oxytocin, 94, 96, 158
       in breast milk, 271
       the hormone of between, 94
Oz, Mehmet (Dr. Oz), 39

P

Palin, Sarah, 134, 135
parenting, 59, 105, 180-181, 245
       and feeling needed, 59
       "this is only a moment...," 245
Paycheck Fairness Act, 129
perspiring, 60, 61
pets, 230
       letting go, 243-244
photographing what you eat, 18, 19
photography, 67-68
physical activity, measuring, 19
picky eater, 10, 21

pioneer spirit, 239-240
poetry, 130
polarization in a relationship, 175, 176
posture, 26-27
       exercises for better, 26-27
power, 121-123
       fearing, 128
       leading, 127
       money and, 121-123
       speaking up, 125
       spiritual, 149
prayer, 143
pregnancy, 269, 270
       eating during, 185-187
       triplets, 268-275
premature birth, 270, 271
priority list, 35
pudding, 98
purpose in life, 110, 149

R

radio, 100
rape, 304, 305, 306
rebellion, humor as, 135-136
responsibility, 281
       accepting, 87
       in relationships, 175
       of sexually active teenager, 181
       teaching children, 105, 284, 297
retirement account, 90, 91
rudeness, 178-179
Rwanda, 298-306

S

salad dressing, recipe for, 38
same-sex relationships, 166-172
       communication in, 172
       emotional connection, 170, 171
saying no, 73, 85, 112, 122
scholarships, 259, 290, 292
scrapbook, 100
self-care, 33, 35, 36
self-discipline with finances, 90
self-discovery, 206-209
self-image, 16, 56, 57, 58, 59, 62, 63, 64, 65, 113
       how others perceive us, 112
       what you tell yourself, 105
selling hand-crafted goods, 298-306
sewing legacy, 221-225
sex, 104, 158, 170, 171
       and love, 158
sexual fluidity, 169, 183
sexually active teenager, 181
shyness, 104, 105
Slim Peace, 218-220
       symbol of hope, 220
solar power, 79, 81

stress relief, 93-97
success, 85
suicide, 237, 238
       warning signs of, 238
support
       building in caring for elderly, 198
       communication, 12

T

teasing, 64, 65
testosterone, 158
thyroid, 35
tithing, 296-297
       sacrifice, 297
treasures, 99, 106

V

vegan, 87
vegetables
       frozen, 43
       grow your own, 45, 46, 47
       Organics: When are they worth it?, 44
vegetarian, 45
"voluntary simplicity," 74-81
volunteering, 77, 96, 97, 293-295

W

war, 145, 146, 220, 222
weight, 13-17, 71
       fitness level, 25
       and thyroid, 35
       weight-seesaw, 14
weight gain, 33
weight loss, 10, 11, 12, 18-23, 137
       Bob Greene's "Back to Business"
          Plan, 34
       after having kids, 10, 14
       Slim Peace, 218-220
       "Weekend Effect" on, 19
Weight Watchers, 11, 14, 137, 218
Wellspring, 11, 12
What I Know for Sure: Oprah, 106, 149,
       311
will, creating a, 91
Women Rule! 2008 conference
       accomplishments, 307
       healthcare clinic, 308
       NeighborGoods, 309
       Save-a-Lot grocery, 310
work, 73, 110, 116
       defined by, 115
       setting career goals, 104
writing, 68, 69, 116-117, 134-139, 148

Y

yoga, 95, 96

Published by Time Home Entertainment Inc.
135 West 50th Street, New York, NY 10020

ISBN-13: 978-0-8487-3365-0
ISBN-10: 0-8487-3365-7
Library of Congress Control Number: 2008942160
Printed in the United States of America
First printing 2010

To order more books, call 1-800-765-6400 or 1-800-491-0551.

O, The Oprah Magazine
Founder and Editorial Director: Oprah Winfrey
Editor in Chief: Susan Casey
Editor at Large: Gayle King
Editor: Brooke Kosofsky Glassberg
Production Director: Kristen Rayner
Associate Photo Editor: Kathy Nguyen
Editoral Assistant: Rachel Mount

HEARST BOOKS
VP, Publisher: Jacqueline Deval

OXMOOR HOUSE
VP, Publisher: Jim Childs
Director, Direct Marketing: Laura Sappington
Editorial Director: Susan Dobbs
Managing Editor: Laurie Herr
Brand Manager: Victoria Alfonso

TIME HOME ENTERTAINMENT INC.
Publisher: Richard Fraiman
General Manager: Steven Sandonato
Executive Director, Marketing Services: Carol Pittard
Executive Director, Retail & Special Sales: Tom Mifsud
Director, New Product Development: Peter Harper
Director, Publicity: Sydney Webber
Associate Counsel: Helen Wan

Love Your Life!
Editor: Susan Hernandez Ray
Project Editor: Vanessa Lynn Rusch
Senior Production Manager: Greg A. Amason

CONTRIBUTORS
Designer: Suzanne Noli
Copy Editor: Carmine B. Loper
Indexer: Mary Ann Laurens
Interns: Christine T. Boatwright, Perri Hubbard, Allison Leigh Sperando, Caitlin Watzke